ADHD

Cognitive–Behavioral Therapy with ADHD Children

Cognitive–Behavioral Therapy with ADHD Children
Child, Family, and School Interventions

Lauren Braswell, Ph.D.
Michael L. Bloomquist, Ph.D.

Foreword by Russell A. Barkley, Ph.D.

THE GUILFORD PRESS
New York   London

© 1991 The Guilford Press
A Division of Guilford Publications, Inc.
72 Spring Street, New York, NY 10012

Printed in the United States of America

This book is printed on acid-free paper.

Last digit is print number: 9 8 7 6 5 4 3

Library of Congress Cataloging-in-Publication Data
Braswell, Lauren.
    Cognitive–behavioral therapy with ADHD children: child, family, and school interventions / Lauren Braswell, Michael L. Bloomquist.
        p.   cm.
    Includes bibliographical references and index.
    ISBN 0-89862-764-8 (cloth)   0-89862-529-7 (paperback)
    1. Attention deficit disorders—Treatment.   2. Hyperactive child syndrome—Treatment.   3. Cognitive therapy for children.
    I. Bloomquist, Michael L.   II. Title.
    [DNLM: 1. Attention Deficit Disorder with Hyperactivity—therapy.
    2. Behavior Therapy.   WS 340 B823c]
    RJ496.A86B73   1991
    618.92'8589—dc20
    DNLM/DLC
    for Library of Congress   91-16596
                                                                              CIP

This book is dedicated to our spouses:

*To Chris Fondell, whose energetic
yet reflective approach to life
continues to amaze me.—L. B.*

*To Rebecca Syverts, whose capacity
to love and to be creative
is greatly appreciated.—M. L. B.*

Foreword

Almost 100 years ago, William James noted in his classic text, *Principles of Psychology* (1898), that self-directed speech could be used as a means of increasing sustained attention and behavioral inhibition, particularly under conditions that otherwise sorely taxed these abilities. Regrettably, it was not until 20 years ago that Meichenbaum and Goodman (1971) first reported the results of an experiment in which James's recommendation was finally put to the test with impulsive children. The results were quite positive and a new intervention in the field of clinical child psychology for impulsive, hyperactive children was born. Over the next decade, self-control training, or cognitive-behavior modification, would be viewed with great promise as either an adjunct to stimulant medication and more traditional behavioral (contingency management) methods for treating hyperactive children or even an alternative to them. Early efforts to replicate Meichenbaum and Goodman's results with primarily school-identified impulsive children also proved successful (Bornstein & Quevillon, 1976; Douglas, Parry, Martin, & Garson, 1976; Kendall & Braswell, 1982), further buttressing the belief that cognitive–behavioral treatment might actually become the treatment of choice for inattentive, overactive, and impulsive children, those now referred to as having Attention-Deficit Hyperactivity Disorder (ADHD). By 1980, studies of relatively complex, sophisticated, and multitiered cognitive–behavioral interventions were under way with more seriously impaired, clinically referred hyperactive children (Barkley, Copeland, & Sivage, 1980; Douglas, 1980) and by 1985, a detailed manual for conducting such treatment was authored by Philip Kendall and the first author of the present book, Lauren Braswell. The place of self-control training in the armamentarium of child clinical psychological therapies seemed well cemented.

Cracks began to appear in this early facade of success, however, when efforts to replicate several of the early promising studies proved negative (Billings & Wasik, 1985; Friedling & O'Leary, 1979). Even where positive results were noted, they did not seem to generalize to other, no-treatment environments, to maintain themselves after intervention was terminated, or to generalize to measures of academic achievement (Barkley et al., 1980; Borden, Brown, Wynne, & Schleser, 1987; Brown, Wynne, & Medenis, 1985). Particularly problematic was the observation that what might work with mildly impulsive children recruited from screenings of school classrooms was not so successful with the more serious degrees of impulsivity, inattention, or hyperactivity witnessed in clinically referred children. Subsequent reviews of this literature by Abikoff (1985, 1987) even concluded that the clinical benefits of cognitive–behavioral therapies for ADHD children remain unproven. Others have even ventured the more heretical notion that children actually do not or cannot engage in self-control apart from external contingencies established to prompt, reinforce, and maintain its occurrence (Gross & Wojnilower, 1984; Hayes et al., 1985). Adult supervision to prompt and rehearse cognitive strategies and preclude cheating, the need for public goal-setting, and the requirement that there exist external reinforcement to back up self-reinforcement programs were said to account for any initial positive results from cognitive–behavioral therapies.

Where, then, does the field stand on the efficacy of such interventions for ADHD children? Certainly, the topic is controversial and the opinions from leading experts studying ADHD quite varied. The findings from more recent studies of this treatment with ADHD children are also conflicting. I am very pleased to see that Lauren Braswell and Michael Bloomquist provide a quite scholarly review of these studies in this book and do not pale from the controversy in making their case for the use of these interventions with ADHD children. Admittedly, my own enthusiasm for these methods when provided through individually delivered, clinic-based mechanisms has waned considerably in the past 5 years. Instead of the naive myopic optimism for this approach as a clinical treatment that characterized my own early views and that was frequently found in the initial years of promulgation of this therapy, I am much more cautious, circumspect, yet favorably predisposed to the continued scientific study and clinical use of these therapies with ADHD children—provided that certain limitations and preconditions be clearly recognized. I am delighted to note that many of these precautions are nicely addressed in the present book.

First, it is my opinion that, for cognitive–behavioral therapy to succeed with clinically referred children, it must be taught to the primary caregivers (parents, teachers, etc.) of these children who, on a daily basis, in myriad contexts and social exchanges, encounter and manage the impulsive, disinhibited, inattentive, and poorly regulated behavior for which ADHD children are notorious. It is these adults who must become the therapists for these children, placing the clinician now in the role as consultant-trainer to these adults. This approach results in (1) more frequent, intensive, and naturalistic opportunities for acquisition, rehearsal, and demonstration of self-control strategies by the children; (2) less trouble for the generalization and maintenance of these skills from treatment to no-treatment settings since they are taught and reinforced within ecologically valid circumstances; and, it is hoped, (3) greater likelihood that such training will "take" and become "internalized" by the children for later use in other social contexts. The jury is still out on whether this ecological approach will, in fact, achieve its promised goals but it certainly seems to be the correct direction in which to proceed at this time. The authors could not have been more timely in providing us with the detailed methods for conducting this next-generation approach to self-control training in which parents and teachers become therapists in the self-control training of their ADHD children.

A second cautionary note is the need for this treatment approach and its proponents to stay abreast of the rapid developments and reconceptualizations concerning the nature of ADHD. Very few scientists studying ADHD continue to view it as an attention deficit and are gradually shifting to the view that it may be a disorder of motivational regulation in behavioral terms, or "resource allocation" in information processing terms (Barkley, 1989; Haenlein & Caul, 1987; Quay, 1988; Sergeant & Scholten, 1985; van der Meere & Sergeant, 1988). ADHD does not seem to be so much a skills deficit as a performance deficit. That is, ADHD is not the result of a lack of cognitive skills, abilities, or strategies but an inability to use or sustain the use of an existing, appropriate behavioral repertoire that is required in a particular setting. In short, it is not a deficit in knowing what to do, but in doing what you know. This, then, is a problem with motivation that is unlikely to be successfully addressed by approaches that exclusively emphasize skill training. ADHD may well be, in part or wholly, a relative insensitivity to social consequences that leaves the individual more under the influence of moment-by-moment contingencies and less governed by societal rules and future consequences (Barkley, 1990). If this reconceptualization of ADHD proves correct, it accounts for one of the more exasperating aspects of clinical work with ADHD children: their failure to use what they have been previously taught and apparently know in social contexts where it is in their best interests to do so. I am encouraged by the authors' incorporation into this text of intervention strategies designed to address this motivational deficit as opposed to exclusively relying on skill training. This book offers a fine compromise of these two approaches to ADHD: one that trains and rehearses with the child the meta-cognitive strategies and skills seemingly necessary for adequate behavioral self-regulation, the other focusing on establishing the environmental cues and consequences crucial to its display and maintenance.

The third precondition to engaging in cognitive–behavioral interventions with ADHD children must be the tacit acknowledgment that most children with this disorder are unlikely to be cured, in the strict sense of that term, by any existing interventions. The goal of treatment, therefore, is not so much to eliminate or correct an underlying deficit as to symptomatically manage what is best viewed as a chronic, disabling condition. Such symptomatic treatment (1) reduces the severity of the behavioral symptoms as much as possible; (2) attempts to preclude or diminish the risks for secondary problems developing over time from these primary symptoms; (3) provides periodic reintervention as required to manage crises that emerge with the changing developmental demands made on the disabled child; (4) better prepares the primary caregivers and other family members for the raising of a behaviorally handicapped child; and (5) prevents or diminishes the likelihood of deterioration in the adjustment of other family members as a consequence of the presence of the handicapped ADHD child within that family. Workers in the field of physical disabilities, mental retardation, and autism will readily recognize these as longstanding tenets of their own efforts at intervention. It is time that those dealing with ADHD children did so as well. No one should be misled into thinking that cognitive–behavioral interventions, as all other effective therapies for ADHD, will rid the child of ADHD such that subsequently he/she requires no further special treatment. The authors have done a superb job making this case in their initial chapters and re-emphasizing it throughout their explication of their treatment procedures, whether with parents, educators, or the children themselves.

With these caveats in mind, Braswell and Bloomquist have done an excellent job in articulating their complex, state-of-the-art cognitive–behavioral therapy for ADHD children. Their ecological–developmental model provides an accurate depiction of the changing nature of ADHD over development and acknowledges the complex interaction between the child and his/her social environment that shapes each case of ADHD uniquely. Correctly, this model articulates the significant impact such children have on their families and caregivers and provides recommendations for its redress rather than seeing the child as purely the passive vessel storing up the effects of its environment. The cognitive–behavioral view espoused here also picks up where more traditional models have left off, stressing the need for caregivers of ADHD children, and not professionals, to serve as the primary therapists in their children's management and training. Most valuable in my opinion, however, is the clear, concise, detailed explication of the cognitive–behavioral techniques themselves in the latter sections of the volume. The richness of clinical detail, samples of therapy applications, numerous charts and outlines for aiding their clinical implementation, and recommendations for managing possible obstacles in therapy are commendable. They make this book obviously the fruitful collaboration of two scholarly, well-grounded scientist-practitioners whose depth of clinical wisdom permeates their empirical model of intervention. It is at once clear that they have seen many ADHD families and, most importantly, have listened intently to them.

RUSSELL A. BARKLEY, Ph.D.
Worcester, Massachusetts

References

Abikoff, H. (1985). Efficacy of cognitive training intervention in hyperactive children: A critical review. *Clinical Psychology Review, 5,* 479–512.

Abikoff, H. (1987). An evaluation of cognitive behavior therapy for hyperactive children. In B. Lahey & A. Kazdin (Eds.), *Advances in clinical child psychology* (Vol. 10, pp. 171–216). New York: Plenum.

Barkley, R. A. (1989). The problem of stimulus control and rule-governed behavior in children with Attention Deficit Disorder with Hyperactivity. In J. Swanson & L. Bloomingdale (Eds.), *Attention deficit disorders.* New York: Pergamon.

Barkley, R. A. (1990). *Attention-deficit hyperactivity disorder: A handbook for diagnosis and treatment.* New York: Guilford.

Barkley, R. A., Copeland, A. P., & Sivage, C. (1980). A self-control classroom for hyperactive children. *Journal of Autism and Developmental Disorders, 10,* 75–89.

Billings, D.C., & Wasik, B. H. (1985). Self-instructional training with preschoolers: An attempt to replicate. *Journal of Applied Behavior Analysis, 18,* 61–67.

Borden, K. A., Brown, R. T., Wynne, M. E., & Schleser, R. (1987). Piagetian conservation and response to cognitive therapy in attention deficit disordered children. *Journal of Child Psychology and Psychiatry, 28,* 755–764.

Bornstein, P. H., & Quevillon, R. P. (1976). The effects of a self-instructional package on overactive preschool boys. *Journal of Applied Behavior Analysis, 9,* 179–188.

Brown, R. T., Wynne, M. E., & Medenis, R. (1985). Methylphenidate and cognitive therapy: A comparison of treatment approaches with hyperactive boys. *Journal of Abnormal Child Psychology, 13,* 69–88.

Douglas, V. I. (1980). Higher mental processes in hyperactive children: Implications for training. In R. Knights & D. Bakker (Eds.), *Treatment of hyperactive and learning disordered children* (pp. 65–92). Baltimore, MD: University Park Press.

Douglas, V. I., Parry, P., Martin, P., & Garson, C. (1976). Assessment of a cognitive training program for hyperactive children. *Journal of Abnormal Child Psychology, 4,* 389–410.

Friedling, C., & O'Leary, S. G. (1979). Effects of self-instructional training on second- and third-grade hyperactive children: A failure to replicate. *Journal of Applied Behavior Analysis, 12,* 211–219.

Gross, A. M., & Wojnilower, D. A. (1984). Self-directed behavior change in children: Is it self-directed? *Behavior Therapy, 15,* 501–514.

Haenlein, M., & Caul, W. F. (1987). Attention deficit disorder with hyperactivity: A specific hypothesis of reward dysfunction. *Journal of the American Academy of Child and Adolescent Psychiatry, 26,* 356–362.

Hayes, S. C., Rosenfarb, I., Wulfert, E., Munt, E. D., Korn, Z., & Zettle, R. D. (1985). Self-reinforcement effects: An artifact of social standard setting? *Journal of Applied Behavior Analysis, 18,* 201–214.

James, W. (1898). *Principles of psychology.* New York: Britannica.

Kendall, P. C., & Braswell, L. (1982). Cognitive–behavioral self-control therapy for children: A component analysis. *Journal of Consulting and Clinical Psychology, 50,* 672–689.

Kendall, P. C., & Braswell, L. (1985). *Cognitive–behavioral therapy for impulsive children.* New York: Guilford.

Meichenbaum, D., & Goodman, J. (1971). Training impulsive children to talk to themselves: A means of developing self-control. *Journal of Abnormal Psychology, 77,* 115–126.

Quay, H. C. (1988). Attention deficit disorder and the behavioral inhibition system: The relevance of the neuropsychological theory of Jeffrey A. Gray. In L. Bloomingdale & J. Sergeant (Eds.), *Attention deficit disorders: Criteria, cognition, and intervention* (pp. 117–126). New York: Pergamon.

Sergeant, J. A., & Scholten, C. A. (1985). On resource strategy limitations in hyperactivity: Cognitive impulsivity reconsidered. *Journal of Child Psychology and Psychiatry, 26,* 97–109.

van der Meere, J., & Sergeant, J. (1988). Controlled processing and vigilance in hyperactivity: Time will tell. *Journal of Abnormal Child Psychology, 16,* 641–656.

Preface

We owe the existence of this book to many different groups and individuals who have shaped our understanding of the needs of children struggling with Attention-Deficit Hyperactivity Disorder. Most notably, our clients have been quick to help us see the shortcomings of some of our earlier notions about treatment. These clients, along with their families and teachers, have made sure that we understand how crucial it is to pursue developmentally appropriate forms of intervention that actively involve parents, peers, and school personnel. We hope to remain open to the lessons our clients are eagerly trying to teach us.

We wish to extend special thanks to the children and staffs of several schools in the Twin Cities area, including North Star Elementary, Grove Learning Center, and Echo Park, Cedar Park, and Westview Elementary Schools of the Rosemount School District, for providing educational settings in which the school-based curriculum could be developed.

Since the original draft of the manuscript was prepared, we have learned that the National Institute of Mental Health (NIMH) has awarded funding to Gerald August, Principal Investigator, and Rick Ostrander and ourselves as Co-Investigators to study the extent to which a variant of the intervention detailed in this volume can prevent the emergence of secondary difficulties in ADHD children. We wish to thank NIMH and the 22 Twin Cities elementary schools that will be participating in the Minnesota Competence Enhancement Program.

We also wish to thank the Division of Child and Adolescent Psychiatry at the University of Minnesota Hospitals and North Memorial Child Guidance Clinic of Robbinsdale, Minnesota, for their role in fostering the development of the clinic-based treatment program described in this volume. We particularly benefitted from the input of Gerald August, Martha Bordwell, Rochelle Brandl, Dan Dossa, Diane Felton, Susan Maise, Rick Ostrander, Steve Schnell, and many others who served as cotherapists with us.

We extend special thanks to our former academic advisors, Philip Kendall (L. B.) and Robert Schleser (M. L. B.). We feel very fortunate to have belonged to research teams that helped us understand the need for careful delineation and evaluation of therapeutic procedures. We are grateful to have the continued input of Phil and Bob with our current efforts.

We have no idea how Lois Laitinen and Janet Bockenstedt ever put up with typing the multiple drafts of the manuscript, but we are really glad that they did, and we deeply appreciate their excellent work.

We also appreciate the valuable input of Deborah Anderson, James Bruce, and JoAnne Gardner, who read and commented on earlier drafts of this book.

Finally, as we indicated in the dedication, we wish to thank our spouses. Chris Fondell (L. B.) and Rebecca Syverts (M. L. B.) provided us with the time to write, tolerated the hassles created by the writing, and were encouraging of our efforts at each step of the process. We only hope to return the favor by allowing them the same opportunity to pursue quests of their choosing.

LAUREN BRASWELL, Ph.D.
North Psychology Clinic

MICHAEL L. BLOOMQUIST, Ph.D.
University of Minnesota
Division of Child and Adolescent Psychiatry
and North Psychology Clinic

Contents

Cognitive–Behavioral Therapy with ADHD Children

Introduction

The parents of children with Attention-Deficit Hyperactivity Disorder (ADHD) and professionals working with these children are faced with the almost overwhelming task of sifting through the reams of available information on ADHD in an effort to make intelligent choices about treatment. Not only does the size of this task make it formidable, but controversies about this condition within both professional circles and the general population make it difficult for parents and professionals to develop a clear understanding of ADHD and the treatment needs of children displaying symptoms of this disorder.

Among the general population, much of the current controversy has been encouraged by the Citizens Commission on Human Rights (CCHR), a group sponsored by the Church of Scientology. In CCHR Information Letter #1 (Citizens Commission on Human Rights, 1987a), the group maintains that the condition of ADHD does not exist and that observations to the contrary are simply the result of personal variations in activity level and attention span. CCHR goes on to suggest that this diagnosis was "created" for the financial benefit of mental health professionals. While opposing the diagnosis, CCHR's most vehement criticisms are focused on the use of psychostimulant medication as a form of treatment for the condition. In CCHR Information Letter #2 (Citizens Commission on Human Rights, 1987b) and in numerous media presentations made by CCHR spokesperson Dennis Clarke, a number of extremely frightening claims are made regarding such medication treatment. In their *Los Angeles Herald Examiner* article, Bayles and McCartney (1988) provide clarification about the weakness of the data sources on which CCHR's more extreme claims are based and emphasize that CCHR's stance against psychostimulant medication is based more on the Scientologist philosophy than on data.

Putting aside these extreme claims, there are other excellent, data-based reasons for parents and professionals to make careful choices about the application of the ADHD diagnostic label and cautious choices about treatment. In Chapter 1, we discuss both what is understood and what is not yet known about ADHD, including the sorts of issues or symptoms that might suggest ADHD but in reality do not. We also discuss areas of research and theorizing still debated in professional circles. In Chapter 2, we provide a relatively brief overview of the elements of an assessment of the ADHD child, as well as suggestions for methods of monitoring the effectiveness of any attempted treatments. An overview of currently accepted modes of treatment is presented in Chapter 3. In addition, we discuss the training experiences, clinical work, and research efforts that have contributed to the development of the treatment approach, detailed in Chapters 4–9. An overview of our ecological–developmental approach to cognitive–behavioral treatment is presented in Chapter 4, and Chapter 5 describes the treatment-planning and preparation-for-change phases of intervention. Child skills training is discussed in Chapter 6, and the parent and family components of the treatment are articulated in Chapter 7. In Chapter 8, we discuss consultation to the child's school setting regarding his/her general educational plan and the implementation of cognitive–behavioral methods in the school setting. We also consider different models for implementing school-based treatment programming. Chapter 9 presents a specific treatment manual that can be used to guide clinic- or school-based treatment efforts. Finally, in the epilogue we consider continuing concerns in the understanding, assessment, and treatment of ADHD.

Importance of a Developmental Perspective

In this volume, we discuss the application of cognitive–behavioral methods with elementary school-age children and adolescents presenting with symptoms of ADHD and ADHD with features of Oppositional Defiant or Conduct Disorder. We also present a manual detailing a particular program for working with 8- to 12-year-old children with these difficulties. Prior to detailing this intervention, we would like to argue for the importance of adopting a developmental perspective when thinking about the possible treatment needs of ADHD children. We urge the reader to view this intervention as one component of a comprehensive, developmentally oriented treatment plan. To be more explicit, many investigators (Barkley, 1989; Garfinkel, 1987; Kuperman, 1988) have suggested age-based overviews of treatment needs for ADHD children, such as that presented in Table 1.

During the preschool years, when the significance of the child's symptomatology is just being recognized, it is most important for parents to obtain medical evaluations by physicians who are experienced in working with ADHD children, such as developmental pediatricians,

TABLE 1
Possible Treatment Needs of ADHD Indiduals across the Life Span

Preschoolers
   Adequate medical evaluation
   Appropriate treatment for any speech/language or motoric difficulties
   Child management training for parents
   Careful choices about early educational programming

Elementary school-age child
   Appropriate educational plan
   Child management training for parents
   Cognitive–behavioral self-control training for child and family
   Social skills group participation for child
   Appropriate physical and special interest activities
   Medication

Adolescents
   Appropriate education plan
   Individual or group treatment for depression or demoralization
   Social skills group participation
   Family therapy
   Vocational guidance
   Appropriate physical and special interest activities
   Medication

Adults
   Individual or group intervention for depression or low self-esteem
   Group therapy for interpersonal difficulties
   Marital therapy if symptoms impact marriage
   Medication

Note. Adapted from Barkley (1989); Garfinkel (1987); Kuperman (1988).

child psychiatrists, and/or pediatric neurologists. Such an evaluation could rule out other possible organic causes for the observed difficulties. The findings of such an evaluation might suggest the need for more assessment of personality features, family functioning, speech and language development, and/or motoric development. When features such as significant aggression, intense anxiety or depression, and/or delays in speech and motoric development are observed, the parents can arrange for intervention by an appropriate health or mental health professional.

   Whether or not such features are present, parents could choose to participate in a behaviorally oriented parent training group. Such groups are conducted by professionals in mental health clinics, but churches and community education programs also offer groups that may be quite adequate (and usually much less expensive). To determine whether or not a certain group might be appropriate, the parent should speak with the group leader to learn about the group's curriculum. The parent can ask if the group will provide training in the use of explicit behavioral methods, such as learning to observe and carefully define both appropriate and inappropriate child behaviors, learning to create a reward system that is appropriate for one's family, and learning which behaviors are best dealt with through ignoring versus through negative consequences, such as time-out. Other common elements in widely used parent training systems include increasing the parents' awareness of possible reasons behind the child's misbehavior, learning better communication methods to use with the family, and examining the impact of how one was parented on one's own parenting skills. According to the reports of various parents, all these elements can be very useful in improving one's child management skills; however, we maintain that it is crucial to attend a program that includes some explicit training in behavioral methods, as these types of programs have been reliably and repeatedly demonstrated as being effective with children presenting a wide variety of difficulties, including inattention and hyperactivity (Barkley, 1981, 1987; Dubey, O'Leary, & Kaufman, 1983; Forehand & McMahon, 1981; Pisterman et al., 1989).

At the preschool level, one may have a choice about whether or not to have a child participate in an early childhood education program. For ADHD children presenting early signs that they may experience achievement difficulties, such programming may be an important component of the overall treatment plan. But in the absence of other disabilities, it is important to consider whether a child would benefit more from another year of greater freedom and less structure than from any special programming.

The most important element of the treatment plan for the elementary school-age child is making sure the child is in an educational environment that provides him/her with the support necessary to develop basic academic skills and self-esteem. No therapy or adjunctive treatment can overcome the impact of spending approximately 35 hours a week in an educational environment that is inappropriate. When a child is beginning school, the parents may wish to meet with the principal to discuss the child's placement with a teacher who has a reputation for being able to help inattentive, overactive children be successful in the classroom. We would hope that most parents would not have the experience of one of our clients who called the principal and said, "I would like to meet with you to discuss my ADD child," to which the principal responded, "I don't want any child with AIDS in my school!"

The parents' use of clear, consistent rules and consequences with the child continues to be important throughout the elementary school years. Thus, the parents might benefit from periodic "refresher courses" in behavioral child management. In addition, by the age of 7 or 8 years, other therapeutic interventions may be appropriate. Cognitive–behavioral interventions that are oriented toward increasing the child's capacity for self-monitoring, reflective problem-solving, and anger management may be initiated. The specific program described in Chapter 9 is recommended for children 8 to 12 years of age who are in at least third grade, but more simplified versions of cognitive–behavioral therapy might be appropriate for use with some 7-year-old children. The current authors do not recommend use of cognitive–behavioral interventions with children younger than 7 years because experimental studies have achieved poor or, at best, extremely inconsistent results with younger children (see Kendall & Braswell, 1985). From a developmental perspective, one would find that many "normal" 5-year-old children are just developing the form of self-regulating thought that most cognitive–behavioral interventions attempt to train (Luria, 1961).

By the age of 7 or 8 years, many ADHD children may also be exhibiting peer difficulties, so participation in a social skills or friendship group program may be of some benefit. Some programs, such as the one described in this volume, combine cognitive–behavioral self-control training with some elements of social skills training. But some ADHD children have social skills deficits of such magnitude that they would benefit from participation in intensive social skills programming in addition to or instead of self-control training. As is the case with parent training, social skills groups are conducted through mental health agencies but also through many community agencies, including public schools. Parents can contact the group leader to learn about the curriculum used in a specific group. The current authors would recommend the use of groups that offer a structured curriculum rather than those offering an opportunity for a more unstructured social interaction. Of course, the opportunity for more unstructured social relating is important, but we would suggest that the child obtain this kind of experience through involvement with sports and/or participation in organizations such as Boy Scouts or Girl Scouts, church youth groups, and special activity-oriented groups. Some ADHD children may have such attentional and coordination difficulties that participation in team sports could be a formula for failure and ridicule. To address this problem, many experts in this area (Garfinkel, 1987) have advised parents to get their ADHD child involved in sports that emphasize individual accomplishment or working against oneself, such as swimming or martial arts training. Obviously, regardless of the specific activity with which the child becomes involved, it is important that he/she has a leader, coach, or trainer that is as sensitive to the child's sense of self-esteem as to the development of specific athletic skills.

For some elementary school-age children, treatment with medication may also be a very important component of their treatment plan. In all cases, the benefits and costs of medication use must be carefully considered and periodically reviewed, but there is no question that many ADHD children do derive significant short-term behavioral benefits from medication use (Barkley, 1977; Cantwell & Carlson, 1978; Taylor, 1986). Issues regarding the use and efficacy of medication are discussed in detail in Chapter 3.

As the child enters adolescence, maintaining an appropriate educational environment continues to be the most important component of the overall treatment plan. Both the need for medication and that for psychotherapeutic interventions may vary widely across the population of ADHD teens. The type of psychotherapeutic intervention needed may vary as well. It is now recognized that some teens continue to derive benefits from medication use that outweigh the possible costs; however, others have developed in their capacities for self-regulation so that the additional benefits of medication use may not be worth the perceived costs. Some ADHD teens continue to need social skills group intervention to improve the quality of their social behaviors and their judgments about social relations. Other ADHD teens may have adequate peer relations but have developed low self-esteem, particularly regarding their academic competence, and possibly other indicators of significant anxiety or depression. Such teens may be best treated through individual or group interventions that specifically address these self-image concerns and help the young person develop more productive methods of social comparison and self-evaluation, as illustrated by the work of Stark, Reynolds, and Kaslow (1987). Still other teens have developed significant communication difficulties and conflicts with their parents and might benefit from family therapy approaches that train more effective methods of communication and conflict resolution (see Foster & Robin, 1989). During the high school years vocational guidance and planning may also be extremely beneficial in helping the ADHD child develop realistic, achievable long-term goals that are consistent with his/her career interests. The junior high and high school-age ADHD child can continue to benefit from special physical activities, such as Outward Bound or other self-reliance training programs that focus on enhancing the child's sense of competence. Involvement in dramatic and musical endeavors also provides an opportunity to emphasize other areas of competence.

Recognition that some of the difficulties of ADHD children may continue into adulthood is relatively recent, and, as will be discussed in a subsequent chapter, there is debate about the percentage of ADHD children continuing to manifest problematic behavior into adulthood and the magnitude of their continuing difficulties. It does appear that, as adults, some ADHD persons manifest symptomatology that is significant enough to warrant treatment due to its disruptive effect on work performance and interpersonal relationships (Wender, 1987).

TABLE 2
Child and Family Model for Learning-Disabled and Attention-Deficit Disordered Children

Step in process	Goals		
	1	2	3
Therapeutic objective	Increase behavioral controls and problem-solving abilities.	Define realistic behavioral and educational goals while anticipating progress (realistic grieving).	Support tolerance for frustration while maintaining effort and developing new compensations.
Task for child	Accept behavior charts and discuss problem areas. "I can boss myself. I can talk about my mistakes."	Accurate but positive acceptance of self. "Some things are hard for me." "I can still do OK."	Recognize anger and the wish to quit. "This makes me mad." "I can try." "I can ask for help and learn new ways to do it."
Task for parent	Learn behavior-shaping skills. Provide structure. Discuss problems in neutral way.	Accurate but positive acceptance of child. Manage grief. Accept disability.	Tolerate frustration. Support new and varied effort.
Desired outcome	Self-control. Increased trust between parent and child. Increased ability to communicate.	Increased self-esteem. Decreased anxiety.	Positive management of frustration. Recognition of compensations. Support for new avenues of development.

Note. From "Family Therapy for Learning Disabled and Attention Deficit Disordered Children" by R. Ziegler and L. Holden, 1988, *American Journal of Orthopsychiatry, 58*(2), 196–210. Copyright 1988 by the American Orthopsychiatric Association. Reprinted by permission.

Key Treatment Themes

In addition to viewing treatment needs from a chronological perspective, Ziegler and Holden (1988) have offered an overview of treatment themes and tasks that they have found to be relevant for both the ADHD and learning-disabled (LD) child and his/her family. The Ziegler and Holden model is represented in Table 2. These authors emphasize that the presence of ADHD and/or LD symptoms in a child impedes the child's development in three major areas: self-control, self-esteem, and frustration tolerance. They further argue that certain aspects of the family's functioning may interact with these features of the child to produce opportunities either for appropriate development or for maladaptive responses. It is their opinion that:

> Children and adolescents with LD/ADHD seem to do best in families
> whose lives reflect several related traits: the child is expected to func-
> tion with normal children; concerted efforts at compensation in both
> learning and self-control are reinforced; aspects of the child's difficulty
> are accepted as medically determined and not fully under either the
> child's or family's control; and the parents maintain their commitment
> and concern for the child at the same time as a certain detachment from
> "the problem" so that none of the family members are overwhelmed by
> frustration. (Ziegler & Holden, 1988, p. 199)

While the viewpoint held by Ziegler and Holden (1988) awaits empirical
confirmation, from our clinical experience we find many aspects of their
model quite appealing.

At the outset of our professional careers, both of us were trained in
the use of cognitive–behavioral methods with individual children. As we
gained experience and worked with more impaired children, we both
came to the firm conclusion that parents and other significant people in
the child's life (including siblings, teachers, and, perhaps, day-care providers) must be incorporated into the treatment process if there is to be
any hope of maintenance and generalization of positive changes. The
practice of working with individual children in isolation from powerful
others in their lives left these early cognitive–behavioral efforts vulnerable to critique from both traditional behaviorists and developmentalists.
From a behavioral perspective, the early cognitive–behavioral efforts
chose to ignore the wealth of data provided by traditional behavioral
researchers and clinicians on the role of the environment in shaping the
child's behavior. In retrospect, this oversight seems particularly difficult
to comprehend, given the fact that, by name, cognitive–behavioral
approaches are presumed to incorporate a number of behavioral features. From a more developmental perspective, Mahoney and Nezworski (1985) cogently argued that cognitive–behavioral formulations must
move beyond their "portrayal of the nervous system as an isolated island
of (albeit mediated) adaption" (p. 72) to give appropriate recognition to
the powerful role of family and affectional systems in shaping the
development of difficulties such as poor self-control, limited problem-
solving, and/or inadequate social skills.

In the case of ADHD children, we agree with Ziegler and Holden
(1988) and many others who argue that some aspects of the child's
difficulties are biologically determined and that, in some cases, biological
factors may set limits on some of the child's capacities at a given age and
stage (as is true in the development of all children). But it seems most
probable that with ADHD, as with so many disorders that are partially or
completely biologically determined, there is a range of possible outcomes, and environmental features may play a very strong role in de-

termining whether a child is functioning near the top or bottom of his/her particular reaction range.

While the specific intervention strategies we shall detail clearly emphasize cognitive–behavioral methods, our view of working with families has also been influenced by developmental theorists. In particular, Sameroff's (1987) transactional model of family functioning has led us to pay greater attention to the bidirectional influences that occur between parent and child. According to this model, family functioning affects child development via a three-part process in which a particular child behavior triggers a parental interpretation of that behavior and that interpretation, in turn, triggers a parental behavioral response. In recognition of the three stages of this system, Fiese and Sameroff (1989) have proposed that intervention around child behavior issues involves three possible components: *remediation,* or change in the child's behavior; *redefinition,* or change in the parent's interpretation of the behavior; and/or *reeducation,* or changing the parent's response to the child.

An ideal application of the methods proposed in this volume would include all three elements of the Fiese and Sameroff (1989) model. Remediation occurs as a result of training the child in more effective methods of problem recognition, problem-solving, and arousal-regulating self-talk. Redefinition of some of the child's behavior occurs as a result of educating the parent and/or teacher about ADHD and helping these significant adults recognize and change any dysfunctional beliefs they have about the child's behavior. Reeducation is accomplished by helping parents and/or teachers respond to the child in a manner more likely to encourage the child's development of more effective problem-solving and appropriate behavior.

Obviously, we believe that the model and ideas for intervention presented in this volume could be of use to other clinicians working with ADHD children. We also hope that the explication of this approach can lead to its careful empirical evaluation. As emphasized in Chapter 3, however, we consider selected cognitive–behavioral methods to be a third option to be explored *after* an ADHD child and his/her family have implemented or considered potentially more appropriate behavioral and/or pharmacological approaches to treatment. We hope this volume will guide some parents and professionals toward the use of this mode of intervention, when appropriate, while simultaneously guiding others away from its use and toward more suitable treatment methods.

Chapter One

Attention-Deficit Hyperactivity Disorder: What Is It?

Attention-Deficit Hyperactivity Disorder (ADHD) has been the object of intense research by physicians, biologists, and psychologists. This high level of interest may stem from the fact that approximately 3%–5% of school-age children manifest the symptoms of this condition (Barkley, 1988a; Lambert, Sandoval, & Sassone, 1978). Thus, a significant number of children and both their families and educators struggle with difficulties associated with this condition.

This chapter provides an overview of current conclusions and hypotheses about various aspects of the ADHD diagnosis and children displaying the symptoms of this disorder. The history of the diagnosis is discussed, and the primary and secondary symptoms are described. Developmental and environmental factors associated with symptom expression are considered, and hypotheses about the underlying mechanisms causing the observable symptoms are reviewed. Recognizing that children with ADHD often manifest other difficulties and that other disorders can be mistaken for ADHD, common coexisting conditions and/or alternative diagnoses are described. Current findings and hypotheses about the cause(s) of ADHD are presented, followed by information on the prognosis of ADHD children.

We view the information presented in this chapter as the absolute minimum the clinician should know in order to provide appropriate services to this client population. As will become obvious from this overview, many aspects of ADHD continue to be poorly understood. It is our hope that ongoing research will render this chapter obsolete in a very short period of time. In the meantime, the reader is strongly encouraged to study sources offering more detailed coverage of the topics highlighted in this chapter. A list of suggested readings for clinicians and parents is presented in Appendix A.

History of the Diagnosis

Many authors have detailed the history of the diagnosis now referred to as *Attention-Deficit Hyperactivity Disorder* (Barkley, 1988a; Cantwell, 1987; Ross & Ross, 1982). To briefly summarize this information, Cantwell (1987) credits a 19th-century German physician, Heinrich Hoffman, as being among the first to write a case description of a child exhibiting symptoms of this disorder. Still (1902) discussed hyperactive children in the *Lancet*, but widespread interest within the United States medical community developed following the encephalitis outbreak of 1917–1918. Many children recovering from encephalitis manifested symptoms of hyperactivity, short attention span, and impulsivity without prior history of these symptoms (Strecker & Ebaugh, 1924). This constellation of symptoms was labeled *brain damage syndrome,* which, Cantwell (1987) notes, was probably an accurate label for this specific sample of children; however, the term was then applied to children who displayed these behavioral symptoms without any physical evidence of brain damage. Later findings did not support the contention that all children manifesting these symptoms had brain damage, so the term was changed to *Minimal Brain Dysfunction* (MBD). This terminology still carried the obvious implication that children exhibiting these difficulties must have some type of neurological impairment, if not clear brain damage. The MBD label fell out of favor in light of the consistent data that only 5% of children with this behavioral constellation exhibited clear physical evidence of structural brain damage and that many children with known brain damage did not exhibit the symptoms of hyperactivity, short attention span, and impulsivity (Rutter, 1977).

As the MBD label became less popular, the terms *hyperkinetic reaction* or *hyperactive child* were used, with *Hyperkinetic Reaction of Childhood or Adolescence* becoming the formal diagnostic term in the second edition of the *Diagnostic and Statistical Manual of Mental Disorders* (DSM-II) (American Psychiatric Association, 1968). The use of these terms signaled a shift from using a label that implied an underlying etiological process that could not be confirmed to the use of a label that denoted the most salient symptom of the disorder.

This emphasis on highlighting the key symptom has been continued in more recent labels for this phenomenon. In light of increasing evidence on the significance of the attentional difficulties of these children, in the third edition of the *Diagnostic and Statistical Manual of Mental Disorders* (DSM-III) (American Psychiatric Association, 1980) the diagnostic label was changed to *Attention Deficit Disorder* (ADD) with or without hyperactivity. For this disorder, as for many others, DSM-III represented a significant advance over DSM-II in the delineation of specific diagnostic criteria. According to the DSM-III criteria, to receive the diagnosis, the child must present with specific behavioral evidence of *inattention, impulsivity,* and, in the case of ADD with hyperactivity, a history of *overactivity.* Thus, the presence of a certain combination of symptoms was required. The usefulness and/or validity of the distinction of ADD with or without hyperactivity has been debated (Barkley, 1981; Carlson, 1986), and in the revised edition of DSM-III (DSM-III-R) (American Psychiatric Association, 1987) the label was again modified to *Attention-Deficit Hyperactivity Disorder* (ADHD). In addition to changing the name, the format of the diagnostic criteria was changed from requiring specific signs of certain core symptoms (inattention, impulsivity and hyperactivity) to requiring any 8 of 14 possible behavioral manifestations.

Some major ADHD investigators consider the DSM-III-R criteria to be less precise and, therefore, a step backward from the criteria of DSM-III (Cantwell & Baker, 1988; Werry, 1988). In support of this view, Newcorn et al. (1989) assessed the relationship between the two methods of diagnosis and found that, while virtually all those meeting the criteria for the DSM-III category of ADD with hyperactivity also met DSM-III-R criteria for ADHD, another group of children whose symptoms emphasized impulsivity and hyperactivity but not necessarily inattention also met criteria for ADHD. Investigators have also criticized the loss of the distinction between ADD with and without hyperactivity. Lahey and colleagues (Lahey, Pelham, et al., 1988; Lahey, Schaughency, Hynd, Carlson, & Nieves, 1987) have argued that ADD with and without hyperactivity should be considered distinct conditions. Their research, as well as that of others (Edelbrock, Costello, & Kessler, 1984; King & Young, 1982), suggests that children with ADD with hyperactivity tend to exhibit greater impulsivity as well as more serious types of externalizing conduct difficulties. In contrast, children manifesting ADD without hyperactivity display a more sluggish cognitive tempo and are more likely to present with coexisting internalizing disorders. Lahey and colleagues argue that the greater lack of specificity in the DSM-III-R criteria increases the possibility that children with these dissimilar conditions could receive the same diagnosis. The creators of DSM-III-R added the diagnosis of Undifferentiated ADHD to be assigned to those children presenting with attentional difficulties but not other symptoms of ADHD. Unfortunately, no formal criteria for this diagnosis are presented in DSM-III-R. Interestingly, using DSM-III-R ADHD criteria to identify a target sample, August and Garfinkel (1989) identified behavioral and cognitive subtypes of ADHD. The behavioral subtype manifested inattention, impulsivity, hyperactivity, and varying degrees of conduct problems but no specific skills deficits characteristic of reading-disabled children, while the cognitive subtype demonstrated inattention, impulsivity, and hyperactivity, as well as severe academic underachievement associated with specific skills deficits related to reading disabilities. The findings of August and Garfinkel (1989) suggest that the DSM-III-R criteria do tend to combine subtypes that can be meaningfully distinguished and that seem consistent with the DSM-III view of separating ADD with and without hyperactivity. At the time of this writing, the extent to which some of these issues and concerns will be addressed by future diagnostic standards (i.e., the fourth edition of the *Diagnostic and Statistical Manual of Mental Disorders)* is not known.

Symptoms and Factors Affecting Their Expression

Primary Symptoms

Despite numerous changes in the diagnostic label and the relative emphasis given particular symptoms, the core symptoms of the condition have not been the subject of change. The DSM-III-R (American Psychiatric Association, 1987) criteria for the diagnosis of ADHD appear in Table 3. Developmentally inappropriate attention difficulties, impulsivity and overactivity are the core features manifested in the specific behavioral characteristics noted in the diagnostic criteria.

The term attentional difficulties has traditionally referred to both vigilance, or sustained attention, and distractibility, or difficulty with selective attention. Manifestations of this type of difficulty include inadequate attending to visual and/or auditory instructions or presentations and difficulty sticking with an assignment or play activity. As will be discussed in a subsequent section, investigators have had difficulty consistently demonstrating that ADHD children differ significantly from unaffected controls or other psychiatric groups on tasks assessing distractibility or selective attention, with study outcomes appearing to be highly task-specific, but differences have been more consistently demonstrated on measures of sustained attention or vigilance (Douglas, 1983; Krupski, 1986).

Impulsivity refers to a tendency to act before or without thinking. This characteristic is evidenced by behaviors such as blurting out verbal responses in class, having difficulty awaiting one's turn in line or in a game, intruding on others' activities, and shifting frequently from one task or activity to another. Impulsivity can also take the form of engaging in a dangerous activity seemingly without an awareness of the potential for unfortunate consequences, such as failing to look for cars before dashing into the street to retrieve a ball, diving into water without considering the depth and one's ability to swim, or attempting to walk on high ledges or fences.

TABLE 3
DSM-III-R Diagnostic Criteria for Attention-Deficit Hyperactivity Disorder

Note: Consider a criterion met only if the behavior is considerably more frequent than that of most people of the same mental age.

A.   A disturbance of at least six months during which at least eight of the following are present:
   1.   Often fidgets with hands or feet or squirms in seat (in adolescents, may be limited to subjective feelings of restlessness).
   2.   Has difficulty remaining seated when required to do so.
   3.   Is easily distracted by extraneous stimuli.
   4.   Has difficulty awaiting turn in games or group situation.
   5.   Often blurts out answers to questions before they have been completed.
   6.   Has difficulty following through on instructions from others (not due to oppositional behavior or failure of comprehension), e.g., fails to finish chores.
   7.   Has difficulty sustaining attention in tasks or play activities.
   8.   Often shifts from one uncompleted activity to another.
   9.   Has difficulty playing quietly.
   10. Often talks excessively.
   11. Often interrupts or intrudes on others, e.g., butts into other children's games.
   12. Often does not seem to listen to what is being said to him or her.
   13. Often loses things necessary for tasks or activities at school or at home (e.g., toys, pencils, books, assignments).
   14. Often engages in physically dangerous activities without considering possible consequences (not for the purpose of thrill-seeking), e.g., runs into street without looking.

Note: The above items are listed in descending order of discriminating power based on data from a national field trial of the DSM-III-R Criteria for Disruptive Behavior Disorders.

B.   Onset before the age of seven.

C.   Does not meet the criteria for a Pervasive Developmental Disorder.

Note. From *Diagnostic and Statistical Manual of Mental Disorders* (3rd ed., rev.) by the American Psychiatric Association, 1987, Washington, DC: Author. Copyright 1987 by the American Psychiatric Association. Reprinted by permission.

Overactivity or hyperactivity is commonly, although not always, observed in children who manifest difficulties with attention and impulsivity. This symptom is easily observed in the young child who is literally "on the go" all the time and, when not climbing the walls, is causing his/her caretakers to want to do so themselves! As children reach puberty, this overactivity may be manifested in fidgety, restless behavior, but a subgroup of children continue to exhibit greater than average rates of activity into adolescence (Lambert, Hartsough, Sassone, & Sandoval, 1987). Current conceptualizations of this symptom emphasize an inability to modulate one's activity level to match the demands of the environment. Thus, ADHD children are rarely judged as significantly more active than others in free play situations but are frequently observed to be so in more structured interactions or classroom situations (Jacob, O'Leary, & Rosenblad, 1978; Schleifer et al., 1975; Weiss, 1975).

In the past, the necessity of situation-specific versus cross-situational symptom expression has been debated (Cohen & Minde, 1983; Schleifer et al., 1975). The DSM-III criteria support the view that the symptoms must be observed in multiple environments but are not specific regarding exactly how many situations or domains of the child's functioning must be affected (Barkley, 1982). Work by Rutter and colleagues (Rutter, 1983a; Sandberg, Rutter, & Taylor, 1978; Schachar, Rutter, & Smith, 1981) has suggested that cross-situational or pervasive ADHD may constitute a true syndrome, with a more predictable course, prognosis, and set of associated features, relative to situational ADHD. Other investigators have observed that children manifesting pervasive symptoms have lower verbal IQs and greater reading difficulties (Boudreault et al., 1988). Goodman and Stevenson (1989a) studied children described as pervasively hyperactive, situationally hyperactive, situationally antisocial, and pervasively antisocial. These investigators observed that children with pervasive hyperactivity demonstrated significantly more attentional and educational difficulties than nonhyperactive children who were pervasively antisocial, but differences between situationally hyperactive versus situationally antisocial children were much less pronounced. As will be discussed in Chapter 2, Barkley (1981) has offered a unique method of quantifying the number of affected settings via his Home and School Situations Questionnaires. He suggests that a child must be rated as experiencing difficulty in at least half of the situations listed on either scale in order to qualify for the diagnosis. Before rigidly adhering to a standard of requiring extreme ratings on both parent and teacher measures, however, one would do well to attend to the findings of Rapoport and colleagues (Rapoport, Donnelly, Zametkin, & Carrougher, 1986). These investigators observed that in a select number of cases in which teachers had rated a child as hyperactive and the parents did not, the children were not found to differ from those with high parent *and* teacher ratings on direct observational measures or actometer measures of activity. Those rated high by teachers but not by their parents were less likely to actually be living with their biological parents and these nonbiological caretakers were observed to be defensive and eager to minimize symptoms. Thus, Rapoport et al. (1986) concluded that, at least in some cases, "situational" hyperactivity may reflect the caregiver's status or attitude rather than attributes of the child.

Despite these various areas of debate, Barkley (1988a) has noted that efforts to define the condition have consistently shared several features, including:

> (1) an emphasis on *age-appropriate* levels of inattention, impulsivity and overactivity; (2) the inability of the children to restrict their behavior to situational demands (self-regulation), relative to same-age children; (3) the emergence of these problems by early childhood; (4) the pervasiveness of these problems across several settings and/or caretakers; (5) the chronicity of these symptoms throughout development; and (6) the inability to account for these behavioral deficits on the basis of obvious developmental disabilities . . . or severe psychopathology. (p. 70)

Processes Producing the Primary Symptoms

There is a debate about the exact nature of the mediating cognitive–affective mechanism(s) that produce(s) the primary symptoms of ADHD. The efforts of Virginia Douglas and colleagues at McGill University have been central to the identification of possible defective processes. As summarized by Douglas (1983), processes under consideration include:

> (1) the investment, organization, and maintenance of attention and effort; (2) the inhibition of impulsive responding; (3) the modulation of arousal levels to meet situational demands; (4) an unusually strong inclination to seek immediate reinforcement. (p. 280)

Douglas (1983) notes that any one of these four processes could play a dominant role in creating the observed behavioral difficulties of these children, or all four mechanisms could be interacting in a complex manner.

Considering attentional processes, many different terms have been used to label different aspects of attentional functioning, with much past research focusing on either sustained attention or selective attention. There is a growing consensus that selective attention is a less useful concept when one is attempting to distinguish ADHD children from other groups. Research on selective attention indicates that there is significant confusion about the meaning of the term, and study outcomes tend to be highly influenced by the specific task chosen to operationalize the process of selective attention (Douglas, 1983; Krupski, 1986).

Sustained attention is also referred to as vigilance. ADHD children, as well as learning-disabled children have been found to perform more poorly than normals on vigilance tasks (Krupski, 1986). Douglas (1983) has noted that sustained attention or vigilance is, by itself, a complex process, involving at least the sustaining of attention over time, the degree of self-direction and organization of attention, and the amount of attention being used or invested. While observing deficits in the performance of ADHD children on a measure of sustained attention, Seidel and Joschko (1990) also observed significant age-related changes in performance, suggesting that within-age group performance comparisons between ADHD and normal children may be more sensitive to differences than across-age group comparisons.

In addition, we would argue that memory capacities/mechanisms are also tapped by many of the measures of attentional processing of ADHD children. Interestingly, ADHD children have been found to perform no differently than controls on tasks requiring automatic or relatively effortless processing, but on tasks requiring increasing levels of organization in attention, memory, or both, ADHD children perform worse than both normals and reading-disabled, nonhyperactive controls (August, 1987; Borcherding et al., 1988; Tant & Douglas, 1982). Tant and Douglas (1982) have interpreted such findings as indicating that the difficulties that ADHD children have with attention interfere with the development of strategies for solving complicated problems. In partial support of this view, August (1987) found that when ADHD children were given a strategy to aid the process of clustering related words in a recall task, their performance equaled that of normal controls initially. Over successive trials, however, the ADHD children were unable to maintain this more successful level of performance, seemingly as a result of failure to maintain effort. Thus, inadequate strategies for solving complex problems *and* motivational factors may be involved.

Douglas (1983) has also argued that inhibitory processes, or rather the failure of inhibitory processes, must be involved in addition to possible deficits in attentional processes. Failures in inhibitory processes are easily observed in the ADHD child's impulsive responsive style. Douglas notes that for many ADHD children, however, they not only respond "too quickly" but also fail to use available processing time in a manner that aids their task performance. Quay (1989) suggests that decreased activity in the behavioral inhibition system of the brain may account for the ADHD child's seeming resistance to the impact of punishment and/or its threat.

The ADHD child's difficulty maintaining appropriate levels of arousal has also received attention as a possible underlying mechanism. Douglas (1983), summarizing past research, suggested that ADHD children do not seem to be different from normal peers in their resting arousal level, but they may have difficulty modulating their arousal level to coincide with situational demands. In a series of experiments, Zentall and colleagues (Zentall, 1985; Zentall & Meyer, 1987; Zentall, 1989) have demonstrated that the performance of ADHD children can be normalized if the task is modified to allow a more active mode of response and greater intratask stimulation; however, with more difficult tasks, their performance may deteriorate more than normal controls if too much stimulation is present. Zentall and Meyer (1987) interpret these findings as supportive of the viewpoint originally put forth by Douglas and Peters (1979) that ADHD children have difficulty modulating their arousal at either end of the continuum of stimulation, both for conditions of boredom and for those of high stimulation, impairing performance and resulting in more disruptive behavior.

Significant research and theoretical attention has also focused on the ADHD child's apparently strong tendency to seek immediate reinforcement (Barkley, 1981; Douglas, 1984; Kinsbourne, 1984). Generally speaking, ADHD children seem to perform as well as others in situations of consistent, immediate, positive reinforcement. Although as an aside, Douglas (1984) has noted that if the reward is too attractive/strong, it may lead the ADHD child to focus on the reward rather than the task. Significant differences between ADHD children and normal controls are most commonly observed in situations involving infrequent, partial reinforcement schedules or under conditions of noncontingent, negative feedback (Douglas, 1984; Kinsbourne, 1984; Rosenbaum & Baker, 1984). As Kinsbourne (1984) nicely summarizes:

> The ADD child needs something solid and concrete or frequent and salient before he too can control his behavior the way the rest of us can under a much wider range of conditions, but then he can. The attention deficit in ADD is not invariant. The machinery for efficient behavioral control exists in the ADD child. Extra activation is needed, however, to enable it to participate consistently in controlling the way these children live. (p. 145)

Barkley (1981, 1988a) has argued that the ADHD child's difficulty applying strategies when problem-solving, as well as his/her tendency to be shaped by the immediate contingencies of the environment, can both be explained by apparent deficits in rule-governed behavior. Barkley notes that as most children develop, they slowly shift from being governed by immediate contingencies to being governed by rules or principles. But for ADHD children, this developmental shift does not occur or they lag significantly behind their peers in their capacity to demonstrate rule-governed behavior. This conceptualization dovetails nicely with interesting observations from problem-solving research. For example, Tant and Douglas (1982) observed that even when ADHD children could clearly state the rules or principles they should be using when attempting to solve a problem-solving task, they could not seem to make their own behavior consistent with the rules they had voiced just seconds earlier.

A somewhat related line of thought has addressed the role of the verbal mediation of behavior. The soviet psychologists Luria (1961) and Vygotsky (1962) put forth a theory of how the child moves from being "controlled" by the overt verbalizations of others to being controlled by his/her own overt verbalizations, to a final stage in which his/her behavior is regulated by his/her own covert verbalizations. Klein (1963) has also maintained that in the normally developing child, private speech gradually becomes less audible and more task-relevant. These viewpoints have led others to speculate that at least some children with ADHD symptoms may have deficits in their capacity for internal, verbal self-regulation (Kendall & Braswell, 1985). Copeland (1979) found that hyperactive 6- to 10-year-old boys used more overt private speech during problem-solving than same-age controls. In addition, the hyperactive children tended to use more immature types of speech and made fewer task-planning statements. As will be discussed in Chapter 3, this line of research has fostered the development of various forms of cognitive training.

Levine (1987) has written extensively on a conceptualization of the underlying deficits of ADHD children that, to a large degree, encompasses all of the previously discussed viewpoints. Levine holds that ADHD children manifest dysfunction in nine "neurobehavioral control systems" that regulate learning and social adaptation. For example, difficulties in *focal control* are reflected in dysfunction in investing the right amount of time and intensity in information to be learned. Levine's model provides a valuable heuristic for understanding the numerous manifestations of this condition as well as the inconsistency of symptom expression, but a literal interpretation of the existence of these nine control systems awaits empirical support.

At the current time, it is probably wisest to conclude that the available data make it difficult to select one process or mechanism that is explanatory for the majority of ADHD children. Greater understanding in this area must await clarification of the ultimate cause(s) of this condition. For example, if it is established that dysfunction in a specific region of the brain is characteristic of these children, then the search for the specific mechanisms involved in producing observed symptoms could be narrowed to those mechanisms controlled or impacted by that particular region.

Common Secondary Problems

Unfortunately, many ADHD children, or at least many of those seeking professional assistance, struggle with other difficulties in addition to the primary symptoms of their condition. These difficulties are referred to as secondary because they are presumed to result, at least in part, from the interaction of the child's primary symptoms and his/her academic and social environment (Paternite, Loney, & Langhorne, 1976).

Poor School Achievement

Numerous investigators have observed that ADHD children demonstrate poor school achievement (Cantwell & Satterfield, 1978; Minde et al., 1971; Safer & Allen, 1976), with Mendelson, Johnson, and Stewart (1971) reporting that 58% of their sample of ADHD children had failed one or more grades by the time they reached adolescence. This poor academic success seems attributable both to the direct effects of limited attention on learning and to the fact that many ADHD children have coexisting learning disabilities, with some investigators finding rates of co-occurrence of 50% or higher (Lambert & Sandoval, 1980). The reader is referred to a subsequent discussion of learning disabilities in this chapter for additional discussion of the relationship between learning disabilities and ADHD.

Poor Peer Relations

The peer relations of both normal and emotionally or behaviorally disturbed children have emerged as an important area of study in recent years, perhaps in recognition of the role of peer relations in the prediction of long-term adjustment (Parker & Asher, 1987). In summarizing the literature on the peer relations of ADHD children, Pelham and Milich (1984) conclude that teachers, mothers, and the children agree that the children's peer relations are quite poor. Sociometric studies indicated that ADHD children are both low in frequency of positive ratings and high in frequency of rejection. Peer rejection seems to occur for both those with and those without hyperactivity, even in the absence of a coexisting diagnosis of conduct disorder (Carlson, Lahey, Frame, Walker, & Hynd, 1987). The reader is also referred to the excellent discussion by Henker and Whalen (1989) of the peer difficulties of ADHD children.

What accounts for these negative peer responses? At the behavioral level, ADHD children have been observed to engage in more negative social behaviors than either normal or other clinic-referred children. For example, ADHD children observed in play groups were found to produce ten times as many negative verbal statements and three times as many aggressive behaviors as peers (Pelham & Bender, 1982).

Grenell, Glass, and Katz (1987) examined both the social knowledge and the social performance of ADHD children and normal peers. The two groups were found to be similar in knowledge of strategies for initiating friendships but children with ADHD were less knowledgeable regarding strategies for maintaining friendships and for promoting conflict resolutions. In terms of social performance, consistent with previous research, Grenell et al. (1987) also found no differences in a free play situation and, interestingly, no differences were observed on a structured cooperative task when the ADHD child had the more active role of worker. When the ADHD child had the more passive role of helper/advisor, he was significantly more likely to cheat and was less effective in communicating with his partner. When the peers were asked to rate their partners in terms of desirability as a friend and as a schoolwork partner, peers rated the ADHD child as less desirable as a schoolwork partner but not as a friend.

In addition to studies of social knowledge and social performance, some investigators have explored some aspects of the ADHD child's social information processing. Milich and Dodge (1984) examined the social information processing patterns of children diagnosed as hyperactive, aggressive, hyperactive–aggressive, and normal. The hyperactive–aggressive group was observed to be deficient in their attention to relevant cues on encoding and cue utilization tasks. They exhibited poorer recall of relevant cues but only for those cues that were affectively neutral (as opposed to being hostile or benevolent). The hyperactive–aggressive boys were more likely than the normal controls to attribute hostile intent to ambiguous provocation by peers and, along with hyperactive and aggressive groups, were more likely to assume that the peer would continue to be hostile. Considering their response to provocation, the hyperactive–aggressive boys were 60% more likely than the controls or the other psychiatric groups to choose to respond aggressively.

The findings of Carlson et al. (1987) would suggest that even ADHD children without coexisting conduct disorder have very poor peer relations, but other data suggest that perhaps the coexistence of significant conduct problems affects the stability of negative peer ratings. Pelham and Milich (1984) note that while negative sociometric ratings have been observed for ADHD children in preschool, kindergarten, and elementary school settings, it appears that the ratings of those ADHD children who are relatively less aggressive become normalized over time, while those of the more aggressive ADHD children continue to be quite negative (Johnson & Pelham, cited in Pelham & Milich, 1984). These results highlight the potential significance of coexisting conduct difficulties.

Conduct Problems

The development of significant conduct problems, particularly aggressive behavior, may represent the most serious secondary difficulty for ADHD children in that such behavioral difficulties seem to mediate both peer relations and behavioral adjustment to the school and home environments. Conduct problems may create social difficulties for the child even if such difficulties are not so severe as to meet the criteria for the formal diagnosis of Conduct Disorder or Oppositional Defiant Disorder. Obviously, even those children who manifest only the core symptoms of ADHD are likely to exhibit some conduct difficulties, if only because their overactive behavior leads to unintended intrusiveness on the activities of others. When discussing conduct difficulties as a secondary problem, one is typically referring to more than just unintended conflicts with others. Rather, one is concerned with more persistent noncompliance or aggression. As will be discussed in greater detail in the section on long-term prognosis, some researchers maintain that the prognosis of ADHD children is largely dependent on the presence or absence of significant conduct difficulties, with those manifesting coexisting conduct disorders being at elevated risk for engaging in delinquent behaviors in adolescence.

Factors Affecting Symptom Expression

Sex Ratio

All investigators find that ADHD is more common in boys than in girls, with the 3:1 ratio observed in a general population sample considered a conservative estimate (Trites, Dugas, Lynch, & Ferguson, 1979). In the past, some researchers have maintained that girls with ADHD exhibit fewer signs of impulsivity and conduct problems (Kashani, Chapel, Ellis, & Shekim, 1979; de Haas & Young, 1984) and show more severe cognitive deficits and learning difficulties (Berry, Shaywitz, & Shaywitz, 1985; Kashani et al., 1979). But more recent data suggest that among boys and girls who demonstrate ADHD symptoms across a number of different settings and raters, the sexes may be quite similar with regard to both the degree of primary symptoms displayed and the presence of secondary problems, such as learning difficulties, externalizing symptoms, internalizing symptoms, peer difficulties, and self-perception (Breen, 1989; Breen & Barkley, 1988; Horn, Wagner, & Ialongo, 1989; McGee, Williams, & Silva, 1987). As the primary and secondary symptoms of ADHD girls have been the object of study much less frequently than has been the case for ADHD boys, firm conclusions regarding the relative equality of symptom expression and degree of impairment cannot be drawn without additional data.

Development

The child's developmental status has a clear influence on symptom expression. As infants, these children are often, though not always, described as colicky, difficult-to-soothe babies who are somewhat irregular in their physiological functioning (Ross & Ross, 1982; Wender, 1987). It must be noted, however, that children manifesting a difficult temperament may later manifest problems other than ADHD or display no form of psychiatric disorder (Chess & Thomas, 1984; Thomas, Chess, & Birch, 1968).

These children typically grow to be active, fearless toddlers. Parents often describe their ADHD child as having moved from crawling to running to climbing in a very short period of time, leaving the parents feeling like they, too, have been running ever since. To make the situation even more frustrating, parents also report that their ADHD child seems less responsive to methods of discipline that the parent may have successfully employed with their non-ADHD children. Judging the significance of the child's difficulties may be complicated at this age and stage, for most children exhibit the "terrible twos" or present at least some degree of challenge to their parents as they attempt to explore the world. Many parents report thinking their ADHD child would outgrow his/her extreme overactivity, while others report attempting to discuss their child's behavior with professionals only to be told that such behavior was within normal limits.

As preschoolers, these children continue to seem quite active, and even ADHD children with average or above average intelligence may appear immature relative to their age-mates. While parents may be keenly aware of their children's difficulties at this age, the extent to which day-care providers or preschool teachers view the child's behavior as unusual may vary. Caregivers or teachers in relatively unstructured settings may view the child as active but not necessarily problematic, while staff in more structured settings may begin labeling the child's behavior as inappropriate.

On entering school, ADHD children are likely to have greater difficulty following classroom rules, particularly those requiring the child to stay seated, remain on-task, and refrain from talking at certain times. They may be less able to apply themselves to the learning of basic academic skills and have special difficulty with written language tasks. Teachers may continue to describe these children as seeming behaviorally immature relative to their peers. Both parents and teachers may be confused by the child's ability to perform well or attend to certain highly interesting tasks or projects, while attending so poorly to more routine assignments. Elementary school-age ADHD children may rush through daily work, missing many items that are believed to be within their ability, or may be so inattentive that no classroom work can be completed without intensive support. Levine (1987) provides an excellent discussion of the inconsistency that seems to characterize these children's performance on various tasks. Significant peer difficulties may also emerge during the elementary school years.

It is widely believed that, on undergoing puberty, most ADHD children displayed decreased overactivity but continuing attentional difficulties. In an interesting follow-up of ADHD adolescents originally diagnosed during their elementary school years, Lambert et al. (1987) observed that one fifth of their sample appeared behaviorally and cognitively normal by adolescence. The remaining 80% were still manifesting some degree of cognitive–developmental and/or behavioral deficits, with 43% continuing to need treatment for ADHD or related behavioral or emotional difficulties. Children continuing to manifest ADHD symptomatology into adolescence appear to be at elevated risk for the emergence of various types of antisocial behavior (Cantwell, 1985). In the sections on coexisting conditions and long-term prognosis, we provide additional discussion of the complex relationship between ADHD and conduct disorder.

Among ADHD children still manifesting difficulties in adolescence, many continue to display difficulties in adulthood (Cantwell, 1985). As noted by Barkley (1989), in adults manifesting difficulties, outcomes range from those who experience a continuation of the original ADHD symptoms to those manifesting significant antisocial behavior, substance abuse, and/or depression.

Environmental Factors

Certain features of the ADHD child's environment have been reliably observed to mediate the degree of symptom expression. DSM-III-R (American Psychiatric Association, 1987) notes that "Signs of the disorder may be minimal or absent when the person is receiving frequent reinforcement or very strict control, or is in a novel setting or a one-to-one situation (e.g., being examined in the clinician's office, or interacting with a video game)" (p. 50). In her discussion of manipulations found to increase the probability that an ADHD child can complete a task, Douglas (1983) lists "having an authority figure present while the children work; administering tests individually; increasing the interest value of tasks; delivering auditory stimuli through earphones; treating the children with stimulant medication; and using rewards or response costs to encourage correct performance" (p. 283). The reader is referred to

Chapter 3 for a discussion of the impact of major forms of treatment for ADHD, but the following discussion highlights available research on several of the factors influencing symptom expression as identified by DSM-III-R and Douglas (1983).

The level of activity allowed within a given setting or task appears to be a key factor in determining how deviant an ADHD child will appear in comparison to age-matched controls. As previously discussed, it is widely accepted that one will not observe significant differences between ADHD children and normal controls in free play situations (Grenell et al., 1987; Schleifer et al., 1975; Weiss, 1975), in which the child's activity is basically not under the constraints of any particular task requirements. But these children do appear more deviant when the situation demands less activity (Jacob et al., 1978). In dyadic, cooperative work interactions, ADHD children were not found to differ from normals when they were allowed to assume the more active role of the worker, but did demonstrate more inappropriate behavior and less effective communication when forced to act in the more passive role of helper (Grenell et al., 1987). These findings are consistent with Zentall and Meyer's (1987) observation that the behavior of ADHD children and their performance on a vigilance task were normalized when the task conditions were altered to allow for a more active response that produced increased visual stimulation during the task. With a more difficult reading task, however, ADHD children exhibited worse behavior in the active-response and high-stimulation condition.

Zentall has also explored other aspects of a task that influence the ADHD child's performance, finding that the introduction of color to increase the stimulation value of a vigilance task can normalize the ADHD child's performance. With a more challenging concept-formation task, the introduction of additional stimulation (e.g., adding color to the visual presentation) early in the learning process could be disruptive for ADHD children, as it is for normal controls (Zentall & Shaw, 1980). Introducing additional stimulation in later trials, however, may have a beneficial effect (Zentall, 1986). Zentall interprets these findings to suggest that ADHD children have difficulty modulating stimulation at either end of the continuum. Thus, low stimulation, rote tasks may set the occasion for increased hyperactivity and poorer task performance, as will conceptually difficult tasks that are introduced with too much intratask stimulation.

The role of reinforcement is another interesting environmental factor, with ADHD children achieving normal levels of performance under conditions of consistent, contingent, positive reinforcement. When faced with performing in conditions of noncontingent, negative feedback, the performance of ADHD children deteriorates more rapidly and they make more statements indicative of negative affect and solution-irrelevant comments (Rosenbaum & Baker, 1984).

Coexisting Conditions and/or Alternative Diagnoses

Clinicians and researchers must be sensitive to identifying all the behavioral and emotional issues presented by an ADHD child. In addition to their primary and secondary symptoms, ADHD children are at high risk to manifest certain other conditions. For example, Munir, Biederman, and Knee (1987) carefully examined a sample of ADHD children to determine the presence of coexisting disorders and observed the following rates: Conduct Disorder, 36%; Oppositional Defiant Disorder, 59%; Major Affective Disorder, 32%; tics (other than Tourette's syndrome), 32%; language/speech difficulties, 23%; encopresis, 18%; and attendance in special education classes, 32%. The clinician must also be aware that many children present with difficulties that appear to be ADHD but actually represent different disorders or problems in living. Failure to recognize serious coexisting conditions or alternative diagnoses could lead to an inappropriate, or at least inadequate, treatment plan.

Learning Disabilities

ADHD and learning-disabled (LD) children share several important features. Both typically have difficulties with school achievement, and, without intervention, these difficulties seem to become greater as the child advances in school. While the hallmark of ADHD is attentional difficulties, LD children have also been found to perform worse than normal controls on measures of sustained attention (Krupski, 1986), and, as is the case with ADHD children, it is expected that the attentional difficulties of LD children will be most evident in the classroom setting. Douglas (1983) maintains that via careful history taking, the clinician can establish whether the attentional difficulties and overactivity preceded the onset of formal schooling, as would be expected with the ADHD child, or did not begin until the child was faced with academic content he/she had difficulty processing, as would be more characteristic of a child with primary learning disabilities. Factor analytic techniques have identified *hyperactivity* and *learning disabilities* as independent dimensions of behavior but, as noted by Rutter (1983a), factorial independence does not, by itself, establish the independence of the disorders. To complicate the differential diagnosis of ADHD and LD, these two conditions manifest a high rate of comorbidity. As previously stated, estimates of the rate of co-occurrence range from 50% to 80% (Barkley, 1981; Lambert & Sandoval, 1980; Safer & Allen, 1976). A particularly strong relationship may exist between ADHD and language disorders, at least in samples gathered through child guidance clinic contacts (Baker & Cantwell, 1982; Love & Thompson, 1988). For some investigators, the question has, in fact, become not whether the two disorders occur together but whether these disorders can be considered as independent entities (McGee & Share, 1988).

A growing number of investigators have attempted to clarify the extent to which ADHD children manifest unique cognitive deficits relative to non-ADHD children with learning disabilities, particularly with regard to reading difficulties. Unfortunately, this area of research has been plagued by significant methodological difficulties, with some of these difficulties resulting from the high degree of co-occurrence of these conditions. For example, Ackerman and colleagues (Ackerman, Dykman, & Oglesby, 1983; Ackerman, Anhalt, Dykman, & Holcomb, 1986; Ackerman, Anhalt, Holcomb, & Dykman, 1986) compared ADD, ADD with hyperactivity, reading-disabled (RD), and normal control boys on a number of different measures and generally concluded that all three disordered groups perform more poorly than controls on tests of memory and rapid arithmetic skills. ADD, but not RD, boys were more deficient in judgments of occurrence information on memory tasks, but otherwise no group displayed a distinctive pattern of deficits. As noted by McGee, Williams, Moffitt, and Anderson (1989), however, the RD group had been rated as significantly higher than normal controls on teacher ratings of ADD symptoms. Thus, the distinctiveness of the groups is open to question. In a similar study, Felton, Wood, Brown, Campbell, and Harter (1987) found that ADD children manifested deficits in verbal learning and memory, while RD children manifested naming and linguistic fluency deficits. In this study, the RD group's reading levels were far below those of the non-RD groups, but even the "pure" ADD group had reading scores that were significantly below those of the normal controls (McGee et al., 1989). In a neuropsychological comparison of normal 13-year-old boys with those manifesting ADD, ADD and RD, and RD only, the only measure distinguishing the ADD group was slightly lower IQ, while RD boys displayed other deficits in memory and verbal skills (McGee et al., 1989). While McGee et al. employed careful group selection procedures, they used shortened versions of three of their seven measures because pilot work indicated that "the longer versions proved boring or frustrating for many of the adolescents" (p. 47). The decision to use shorter versions seems odd when it is accepted that the difficulties of ADHD children are most likely to be observed in later trials of a task to which the child has habituated.

Given the current state of affairs in this area of research, it is extremely difficult to draw firm conclusions about the distinctions, or lack thereof, between the cognitive functioning of ADHD and LD children. Functional differences may be a matter of degree rather than form of difficulty. The findings of August and Garfinkel (1989) also suggest that one subgroup of ADHD children may manifest cognitive deficits while another subgroup does not.

Attempting to detect the presence of specific learning disabilities in the ADHD child is, however, quite important for developing a treatment plan that adequately addresses academic as well as social and behavioral issues.

Conduct Disorder/Oppositional Defiant Disorder

As noted in an earlier section, many ADHD children manifest conduct problems in addition to their attentional difficulties and overactivity (Safer & Allen, 1976). For some children, these problematic behaviors seem to be a direct result of the child's primary symptoms, such as the extremely active little boy who cannot stand in line without pushing someone but never seems to intend to cause harm. For other children, it is less clear that their disruptive behaviors can be completely accounted for by a diagnosis of ADHD.

According to DSM-III-R, children manifesting persistent difficulties with losing their temper, arguing with and defying adults, deliberately antagonizing others, and blaming others for their difficulties are most accurately diagnosed as manifesting Oppositional Defiant Disorder (ODD). If these behaviors escalate into violations of societal norms and the basic rights of others, as illustrated by behaviors such as stealing, destruction of property and physical violence, then the diagnosis becomes one of Conduct Disorder (CD).

To read the DSM-III-R criteria for ADHD, ODD, and CD, it would appear to be a simple matter to distinguish among these three diagnoses. But, in reality, both clinical and research efforts have been plagued by the difficulty of making these distinctions. For example, Schachar, Sandberg, and Rutter (1986) observed that children considered to be defiant are also likely to be rated as inattentive in the absence of objective evidence of inattentiveness. Thus, negative "halo effects" can confound attempts to distinguish these diagnostic categories. In their investigation of the distinctiveness of the categories of ADHD, CD, ODD, and Anxiety Disorder, Reeves, Werry, Elkind, and Zametkin (1987) found that children with CD and ODD resembled each other greatly and that these conditions rarely occurred in the absence of ADHD, so they combined conditions to create an ADHD plus conduct group. They did, however, detect a group manifesting ADHD in the absence of CD or ODD. When comparing these two ADHD groups, the group with conduct problems manifested greater social disability and had experienced more adverse family environments. CD and ADHD plus CD children have also been observed to have parents manifesting greater psychopathology, particularly antisocial spectrum disorders than is the case for the parents of children with ADHD alone (Biederman, Munir, & Knee, 1987; Lahey, Piacentini, et al., 1988; Schachar & Wachsmuth, 1990).

In a thorough review of data on the distinctiveness of ADHD and conduct problems and aggression, Hinshaw (1987) concludes that despite substantial overlap between these conditions, consistent differences do emerge. CD children are more likely to have antisocial parents and family environments noted for conflict and are also more likely to be of lower socioeconomic status. ADHD children are less likely to have these accompanying family characteristics but more likely to exhibit cognitive and achievement deficits. ADHD children are also more likely than children with CD to be observed as off-task in classroom and playroom settings. Finally, Hinshaw (1987) notes that children manifesting both conditions have the worst features of both, including particularly negative long-term outcomes.

Lahey, Stempniak, Robinson, and Tyroler (1978) observed that the diagnostic distinctions between hyperactivity and CD have been particularly unclear because many of the most commonly used rating scales (see those developed by Conners, 1969; Stewart, Pitts, Craig, & Dieruf, 1966; and Werry, 1968) confound items that load on a more conduct disordered factor with those loading on the factor labeled hyperactivity. Commenting on this state of affairs, Hinshaw (1987) notes that much of the literature that purports to give information about ADHD children is actually about ADHD children who are aggressive or manifesting other symptoms of CD. Within the past 8–10 years, researchers have attempted to be more sensitive to this issue. Factor analytic studies have clarified that separate, though overlapping, dimensions of hyperactivity and conduct disorders can be identified (Achenbach & Edelbrock, 1983; Milich, Loney, & Landau, 1982; Roberts, Milich, Loney, & Caputo, 1981). Measures such as the daily behavior checklist devised by Prinz, Connor, and Wilson (1981) attempt to distinguish hyperactive from aggressive symptomatology.

Whether the ADHD child's apparent difficulty with rule-governed behavior (Barkley, 1988a) is the result of specific neurodevelopmental anomalies and more unconscious, relative to the CD child's seemingly conscious choice to violate societal norms, remains unclear and must be the object of much further research. The long-term implications of the presence of conduct disordered behavior will be discussed in greater detail in the prognosis section of this chapter.

As an interesting aside, the United States and Great Britain have had longstanding differences in the relative rates of the diagnoses of ADHD and CD. Clinicians in the United States assign the diagnosis of ADHD 20 times more often than their counterparts in the United Kingdom (Taylor & Sandberg, 1984), while United Kingdom clinicians are more likely to assign the diagnosis of CD. Some British investigators maintain that there is little evidence to justify an independent category of ADHD and that it would be more accurate to use the labels of CD with and without hyperactivity (Prior & Sanson, 1986, 1988; Taylor, 1988). Attempts to explore these difficulties suggest, not surprisingly, that when a child presents with both ADHD and CD symptoms, United States-trained clinicians prefer to assign ADHD, while those trained in the United Kingdom prefer CD. The co-occurrence of ADHD and CD can be fully noted when using the DSM-III-R system, which allows for the assignment of more than one condition, but the *International Classification of Diseases* (ICD-9) diagnostic system (World Health Organization, 1978) requires that only one primary disorder be specified, so clinicians from the two countries were more likely to disagree when required to use ICD-9. Greater agreement was observed between United States and United Kingdom panels of research teams who had extensive experience with both sets of diagnostic criteria (Prendergast et al., 1988).

While both ADHD and CD are considered chronic conditions requiring a life-span approach to treatment, recognizing the presence of CD is important for determining the particular components of treatment that are most (and least) appropriate for a particular client.

Tourette's Syndrome

Gilles de la Tourette's syndrome (TS) is an organic neurological disorder characterized by multiple motor tics and at least one vocal tic. These symptoms must be present before age 21 years and usually emerge at age 6 or 7 years. Being anxious, fatigued, excited, or watching television may cause the tics to increase in frequency, with tics usually most severe in the evening and when with family and close friends (Shapiro & Shapiro, 1989). The symptoms wax and wane over the lifetime of the patient, with up to 73% indicating that their symptoms improved markedly or disappeared at late adolescence or early adulthood (Erenberg, Cruse, & Rothner, 1987). Originally viewed as a rare disorder, improved detection has resulted in estimates that one in 200 people has TS (Shapiro & Shapiro, 1989), and up to 3% of all children may manifest at least one tic at some point during childhood (Barabas, 1988).

High rates of symptoms of both ADHD and LD have been observed in children with TS. For example, in one study based solely on patient questionnaires, 62% reported experiencing learning difficulties and 57% reported concentration difficulties. The incidence of ADHD may increase with the severity of TS, with ADHD symptoms present in 70% of those with severe TS, 50% of those with moderate TS, and approximately 33% of those with mild TS (Matthews, 1988). It should be noted, however, that other investigators have found both mild and severe TS cases to receive high ratings of behavioral disturbance from their classroom teachers (Sverd, Curley, Jandorf, & Volkersz, 1988). Some investigators have even proposed that a common genetic factor may be responsible for both ADHD and TS (Comings & Comings, 1984). Initial family study data are in conflict over the existence of such a genetic link, with some studies obtaining evidence supportive of such a link (Golden, 1986; Kidd, Prusoff, & Cohen, 1980), while others do not (Kruger, 1984; Pauls et al., 1986). It must be noted that sample sizes have been small in such investigations and, therefore, may not have the statistical power to detect the presence of small but significant relationships. Inflated estimates of the co-occurrence of ADHD and TS may also be the result of an ascertainment bias in which individuals with both conditions are more likely to come to the attention of medical or mental health professionals (Pauls et al., 1986; Shapiro & Shapiro, 1989).

Probably the most controversial issue linking TS and ADHD concerns the use of psychostimulant medication and its possible role in precipitating TS. Golden (1988) and others maintain that, in some patients, the use of psychostimulant medication, and possibly imipramine, can precipitate the onset of TS (Fras & Karlavage, 1977; Golden, 1974; Lowe, Cohen, Detlor, Krimenitzer, & Shaywitz, 1982; Price, Leckman, Pauls, Cohen, & Kidd, 1986). Denckla, Bemporad, and MacKay (1976) report that 1.3% of 1,529 children receiving stimulant medication developed transient motor tics, but no cases of TS were observed. Shapiro and Shapiro (1989) maintain that psychostimulants do not precipitate TS or make tic symptoms worse; in fact, they indicate that stimulants can be given to counteract the side effects of common drug treatments for TS with no worsening of TS symptoms (A. K. Shapiro & Shapiro, 1981; E. Shapiro & Shapiro, 1989). Golden (1988) maintains that the conclusions of Shapiro and Shapiro are at odds with the findings of the majority of investigations in this area.

In light of such controversy within the field, it becomes important for clinicians to be sensitive to the presence of a possible tic disorder when evaluating children for ADHD symptoms. The co-occurrence is relatively high, at least in those with severe symptoms, and the presence of tic symptoms would suggest the need for a conservative approach to some medication treatments.

Anxiety Disorders and Response to Trauma

Children manifesting anxiety disorders present with some symptoms that resemble those of the ADHD child. Disrupted concentration, fidgetiness, and some types of impulsive behavior may be observed in children experiencing Overanxious Disorder. ADHD children can certainly appear to be nervous but, in contrast to the overanxious child,

ADHD children do not appear to be unusually self-conscious or overly concerned about their past or future behavior (American Psychiatric Association, 1987). Many parents of ADHD children might, in fact, welcome increased self-consciousness and greater concern about behavior on their child's part! In a comparison of children manifesting Anxiety Disorder and those with ADHD and/or CD, Reeves et al. (1987) observed that Anxiety Disorder was less predominantly male than is the case with ADHD and/or CD and that children with Anxiety Disorder were less academically and socially disabled. In addition, Anxiety Disorder children were more likely to have mothers with Anxiety Disorder. Certainly some ADHD children may develop anxiety symptoms, particularly in relation to their school performance when faced with an extremely demanding teacher and/or repeated failure experiences. But such anxiety may be reality-based and in proportion to the situation, whereas the worries of the child with Overanxious Disorder are, by definition, considered to be excessive or unrealistic.

Children who have experienced major traumas, such as natural, accidental, or deliberate disasters, or have undergone extensive physical or sexual abuse, may develop Posttraumatic Stress Disorder. This condition includes a complex array of symptoms, but of relevance to the current discussion is the fact that such children may have some symptoms resembling those of ADHD. As described in DSM-III-R, these symptoms include difficulty concentrating, being easily startled and overreactive to their environment, and difficulty falling asleep. When viewed in cross-section, children experiencing Overanxious Disorder or Posttraumatic Stress Disorder may superficially resemble the ADHD child, but when the symptoms are placed in the context of other symptomatology and life events, diagnostic distinctions become more clear.

Assessing the presence and degree of anxiety symptoms in even a seemingly "classic" ADHD child is important in designing an effective treatment plan, for some research suggests that ADHD children high in anxiety are less responsive to psychostimulant medication. Swanson, Kinsbourne, Roberts, and Zucker (1978) observed that hyperactive children who also met the full criteria for a diagnosis of Overanxious Disorder responded adversely to methylphenidate on cognitive measures. Aman and Werry (1982) found high scores on the Children's Manifest Anxiety Scale (Castenada, McCandless, & Palermo, 1956) predictive of a poor response to methylphenidate (at dosages of 0.35 mg/kg) on cognitive measures. Such findings have led Gittelman and Koplewitz (1986) to conclude that psychostimulants are clearly not a medication of choice for those presenting with anxiety disorders and may not be an appropriate medication for other conditions when anxiety symptoms are also prominent.

Our understanding of both anxiety disorders and ADHD may be advanced by future research addressing the possible mediating links between anxious feelings and impulsive behavior.

Mood Disorders

A frequent association has been noted between depressive disorder, CD, and ODD (Jensen, Burke, & Garfinkel, 1988). Although less common, some investigators have also observed an association between ADHD and depressive disorder, with reports of depression being relatively common in young adults who had previously been diagnosed with symptoms of ADHD (Wender, Reimherr, & Wood, 1981; Weiss, Minde, Werry, Douglas, & Nemeth, 1971). More recently, Jensen, Burke, and Garfinkel (1988) found that while few ADHD symptoms were present in boys diagnosed with Major Depressive Disorder, boys with ADHD as a primary diagnosis did manifest symptoms of depression, although they did not meet the full criteria for a diagnosis of Major Depressive Disorder. Biederman, Munir, Knee, et al. (1987) found that approximately one third of a sample of ADHD probands met DSM-III criteria for depression and their first-degree relatives displayed greatly elevated risk for depression compared to the rate observed in the relatives of non-ADHD probands.

Early conceptualizations of depression in children emphasized that the depression might be "masked" and manifest itself through behavioral disorders including hyperactivity (Malmquist, 1975). The concept of masked depression is no longer considered useful (Lefkowitz & Burton, 1978), but, as is the case with anxiety disorders, certain isolated symptoms of depression could be misinterpreted as indicative of ADHD. For example, the child experiencing a depressive episode may manifest increased irritability, poor concentration, psychomotor agitation, and difficulty completing assignments. But the depressed child is also likely to display diminished interest or pleasure in previously preferred activities, a significant weight gain or loss (or failure to grow at the expected rate), and excessive feelings of worthlessness.

ADHD children can certainly manifest a depressive episode; however, Cantwell (1987) maintains that both ADHD and LD children are much more likely to present with what Weiss and Hechtman (1986) refer to as a "demoralization syndrome." Cantwell describes this syndrome as being characterized by feelings of worthlessness and self-derogation in relation to the child's school performance. When at school, such children may appear to be depressed, but they do not manifest these symptoms in other areas of functioning, such as at home or with peers in their neighborhood.

The relationship between ADHD and Bipolar Mood Disorder may be even more complex. There is growing awareness that early manifestations of childhood mania may resemble ADHD (Bowdan, 1977; Coll & Bland, 1979; Dvoredsky & Stewart, 1981). But distinguishing ADHD from early manifestations of Bipolar Disorder is a difficult task. Hyperactivity may be more indicative of mania than of ADHD if it occurs in an episodic or phasic manner, is accompanied by an irritable mood state, fails to respond to psychostimulants, and occurs in a child with a family history of Bipolar Disorder (Akiskal et al., 1985; Coll & Bland, 1979; Weinberg & Brumback, 1976). More recent efforts have attempted to identify interview methods and psychometric instruments that can accurately distinguish ADHD from Bipolar Disorder (Nieman & Delong, 1987). The difficulty lies in the field's lack of knowledge about the prepubertal manifestations of Bipolar Disorder, particularly manifestations of mania and hypomania.

Recognizing a coexisting mood disorder in an ADHD child or determining that the observed symptoms are consistent with a primary diagnosis of Mood Disorder is extremely important for treatment planning. Such a distinction could influence the clinician's choice of both pharmacological and psychological treatments. For example, an initial trial of antidepressant medication might be considered more appropriate than starting with psychostimulant treatment, and psychotherapeutic interventions might be directed to first address the symptoms of Mood Disorder rather than ADHD symptoms.

Response to Chaotic Environment

DSM-III-R clearly recognizes that children living in "inadequate, disorganized or chaotic environments may appear to have difficulty in sustaining attention and in goal-directed behavior" (p. 52). The diagnostic manual also acknowledges that when such circumstances are present, it may not be possible to clarify whether the child's behavioral difficulties are *primarily* the result of the environment or the result of features internal to the child. It is quite easy to believe that children who have never had stable caregivers, guidelines, or limits will have difficulty with rule-governed behavior.

When a young child from such an environment is placed in a more stable setting, the child's adaptation to the new environment can yield information that clarifies the primary source of the difficulties. But we would speculate that there is a point in development beyond which the features of the chaotic environment have been so incorporated by the child that efforts to distinguish internal versus external etiologies become meaningless. From a more speculative, ethological perspective, it may be the case that in certain environments, perhaps those with limited resources, an impulsive response style may be at least somewhat adaptive. Children in such environments may experience significant conflict between the style of responding that is adaptive at home and in their neighborhood versus the style considered more appropriate for traditional educational environments.

The degree of chaos in the home could affect treatment planning in several ways. If the family's coping skills are quite limited, the clinician may choose to work initially with the family on developing basic daily routines that incorporate a few simple child management techniques that are applicable for all children in the family. The clinician may also need to problem-solve with the family and enlist the assistance of social service agencies to insure that the family's needs for food, clothing, and shelter are met. In extremely disorganized home situations, it may be unwise and potentially unsafe for family members to be responsible for administering medication to the child. If the child is a good medication candidate, school personnel, public health nurses, or home health aides could be enlisted to help the child receive medication in an appropriate manner.

Possible Causes

Biological Causes

Genetic Factors

Evidence from a number of different lines of genetic research is converging to indicate that hereditary factors may be involved in the development of at least some children's ADHD symptoms. Data from family risk, adoption, and twin research are supportive of this conclusion.

When compared with the families of non-ADHD psychiatric referrals, the families of ADHD children have a higher incidence of antisocial personality and hysteria, with both groups of families of psychiatric referrals displaying higher rates of alcoholism than normal controls. Interestingly, parents of non-ADHD psychiatric referrals exhibited higher rates of Schizophrenia Spectrum Disorder (Befera & Barkley, 1985; Cantwell, 1975; Morrison, 1980; Morrison & Stewart, 1973). August and Stewart (1983) analyzed the contribution of having at least one parent with antisocial spectrum disorder to the presence of conduct-disordered symptoms in the ADHD child. Children with an antisocial parent were much more likely to display conduct-disordered symptoms, to have a sibling with CD, and to come from broken homes. Children with ADHD symptoms whose family histories were negative for antisocial behavior displayed relatively more achievement problems, as did their siblings. Their findings lend support to the view that the higher rates of dysfunction in families of ADHD children may be related to the comorbidity of other psychiatric disorders, particularly antisocial spectrum problems (Biederman, Munir, & Knee, 1987; Lahey, Piacentini, et al., 1988; Schachar & Wachsmuth, 1990).

Family risk studies can yield data supportive of a possible hereditary mechanism, but such investigations do not allow the separation of genetic and environmental influences. To some extent, adoption studies can tease apart the relative contributions of biology and environment. Adoption study findings demonstrate a greater incidence of psychiatric disorders in the biological parents of ADHD children than in their adoptive parents (Morrison & Stewart, 1973; Safer, 1973). When the biological parents of ADHD adoptees have been compared to their adoptive parents, as well as to the biological and adoptive parents of non-ADHD adoptees, the biological parents of the ADHD children exhibit significantly greater attentional difficulties than the other three groups (Alberts-Corush, Firestone, & Goodman, 1986). Comparing the biological parents of ADHD adoptees with those of non-ADHD adoptees was an important step in demonstrating that attentional difficulties are not a feature common to all biological parents of adopted children. Even greater information will result if future adoption studies compare the families of ADHD children with those of other psychiatrically impaired adoptees.

Limited twin data also provide support for the contribution of a genetic factor in the expression of ADHD. Observations of a small sample of monozygotic twins (sharing 100% genetic overlap) and dyzogotic twins (sharing approximately 50% genetic overlap) typically find higher concordance or agreement for the presence or absence of symptoms for monozygotic than for dizygotic twins (Heffron, Martin, & Welsh, 1984; McMahon, 1980). For example, Lopez (1965) observed concordance rates of 100% for the monozygotic twins but only 17% for the dizygotic pairs. In their case report of three sets of monozygotic twins concordant for ADHD symptomatology, Heffron et al. (1984) emphasize that while their findings suggest a genetic component, factors such as prematurity, intrauterine difficulties, abuse, and chaotic family circumstances were also implicated. Using a larger sample than is common in twin research, Goodman and Stevenson (1989b) were able to control for the expectancy bias of greater similarity between monozygotic twins than between dizygotic twins by comparing the results for recognized and unrecognized monozyotic pairs. They found that even when controlling for such bias, genetic effects seemed to account for about half of the variance in the characteristics of hyperactivity and inattentiveness.

Brain Damage or Dysfunction

Many investigators in this field share the viewpoint that ADHD children must have experienced some type of prenatal or perinatal stress. Such stress could produce brain damage or dysfunction that plays a causal role in the etiology of the condition (Stewart, 1980; Wender, 1987). Investigations directly addressing this contention have produced contradictory findings. As previously stated, only about 5% of ADHD children have hard evidence of neurological impairment (Rutter, 1977), and many children with clear evidence of neurological impairment do *not* manifest ADHD symptomatology (Rutter, Chadwick, & Shaffer, 1983). ADHD children have not been found to display significant differences in brain structure as assessed by computed tomography (Shaywitz, Shaywitz, Byrne, Cohen, & Rothman, 1983). Additionally, prenatal and perinatal stresses were not observed to play an etiological role in two large prospective studies (Nichols & Chen, 1981; Werner & Smith, 1977). But in examining events in the prenatal, perinatal, and early medical history of ADHD children and normal controls, Hartsough and Lambert (1985) found a number of factors to be predictive of later hyperactivity. Listed in order of their predictive power, these factors include: health problems in infancy, postmaturity of the fetus, poor maternal health during pregnancy, first pregnancy for the mother, toxemia or eclampsia during pregnancy, young age of mother (under 20 years), poor coordination as an infant, long labor, four or more serious accidents in childhood, delay in bowel control, and delay in talking and speech difficulties. Hartsough and Lambert (1985) argue, however, that these factors alone are not particularly successful at predicting later hyperactivity and must be combined with a number of social, familial, and environmental events to have adequate predictive power. Their views on the multiple etiological factors of ADHD are discussed in the conclusion of this section.

As summarized by Anastopoulos and Barkley (1988), while observable structural brain damage does not appear to be a major cause of ADHD symptomatology, there is emerging evidence to suggest that some form of dysfunction may be occurring in the frontal and prefrontal regions of the brain associated with the control and regulation of attention and the inhibition of sensory and sensorimotor information. In a series of studies examining cerebral blood flow via positron emission tomography, Lou and colleagues (Lou, Henriksen, & Bruhn, 1984; Lou, Henriksen, Bruhn, Borner, & Nielsen, 1989) have observed ADHD children to exhibit hypoperfusion and, by inference, low neural activity, in the striatum, which is located at the head of the caudate nucleus and interfaces with the prefrontal cortex. This hypoperfusion was observed for both ADHD children who evidenced no other indication of neurological impairment and for those with ADHD and other signs of central nervous system dysfunction (e.g., cerebral palsy). The group with other central nervous system signs displayed relatively larger affected regions. Other investigators have implicated this region as being involved in attention and memory consolidation (Iversen, 1977; Luria, 1973). In addition, Lou's group observed the sensory and sensorimotor regions of ADHD children to be hyperperfused relative to normal controls, suggesting a lack of neural inhibition of sensory perception. Interestingly, administrations of methylphenidate and amphetamine resulted in normalized neurochemical activity in the affected regions, particularly the left striatum. Zametkin et al. (1990) obtained similar findings when using positron emission tomographic scans to study cerebral glucose metabolism in adults who were both hyperactive as children and the biological parents of currently hyperactive children. Relative to controls, these adults were found to have reduced glucose metabolism in a number of specific brain regions, with some of the greatest reductions observed in the superior prefrontal cortex and the premotor cortex. Clearly, studies of large samples of ADHD children will be necessary to validate these interesting but preliminary findings. Investigations contrasting the cerebral blood flow or glucose metabolism of ADHD children with that of other psychiatric groups will also be needed to determine if these frontal and prefrontal anomalies represent a pathogenic mechanism specific to ADHD or one shared with other conditions, particularly other types of externalizing disorders. Anastopoulos and Barkley (1988) note that the findings of neuropsychological investigations are consistent with the hypothesis that ADHD children experience some type of frontal lobe impairment. In their analysis of the pathophysiology of ADHD, Zametkin and Rapoport (1986) also concluded that psychopharmacological and neuroanatomical studies implicate frontal regions, particularly those interfacing with the prefrontal cortex.

Neurochemical Factors

The ADHD child's positive response to psychostimulant medications that increase levels of certain neurotransmitters or neural receptivity to neurotransmitters, most notably dopamine and/or norepinephrine, has led to speculation that ADHD children have some type of disorder-specific deficit in their levels of these neurotransmitters. It was originally argued that these children were displaying a specific, apparently paradoxical, reaction to these medications. The work of Rapoport and colleagues (Rapoport, et al., 1978) indicated that, in fact, normal children respond similarly to psychostimulant medications, so the response of ADHD children is no longer viewed as paradoxical. But, as Anastopoulos and Barkley (1988) point out, dopamine and/or norepinephrine mechanisms mediate the affected brain regions identified by Lou and colleagues. Thus, some combination of neurological dysfunction and neurochemical imbalance may be implicated.

Neurological Immaturity

Kinsbourne (1977) advocated that ADHD was the result of neurological immaturity rather than dysfunction, emphasizing that the ADHD child's behavior would be considered normal for a younger child, rather than deviant at any age. Anastopoulos and Barkley (1988) summarize evidence from investigations of social interactions, attention span, activity level, electroencephalographic results, and evoked potential findings that are consistent with the hypothesis of neurological immaturity. Ultimately, however, this immaturity has to be manifested in some structural or functional features of the brain. Thus, the neurological immaturity conceptualization may be quite consistent with emerging data on dysfunction of neurochemical activity in specific regions of the brain.

Bioenvironmental Causes

Another group of postulated causes of hyperactivity involves the interaction of the individual's biology with some type of environmental agent. While any one of these causes may be quite significant in the case of an individual, it is not believed that such agents account for all or even most of the observed cases of ADHD (Anastopoulos & Barkley, 1988; Wender, 1987).

Dietary Factors

The bioenvironmental causes that have received the most attention in the popular press conceptualize hyperactivity as the result of food additives, sugar, or specific food allergies.

Feingold (1975) established the hypothesis that hyperactivity is a reaction to artificial colorings, flavorings, salicylates, and some preservatives. Feingold maintained that a diet free of these elements will cure or significantly reduce hyperactivity in children who have demonstrated a sensitivity to these ingredients. This viewpoint has achieved popularity with parents, and a number of cities have chapters of the Feingold Association, an organization that provides information about the recommended diet and sponsors social gatherings for the ADHD child and his/her family at which only additive-free foods are served. As Wender (1987) nicely summarized, many parents report benefits from placing their child on this diet; however, virtually every carefully controlled investigation on this topic has demonstrated that additives do not produce significant increases in hyperactivity, and the additive-free diet does not produce clinically significant improvement (Conners, 1980; Mattes & Gittelman, 1981; Taylor, 1980; Werry, 1976).

Ingestion of too much refined sugar has been proposed as another possible dietary cause of ADHD (Smith, 1976). The question is not "Does sugar produce an effect in children?" but rather "Does sugar produce a differential effect in children we observe to have ADHD?" It is entirely probable that all of us have our behavior affected by certain dietary substances, but this effect may not be specific to ADHD children (i.e., perhaps most children will display increased hyperactivity or mood lability following ingestion of large amounts of sugar).

More recent work by Kaplan, McNicol, Conte, and Moghadam (1989) found that if one eliminated a number of suspected elements from the child's diet (including food dyes, food flavors, preservatives, monosodium glutamate, chocolate, and caffeine) and reduced simple sugar intake, then some evidence of the impact of diet could be achieved. Kaplan et al. (1989) found that ten of 24 hyperactive preschoolers were rated by parents as displaying at least a 25% improvement in behavior. But ratings from day-care providers did not demonstrate treatment effects, and attempted laboratory psychometric measures could not be consistently obtained due to the untestability of the children. Thus, reliable treatment effects could not be demonstrated across settings or different domains of behavior. Curiously, analyses of nutritional status (as assessed by measurements of white and red blood cells, hemoglobin, mean corpuscular volume and hemoglobin, platelets, calcium, magnesium, phosphorus, copper, zinc, lead, serum folate, red blood cell folate, and serum vitamin B_{12} levels) revealed no meaningful treatment effects.

From a clinical perspective, it seems important to note that perhaps the greatest danger of trying major diet modifications could come from implementing it with only the ADHD child rather than the entire family. It could be deleterious for the ADHD child to be singled out in a manner that involves deprivation from desirable foods, particularly if other family members are allowed to continue to consume them (Pastor, 1987). Thus, if a family chooses to try the diet, it should be undertaken as a family project. In addition, Barkley (1981) has cautioned that pursuit of dietary treatment should not prevent the parents from obtaining interventions for their child that have demonstrated effectiveness.

Food and Inhalant Allergies

Allergies have also been suggested as a cause of some ADHD behavior. With most discussion focusing on food allergies, Taylor (1980) and Wender (1987) described how the tension–fatigue syndrome that some children manifest when having an allergic reaction to a particular food may include increased restlessness and irritability but does not include all of the symptoms of ADHD. He notes, however, that if a child manifesting ADHD also has untreated allergies, it is quite possible that these allergies make the ADHD behavior worse—much as untreated allergies could cause anyone to feel worse and perform more poorly on tasks requiring highly focused attention. While careful to note that most children with allergies do not exhibit ADHD behavior and many ADHD children do not have allergies, Marshall (1989) has hypothesized that a small subset of children may exhibit ADHD symptoms as a result of food and/or inhalant allergy-related imbalances in central nervous system cholinergic–adrenergic activity, as such imbalances are known to lead to poor regulation of arousal levels.

At the current time, the weight of scientific evidence does not support the view that allergies play a major causal role in the symptomatology of most ADHD children, but hypotheses such as Marshall's (1989) merit further research.

Lead Poisoning

In contrast to the lack of support for the role of diet as a contributing factor to the expression of ADHD symptoms, there is growing evidence implicating lead poisoning as a possible bioenvironmental cause (Anastapoulos & Barkley, 1988; Wender, 1987). Children are thought to acquire elevated lead levels through eating lead-based paint or through inhaling lead fumes, such as automobile emissions. While it does not seem probable that lead poisoning accounts for the majority of cases of ADHD, an association between elevated blood lead levels and hyperactivity has been demonstrated and replicated (Baloh, Sturm, Green, & Gleser, 1975; David, Clark, & Voeller, 1972; Gittelman & Eskenazi, 1983). In a more recent evaluation, McMichael and Baghurst (1988) studied children from birth to age 4 years who lived near a lead smelting factory. The more elevated the child's blood lead levels, the less maturity shown by his/her scores on developmental measures of memory, perception, and motor activity. Controlling for the parents' educational level, mother's IQ, father's occupational level, and features of the home environment reduced the correlation, but the relationship between lead levels and developmental status remained significant. The investigators noted that the effects seem to be enduring and cumulative.

The reader is referred to Ross and Ross (1982) and Wender (1987) for further discussion of this issue. Rutter (1983b) also provides an excellent discussion of the data on the possible side effects of relatively low-level lead exposure on intelligence and behavior and the public policy implications of such findings.

Maternal Use of Alcohol and Nicotine

Women who are heavy consumers of alcoholic beverages during pregnancy are at high risk to have children manifesting fetal alcohol syndrome. The clinical features of fetal alcohol syndrome vary with the duration and timing of prenatal alcohol use, but the principal characteristics include growth retardation, microcephaly, mental retardation, and certain craniofacial anomalies. The most commonly observed neurological findings include hypotonia, ataxia, and hyperactivity. Interestingly, these children appear to outgrow the hypotonia and ataxia, but the hyperactivity persists (Steinhausen & Spohr, 1986).

In a detailed, controlled series of studies, Steinhausen and colleagues (Steinhausen, Nestler, & Spohr, 1982; Steinhausen, Nestler, & Huth, 1982) demonstrated that children with fetal alcohol syndrome may demonstrate a number of different types of symptoms in addition to hyperactivity, including attention deficits and peer difficulties. These investigators observed that the severity of the fetal alcohol syndrome (in terms of dysmorphic features) was a better predictor of psychopathology than age, sex, socioeconomic status, and social environment.

Streissguth and colleagues conducted a large prospective investigation of the behavioral effects of social drinking (Streissguth, Martin, Martin, & Barr, 1981; Streissguth, Barr, & Martin, 1983; Streissguth et al., 1984). In their follow-up of 4-year-old children (Streissguth et al., 1984), they observed that maternal alcohol use during early pregnancy was related to poor attention and longer reaction times on cognitive measures, even when controlling for the effects of maternal use of caffeine and nicotine, nutrition, maternal education, and birth order.

Steinhausen and Spohr (1986) caution that paternal alcoholism may also be a contributing factor to some of the observed symptoms of children with fetal alcohol syndrome (Steinhausen, Göbel, & Nestler, 1984). In addition, Steinhausen and Spohr (1986) note that it is likely that the observed outcomes of these children represent an interaction of genetic and teratogenetic effects. There is clear evidence from animal studies that alcohol is a teratogenic agent (Abel, 1981, 1984), but its relative contribution is unclear.

It is important to note that fetal alcohol syndrome does not explain all or most cases of ADHD, but given the fact that medical and mental health professionals have become sensitive to the presence of fetal alcohol syndrome only within the last decade and that milder cases with few craniofacial and internal malformations may nonetheless have significant psychiatric problems (Steinhausen & Spohr, 1986), it seems entirely possible that fetal alcohol syndrome plays a contributing role in at least a subgroup of children diagnosed with ADHD.

More recently, investigators have coined the term "fetal tobacco syndrome" to refer to infants with mothers who smoked at least five cigarettes per day during pregnancy and who display symmetrical growth retardation at term, resulting in low birth weight that cannot be explained by other factors (Nieburg, Marks, McLaren, & Remington, 1985). While our current understanding of the long-term impact of nicotine on the developing child lags behind our knowledge of the effects of alcohol, it appears that smoking during pregnancy is correlated with an increased risk that the child will manifest hyperactivity and attentional deficits as well as other deficits in intellectual and emotional development (Denson, Nanson, & McWatters, 1975; Dunn, McBurney, Ingram, & Hunter, 1977; Naeye & Peters, 1984; Streissguth et al., 1984; Wilcox, 1983).

Environmental Viewpoints

The research literature has offered little support for a purely environmental formulation of the cause of ADHD and, in fact, few purely environmental hypotheses have been offered (Barkley, 1989). From a traditional behavioral perspective, Willis and Lovaas (1977) postulated that ADHD was the result of the parents' commands having poor stimulus control over the child's behavior, with the implication that it is something about the parents' methods of child management that produces such poor compliance (Barkley, 1981). It has been reliably observed that mothers of ADHD children provide more commands and supervision to their ADHD child, but these behaviors on the mother's part seem to be a direct function of the behavior of the ADHD child. In a fascinating line of research, Barkley and colleagues have demonstrated that such behavior on the mother's part is diminished when the child exhibits improved behavior as a result of stimulant medication (Barkley & Cunningham, 1980; Barkley, Karlsson, Pollard, & Murphy, 1985). These findings have led Barkley to conclude that the mother's behavior is more likely to result from, rather than cause, the child's ADHD symptoms (Barkley, 1988b).

The view that ADHD is the result of environmental overstimulation has been put forth in two forms, one view implicating contemporary culture and the other concerning features of mother–child interaction. Block (1977) has argued that general increases in the cultural tempo or pace of modern living may result in overstimulation of children who may be already at risk for such behavior. At the level of the individual family, Jacobvitz and Sroufe (1987) report that an overstimulating manner of interacting on the part of mothers with their toddlers was the variable most predictive of teacher-reported hyperactivity when these children entered kindergarten. Making a similar point from a different perspective, Wahler and Dumas (1989) view a variety of childhood problems as the result of dysfunctional parent–child interactions, with such interactions caused by a stress-induced attentional deficit on the *mother's* part which causes her to be out of synchrony with the cues offered through the child's behavior. While quite interesting, such viewpoints are clearly in need of more empirical validation.

In contrast to the weak evidence for environmental *causes* of ADHD behavior, there is growing, compelling evidence supporting the impact of environmental (primarily family) factors upon the *course* and ultimate *outcome* of ADHD children. In a seminal study, Paternite et al. (1976) demonstrated that while primary symptoms of ADHD (hyperactivity, attentional difficulties, and impulsivity) appeared to be unrelated to socioeconomic status or parenting variables, the presence of secondary difficulties, particularly aggression, was significantly related to both socioeconomic and parenting factors, with lower socioeconomic status and less adequate parenting associated with the presence of aggression in the child. Kendall and Braswell (1985) summarized developmental research suggesting that, while parental actions do not directly cause the development of self-regulation in their children, their actions may reinforce, enhance, or possibly inhibit the natural emergence of these capacities. It must be noted, however, that the heightened risk a child experiences from having an inadequate, possibly antisocial parent is not just an environmental liability but also a genetic risk factor. Thus, clarifying the extent to which certain features of the child's background pose an environmental versus biological risk may be quite difficult.

Recognition of Multiple Causal Pathways

The available data suggest that it is crucial for the field to move beyond unidimensional conceptualizations of the cause of ADHD. Hartsough, Lambert, and colleagues (Hartsough & Lambert, 1982, 1984, 1985; Lambert, 1988; Lambert & Hartsough, 1984; Sandoval, Lambert, & Sassone, 1980) have put forth a complex causal model arguing that "both individual differences in the organic and psychological make-up of the child and individual differences in the family and social environment contribute to whether or not a child is identified as hyperactive. This multidimensional or interactive model posits a complex interaction between the child's environment and his physical and psychological status" (p. 273). Their model addresses not only various causal factors but also specified mediational factors that contribute to different aspects of the cause and/or outcome of these children. For example, Lambert (1988) has demonstrated that certain mental health outcomes, such as depression, aggressive Conduct Disorder, and the receipt of psychiatric treatment, are most attributable to general factors such as prenatal and perinatal conditions and the child's early temperament, while educational outcomes appear to be more related to specific family, social, and cognitive capacity factors. In the following section, we provide more discussion of the prognosis of ADHD children, but the work of Lambert and colleagues provides an excellent example of how our understanding of the causes of ADHD and our predictions regarding the course of the disorder can be improved by the use of more complex, multidimensional models.

Prognosis

A growing number of investigators have published accounts of the long-term outcomes of ADHD children (see reviews by Thorley, 1984; Wallander & Hubert, 1985; Weiss & Hechtman, 1986). Unfortunately, a number of significant methodological problems have plagued efforts to study the adolescent and adult outcomes of individuals presenting with ADHD in childhood.

Commonly used assessment tools may actually confound the diagnosis of ADHD with that of CD and ODD. Hinshaw (1987) echoed the concerns of Loney and Milich (1982) when noting that much of the literature that purports to provide data about the long-term outcome of ADHD children is actually, in large part, about ADHD children who are also aggressive or manifesting other antisocial spectrum symptoms. This lack of diagnostic homogeneity plagues all research concerning ADHD, but it is particularly disruptive to attempts to establish the long-term prognosis, given the solid data on the poor outcomes associated with persistent conduct disturbances (Loeber, 1982; Robins, 1966).

Subject attrition or dropout is another serious methodological concern that plagues efforts to determine the natural history of the diagnosis as well as long-term treatment outcome studies (Thorley, 1984). In their excellent discussion of both subject dropout and condition changes, Firestone, Crowe, Goodman, and McGrath (1986) note that only 22% of their original sample "survived" for 2 years in their original treatment conditions. Thus, with data lacking on 78% of their sample, Firestone et al. (1986) emphasize the need for caution in attempting to generalize the results of the 22% to the general population of ADHD children and their families.

Follow-up studies of ADHD children have also been criticized for failing to include psychiatric controls (Rutter, 1983a; Thorley, 1984). Typically, the outcomes of ADHD children and age-matched normal controls are compared. Such comparisons can yield general information about prognosis, but cannot yield differential information about the outcome of ADHD children as compared with children displaying similar levels of disturbance but without ADHD symptomatology. Thorley (1984) notes that follow-back studies, in contrast to follow-up studies, have tended to use psychiatric controls. These studies present their own difficulties, however, for they typically follow back the histories of a deviant adolescent or adult sample, such as psychiatric inpatients. Thus, these investigations offer no information concerning the potentially large group of ADHD children who do not become psychiatric inpatients or do not fall into other categories of individuals on whom follow-back studies are typically conducted.

Keeping all these methodological cautions in mind, some findings of follow-up and follow-back studies have emerged with such consistency across different research groups that they do warrant reporting.

Summarizing prospective and retrospective research, both Cantwell (1985) and Wallander and Hubert (1983) suggest that a significant minority of ADHD children are no longer manifesting symptoms at adolescence, while the majority do continue to manifest at least some degree of psychopathology into adolescence. Those who continue to manifest symptoms are at elevated risk for the development of more antisocial spectrum behaviors, but do not seem to be at elevated risk for other disorders. A smaller percentage of those manifesting ADHD symptoms in adolescence will continue to display symptomatology into adulthood. For many, these symptoms may present some difficulties but do not result in diagnosable psychiatric conditions, but those with significant conduct difficulties in adolescence appear to go on to experience major adjustment difficulties in adulthood. This conclusion is supported by the more recent findings of Mannuzza, Klein, Konig, and Giampino (1989) who observed that childhood hyperactivity is a risk factor for later criminality, but the relationship between these factors is almost completely determined by the development of Antisocial Personality Disorder in early adulthood. Continuing ADHD by itself was not associated with a significantly elevated risk for arrest.

Summary

Children manifesting the primary symptoms of ADHD (inattention, impulsivity, and hyperactivity) have been recognized for a number of years, but the specific diagnostic label assigned these children has undergone numerous changes in response to emerging scientific data and changing theoretical viewpoints. This condition occurs in approximately 3%–5% of United States elementary school children and is at least three times more common in boys. The specific manifestations of the condition change somewhat as the child develops, but difficulties with attention persist, for some, into adulthood. The degree of symptom expression is affected by certain features of the child's environment, including the degree of structure, amount of activity permitted, and overall level of stimulation in the setting. The primary symptoms of ADHD tend to result in secondary difficulties such as poor school achievement, poor peer relations and conduct difficulties. In addition, ADHD can occur along with a formal learning disability or other psychiatric condition. In diagnosing ADHD, it is extremely important to recognize and/or rule out a number of other biological or environmental conditions that could account for all or part of the child's seemingly ADHD-type behavior. Controversy exists concerning both the ultimate cause of this condition and the intervening cognitive–emotional mechanisms that are responsible for the observed behaviors. The field seems to be moving away from more simplistic, single-cause explanations to a more sophisticated viewpoint that recognizes the combined effects of multiple causal agents; however, for a small subset of ADHD children, individual causal agents/ events may totally account for the observed symptomatology. Our understanding of the long-term prognosis for these children is hampered by a number of serious methodological problems that plague this type of research, but it does appear that the combination of ADHD and more conduct-disordered behavior in adolescence predicts a negative outcome in adulthood.

Chapter Two

Assessment Methods with Children Exhibiting Attentional Difficulties

This chapter addresses methods for establishing an initial understanding of a child's strengths and areas of difficulty, particularly as these difficulties may relate to the symptoms of ADHD. In our discussion, we shall also note which tools may be valuable for monitoring the impact of the various types of intervention the ADHD child may experience. Implicit in this discussion is the notion that the need for assessment or monitoring does not stop once a formal diagnosis has been assigned. Rather, the initial evaluation may establish the presence of some issues in the child and/or family that require continuing measurement. In addition to our discussion of assessment methods, we would also refer the reader to other resources that provide detailed discussions of assessment concerns (Barkley, 1981, 1988; Kendall & Braswell, 1985; Kirby & Grimley, 1986; Wender, 1987).

Before discussing specific methods, a few general assessment issues merit consideration. With the popularization of the diagnosis of ADHD, this diagnostic entity is vulnerable to being the target of oversimplified conceptualizations that suggest that one can diagnose the condition on the basis of a certain score on one rating scale or computerized testing instrument. It is our hope that this chapter will offer clear guidelines for preferred methods of diagnosing ADHD and monitoring treatment efforts, while avoiding mindless oversimplification of the issues involved. It is no longer, if it ever was, acceptable practice to assign this diagnosis on the basis of a brief examination in a physician's or mental health professional's office and a score above 1.5 on the ten-item Conners Abbreviated Teacher Rating Scale (Conners, 1969, 1973). The use of such loose and inadequate diagnostic practices has made the entire field vulnerable to critique from many quarters.

One guideline for moving away from an oversimplified view of assessment involves adopting a whole-child approach rather than a diagnosis-focused viewpoint. As discussed by Masten and Braswell (in press), professionals coming from backgrounds emphasizing descriptive psychopathology and those espousing traditional behaviorism may have a tendency to focus exclusively on symptoms or problem behaviors, respectively. This narrow focus can be misleading if it results in a failure to place symptoms and behaviors in a developmental context and in a failure to recognize areas of strength or competency that may mitigate the impact of the symptoms on the child's level of adaptive functioning. To this end, we also find it helpful to think of areas of difficulty from both a diagnostic and a functional perspective. This approach helps us conceptualize the overall pattern of the child's difficulties, while also addressing the specific functioning impairments that are relevant to a particular child. In other words, children sharing the diagnostic label of ADHD may differ in the specific targets to be addressed in therapy. Recognition of both child and family strengths, as well as weaknesses, is also extremely important in developing an appropriate treatment plan.

Viewing the diagnostic process as a team effort can also minimize the possibility of developing an oversimplified view of a child and his/her family. At a minimum, such a team could include a physician with expertise in this area (child psychiatrist, developmental pediatrician, or pediatric neurologist), a psychologist or educational diagnostician, and the child's teacher. As will be elaborated in this chapter, other professionals, such as speech and language clinicians, can also provide very helpful data for learning how the child is understanding and responding to his/her world. Obviously, urban settings with many professionals or large medical centers are more likely to have established diagnostic teams, but such an approach does not have to be limited to these sites. Smaller communities can establish their own teams through communication among local pediatricians, community mental health center staff, and school psychologists, social workers, and teachers. Establishing clear lines of communication and reaching agreement about assessment methods require an initial investment of time and effort that may be met with resistance by some potential team members. But those seeking to establish such a team should emphasize that, given the chronic nature of ADHD and the high risk for escalating academic and behavioral problems, developing systematic methods of assessment and treatment monitoring may actually save time and effort in the long run.

We would also like to emphasize that it is crucial for the child to have an adequate medical evaluation. As discussed in Chapter 1, there are organic conditions, such as Tourette's syndrome, that can present as or along with ADHD-type symptoms. Very young children may also be manifesting responses to unrecognized allergies to major food groups and/or serious sensory deficits. In very rare cases, extremely serious medical conditions, such as brain tumors, can first manifest through behavioral changes. Obtaining such an examination is not difficult if the family's first contact is with a medical professional who is knowledgeable and skilled in the differential diagnosis of such conditions. If a family's first contact is with a nonmedical mental health professional, then this professional needs to inform the family of the importance of obtaining such an evaluation and, if necessary, help the family arrange a screening appointment with an appropriate physician.

With these general concerns in mind, we shall now discuss specific methods for evaluating the child and his/her family. It is assumed that the reader is familiar with the basic content and methods of child interviewing and assessment, for the current review will highlight selected issues and methods as they relate to the assessment of possible ADHD symptoms and should not be considered a guideline for effectively evaluating all forms of childhood difficulty.

Parent and Child Interviews

The interview with the child and his/her parents or primary caregivers is the cornerstone of virtually any child evaluation process. In this section, we shall discuss methods and concerns relevant to both parent and child interviewing, as well as some thoughts about information that may be helpful to obtain with the parent and child together. Obviously, the exact content of the interview will vary with its purpose. For example, a diagnostic interview that is the family's first effort to explore and understand their child's problematic behavior will differ from an interview with a family that has undergone multiple diagnostic evaluations and is now being screened for participation in a particular treatment program. The reader is also referred to other references addressing the details of interviewing parents and children (Bierman, 1983; Kendall & Braswell, 1985; Yarrow, 1960).

Given that many of our treatment efforts require the active involvement of parents and child, we prefer to set the tone for this type of involvement by having the parents and child begin the interview process together. During this time together, the clinician can address the family's questions or fears about what will be involved in the evaluation process. The clinician can also explain general issues such as confidentiality and its limits. In this context, the interviewer can explain that some of the interview time will be spent together and some parts will be conducted separately for the child and parents. Thus, the parents and child can make decisions about what information they choose to disclose together or in private. In addition to aiding the disclosure of certain types of information, announcing that there will be both conjoint and separate

interview time permits the clinician to observe the social judgment exhibited by both parties in terms of the material they choose to disclose in
either context.

During the conjoint phase of the interview time together, it is valuable to ask for the child's understanding of the purpose of the appointment and have the parents discuss their major concerns about the child.
Besides being crucial information in its own right, this allows the clinician to observe the extent to which the child was prepared for the
interview experience and the degree to which family members agree
about the major concerns to be addressed. Having the parents and child
review the child's school history together can also be quite informative,
both for its pure information value and for the interaction it generates
between the parents and child. Can the family communicate a school
history that allows for differences in parent and child perception on
some points or does the family's discussion easily slip into arguments
about whether a certain event occurred in first or second grade? Do the
parents try to change or deny the child's reported feelings about a
particular teacher? Do the parents begin to blame each other or puni-
tively blame the child for difficulties?

We caution, however, that there are some family circumstances that
indicate that such a conjoint discussion is not advisable. For example, if
conducting the interview together becomes one more opportunity for
either or both parties to resort to significant blaming and name-calling,
then the clinician should proceed with separate interviews for the parents and child. In such situations, the information to be obtained about
the family's functioning is immediately apparent and does not require
endless repetition. Drawing upon the work of Alexander and colleagues
(Alexander & Parsons, 1982; Alexander, Waldron, Barton, & Mas,
1989), it is our concern that allowing such forms of interaction to
continue indefinitely "for diagnostic purposes" conveys an implicit message that such forms of communication, and the problem definitions
they imply, are acceptable. If subtle messages are to be conveyed, we
prefer to send one emphasizing the value of productive communication.
We might choose to end an intrafamilial debate with a nonblaming
statement such as: "It is clear to me that you are all *very concerned* about
what we are discussing. The concern is so deep that it is even hard to talk
about it together. For right now, I'm going to talk separately with each of
you to be sure I can understand each of your viewpoints on these issues."

When interviewing the parents separately, it is important to clarify
any other concerns they may not have discussed in the child's presence.
Parents are usually quite clear about their major concerns, but they are
likely to need encouragement to translate these concerns into specific
behaviors or symptoms. Once these concerns have been translated into
specifics, the interviewer can, in classic behavioral style, help the parents

describe the frequency, intensity, and duration of these symptoms, as well as the common antecedents and consequences of symptom occurrence. Having parents describe any attempted interventions, their theories about the cause of these behavioral concerns, and their feelings about their ability to cope with these behaviors is also quite valuable. Given the chronic nature of the ADHD child's symptomatology, it is interesting and important to understand why the parents are choosing to seek help at this particular time. Are they receiving more pressure from the child's school personnel to "do something"? Is conflict over child management starting to affect their marriage?

After major concerns have been sufficiently delineated, the interviewer can survey the parents for the presence of other signs and symptoms in the child. Therein lies the utility of a number of the currently available structured interview schedules, such as the Diagnostic Interview Schedule for Children (Costello, Edelbrock, Kalas, Dulcan, & Klaric, 1984) or the Diagnostic Interview for Children and Adolescents—Revised (Herjanic & Reich, 1982). The use of such schedules assures that the parents will be questioned about a wide range of possible difficulties that may or may not appear to be related to the major concerns. Such schedules also aid conceptualizing the major concerns in terms of current diagnostic categories or groupings.

Obtaining information about the child's developmental history, including the age of onset of the current difficulties, and the family's social and psychiatric history is also extremely important for understanding possible causes of the child's current difficulties, as well as revealing concerns that are now resolved but may have contributed to the current state of affairs. For example, learning that the child had a significant delay in expressive language development is valuable information even if this difficulty is largely resolved, or knowing that the parents were separated for a lengthy period during the child's preschool years may be of great relevance to the child's difficulties. Learning that the family has a strong history of mood disorder or tic disorders is extremely important information for clarifying the existence of concurrent difficulties or alternative diagnoses. As discussed by Kendall and Braswell (1985), the interviewer must be sensitive to what the shared information reveals about the parent's problem-solving capacities and frustration tolerance, as well as what is directly communicated about the child.

The child interview is not particularly valuable for revealing direct evidence of the child's hyperactivity or inattentiveness, for in the novel, one-to-one interview setting, many ADHD children are able to display appropriate behavior. The child interview may, however, be helpful in determining what aspects of the child's behavior he/she actually perceives or experiences as problematic. Certainly, some ADHD children are completely oblivious to the havoc their behavior creates. Many others are, however, keenly aware that they have more difficulty completing their schoolwork than their classmates or are aware that they are reprimanded by their parents more frequently than is the case for their siblings. Some children may use labels such as "being hyper" or even "being ADHD" to describe themselves. The clinician needs to clarify what the child thinks such labels mean. Asking the child how he/she explains the problematic behavior and what seems to make it better or worse can be very revealing. When asking such complex questions, it is particularly valuable to keep in mind Bierman's (1983) suggestions for aiding the child's comprehension. For example, Bierman recommends that, in contrast to what one might do when interviewing an adult, offering structured response alternatives or questioning in a manner analogous to an incomplete sentences questionnaire may be beneficial with children.

Like parents, children need to be asked about other possible symptomatology. Interestingly, it has been reliably demonstrated that while parents and children tend to agree on the occurrence of discrete events, children are better informants about symptoms reflective of their subjective emotional distress (Herjanic & Reich, 1982). Thus, it is particularly important that children as well as their parents be questioned about signs and symptoms of anxiety, depression and distortions in thinking. Child versions of structured interviews, such as the previously mentioned Diagnostic Interview Schedule for Children and Diagnotic Interview for Children and Adolescents, and interview schedules specifically focused on depression, such as the Child Depression Rating Scale (Pozanski, Cook, & Carroll, 1979), can be valuable for this purpose.

As discussed by Karoly (1981) and Kendall and Braswell (1985), how the child discusses himself/herself in the initial interview offers an excellent opportunity to form a preliminary view of the child's problem-solving capacities and sophistication. Does the child seem mystified by his/her behavior and make no active attempts to cope with it, or has the child developed his/her own theories about the problematic behaviors and attempted to carry out coping efforts consistent with these theories? For example, one of our clients attributed some of his difficulties to "getting too hyper" when he was with too many friends, so he had told his mother he thought he would do better if he just played with his friends individually. Such reasoning suggests that the child is clearly developing his own conscious problem-solving strategies and further indicates that he may be an excellent candidate for a cognitive–behavioral intervention program. Kirby and Grimley (1986) offer an excellent discussion of how the child interview can be used to gain insight into the child's attributional style, awareness of the role of attentional difficulties, and views of common treatments, as well as his/her general perception of his/her functioning at home and school.

Other semistructured interview formats that assess factors of interest to cognitive–behavioral therapists include the interview of Asarnow and Callan (1985) that elicits the child's response to social problem-solving dilemmas and the attribution-focused interview of Dodge, Murphy, and Buchsbaum (1984) that explores the child's perception and interpretation of the aggressive behavior of others.

Clearly, the information presented suggests that the parent and child interviews must be comprehensive in order to rule in or rule out the presence of ADHD symptoms and/or recognize the existence of a coexisting condition or alternative explanation for the observed difficulties.

Parent and Teacher Rating Scales

Parent and teacher ratings of children's behavior have been widely used in the evaluation of many types of childhood difficulties but have been particularly prominent in efforts to identify ADHD symptoms in children. As discussed by Barkley (1988a) and Conners (1987), there are both advantages and disadvantages to the use of such scales.

On the positive side, parent and teacher rating scales provide an efficient, cost-effective means of gathering information from the most significant adults in the child's life. They provide a means of quantifying the myriad of observations these important adults have made and a more objective method of comparing the child's behavior in his/her two major life settings—home and school. As noted by Achenbach (1987), if the scales have been well-developed, they also provide a means of comparing a child's behavior to that of peers of the same age and sex.

On the negative side, such scales are clearly subject to the effects of both positive and negative biases. For example, a teacher may tend to rate a bright, engaging child with ADHD symptoms more positively because the child is so likeable, minimizing or excusing evidence of behavioral difficulty. On the other hand, a child who is quite aggressive and much less appealing may be rated highly on other negative behavioral traits that he does not actually manifest (Schachar et al., 1986). Rating scales also assume that the rater possesses adequate knowledge to produce a valid rating of the child. This assumption may be safe if an elementary teacher is asked to rate a pupil in the mid to late school year, but the teacher may not possess adequate knowledge if asked to make the rating too early in the school year. Generally speaking, junior high and high school teachers have much more limited interaction with a pupil, and it may take them longer to acquire a realistic appraisal of the child. In addition, in the secondary school setting, it is certainly recommended that more than one teacher complete the desired ratings. Finally, difficulties with parent and teacher rating scales emerge when they are used in treatment outcome studies or for any other purpose that demands repeated administrations. At least one widely used rating scale, the Conners Parent and Teacher Rating Scales (Conners, 1970; Goyette, Conners, & Ulrich, 1978), has reliably demonstrated a tendency to yield a lower score on second administration, even if the interval between administrations is relatively brief and/or no intervention has occurred. To avoid false evidence of "improvement," Conners and Barkley (1985) advise administering the scale more than once during the baseline period. In addition, problems of bias arise if parents and/or teachers have been involved in some aspect of the attempted interventions. Clearly, whether or not parents and teachers have been involved in the intervention efforts, it is important to obtain their observations of any perceived effects; however, if these key figures were involved in the treatment process, an investigator would also want to demonstrate effects via more unbiased observers or additional sources of data.

A final issue to consider before presenting specific examples of parent and teacher scales is that such scales vary tremendously in the range of psychopathology and behavioral difficulties they attempt to cover and, thus, vary to some degree in their purpose. Some scales are designed to cover many different areas of possible difficulty and can, therefore, yield information about the simultaneous presence (or absence) of symptoms reflective of a number of different types of disorders or difficulties. In subsequent discussions, we shall refer to these measures as broad-spectrum rating scales. Other commonly used scales are designed with the explicit purpose of detecting the presence or absence of symptoms associated with a specific disorder or difficulty. Obviously, such scales, which we shall refer to as narrow or focused scales, cannot yield information about the presence of another disorder, unless the symptoms of another condition have significant overlap with the symptoms of the disorder targeted by the scale. Given their comprehensive coverage, broad scales are extremely valuable for use during an initial screening or diagnostic evaluation. Such measures help guard against the possibility of attending to one area of symptomatology while ignoring another domain equally worthy of concern. Given their length, they may be more difficult to use repeatedly, especially over the course of a limited time frame. Narrow scales are valuable for confirming the presence of a difficulty that emerged from a broad measure. Such scales tend to be brief and are, therefore, easy to use as repeated measures for monitoring the impact of treatment focused on that specific disorder. Thus, both types of scales have an important place in an adequate evaluation process, but the user must be clear on the purpose for which he/she is using a particular scale.

The preceding discussion of difficulties with rating scales is not meant to discourage their use, but rather to make clinicians, parents, and teachers more informed users of such scales and wiser consumers of the information such instruments yield.

The Child Behavior Checklist (Achenbach, 1978; Achenbach & Edelbrock, 1979; Edelbrock & Achenbach, 1984) is an excellent example of a well-developed broad-spectrum scale that is available in both parent and teacher forms. The Child Behavior Checklist assesses a number of different areas of psychopathology as well as adaptive capacities, and the scoring has been separately normed for boys and girls at three different age levels (4 to 5 years, 6 to 11 years and 12 to 16 years). Computerized scoring programs are available for both the parent and teacher forms (Thomas Achenbach, PhD, Department of Psychiatry, University of Vermont Medical School, Burlington, VT 05401). There is also a self-report version of the Child Behavior Checklist for children 11 years and older. ADHD children may show elevations on a number of different scales, particularly those reflecting externalizing problem behaviors. The value of this, and other broad rating scales, is not so much in producing a classic ADHD profile but rather in providing a better understanding of all dimensions of the child's functioning. Other examples of broad-spectrum measures include the Personality Inventory for Children (Wirt, Lachar, Klinedinst, & Seat, 1981), the Conners Parent and Teacher Rating Scales (Conners, 1969, 1973; Goyette et al., 1978), and the Walker Problem Behavior Identification Checklist (Walker, 1970).

A number of focused scales have been used in research and treatment of ADHD children. The most widely used, but currently controversial, measure is the Conners Abbreviated Scale (Conners, 1969; Goyette et al., 1978), which was originally constructed from the ten items from the longer teacher version that loaded most highly on the factors of the longer scale. Unfortunately, as Ullmann, Sleator, and Sprague (1985) clearly discuss, a number of different versions of this ten-item scale have been employed, with some having significantly different wording of items than the original scale. In addition, despite the fact that this scale is, for unclear reasons, referred to as the Hyperactivity Index, it was constructed to be, and in reality is, a psychopathology index, since the items were selected by virtue of their high loadings on all factors of the longer Conners, not just their loading on the hyperactivity scale (Conners, 1987). As discussed by Conners and Barkley (1985), when used as a screening measure, the ten-item Hyperactivity Index tends to select children demonstrating symptoms of both hyperactivity and aggressive conduct disorders. As discussed in Chapter 1, many of the existing long-term outcome data on ADHD are difficult to interpret due to the use of measures such as the Hyperactivity Index as the original screening instrument. Use of the measure has also been problematic as a result of the use of a uniform cutoff score (raw score of 15 or mean item score of 1.5), despite clear evidence of significant sex and age variations in average scores in normal populations (Barkley, 1981; Ullmann et al., 1985).

In an attempt to recognize but also distinguish the presence of inattentive and aggressive symptomatology, Loney and Milich (1982) created the Iowa Conners Teacher Rating Scale. This measure consists of two five-item scales that assess inattention/overactivity and aggression. The scales are composed of those items from the full-length Conners Teacher Rating Scale that correlated with either (but not both) empirically derived hyperactivity or aggression factors that were based on psychiatric chart data. The Iowa Conners appears to have both adequate internal consistency and test–retest reliability (Loney & Milich, 1982). The inattention/overactivity and aggression subscales have also demonstrated unique prediction validity (Atkins, Pelham, & Licht, 1989; Johnson & Pelham, 1986), with the inattention/overactivity factor related to high activity in the classroom and playground, having a disorganized desk, low academic achievement and aptitude, and poor peer relations. The aggression factor related to disruptive classroom behavior and peer ratings of aggression. Norms are available for boys and girls in grades K–5 (Pelham, Milich, Murphy, & Murphy, 1989).

Several other attempts have been made to overcome the problems of the Conners Abbreviated Rating Scale. Ullmann and colleagues (Ullmann et al., 1985; Ullmann, Sleator, & Sprague, 1984) developed the ADD-H Comprehensive Teacher Rating Scale (ACTeRS). This scale has 24 items that are organized into four factors: attention, hyperactivity, social skills, and oppositional behavior. Scoring yields separate percentile scores on each of these four factors. The higher the percentile score, the more appropriate the behavior. The authors emphasize that, given the central role of attentional difficulties in making the diagnosis of ADHD, this diagnosis should not be assigned unless the child is scoring low in the attention factor, regardless of his/her scores on the other factors. The scale is designed for use with kindergarten through fifth grade children and separate norms are used for boys and girls. Pelham and his colleagues developed a symptom checklist based on the *Diagnostic and Statistical Manual of Mental Disorders,* third edition (DSM-III) criteria for Attention-Deficit Disorder with and without hyperactivity (Pelham, Atkins, Murphy, & White, 1981). Like the ACTeRS, the SNAP checklist has separate norms for boys and girls and is designed for children in grades K–5.

Taking a somewhat different approach, Kendall and Wilcox (1979) developed the Self-Control Rating Scale to assess a number of different cognitive and behavioral manifestations of self-control. This measure may be of particular interest to those conducting cognitive-behavioral interventions with ADHD children, for the Self-Control Rating Scale has repeatedly demonstrated sensitivity to cognitive–behavioral treatments (Kendall & Braswell, 1982b; Kendall & Wilcox, 1980; Kendall & Zupan, 1981). In addition, mean Self-Control Rating Scale scores have been found to vary with the diagnostic status of the child (Robin, Fischel, & Brown, 1984), with hyperactive children achieving the highest mean score relative to conduct disordered children or those with more internalizing symptomatology.

The Barkley Home and School Situations Questionnaires (Barkley, 1981) are unique among the rating scales discussed in that they require the parent or teacher to rate whether or not a child has difficulty in a number of situations that occur commonly in the home or school setting. If a problem exists, the rater then indicates the degree of difficulty associated with each problematic situation on a scale ranging from one to nine. Barkley (1981) suggests that the truly ADHD child will evidence difficulty in over 50% of the situations on both the home and school measures. Relative to the other measures described, these scales provide more specific information concerning where one might choose to focus intervention efforts with the child. Barkley (1981) presents some normative data on these scales, but Conners and Barkley (1985) caution that more adequate norms are needed.

As the preceding examples indicate, the evaluator has a number of choices of both broad and focused rating scales that are appropriate for use with children believed to exhibit ADHD symptomatology. The evaluator can combine data obtained from both broad and narrow rating scales to examine the consistency with which specific symptoms and problematic behaviors are reported by both parents and teachers. The revised third edition of the *Diagnostic and Statistical Manual of Mental Disorders* (DSM-III-R) suggests that, given their more extensive experience with children, greater weight should be given to the teacher ratings. As discussed in Chapter 1, the findings of Rapoport et al. (1986) also support a weighting in favor of teacher ratings.

Observational Data

As discussed in the previous section, while rating scales have the advantage of being easy and cost-effective to administer, they are subject to both positive and negative bias effects. Objective behavioral observation data has the opposite profile of strengths and weaknesses. Observational methods that are based on the occurrence of clearly defined behaviors and that are conducted by blind behavioral raters are not subject to pervasive positive or negative bias effects, but relative to most rating scales such observations are more time consuming and potentially expensive to conduct.

Despite this disadvantage, we think there are some compelling reasons to conduct behavioral observations with ADHD children when attempting to establish an initial diagnosis and, even more importantly, when determining the effectiveness of a given treatment. In addition to being less subject to biasing effects, behavioral observations permit the gathering of information about specific behaviors that may have been the targets of change efforts and the simultaneous gathering of data on normal children so the investigator can determine the extent to which a child's behavior has been normalized (Abikoff, Gittelman, & Klein, 1980; Abikoff, Gittelman-Klein, & Klein, 1977). Behavioral observation systems have been developed for use with ADHD children in the classroom, home, and clinic settings.

One example of a carefully researched system of classroom observations has been developed by Abikoff and colleagues (Abikoff & Gittelman, 1985a; Abikoff et al., 1977, 1980). Referred to as the modified Stony Brook Classroom Observation Code, this system is designed for use during periods of teacher-led instruction or independent work under teacher supervision. As described in Abikoff and Gittelman (1985a), this system includes ten categories for rating behavior. Previous research has found that code category cutoff scores can distinguish between hyperactive and normal students, with the two-category dyad of *interference* and *off-task* producing the greatest between-group discrimination. This system is an excellent evaluation tool for research purposes, but the extensive observer training required to achieve adequate levels of reliability may render this method impractical for many clinical settings (see Abikoff et al., 1977, for observer training information).

Rapport and colleagues (Rapport, Stoner, DuPaul, Birmingham, & Tucker, 1985; Rapport et al.,1987) employed a behavioral observation system that assesses the extent to which a child is off-task during periods of in-seat academic work. Evaluations of the effects of different doses of psychostimulant medication have found this observational measure to be quite sensitive to both overall and between-dose differences (Rapport et al., 1985, 1987). Interestingly, this in-setting observational approach was more sensitive to such differences than clinic-based assessments using tasks of the Continuous Performance Test type (Rapport et al., 1987) or paired-associate learning tasks (Rapport et al., 1985). Unfortunately, neither of the Rapport articles nor the articles in which this system was first used describe the length of training time required to achieve observed reliability (Iwata & Bailey, 1974; Rapport, Murphy, & Bailey, 1980, 1982).

Several well-documented systems for conducting in-home observations have also been developed. The system created by Patterson and colleagues (Patterson, Ray, Shaw, & Cobb, 1969) for use with conduct-disordered children is probably the most well known of the available systems. This coding system allows the ongoing recording of family interactions, not just child behaviors. The Response-Class Matrix (Mash, Terdal, & Anderson, 1973) is another behavioral observation system developed for assessing parent–child interactions. Both these systems require significant observer training time and, as previously noted, may not be easily incorporated into a routine clinic assessment.

Given the difficulties involved in conducting observations in the home and school settings, several investigators have developed methods of recording parent and child behaviors in analogue clinic situations (Atkeson & Forehand, 1981; Eyberg & Johnson, 1974; Hughes & Haynes, 1978; Milich, Loney, & Landau, 1982). Barkley and colleagues (Barkley, Fischer, Newby, & Breen, 1988; Breen, 1989) have modified the Milich et al. (1982) system in an attempt to create an analogue academic playroom situation in which the child is asked to remain seated and complete grade-appropriate mathematical problems while his mother reads magazines at the opposite end of the room. Over a 15-minute period, the observer records the extent to which the child is off-task, fidgets, vocalizes, talks to his/her mother, plays with objects, is out-of-seat, or displays negative behavior towards the mother. The number of times the mother makes a command to the child is also recorded. The findings of Barkley et al. (1988) indicate that this measure is sensitive to drug and between-dose effects, and Barkley (1988b) states that coders are easily trained, but neither citation provides an exact statement of the training time required to achieve adequate levels of reliability. The Systematic Observation of Academic and Play Settings (SOAPS) is another analogue observation method developed by Roberts and colleagues (Roberts, Milich, & Loney, 1985; Robert, Ray, & Roberts, 1984). Roberts (1990) reports that analyzing behavior in the restricted academic setting via the SOAPS allowed her to reliably distinguish hyperactive, aggressive and hyperactive–aggressive boys.

The current authors suggest that clinicians might first choose to contact the child's school and learn if certain staff routinely conduct observations of on- and off-task behavior in the classroom. If such staff are available, then it would be preferable to obtain *in vivo* data from the classroom setting, given concerns about setting effects (Rapport et al., 1987). If the school is not willing or able to provide such data, and/or if there are issues in the parent–child relationship that merit direct observation, then the clinician may prefer to use an analogue observation situation such as those developed by Barkley et al. (1988), Roberts et al. (1984), or Forehand and McMahon (1981).

Artifacts of Behavior

In addition to observing behavior directly, desired and undesired behavior produces various artifacts that the clinician or researcher may
choose to measure. For example, Rapport et al. (1987) recorded the
percent of problems completed in a given work period and percent
correct. These measures were then combined to produce an academic
efficiency score. Along with the direct behavioral observations, Rapport
et al. (1987) found this academic efficiency score to be quite sensitive to
overall and between-dose effects of psychostimulant medication. Kendall and Braswell (1985) also discuss the gathering of archival data, such
as the frequency with which the child receives tickets, pink slips, sus-
pensions, or whatever the school-specific indicator of major misbehavior
might be. These measures would not necessarily play a key role in
diagnosing a child, but they could be important real-world indicators of
the success or failure of a given treatment approach.

Intellectual and Achievement Testing

When undergoing initial evaluation, children presenting with possible
symptoms of ADHD need to undergo individual intelligence testing with
a standard, widely accepted instrument, such as the Wechsler Intelligence Scale for Children—Revised (WISC-R) (Wechsler, 1974), the
Stanford–Binet Fourth Edition (Thorndike, Hagen, & Sattler, 1986), or
the Kaufman Assessment Battery for Children (Kaufman & Kaufman,
1983). Assessment with such an instrument is necessary to establish the
child's general level of intellectual functioning and to determine any
existing differences or discrepancies among the child's capacities in
various domains of cognitive functioning. Other test batteries have been
developed with the goal of assessing specific underlying cognitive abilities that may be of particular relevance to the assessment of the ADHD
child. For example, the Detroit Tests of Learning Aptitude (Hammill,
1985) contain a number of subtests that emphasize concentration and
attentional capacity. Such measures can serve as a means to further
explore any areas of deficit that emerge from the initial intellectual
assessment. Such information is crucial for several reasons. The diagnosis of ADHD requires that the child's behavior be inconsistent with
his/her cognitive age or level. For example, perhaps a child's attentional
capacities appear more like those of someone 2 years younger. This
observation might lead to an appropriate diagnosis of ADHD if the
child's cognitive capacities are at age level or advanced. If, however,
the child's performance on intellectual testing suggests that he/she is

exhibiting delays of 2 or more years across all aspects of intellectual functioning, then assigning a diagnosis of ADHD would be inappropriate, for the child's attentional capacities are actually in line with his/her other cognitive capabilities.

For other children, extreme discrepancies between different cognitive capacities may offer a total or partial explanation for observed attentional difficulties. For example, if a child does extremely poorly on subtests requiring verbal reasoning and fluency but quite well on subtests that tap into mechanical or spatial reasoning capacities, this might be an initial sign of a significant language-based learning disability. As discussed in Chapter 1, some types of learning disabilities may cause a child to appear ADHD. In addition, recognition of the existence of a coexisting learning disability is important for adequate treatment planning, even if it does not fully account for the ADHD symptoms.

A full understanding of possible learning disabilities or differences also requires the administration of standard measures of achievement, such as the Woodcock–Johnson Tests of Achievement (Woodcock & Johnson, 1977) or the Peabody Individual Achievement Test—Revised (Markwardt, 1989). The level of knowledge a child has achieved in a certain subject area can then be compared with what might be expected, given the child's general intellectual ability and current grade placement, and any discrepancies can be observed.

In the past, it has been popular to place a great deal of emphasis on the scores a child obtains on certain subtests of standard IQ measures in order to rule in or rule out a diagnosis of ADHD. For example, when using the WISC-R, psychologists would place great emphasis on the Arithmetic, Digit Span, and Coding subtests that make up the Freedom from Distractibility Factor (Kaufman & Kaufman, 1983). The current authors would like to caution against overinterpretation of such information. Once again, it is extremely important to consider the context in which the child's performance occurs. Certainly, if a child performs poorly on subtests assessing attention even in the one-to-one testing situation, this is powerful information, for it is reasonably safe to assume that most environments in which the child must function contain even more possible distractors than is true in the testing environment. On the other hand, if the child performs adequately on these measures in the one-to-one environment, this does not necessarily rule out the presence of significant attentional difficulties in less ideal or more distracting settings. And, finally, it is possible that a child might perform significantly better on these subtests than in other domains of cognitive functioning. Such results may be particularly puzzling and signal the need for an extremely thorough evaluation of all possible alternative explanations for the observed ADHD-like behaviors.

Laboratory Measures of Attention, Learning, Impulsivity, and Activity Level

This class of assessment tools includes a wide range of different types of measures that are purported to assess variables of key relevance to the diagnosis and treatment of ADHD, such as sustained attention and impulsivity. More than seems true for other areas of assessment, the preferred approaches from this class of measures seem influenced by "fads" and trends in the field rather than data-based conclusions about the validity of such measures and the inferences made from them. For example, as we discussed with the use of the WISC-R, low scores on certain attention-sensitive subtests were previously believed to be crucial findings for making the diagnosis of attentional difficulties and, at least in the minds of some psychologists, the absence of such findings negated this diagnosis. But mounting data on the situational variability of children with these difficulties and, most importantly, greater recognition of the typically positive effects of the one-to-one testing situation on performance have led clinicians away from overly simplistic interpretations of such test findings. Our concern with the laboratory measures to be discussed is that researchers and clinicians may now be using more recently developed tools in the same way they once used WISC-R subtest scores and are, again, arriving at overly simplistic conclusions that ignore the rather unique context in which such assessments occur and, sometimes, fail to recognize other types of processing or learning difficulties that might interfere with optimal performance on such measures.

Continuous Performance Test-Type Measures

One large class of in-clinic or laboratory assessment tools is based on variations of the Continuous Performance Test (CPT) (Rosvold, Mirsky, Sarason, Bransome, & Beck, 1956). As described by Swanson (1985), CPT measures are, generally speaking, signal detection tasks in which the subject is supposed to watch a sequence of stimuli to detect an infrequently occurring target. Virtually all versions of the CPT allow the recording of errors of omission, which are presumed to reflect inattention, and errors of commission, which are thought to be indicative of impulsivity (Klee & Garfinkel, 1983). It should be noted, however, that some investigators have argued for a more complex interpretation of commission errors (Halperin et al., 1988). The reader is referred to Conners (1985) and Swanson (1985) for listings of currently available computerized CPT programs.

   The Gordon Diagnostic System (Gordon, 1979; McClure & Gordon, 1984) is one version that has received significant research attention from sources other than the original developers. The Gordon includes a CPT-type task and a task that assesses the child's performance in a situation providing differential reinforcement of low-rate responding (DRL), which is believed to be a measure of impulsivity. Using only the CPT task of the Gordon Diagnostic System, Rapport et al. (1987) found that while the CPT did detect medication effects, it was relatively less sensitive to both overall effects and clearly less sensitive to between-dose effects than direct observations of on-task behavior in the classroom and academic efficiency scores. Barkley et al. (1988) also found the CPT task to be less sensitive to between-dose differences than other measures and, surprisingly, found the DRL task to be insensitive to any medication effect. Rapport et al. (1987) speculated that several factors might account for the poorer-than-expected showing of the CPT task. They found their subjects' scores on this measure to be relatively more variable than the classroom measures used. In addition, the CPT measure at each assessment period involved a 9-minute sample of behavior relative to 3 days of 20-minute behavioral observations in the classroom. Finally, and perhaps most importantly, the clinic setting in which the CPT is administered is vastly different from the "real life" classroom environment, thus the external validity of the measure may be significantly compromised.

Even more troubling data have been reported by Trommer, Hoeppner, Lorber, and Armstrong (1988b). These investigators found that the Gordon CPT yielded high rates of both false negatives and false positives when used to screen a sample of both ADHD and non-ADHD clinic controls. CPT performance was found to be highly correlated with other aspects of cognitive functioning. For example, relative to those classified as normal, those scoring in the abnormal range on the CPT were also significantly lower on measures of abstract and logical reasoning, simple verbal reasoning, nonverbal problem-solving, and simple arithmetic skills. Trommer et al. concluded that accurate performance on the CPT does not rule out ADHD, particularly in bright children, and poor performance on this measure seems to imply cognitive deficiencies, not simply deficits in attention and/or impulsivity. These authors recommend that a poor performance on this measure should prompt referral for additional psychoeducational or neuropsychological assessment rather than lead directly to treatment of ADHD.

While these findings relate specifically to the Gordon Diagnostic System, they clearly raise questions that are relevant to all available CPT programs. The goal of having a simple clinic-based tool for screening for ADHD-type symptoms and monitoring treatment effects is certainly admirable. But currently there are concerns about whether or not computerized CPT measures detect the presence of attentional difficulties with sufficient accuracy, the extent to which the findings are correlated with general cognitive functioning and the extent to which other measures are more sensitive to both overall and between-dose medication effects.

The CPT measures described above all involve some form of visual display. Trommer, Hoeppner, Lorber, and Armstrong (1988a) have offered preliminary reports on a measure of auditory attention that they refer to as the Go–No-Go Paradigm. It remains to be seen whether or not this measure is plagued by the concerns noted with the currently existing CPT measures, but preliminary data indicated that means and patterning of performance on this measure distinguished children with Attention-Deficit Disorder with hyperactivity, those with Attention-Deficit Disorder without hyperactivity, and controls.

Paired-Associates Learning Tasks

Studies examining medication effects have also used various forms of the paired-associates learning task in which the child is given a number of trials to learn specific pairings of stimuli, most commonly word–word or picture–letter pairs. The paired-associates learning task is considered to be a demanding, "high-level" learning task and, as such, it may be particularly powerful in discriminating ADHD children from normal controls (Douglas, Barr, O'Neill, & Britton, 1986), but there is debate about the sensitivity of the paired-associates learning task to the effects of different medication levels (Douglas et al., 1986; Rapport et al., 1985; Swanson, Sandman, Deutsch, & Baren, 1983).

Other Laboratory Measures

As discussed by Swanson (1985), other classes of cognitive measures have been used in evaluating the cognitive functioning of ADHD children. These include *choice reaction time tasks* that were originally developed to study stages in human information processing, *single-trial recall tasks* that study the encoding and retrieval processes in memory and give insight into organization (or lack thereof) in memory, and *match-to-sample tasks* that are assumed to assess the extent to which the subject has an organized and/or reflective versus disorganized and/or impulsive manner of responding. The Matching Familiar Figures test, developed by Kagan and colleagues (Kagan, 1966; Kagan, Rosman, Day, Albert, & Phillips, 1964), has been the most widely used example of a match-to-sample task. This measure has numerous limitations (see Ault, Mitchell & Hartmann, 1976; Block, Block, & Harrington, 1974; Egeland & Weinberg, 1976; Reynolds & Stark, 1986), but Cairns and Cammock

(1978, 1984) have developed a longer version of the Matching Familiar Figures test that is believed to be more reliable and stable than the original. This measure is of some interest, since it is one of the few laboratory measures that has demonstrated sensitivity to both pharmacological and psychological interventions (Barkley, 1977; Meichenbaum & Goodman, 1971). The reader is referred to Homatidis and Konstantareas (1981) for further discussion of other laboratory measures of possible value in distinguishing children with ADHD symptoms from age- and IQ-matched controls.

In the past, greater attention has been given to direct measures of activity level obtained with instruments such as actometers, pedometers, and motion transducers. As Barkley (1989) succinctly summarizes, these measures each present with numerous issues concerning both reliability and validity, and he concludes that these tools do not make a meaningful contribution to the process of treatment planning.

Child Self-Report Measures

The field suffers from a lack of reliable and valid child self-report measures. There are several child self-report measures that reliably assess specific domains of personality functioning or cognitive style, and these are of great relevance for understanding the whole child; however, reliable and valid self-report measures that relate specifically to ADHD symptoms have not yet been developed.

A self-report version of the Child Behavior Checklist, the Youth Self-Report, has been developed for use with children ages 11 to 18 years (Achenbach & Edelbrock, 1983). Use of this measure permits a direct comparison of the child's view of his/her general functioning relative to the views provided by the parent and teacher on their respective versions of the same measure. Adolescent clients can also complete other comprehensive measures such as the Minnesota Multiphasic Personality Inventory (MMPI) (Hathaway & McKinley, 1951).

The clinician can follow up on any more specific concerns emerging from the Youth Self-Report, MMPI, or child interview by using relevant focused scales, such as the Children's Depression Inventory (Kovacs, 1982) or the Revised Children's Manifest Anxiety Scale (Reynolds & Richmond, 1985). We find these two brief self-report measures particularly helpful when clarifying the relative contribution of depression- and/or anxiety-related symptoms to the child's current difficulties. Fortunately, the issue of assessing more internalizing states in children has received increasing attention over the past decade, and a number of potentially useful scales have emerged. Interested readers are referred to discussions of such measures by Kazdin, Cantwell, and Kendall

(1989). For many children, the assessment of self-esteem and/or self-concept may also be quite valuable. Measures such as the Piers–Harris Self-Concept Scale (Piers & Harris, 1969) and the Self-Perception Profile for Children (Harter, 1985) are useful for this purpose.

Locus of control is an aspect of cognitive style that may be of particular interest to those contemplating the use of cognitive–behavioral interventions. The concept of locus of control, as advanced by Rotter (1966), concerns the extent to which a person believes his/her experiences are determined by factors outside or external to himself/herself (such as luck, fate, and powerful others) versus factors internal to himself/herself (such as effort or ability). Previous research has demonstrated that ADHD children tend to be more external in their locus of control relative to age-matched peers (Linn & Hodge, 1982), that cognitive–behavioral interventions can shift children toward a more internal locus of control (Bugental, Collins, Collins, & Chaney, 1978), and that those ADHD children who appear to be relatively more internal prior to treatment may be the most responsive to cognitive–behavioral interventions (Braswell, 1984; Braswell, Koehler & Kendall, 1985; Bugental et al., 1978; Bugental, Whalen, & Henker, 1977). The Nowicki–Strickland Child Locus of Control Scale (Nowicki & Strickland, 1973) has been widely used to assess this dimension in children, but the reader is referred to Kendall and Braswell (1982a) for a discussion of other locus of control measures for use with children.

If the clinician is planning to conduct problem-solving training with the child, other cognitive–behaviorally oriented assessment tools might be relevant. For example, both the Means–End Problem-Solving Scale (Shure & Spivack, 1972) and the Problem-Solving Measure of Conflict (Lochman & Lampron, 1986) were designed to assess the child's ability to articulate a means to reach an end when confronted with a problematic situation.

When working with adolescent clients, Barkley (1988a) recommends the use of the Issues Checklist (Robin, 1981) which can be completed separately by the client and his/her parents. As developed by Robin (1981), this measure lists 44 specific issues that are common areas of conflict between parents and their teenage children. The respondents rate whether or not a specific issue has been discussed in the past 2 weeks and, for those issues discussed, the degree of negative affect associated with the discussion is also rated. In many ways, this measure could be viewed as an adolescent version of the Home Situations Questionnaire that Barkley (1981) developed to specifically define problematic home situations for the younger ADHD child. The Issues Checklist has normative data and has been used to assess outcome following behavioral family therapy interventions (see Foster & Robin, 1989). The Conflict

Behavior Questionnaire (Foster & Robin, 1989) and the Family Beliefs Inventory—adolescent version (Vincent Roehling & Robin, 1986) can also be useful measures if the clinician anticipates conducting problem-solving/communication training with an ADHD adolescent and his/her family.

The Children's Perceived Self-Control Scale was developed by Humphrey (1982) to serve as a child self-report version of Humphrey's parent and teacher self-control rating scales that were derived from the Self-Control Rating Scale (Kendall & Wilcox, 1979). Unfortunately, other investigators have found this measure to have low internal consistency reliability (.61), with 40% of the score associated with error variance (Reynolds & Stark, 1986). Thus, the psychometric limitations of this scale argue against its use. The goal of attempting to create such a measure is clearly admirable, however, and further refinement and validation of this or other types of child self-report measures concerning ADHD symptoms are clearly needed.

Parent Assessment

Barkley (1988a) provides an excellent discussion of various domains of parental assessment that may have great relevance for understanding the child and making realistic decisions concerning treatment. In brief, he recommends screening parents for marital discord with a scale such as the Locke–Thomas Marital Adjustment Scale (Locke & Thomas, 1980) and for depression using the Beck Depression Inventory (Beck, Rush, Shaw, & Emery, 1979). While understanding the status of the marriage and the mental health of the parents is important in conducting an adequate assessment of any childhood difficulty, it is crucial to do so if one is considering referring the family for involvement in treatment methods such as those described in this volume. Such interventions make significant demands on the parents to be able to function as a team in the home setting. Information suggestive of serious marital discord or depression in either parent would mean that involvement in such treatment efforts might be more productive following treatment of the parental concerns.

Other rating scales have been developed to elaborate various aspects of total family functioning, such as the Family Environment Scale (Moos & Moos, 1981) or the Child's Attitude toward Mother, Child's Attitude toward Father, and Index of Parental Attitudes Scales, developed by Hudson (1982). The Parent Locus of Control Scale (Campis Lyman, & Prentice-Dunn, 1986) can be used to understand the parents' perception of their responsibility for the child's behavior and the degree of control they feel they have over such behavior. These measures not only clarify factors of relevance for pretreatment planning, but also serve as indices of posttreatment change.

Adjunct Assessments

Other types of evaluation can add significantly to the understanding of a particular child. We recommend the inclusion of these additional assessments if the information from the initial interview rating scale and psychometric assessments makes such additional evaluation appropriate.

For example, we have found that speech and language assessments emphasizing various aspects of auditory processing add information that is very valuable for educational planning. Such an evaluation would certainly be indicated if the developmental history suggests anomalies in speech and language development or chronic difficulties with ear infection, but we have also found such evaluations quite useful with children having no history of significant delays but presenting with current evidence of deficiencies in the processing of verbally oriented material and/or short-term auditory memory difficulties.

In a similar manner, an evaluation of fine and gross motor capacities by an occupational or physical therapist can help determine if a child would benefit from adaptive physical education in his/her school setting or from carefully planned involvement in special extracurricular physical activities.

Certain patterns of preliminary test results may suggest the need for more comprehensive neuropsychological assessment. The specifics of such an assessment could take many forms. The reader is referred to August (1990) for more detailed discussion of this topic.

Finally, the psychologist may wish to conduct additional personality assessment via more projective techniques *if* the information obtained from interview and rating scale sources suggests the possibility of seriously disorganized thinking or the press of particular needs or conflicts. Data obtained from projective assessment tools does not "make or break" a diagnosis of ADHD, but such information can clarify the strength or pervasiveness of other concerns as they influence the child's perceptions and behavior.

Overview of Assessment

Clearly, obtaining the information necessary to adequately understand the child and his/her presenting complaints demands a comprehensive approach to evaluation. In accord with Barkley (1988a), we suggest that the appropriate assessment of the possibly ADHD child must include different types of data obtained from different sources. Such a comprehensive assessment would include parent and child interviews, along with the use of a broad-spectrum rating scale that could be completed by parents and teacher, a disorder-focused scale to be completed by parents and teacher, the Home and School Situations Questionnaires (Barkley, 1981), and, with adolescents, a measure such as the Issues Checklist (Robin, 1981). An adequate psychoeducational assessment of the child is also required, along with observations of behavior. Ideally, these observations could be obtained in the target environment—usually the classroom but, if not, analogue clinic observations could be conducted. Specific measures of attention are desirable, particularly if a medication trial is to be conducted, but it must be remembered that in-class measures of on-task behavior and academic efficiency may be more sensitive measures of overall and between-dose medication effects. Screening for parental psychopathology, marital discord, and family dysfunction is also necessary. If cognitive–behavioral intervention is being considered, it would be desirable to include the Self-Control Rating Scale (Kendall & Wilcox, 1979) and child, adolescent, or parent measures that target the cognitive constructs and behaviors to be addressed in therapy.

For the sake of ongoing treatment monitoring, one can select a logical subset of these measures. Barkley et al. (1988) have presented a model for repeated assessment of medication effects that includes having the parents complete the Conners Parent Rating Scale—Revised, the Home Situations Questionnaire, and a side effects questionnaire. The child is assessed via in-clinic observations in an analogue academic situation. As previously discussed, a computerized measure of attention and impulsivity was originally included with this battery, but the impulsivity test did not prove to be sensitive to any medication effects, and the attentional portion of the test was sensitive to only the higher medication doses.

We suggest that an adequate repeated evaluation of a cognitive–behavioral intervention program might include having parents complete the Self-Control Rating Scale and Home Situations Questionnaire (plus the Issues Checklist for adolescents) and having teachers complete the Self-Control Rating Scale and School Situations Questionnaire. If the intervention is designed to impact overall family functioning, then scales assessing the family may also be of relevance. The child, and parents if involved, should also be tested on the specific information that is assumed to be trained during the intervention. This limited set of assessments would not be adequate for a full-scale treatment outcome study, but it is offered as an example of a practical set of measures that could be used in virtually any clinic and that would meet minimum standards of documenting adequate quality assurance of one's intervention. We also recommend that each family write down several specific treatment goals, so that the success of the intervention for a particular family can be judged in terms of the concerns most significant to the clients, as well as in terms of the outcomes of interest to the clinician or researcher.

Chapter Three

Common Methods of Treatment of ADHD in Current Medical and Psychological Practice

This chapter presents data and issues concerning the three major current treatments for ADHD: medication, behavioral interventions, and cognitive–behavioral approaches. Our goal in writing this review is to help the reader develop a stance of cautious optimism regarding the use of medication and behavioral intervention and a stance of interested skepticism regarding cognitive–behavioral interventions! Each mode of treatment has significant limitations, and no method provides a "cure" for ADHD (Barkley, 1989).

In addition to these three forms of intervention, we would like to again note that it is crucial for ADHD children to receive appropriate educational intervention. Obviously, medication, behavioral techniques and cognitive–behavioral methods are frequently used in the educational environment, and some of the data we shall be discussing directly concerns the impact of these forms of intervention on academic outcomes. But many ADHD children can benefit from specialized teaching methods and curricula that go beyond the management of attention and behavior that may be afforded by medication, behavioral interventions, or cognitive–behavioral methods. The educational needs of ADHD children are discussed in more detail in the chapter on school intervention, but here we would like to underscore the importance of the child receiving appropriately individualized educational services. With this point in mind, we can now go on to consider the three most common forms of intervention in current practice.

Medication Treatment

Psychostimulants

Psychostimulant medication, in the form of methylphenidate (Ritalin), pemoline (Cylert), and dextroamphetamine (Dexedrine), is the most common form of pharmacologic treatment of ADHD. As noted by Werry (1988), the majority of research in this area has been conducted with methylphenidate, but aside from milligram potency and duration of action, there is little to differentiate its effects (and side effects) from those of dextroamphetamine and pemoline. According to Barkley (1981), these medications exert their greatest effect on behavior approximately 1–2 hours after ingestion. The behavioral effects do not persist beyond 4–5 hours from the point of ingestion unless a sustained-release form of the medication is being employed. Some investigators have found the sustained-release form of methylphenidate to be slightly less effective than regular methylphenidate, but whether this behavioral difference is due to differences in rate of absorption or peak plasma levels is unclear (Birmaher, Greenhill, Cooper, Fried, & Maminski, 1989).

There is no question that psychostimulant medication can produce short-term behavioral improvement in the form of increased attention-to-task and decreased activity in the majority of children diagnosed as ADHD (Cantwell, 1980; Safer & Allen, 1976; Werry, 1988), with effects comparable for both boys and girls (Pelham, Walker, Sturges, & Hoza, 1989). What has been the subject of most recent inquiries are issues such as the age and type of ADHD child most likely to be a positive medication responder, the effect of medication on parent–child relationships and social behavior, the role of medication in affecting academic performance, the long-term efficacy of medication, and concerns about medication side effects.

Age Factors

The positive short-term behavioral effects of psychostimulants on elementary school–age samples have been well-documented. Approximately 70%–80% of a carefully diagnosed sample of latency age ADHD children will display a positive response to psychostimulants (Cantwell, 1980). As Ferguson (1986) has noted, the 20%–30% of nonresponding ADHD children represent a very interesting group for future study because most non-ADHD children will show some improvement on vigilance tasks following the administration of psychostimulant medication! Barkley (1981) indicates that medication is not recommended for use with children 3 years of age and younger, and its effects on 4- and 5-year-old children may be more inconsistent than the generally reliable effects with elementary school-age children.

There is now growing evidence that methylphenidate can produce comparable behavioral and attentional improvements in adolescents with childhood histories of ADHD (Coons, Klorman, & Borgstedt, 1987; Klorman, Coons, & Borgstedt, 1987; Varley, 1983). In a sample of

12- to 19-year-old subjects, Klorman et al. (1987) found that methylphenidate produced reductions in noncompliance and inattention as rated by parents and teachers. This study included a careful examination of emotional and physical side effects. Interestingly, it was observed that four subjects in the placebo condition rated themselves as sad while none did so under methylphenidate; in fact, methylphenidate was found to lower subjective ratings of dysphoria, while leaving ratings of anxiety, euphoria, and differentness unchanged. This observation is of interest in light of past reports of possible stimulant-related dysphoria in some children (Cantwell & Carlson, 1978). Heart rate was observed to rise after methylphenidate administration. Extending their examination of effects to more cognitive measures, Coons et al. (1987) found that methylphenidate enhanced accuracy and precision of responding rather than speed on a memory scanning task. On a vigilance task, medication enhanced accuracy, sensitivity to detection of targets, and speed and precision of reaction time.

While the use of medication with ADHD adolescents is receiving increasing support from the research literature, proposing the use of such a treatment to a person newly diagnosed in adolescence may understandably play into conflicts about control and autonomy that are already raging between the adolescent and his/her family. Thus, eliciting the adolescent's informed support of this treatment option is particularly crucial if use of medication is to be a viable component of the overall treatment plan (Wender, 1987).

Type of ADHD Child

Increasingly, researchers and clinicians are moving toward the recognition that there are different types of ADHD children and that these types are likely to have significant implications for response to treatment (Levine, 1987). As discussed in Chapter 1, ADHD children who also manifest Tourette's syndrome or have a history of tics are not considered good candidates for psychostimulant medication (Golden, 1988). Children with high levels of anxiety, numerous fears, and psychosomatic complaints, in addition to their ADHD symptoms, are also not considered to be good candidates for treatment with psychostimulants (Aman & Werry, 1982; Barkley, 1981; Swanson et al., 1978). However, as will be discussed in the next section, such children may be appropriate for a trial of antidepressant medication. The presence of thought disorder or other major symptoms of psychosis also suggests that psychostimulants would be contraindicated (Barkley, 1981). Thus, psychostimulants are viewed as most appropriate for the child presenting with ADHD alone or ADHD and oppositional/conduct-disordered types of symptoms (Klorman et al., 1988). Stimulants can also be effective with children with both ADHD and learning disability, although if the child's history strongly suggests that the ADHD symptoms are secondary to a primary learning disability, then the response to psychostimulants may be more uncertain. There is some evidence that children with learning disabilities but no ADHD can have certain aspects of their performance aided by psychostimulant medications (Dykman, Ackerman, & McCray, 1980; Gittelman-Klein & Feingold, 1983), but this is not believed to be the case for all forms of learning or information-processing deficits.

Social Behavior

The effects of psychostimulant medication on the interactions of parents and their ADHD children have been extensively examined. Summarizing much of his previous research on this topic, Barkley (1985) concludes that the negative, controlling behavior of parents towards their ADHD children seems in direct response to the child's inappropriate behavior. When the child's behavior improves in response to psychostimulant medication, the parents, in turn, become less controlling and negative. Barkley (1988b) replicated these findings, which were originally observed in school-age hyperactive children, with a sample of 3- and 4-year-old children judged to be ADHD. Schachar, Taylor, Wieselberg, Thorley, and Rutter (1987) have also examined changes in family functioning in responders and nonresponders to methylphenidate, with a responder defined as a child displaying at least a 50% improvement in symptomatology. In the families of responders, significant short-term improvements were observed in terms of an improved affective tone of the parent–child relationship, increased expressed maternal warmth, decreased expressed maternal criticism, and decreased negative encounters between the ADHD child and siblings. Increased contact between the ADHD child and the mother was also reported. The authors noted that responders and nonresponders did not differ in initial family circumstances, and changes were not observed in a placebo control group, suggesting that the findings were not just the result of positive expectancies. Schachar et al. (1987) speculate that the improvement in the affective tone of family functioning could be more important in reducing the child's risk for later conduct disturbance than the actual reduction in activity level. Treatment with psychostimulant medication has also been observed to improve the quality of interactions between ADHD students and their classroom teachers (Whalen, Henker, & Dotemoto, 1981).

Other investigators have examined the effects of psychostimulant medication on the behavior of ADHD children with their peers. Whalen et al., (1987) examined the effects of different doses of methylphenidate on the natural social behavior of 7- to 8-year-old and 9- to 11-year-old hyperactive children. In contrast to past efforts, which have frequently examined social behavior in adult-regulated classroom or laboratory settings, Whalen et al. (1987) conducted their observations during un-structured playground periods that included very little adult regulation. They observed the younger group (7 to 8 years old) to exhibit higher overall rates of negative behavior. This group displayed improvement in their behavior at a dose of 0.3 mg/kg but displayed maximal improve-ment at 0.6 mg/kg. In contrast, the older group displayed maximal improvement at 0.3 mg/kg. Interestingly, despite other reports of possi-ble medication-induced dysphoria and social withdrawal (Whalen, Henker, & Granger, 1989), neither low nor moderate doses produced increased social withdrawal.

As previously discussed, parents and teachers have been repeatedly found to change their appraisals and manner of interacting with ADHD children in relation to medication-induced behavioral improvements. But what about peers? Whalen et al. (1989) observed that medication treatment did improve the ADHD child's standing within his/her peer group, with those on medication receiving increased nominations as being cooperative, fun to be with, and considered a best friend. These improvements were dose-related, with higher doses (0.6 mg/kg vs. 0.3 mg/kg) producing more positive appraisals. Medication did not, howev-er, normalize the status of the ADHD boys relative to their non-ADHD peers. Hinshaw, Henker, Whalen, Erhardt, and Dunnington (1989) found that medication decreased noncompliance as well as physical and verbal aggression in a sample of 6- to 12-year-old ADHD boys. These decreases made the behavior of the ADHD children comparable to that of a comparison group of non-ADHD peers. Medication did not affect rates of nonsocial or prosocial behaviors, but under the placebo condi-tion the ADHD comparison groups were not found to differ in their levels of prosocial behavior.

Whalen et al. (1987) and Henker and Whalen (1989) caution against an overly optimistic interpretation of these findings and suggest that there are features of establishing a positive social reputation, such as skills in making and keeping friends, that medications may be unlikely to impact. On the other hand, research by Hinshaw, Henker, and Whalen (1984b) raises the possibility that psychostimulants can do more than decrease negative social behavior. Hinshaw et al. (1984b) examined the impact of different methods of training children to self-monitor their social behavior and crossed these training conditions with medication or placebo. The impact of the behavioral training methods will be discussed later in this chapter. Of relevance to the current discussion is the finding that psychostimulant medication not only decreased negative social be-havior, but produced more accurate self-monitoring. The children were better able to attend to and accurately label the quality of their own social behavior. Hinshaw, Buhrmester, and Heller (1989) examined the impact of administering methylphenidate during the posttest assessment of ADHD boys who had participated in anger management training. Medication enhanced self-control and modestly increased the display of the trained coping strategies in addition to decreasing physical retaliation. Thus, the findings of Hinshaw, Buhrmester, and Heller (1989) and Hinshaw et al. (1984b) suggest that medication-mediated improvements in attention can do more than decrease negative or inappropriate behaviors.

The specific impact of psychostimulants on social behavior may also depend on preexisting features of the child. For example, Pelham and Bender (1982) observed that the administration of pemoline led to improved social behavior in ADHD children who were also aggressive, but nonaggressive ADHD children became more isolative when medicated. Hinshaw, Henker, et al. (1989), however, did not observe an interaction between type of ADHD child and changes in isolative behavior.

Academic Performance

As Werry (1988) notes in his excellent review of drugs and cognitive functioning in children, the field continues to face the question of whether psychostimulants can produce true improvements in learning and achievement or simply improve a child's ability to perform skills he/she already possesses. In contrast to the negative findings of past efforts addressing this question (Aman, 1980; Barkley & Cunningham, 1978), more recent findings suggest the possibility that psychostimulant medication can enhance learning and achievement.

Douglas et al. (1986) and Gadow and Swanson (1985) discuss the methodological weaknesses and conceptual difficulties that may have limited past efforts to detect effects on learning and academic performance. Using carefully determined, individualized criterion, Douglas et al. (1986) examined the effects of 0.3 mg/kg of methylphenidate and placebo on a number of cognitive, learning, academic, and behavior measures. Assessments were conducted in both laboratory and regular classroom settings. Their results revealed medication-related improvements on the majority of their measures, including increased work output, improved accuracy and efficiency, and better learning acquisition. Improved effort and more self-correcting behaviors were also observed in the medication condition. These findings were interpreted as demonstrating the role of stimulants in enhancing self-regulatory processes.

In addition to general questions about the role of psychostimulants in aiding learning, the findings of Sprague and Sleator (1977) have raised the question of different dose–response curves for behavioral versus cognitive effects. In their widely cited study, they demonstrated that while maximal behavioral improvement (in terms of teacher ratings of behavior) was noted at 1.0 mg/kg, maximal cognitive improvement on a short-term memory task occurred at 0.3 mg/kg, and deterioration of cognitive performance, as well as increased heart rate, was observed at 1.0 mg/kg. Given the fact Sprague and Sleator did not include intermediate dosages, the exact nature of this dose/response curve is unclear. Douglas, Barr, Amin, O'Neill and Britton (1988) examined the impact of three dosages of methylphenidate (0.15, 0.3 and 0.6 mg/kg) on a variety of academic, cognitive, and behavioral measures administered in both laboratory and classroom settings. Their findings generally indicated a pattern of improvement associated with increasing dosage across almost all measures; however, performance on a paired associate learning task seemed maximized at 0.3 mg/kg, suggesting that certain higher-order tasks may be adversely affected by dosages around or above 0.6 mg/kg. This conclusion is consistent with the findings of Gan and Cantwell (1982). Other investigators have found linear relationships between dosage and improvement on academic measures using dosages comparable to those of Douglas et al. (1988) (Kupietz, Winsberg, Richardson, Maitinsky, & Mendell, 1988; Pelham, Bender, Caddell, Booth, & Moorer, 1985; Richardson, Kupietz, Winsberg, Maitinsky, & Mendell, 1988; Rapport et al., 1988), but these authors caution that individual responses to dosages can be highly idiosyncratic. Dosage and the degree of learning mastery of the material may both influence the impact of medication on learning (Rapport, Quinn, DuPaul, Quinn, & Kelly, 1989). Thus, the optimal dose for an individual child cannot be inferred from group data. As discussed in Chapter 2, Rapport et al. (1987) found that observations of classroom on-task behavior and academic efficiency (number of items correct in relation to number attempted) were more sensitive measures of overall medication effects and between-dose effects than a laboratory measure of attention, in this case the Gordon Diagnostic System version of the Continuous Performance Test (Gordon, 1983).

In terms of relative efficacy, a review by Gadow (1985) suggests that behavioral training methods with demonstrated impact have outperformed medication treatment on measures of academic accuracy and productivity. These findings are discussed in greater detail in the subsequent section on behavioral interventions.

Long-Term Outcome

As previously noted, the potentially dramatic, positive short-term effects of psychostimulant medications have been clearly demonstrated, but many questions remain regarding the long-term efficacy of these medications as a treatment for ADHD. Jacobvitz, Sroufe, Stewart, and Leffert (1990) reviewed the findings from five different long-term investigations of the effects of psychostimulant medication and conclude that there is no evidence to support the view that medication treatment yields better academic outcomes, more positive peer relations, or less antisocial behavior. Solid conclusions about the long-term effects of medication are clearly limited by the major methodological flaws that plague most of the follow-up studies of ADHD children (see discussion in Chapter 1), but, as Jacobvitz et al. (1990) assert, the flaws in these studies cannot be interpreted as providing support for the long-term efficacy of psychostimulants. As will be discussed later in this chapter, there is evidence suggesting that multicomponent long-term treatments that include medication have been associated with more positive outcomes relative to drug only treatment regimens (Satterfield, Satterfield, & Schell, 1987).

Side Effects

In addition to questions about the types of gains that psychostimulants are able to produce, investigators have also explored concerns of possible medication side effects. It is generally agreed that some of the most commonly observed side effects, such as appetite suppression and insomnia, resolve after several weeks on the medication or can be minimized through dosage reductions or careful timing of drug administration (Barkley, 1977; Klein, Gittelman, Quitkin, & Rifkin, 1980; Taylor, 1986). Concerns about psychostimulants causing tics or precipitating Tourette's syndrome have already been addressed in Chapter 1 and will not be repeated at this point. The existence and resolution of concerns regarding medication rebound effect, state-dependent learning, growth suppression, and stimulant-induced disturbed thinking merit further discussion.

Psychostimulant rebound effects refer to the behavioral deterioration that occurs in the late afternoon or evening when the child has received medication earlier in the day. Typically, this behavioral rebound includes increased restless and inattentive behavior, as well as elevated levels of hostility and/or emotional lability (Porrino, Rapoport, Behar, Ismond, & Bunney, 1983; Rapoport et al., 1978). In clinical practice, there appears to be huge variability in the degree to which children manifest a rebound effect, with some seeming to have little or no rebound, while for other children the emotional and behavioral rebound is quite noticeable and extreme. Johnston, Pelham, Hoza, and Sturges (1988) examined the effects of two doses of methylphenidate (0.3 and 0.6 mg/kg) and placebo on the evening behavior of ADHD boys.

On one of the two measures the parents were asked to complete, statistically significant differences were observed on evenings following the daytime administration of 0.3 mg/kg of methylphenidate. Differences were not observed at 0.6 mg/kg and no differences were observed at either dose on the other rating scale. The authors note that considerable variability was present, both within child, as demonstrated by fluctuating daily ratings, and across children, as suggested by the standard deviations. Thus, while the rebound effects could be quite significant for certain children on certain days, these children were not consistently affected, and still other children showed no significant rebound effects. The authors conclude that psychostimulant rebound effects are of little clinical significance for most ADHD children, but careful monitoring of each child's medication response is necessary to determine if such effects are of significance for a particular individual.

Another area of inquiry regarding psychostimulants, as well as other medications, concerns possible state-dependent learning. Studies examining state-dependent learning attempt to clarify whether information learned while receiving a medication may be retrieved or recalled only when the subject is again on the medication and not during periods in which the person is off the medication. Examination of this issue with psychostimulants is complex, for there is no question that some children have their performance on learning tasks facilitated while on these medications, at least as a result of improved attention and possibly as a result of other improvements in their information processing capacities (Richardson, Kupietz, Winsberg, Maitinsky, & Mendell, 1988). In their review of this issue, Becker-Mattes, Mattes, Abikoff, and Brandt (1985) conclude that the weight of past research with both ADHD children and other disordered populations does not suggest the view that psychostimulants foster state-dependent learning in children, and Becker-Mattes et al. (1985) present additional data that is supportive of this conclusion. These authors note that concerns about number of daily doses and medication holiday can, therefore, be decided on the basis of concerns other than the possibility of state-dependent learning.

Questions about the role of psychostimulant medication in causing growth suppression have received considerable research attention (Gittelman-Klein, Landa, Mattes, & Klein, 1988; Gittelman-Klein & Mannuzza, 1988; Safer & Allen, 1975; Safer, Allen, & Barr, 1972, 1975). As summarized by Jacobvitz et al. (1990), current findings suggest that methylphenidate does suppress growth during the active phase of treatment, at least if given at moderate dosage levels. The mean height suppression appears to be approximately 1.5 cm, and this growth suppression can be avoided through the implementation of summer medication holidays (see Gittelman-Klein et al., 1988). In addition, there appears to be no overall reduction of height in adulthood for individuals receiving from 6 months to 4 years of medication treatment in childhood (Gittelman-Klein & Mannuzza, 1988). As noted by Jacobvitz et al. (1990), however, the subjects in the Gittelman-Klein and Mannuzza study had their medication treatment stopped by early adolescence, so this data cannot speak to the issue of possible growth suppression if treatment is continued throughout the adolescent years.

A very rare, but potentially serious, reaction to methylphenidate involves the emergence of symptoms of psychosis. Visual and tactile hallucinations are the most commonly reported symptoms of such a reaction, but disturbance in other aspects of thought processes and the development of delusional beliefs have also been observed (Bloom, Russell, Weisskopf, & Blackerby, 1988). Symptoms of psychosis have long been recognized as a sign of stimulant intoxication in adults using large quantities of amphetamines, but there is now growing recognition that a very small number of children may display such signs on medication levels within the normally accepted dose ranges. Such rare, but serious, responses to the medication offer further evidence for the need for careful monitoring of the behavioral and emotional status of stimulant-treated children.

Antidepressants

While the use of antidepressant medications with children manifesting ADHD symptoms appears to be on the increase (Garfinkel, Wender, Sloman, & O'Neil, 1983; Zametkin, Rapoport, Murphy, Linnoila, & Ismond, 1985), the volume of research on this topic still lags far behind that of psychostimulant use with this population (Barkley, 1989). As a result, conclusions concerning this class of medications must be considered more tentative than those made with regard to the psychostimulants. There are two major types of antidepressant medications: tricyclic antidepressants and monoamine oxidase inhibitors (MAOIs). The bulk of research interest with ADHD children has involved the tricyclics, but prior to our discussion of this class of medications, data on the MAOIs will be briefly presented.

In an interesting series of papers, Zametkin and colleagues compared the clinical and biochemical effects of different MAOIs (clorgyline, deprenyl, and tranylcypromine sulfate) to those of a psychostimulant medication (Zametkin, Rapoport, Murphy, Linnoila, & Ismond, 1985; Zametkin, Rapoport, Murphy, Linnoila, Karoum, et al., 1985). Interestingly, they found that the MAOIs produced immediate, clinically significant behavioral improvement. Ratings by clinical staff, teachers, and parents suggested that the MAOI treatment produced behavioral changes highly similar to those produced by psychostimulants. These findings of positive behavioral effects are encouraging. MAOIs, however, in contrast to psychostimulants or tricyclic antidepressants, require that the client carefully avoid foods high in tyramine. Unfortunately, many highly desirable foods are high in tyramine (see Folks, 1983, for a listing of such foods). As a result of the potentially serious health consequences of dietary lapses, some investigators have recommended that MAOIs not be used with clients who are at risk to use drugs, are impulsive or unreliable, or have unreliable families (Ryan et al., 1988). Given that there are no formally diagnosed ADHD children who are not impulsive, this would appear to limit the usefulness of the MAOIs with this population.

Interest in the use of tricyclic antidepressants with ADHD children has grown steadily over the past decade (Donnelly et al., 1986; Gastfriend, Biederman, & Jellinek, 1984). While tricyclics must be taken for weeks to build up a blood level sufficient to produce an antidepressant effect, changes in attention and impulse control have been observed to occur in a matter of days for some patients (Donnelly et al., 1986). Garfinkel et al. (1983) compared the effects of two tricyclics (clomipramine and desipramine) and methylphenidate on ADHD boys via a double-blind, placebo-controlled, crossover design. All medications were administered at 9 A.M. and 12 noon. Methylphenidate produced greater improvement of behavioral symptoms of ADHD during the day but, given their longer half-life, the two tricyclic antidepressants were more effective in producing some behavioral improvement in the evening hours. The tricyclics were also less likely to disrupt sleep and more likely to produce improvement in teacher or childcare worker ratings of the child's mood and self-esteem. Thus, tricyclics may produce a more even but less robust response, without the ups and downs associated with the short half-life of psychostimulant medications. Unlike the antidepressant effect, however, the attentional effects may diminish over time, making tricyclics a less appropriate medication for long-term usage than the psychostimulants (Barkley, 1989). Tricyclics may be of particular value for clients for whom the use of psychostimulants is currently contraindicated. For example, ADHD children who manifest high levels of anxiety and depression may derive particular benefit from tricyclics (Pliska, 1987). Children who have been nonresponsive to trials of stimulant treatment and those with a coexisting tic disorder may also be good candidates for tricyclics, particularly desipramine (Biederman, Baldessarini, Wright, Knee, & Harmatz, 1989; Riddle, Hardin, Cho, Woolston, & Leckman, 1988). The most serious side effect associated with tricyclic use is tachycardia (Biederman, Gastfriend, Jellinek, & Goldblatt, 1985; Puig-Antich, Ryan, & Rabinovich, 1985). Other commonly observed but less serious effects include skin rash, dry mouth, constipation, and drowsiness (Barkley, 1989).

Final Comments

We hope it is clear from our discussion that medication can provide significant symptom reduction for some ADHD children. The longevity of these effects is not clearly understood, and there are some children with attentional difficulties who are not good medication candidates. As this review suggests, parents and physicians face a growing array of choices and cautions concerning the medication treatment of ADHD symptoms. Given the growing complexity of this area, it is crucial for parents to feel that they are working with a medical professional who has a sufficient grasp of the costs and benefits associated with each possible choice.

Behavior Therapy

A number of different types of behavioral approaches have been implemented with hyperactive or ADHD children (see reviews by Hinshaw & Erhardt, 1990; Rapport, 1987; Werry & Wollersheim, 1989). Virtually all behavioral treatments for this population of children are operant or instrumental approaches that involve environmental manipulation of the events that precede a target behavior (eliciting stimuli) and/or the events that immediately follow such behavior (reinforcing or punishing consequences) in order to either increase or decrease the frequency of occurrence of the target behavior. Given that ADHD children can be viewed as manifesting both behavioral deficiencies (e.g., not enough impulse control) and behavioral excesses (e.g., overactive behavior and frequent noncompliance), behavioral interventions often take on the goals of increasing certain desirable behaviors while decreasing more undesirable behavior (Hinshaw & Erhardt, 1990). In addition, Barkley (1989) has summarized current conceptualizations of the core deficit in ADHD as being a lack of rule-governed behavior or a tendency to be governed by immediate consequences rather than overarching principles of behavior. To the extent that such a formulation is true, then interventions that "directly alter the pattern, timing or salience of such consequences by socially arranged means to improve ADHD symptoms should be the treatments of choice" (Barkley, 1989, p. 53).

While respondent or classical conditioning approaches that pair conditional stimuli or signals with physiological responses or reflexes have been used in the treatment of a number of other emotional difficulties in adults and children, this class of behavioral interventions has not been widely implemented with ADHD children. As we shall discuss, relaxation training, which is a key element in the major respondent approach of systematic desensitization, has been attempted with this population. The manner in which such training has been operationalized, however, emphasizes the use of relaxation as an active coping response to be enacted in specific situations. Thus, relaxation training efforts with ADHD children can also be classified under the rubric of operant or instrumentally oriented approaches.

Behavioral interventions will be discussed in terms of direct attempts to manipulate stimuli or contingencies in controlled environments, clinical behavior therapy efforts, relaxation training interventions, and behavioral self-control intervention programs.

Direct Stimulus or Contingency Management in the Laboratory or Classroom

Contingency management systems, as implemented in controlled environments such as the laboratory or classroom, usually involve the awarding of points or tokens for desired behavior. Some programs may also include a response–cost contingency whereby the child can lose points or tokens for certain clearly specified rule violations or undesirable behaviors. Rewards or response–cost contingencies are enacted immediately upon the occurrence of the desired or undesired behavior. Commonly selected target behaviors for reward include being on-task, completing academic work in an accurate manner, and complying with adult requests. Response-cost contingencies are often targeted to punish off-task or disruptive behavior. It is the consensus within the field that such methods of contingency management can be highly successful in increasing time on-task and academic productivity (Barkley, 1989; Hinshaw & Erhardt, 1990; Rapport, 1987; Werry & Wollersheim, 1989) and, in fact, such tightly controlled behavioral methods may be more effective than psychostimulant medication in achieving such goals (Gadow, 1985).

Researchers and clinicians have become increasingly aware of how contingency programs must be structured in order to achieve consistently positive effects with ADHD children. As discussed by Kinsbourne (1984), the ADHD child typically requires more frequent and immediate feedback about the acceptability of his/her behavior. In addition, more powerful or salient backup rewards are usually required and the selection of rewards must be changed or rotated in order to avoid the child's loss of interest. The inclusion of prudent negative consequences is important for achieving the most improved behavior, but the overall contingency system should provide more opportunities for reward than punishment.

Unfortunately, despite their power, such methods have significant limitations. One common concern is that the gains achieved by such programs do not persist once the formal contingencies are discontinued, making these behavioral contingencies similar to psychostimulant medication in their capacity to produce significant, but not long-lasting, behavior change (Hinshaw & Erhardt, 1990). Maintenance of program effects may be somewhat better during the fading of response–cost, rather than reward, contingencies (Sullivan & O'Leary, 1990). In addition to problems with persistence over time, the effects produced by such programs do not generalize across settings unless such generalization has been explicitly programmed (Barkley, 1989). Another difficulty concerns the fact that such programs can be implemented only in environments that afford tight control, such as classrooms or institutional settings, with most home environments being "too loose" for the effective use of such systems (Hinshaw & Erhardt, 1990; Werry & Wollersheim, 1989). Finally, even in tightly controlled environments, such interventions require tremendous effort on the intervenor's part to consistently and continuously reward, punish, or ignore selected target behaviors (Hinshaw & Erhardt, 1990).

A smaller number of investigations have attempted to alter the ADHD child's behavior by changing the stimulus or antecedent conditions that have precipitated undesirable behavior. Barkley (1989) reviewed this area of research, which is dominated by the efforts of Sydney Zentall (Zentall, 1985, 1989; Zentall & Meyer, 1987). Barkley concludes that increasing intratask novelty and the degree of active response allowed, as well as decreasing task length and complexity, can result in reductions in the occurrence of ADHD symptoms such as inattention and non-task-related activity. Barkley further recommends that more concrete representations of time limits and the more frequent statement of task and/or behavioral rules by both the instructor and the child also seem to result in more productive behavior on the part of the ADHD child. The conclusions of these stimulus- or antecedent-oriented studies must be considered more tentative than the conclusions we can draw from the myriad of studies examining the impact of consequent conditions. Nonetheless, these findings are extremely interesting and have obvious implications for the type of instructional style most likely to be effective with ADHD children.

Clinical Behavior Therapy

The term clinical behavior therapy is used in this instance to refer to interventions in which the behavior therapist provides consultation to parents and/or teachers about basic behavioral management procedures and the parents or teachers then carry out the direct implementation of rewards and punishment (Barkley, 1989; Hinshaw & Erhardt, 1990; Rapport, 1987). Obviously, such programs vary in their comprehensiveness and/or intensity. Pelham and colleagues (Pelham, Schnedler, Bologna, & Contreras, 1980) have conducted large-scale programs that include parent training, teacher consultation, and individual tutoring. Working with a more conduct-disordered sample, Patterson and his colleagues at the Oregon Social Learning Center have developed and implemented comprehensive behavioral family intervention programs (Patterson, Reid, Jones, & Conger, 1975). But as more commonly practiced, clinical behavior therapy usually involves the parents attending a time-limited series of group sessions that train them in the use of specific behavioral methods. Barkley (1981, 1987) presents a parent training model that is based on the work of Forehand and McMahon (1981) with oppositional children, but with selected features added to address special issues with ADHD children.

Generally speaking, these programs have been found to produce at least moderate, positive behavior change in ADHD children. As summarized by Hinshaw and Erhardt (1990), such programs seem capable of producing change in 2–4 months, as measured by parent and teacher behavior ratings. Obviously, this type of measurement, while highly valid from a consumer satisfaction standpoint, does not yield "pure" outcome data, since the parents and, often, teachers are directly involved in implementing the treatment and are clearly nonblind raters. But investigators have attempted to include more objective measures of change in child and parental behavior. For example, Pisterman et al., (1989) conducted a behaviorally oriented group training intervention for the parents of ADHD preschoolers. Relative to a waiting list control group, the treatment group evidenced significant improvement in the percentage of child compliance with parental commands, and parents evidenced improved quality of commands and increased reinforcement of child compliance as assessed during in-clinic behavioral observations. Many investigators have observed, however, that few studies provide evidence of parental in-home compliance with program procedures, so to the extent that real change occurs, the mechanism of such change is quite unclear (Pelham & Murphy, 1986; Pisterman et al., 1989; Rapport, 1987).

Hinshaw and Erhardt (1990) note that while parent training programs produce change, they may be less effective at resolving a number of problematic behaviors than relatively high doses of psychostimulant medication. On a brighter note, there is now greater recognition that certain means of conducting parenting training and certain aspects of the trainer's style may affect what parents learn and the effectiveness of their use of the trained procedures (Twardosz & Nordquist, 1987). There is also greater awareness that factors such as maternal depression (Brody & Forehand, 1986; Conrad & Hammen, 1989), maternal social isolation (Wahler & Afton, 1980), and marital discord (Porter & O'-Leary, 1980) can interact in a complex manner with parental perceptions of child behavior and parental use of trained strategies, possibly resulting in a decrease in the consistency and predictability with which the parents use program methods (Barkley, 1989). The optimal form of clinical behavior therapy may also vary with the age of the child. Barkley (1989) suggests that while parenting training may be preferred for families with preschool or elementary school-age children, families with ADHD adolescents may benefit more from problem-focused family approaches that emphasize contingency contracting, family problem-solving and communication skills training. Examples of such approaches will be discussed in the subsequent section on cognitive–behavioral interventions.

Relaxation Training

The hypothesis that ADHD children may manifest abnormal levels of physiological arousal has led some investigators to evaluate the effectiveness of various forms of relaxation training. As reviewed by Fish (1988), there seems to be little question that hyperactive children, like most other human beings, can be trained to reduce their levels of muscle tension via common techniques such as progressive muscle relaxation or electromyographic biofeedback. But the extent to which such training produces meaningful changes in behavior or cognitive–academic performance is much less clear. The small number of adequately controlled studies in this area makes it particularly difficult to draw firm conclusions about possible treatment effects. In an investigation that included both hyperactive and nonhyperactive control groups, Braud (1978) did demonstrate that the hyperactive children had significantly higher muscle tension at pretest. Both electromyographic biofeedback and progressive muscle relaxation decreased muscle tension and resulted in improved parent ratings of behavior, improved scores on a measure of visual–motor functioning, and better scores on the Wechsler Intelligence Scale for Children—Revised (Wechsler, 1974) Digit Span and Coding subtests. While interesting, this finding must be viewed as tentative, given the lack of other controlled investigations and the negative findings of other investigators. In our opinion, it would seem more appropriate to conceptualize relaxation training as one element of a comprehensive program, rather than viewing it as a treatment in and of itself.

Behavioral Self-Control Training

The term behavioral self-control refers to the implementation of self-monitoring, self-evaluation and self-reinforcement procedures. As the names imply, self-monitoring refers to maintaining an active awareness of the occurrence of certain targeted behaviors or thoughts, self-evaluation involves judging the rate or quality of the behavior being modified against some existing standard or criterion, and self-reinforcement refers to the individual administering his or her reinforcement if a certain standard of behavior has been achieved. While this class of interventions could arguably be discussed in the following section on cognitive–behavioral methods, we chose to consider it in the context of behavioral interventions for several reasons. We view this class of techniques or methods as a transitional link between traditional behavioral methods and more heavily cognitive forms of intervention. Also, the originators of behavioral self-control methods seemed more intent on turning behavioral methods on cognitive events than turning cognitive events upon behavior. In addition, we are concerned that the demonstrated efficacy of behavioral self-control methods may be minimized or obscured if such techniques are lumped together with more elaborate cognitive interventions that have weaker or no demonstrated efficacy. That these methods do tend to be ignored is demonstrated by the fact that, with the exception of Barkley (1989), all the previously cited reviews of behavioral methods offered no discussion of behavioral self-control methods under the label of either traditional behavior therapy or cognitive–behavioral therapy.

The literature on behavioral self-control methods with ADHD children is interesting because it contains some findings that conflict with application of behavioral self-control with other problem behaviors. For example, it is generally accepted that self-monitoring alone will produce only weak and highly transient improvement and that it must be combined with self-evaluation and self-reinforcement in order to reliably achieve positive behavior change. But with ADHD children, it may be the case that simply having them self-monitor on-task behavior or work productivity will, in fact, improve attention-to-task and work completion (Harris, 1986). This finding could be explained by the fact that in the case of ADHD children, attention is the target behavior to be changed and, thus, having a structured method of monitoring one's attention can by itself be quite powerful. With other behavior change targets, such as smoking cessation or weight reduction, attention per se is not the variable of interest. The work of a number of other investigators suggests the importance of self-monitoring combined with self-reinforcement for the achievement of agreed-upon standards of attention and behavior (Barkley, Copeland, & Sivage, 1980; Varni & Henker, 1979). In a very interesting study, Hinshaw et al. (1984b) trained ADHD children to accurately evaluate their own social behavior and compared the effects of such training to psychostimulant treatment and the use of a traditional external reinforcement condition. At posttest, the group receiving both self-evaluation training and medication exhibited the most positive social behavior, and the behavior of the self-evaluation alone group was found to be superior to the external reinforcement alone condition. These findings are consistent with those of Chase and Clement (1985) who observed that the combination of psychostimulant medication and self-reinforcement was more effective than either treatment alone in improving the academic performance of ADHD children. Interestingly, while the combined treatment was the most effective, self-reinforcement alone was more effective than psychostimulants alone.

Collectively, these findings suggest that behavioral self-control methods can be extremely valuable in improving the attention-to-task, academic productivity, and, possibly, social behavior of ADHD children. These methods have the advantage of actively involving the child in the process of evaluating his/her behavior and, conversely, demand less teacher/parent/staff time for implementation than may be the case with traditional token systems. One might speculate that these approaches are successful because they demand the use of self-regulatory processes that the ADHD child does not typically enact, much as Douglas et al. (1986) found psychostimulants to "activate" self-regulatory processes.

In summary, direct contingency management in the classroom/ laboratory seems capable of producing highly significant, meaningful behavior change in the setting of implementation, but such interventions can be quite labor-intensive and, currently, effects seem to be limited to the intervention setting. Clinical behavior therapy approaches have demonstrated effectiveness, but the magnitude of effects appears to be less than that obtained with psychostimulant treatment or direct contingency management efforts. Relaxation training approaches are generally successful in achieving their specific goal of decreased muscle tension, but such approaches have not reliably demonstrated a capacity to resolve the major behavioral symptoms of ADHD children. Behavioral self-control interventions have demonstrated effectiveness in increasing appropriate academic and social behavior. Including elements of behavioral self-control with traditional direct contingency management approaches and parent training programs might increase treatment impact by requiring the ADHD child to exercise his/her self-regulatory capacities.

Cognitive–Behavioral Interventions

For the purpose of the current discussion, the term cognitive–behavioral interventions refers to approaches such as self-instructional training, problem-solving training, attribution retraining, and stress inoculation procedures. Self-instructional methods involve training children to use or develop self-guiding speech as an aid to academic or social problem-solving. Self-instruction often incorporates elements of problem-solving training, such as learning to recognize the existence of a problem, generating alternative problem solutions, evaluating the consequences of different alternatives, and reviewing the outcome of the selected alternative. Attribution retraining involves helping a child reappraise his/her explanations for particular outcomes or events, often with the goal of helping the child adopt a more functional belief system regarding the value of his/her effort. Attribution retraining has not been used as a primary intervention with ADHD children, but elements of this approach have been combined with some self-instruction and problem-solving training efforts. Finally, stress inoculation training involves increasing the child's awareness of his/her signals of stress or strong emotion and helping the child develop a menu of different coping methods to be used when faced with stressors. Stress inoculation interventions also emphasize practicing these coping methods via exposure to a graded series of stressors.

The domain of cognitive–behavioral intervention with ADHD children is afflicted by having more reviews of treatment outcome than actual treatment outcome studies! We apologize for adding one more review to a literature already replete with such works. We hope the reader will excuse our actions for two reasons. First, given that one purpose of this book is to present cognitive–behavioral treatment approaches for ADHD children, one would certainly hope that we can demonstrate a familiarity with the works that provide a foundation for the current effort. Second, in the last section of this chapter, we present new outcome data concerning a cognitive–behavioral treatment approach we developed. Thus, while we are adding a review, we shall also contribute some data to the field. If these justifications are not sufficient to help the reader wade through yet another review, we refer you to (or remind you of) previous reviews of the relevant literature (Abikoff, 1985, 1987; Braswell & Kendall, 1988; Kendall & Braswell, 1985; Ryan, Weed, & Short, 1986; Whalen, Henker, & Hinshaw, 1985).

Cognitive–behavioral interventions with samples of mildly to moderately behavior-disordered children have achieved successful outcomes (Kendall & Braswell, 1982b; Schleser, Meyers, Cohen, & Thackwray, 1983; Schleser, Meyers, & Cohen, 1981). In addition, cognitive–behavioral approaches to remediating deficits in academically impaired children have been increasingly successful and broadly applied in the wake of changing perspectives on learning disabilities (Ryan et al., 1986; Wong, 1985). This class of interventions has, however, achieved much more limited success with children meeting the full diagnostic criteria of ADHD and/or has failed to demonstrate incremental benefit beyond the outcomes achieved with psychostimulant medication.

Douglas, Parry, Marton, and Garson (1976) conducted one of the earliest yet most comprehensive evaluations of a cognitive–behavioral intervention with children manifesting clinical levels of ADHD symptomatology. The training included 24 sessions that emphasized self-instruction training as described by Meichenbaum and Goodman (1971). Children were trained using a variety of tasks and games, including some of their actual school work. Training occasionally occurred in pairs to address the social aspects of problem-solving. Contingency management techniques were not a routine part of the training but were used if a child was clearly unmanageable in the session. Teachers and parents were seen in consultation sessions to inform them of the methods the children were using and to suggest ways in which the adults could encourage and reinforce the use of these skills in the home or classroom. Teachers and parents also participated in some of the child training sessions. Treatment effects were assessed via a variety of cognitive and academic measures, as well as teacher and parent behavior ratings, but the parent ratings had to be dropped from the analysis because a mail strike resulted in a low rate of return. Relative to a nontreatment control group, the treated children were significantly improved on several cognitive and academic measures at both posttest and 3-month follow-up; however, the treated group did not evidence significant improvement on the teacher ratings of classroom behavior.

Kirby and Grimley (1986) developed a cognitive–behavioral intervention for ADHD elementary school students that was conducted 2 hours a day, 4 days a week, over the course of a 7-week summer school. Each session included self-instructional training with academic tasks and individual and group games, as well as group discussion and practice of the self-instructional concepts as they related to social skills. Response–cost procedures were used during training to discourage inattentive or impulsive behavior. The children's parents were informed about the content of training and were given access to literature on the training methods, as well as encouraged to observe the training sessions or watch videotapes of the sessions. ADHD children in a control condition received comparable amounts of trainer attention, played the same individual and group games, and did academic tasks, but without the inclusion of the self-instructional training methods or the response–cost contingency. At posttest and at 1-year follow-up, Kirby and Grimley interpret their data as suggesting the superiority of the cognitive training group. An 8-week series of booster sessions did not seem to further improve outcome at 1-year follow-up. We are concerned that the small numbers of children in each condition, the lack of information about the ages of the children in each condition, the existence of pretreatment differences on some of the outcome measures, and missing parent rating data make it difficult to fully understand the meaning and true clinical significance of the observed differences in outcome.

Horn, Ialongo, Popovich, and Peradotto (1987) assessed the combined effects of behavioral parent training and group-administered cognitive–behavioral self-control therapy with ADHD elementary school students. Curiously, these investigators found that the combined treatment was not superior to either behavioral parent training or self-control therapy alone, with all three groups evidencing significant behavioral improvements in the home as assessed at posttest and follow-up via the Conners Parent Questionnaire. Generalization of improvement to the classroom environment was not observed. The absence of a no-treatment control group complicates the interpretation of these findings, particularly in light of the previously noted observation that repeated administration of the Conners often results in score decreases that are believed to be unrelated to real behavior change in the child. Horn et al. (1987) argue, however, that instances in which such practice effects have been documented have typically involved very brief test–retest intervals, and such effects are considered to be unlikely over intervals as long as the 3-month span used in their study (Glow, Glow, & Rump, 1982; Milich, Roberts, Loney, & Caputo, 1980). We speculate that focusing on only behavioral child management skills with the parents while training the children in cognitive–behavioral methods may have left the parents prepared to reinforce positive behaviors but unprepared to cue, prompt, or reinforce fledgling efforts at reflective problem-solving or to engage in problem-solving as a family.

While not developed specifically for ADHD clients, Barkley (1988a) has recommended that family approaches such as problem-solving communication training (Robin, 1981; Robin, Kent, O'Leary, Foster, & Prinz, 1977) can be quite useful in addressing the conflicts that commonly arise between ADHD adolescents and their parents. Problem-solving communication training involves training the teenager and his/her parents to use a structured method of problem-solving to resolve common disputes. In addition, participants receive training in specific communication skills, such as demonstrating effective listening and making nonaccusatory statements. Experimental evaluations have demonstrated the effectiveness of this approach, but response to treatment may vary with the particular skill needs of the family (see review by Foster & Robin, 1989).

Cognitive–behavioral interventions targeted for conduct-disordered and defiant children are also of some relevance, given the high degree of overlap between these conditions and ADHD. Lochman and colleagues have developed the Anger Coping Program for uses with aggressive elementary school children (Lochman, Burch, Curry, & Lampron, 1984;

Lochman & Curry, 1986; Lochman, Lampron, Gemmer, & Harris, 1987). This intervention was designed to be conducted in a school context. Program content includes discussion and practice of components of effective problem-solving, training in the recognition of physiological cues of arousal, and practice in the use of appropriate self-talk during problem situations. Experimental evaluations indicate that this program is effective in reducing aggressive off-task behavior in the classroom, with the addition of behavioral goal-setting producing further behavior improvement (Lochman et al., 1984; Lochman & Curry, 1986). Feindler and Ecton (1986) have developed an adolescent anger control program, referred to as "The Art of Self-Control." This program employs a stress inoculation training format that has three phases, including educational–cognitive preparation, cognitive and behavioral component skill acquisition, and skill application. Experimental evaluations with conduct-disordered junior high school students (Feindler, Marriott, & Iwata, 1984) and adolescent psychiatric inpatients (Feindler, Ecton, Kingsley, & Dubey, 1986) suggest that this program has yet to demonstrate significant, broad-based behavioral effects. Working with an inpatient population of 7- to 13-year-old conduct-disordered children, Kazdin, Esveldt-Dawson, French, and Unis (1987b) did achieve significant, enduring, meaningful effects for their problem-solving skills training program. This program has also produced positive effects when combined with a behaviorally oriented parent training group (Kazdin, Esveldt-Dawson, French, & Uris, 1987a) or with more opportunities for *in vivo* practice (Kazdin, Bass, Siegel, & Thomas, 1989). Another approach that has demonstrated effectiveness with severely conduct-disordered adolescents and their families is Alexander and colleagues' functional family therapy (Alexander & Parsons, 1982). The functional family therapy model of treatment includes behavioral family systems and, more recently, cognitive elements. Functional family therapy has achieved impressive results in terms of improved communication within the family and reduced subsequent court contact for both the target adolescent and his/her siblings. Impressively, these positive outcomes have been achieved by both Alexander and colleagues (Alexander & Parsons, 1973; Klein, Alexander, & Parsons, 1977; Barton, Alexander, Waldron, Turner, & Warburton, 1985) and independent research groups (Gordon & Arbuthnot, 1987).

Of course, when considering treatment for ADHD children, with or without Conduct Disorder, one must evaluate not only the relative efficacy of different psychological interventions, but also the efficacy of these psychological interventions relative to medication treatment. Brown, Wynne, and Medenis (1985) conducted an intervention highly similar to that of Douglas et al. (1976) and contrasted it with the effects of stimulant medication alone, a combined therapy and medication condition, and a no-treatment control group. Both the medication only and combined treatment groups displayed significant improvement on measures of attention deployment and parent and teacher behavior ratings at posttest and 3-month follow-up but insignificant change on academic measures. Cognitive training alone produced significant improvement on measures of attention deployment but not behavior ratings or measures of academic achievement. The authors concluded that cognitive training alone was not efficacious in treating ADHD children and that cognitive training did not produce effects beyond those achieved with psychostimulants alone.

The findings of Brown et al. (1985) are similar to those of Abikoff and Gittelman (1985) who observed that cognitive training did not improve the academic, cognitive, or behavioral outcomes of children being maintained on psychostimulant medications. In addition, Abikoff and Gittelman (1985b) found that the addition of cognitive training did not facilitate the children's withdrawal from medication. In an interesting methodological caveat, Brown, Borden, Wynne, Schleser, and Clingerman (1986) compared cognitive training, medication treatment, and a combined treatment condition and demonstrated that if medication treatment is discontinued prior to posttest, as is the case with the cognitive treatment, no positive treatment effects are demonstrated for any of the three conditions.

Abikoff et al. (1988) explored whether or not an academically focused version of cognitive training in combination with medication could produce benefits beyond those achieved with remedial tutoring plus medication or medication alone in a sample of ADHD boys who were academically deficient. The Abikoff et al. (1988) cognitive training involved self-instructional training, as well as self-monitoring, self-reinforcement, and attack strategy training components. In contrast to Abikoff and Gittelman (1985b), Abikoff et al. (1988) also awarded points for accurate self-monitoring and used response–cue contingencies to encourage accuracy. All three conditions demonstrated comparable levels of improvement, suggesting that the cognitive components did not add to treatment efficacy.

Emphasizing a somewhat different approach to cognitive–behavioral intervention, Hinshaw et al. (1984b) trained small groups of ADHD children in stress inoculation methods designed to help them recognize their own anger cues and to manage themselves in an anger-producing situation, using a variety of coping strategies, including self-talk. The control group was exposed to general principles of social problem-solving and perspective-taking. Half of the children in each condition were receiving methylphenidate while the other half received placebo. Treatment effects were assessed by observing each child's response to a behavioral provocation situation. Relative to pretreatment observations in a similar situation, children in all conditions displayed less laughing, fidgeting, and verbal aggression and were more likely to make neutral statements in response to provocation. The children receiving the cognitive–behavioral intervention were rated significantly higher on global ratings of self-control and displayed significantly more purposeful coping strategies. Medication produced change in the intensity of the child's behavior, with medicated children responding in a less intense manner, but it did not alter the content of the child's response. There was no follow-up assessment or alternative provocation measure, so it is impossible to determine if the posttreatment findings generalized across time or situation, but this study offers interesting insight regarding the type of training that may be capable of changing the content of the child's actions in at least one type of difficult situation.

The findings of this group of studies are quite equivocal and suggest that many cognitive–behavioral programs, at least as they are commonly implemented, are not effective in producing behavior change that generalizes to the home or school environment. In a meta-analysis of self-instructional training outcome studies, Dush, Hirt, and Schroeder (1989) observed that such interventions surpassed no-treatment and placebo conditions, but only by an average of half a standard deviation on common measures of behavior change. As frequently observed (Abikoff, 1985; Braswell & Kendall, 1988; Whalen & Henker, 1987), cognitive–behavioral interventions were originally heralded as techniques that could solve the problems of limited treatment maintenance and generalization that seemed to characterize traditional behavioral approaches. Virtually all investigators in this field agree that this early expectation has not been met. Abikoff (1985) suggests that this expectation has not been fulfilled because treatments are typically too brief to permit adequate skills mastery, training tasks often have little overlap with the demands of outcome tasks, and little attention has been directed towards assessing, much less programming for, maintenance. Mahoney and Nezworski (1985) emphasize that the acquisition of capacities such as self-control or social competence clearly consists of developmental processes rather than events, and they urge cognitive–behaviorists to pay greater attention to the affectional and family systems in which these capacities develop over years of social exchange. Whalen and Henker (1987) have argued that cognitive–behavioral methods must be tailored to the needs of the individual child and his/her family and emphasize that training the child to cope with obstacles or delays may be as important as training other aspects of problem-solving.

In addition to these overarching critiques, which we see as relevant to all current cognitive–behavioral efforts, we also have some specific concerns about the manner in which cognitive–behavioral training was implemented in many of the previously reviewed research efforts. As noted by Braswell and Kendall (1988), amazingly few cognitive–behavioral intervention efforts with ADHD children actually included behavioral contingencies to routinely reinforce appropriate behavior and skill application or punish inappropriate behavior. Douglas et al. (1976) invoked contingencies only when a child was extremely unmanageable. Abikoff and Gittelman (1985b) provided only social praise and noncontingent reinforcement at the end of each session. Brown et al. (1985) and Brown et al. (1986) used no formal contingencies. Of the studies with ADHD samples, only Abikoff et al. (1988) and Kirby and Grimsley (1986) did use contingencies to either reinforce appropriate behavior or punish inaccuracy and/or inattention. In our own work, we have found the use of contingencies to be crucial, given that ADHD children are so likely to exhibit behavioral excesses and deficits that would clearly interfere with the learning process. It is our contention that if such children were going to acquire more reflective behavior through natural social contingencies, this would have already occurred and they would not be in need of our treatment! Clearly, ADHD children need more incentives to work at acquiring and generalizing a mode of thought and action that does not come easily for them. To the extent that such contingencies can provide external feedback and incentives while training the child in accurate self-evaluation and strategy utilization, they may be particularly powerful in facilitating positive behavioral change (Hinshaw, Henker, & Whalen, 1984a).

In addition to our concerns about the failure to include behavioral methods, we are also struck by the fact that earlier efforts typically did not include parents in a substantive manner. Several of the previously cited studies did provide parents with information about the content of the children's training and offered parents the opportunity to observe the training sessions, but only one study with ADHD children (Horn et al., 1987) formally required the parents' involvement. Curiously, Horn et al. chose to train the parents in behavioral skills, while emphasizing cognitive–behavioral capacities with the children. None of the previously cited studies required parents to provide any form of documentation of their efforts to model, cue, or reinforce the use of cognitive–behavioral problem-solving skills in the home environment. As the field has developed, there appears to be a growing consensus that parents must be included in a significant manner if there is to be any hope of obtaining meaningful, generalizable results.

In a similar vein, there have been very few attempts to truly involve the child's classroom teacher in the process of developing the child's capacities for better problem-solving in the classroom environment. As with parents, teachers have been allowed to gain information about the child's training and, perhaps, even observe training sessions, but teachers are not systematically involved in prompting and reinforcing the use of fledgling problem-solving skills in the classroom environment.

Finally, we agree with the concerns of Whalen and Henker (1987) that more emphasis needs to be placed on recognizing when it is and is not appropriate to use cognitive–behavioral efforts and on learning to cope with various types of obstacles to successful problem-solving. We would also suggest that these elements of training content must be addressed not only through the presentation of the formal curriculum, but also as these issues arise in the actual process of training. For example, practicing coping with frustration can be addressed through structured role-play but also through problem-solving about conflicts arising within a training group.

With these concerns in mind, we shall now detail the process of development of our child and family model for cognitive–behavioral intervention.

Development of the Current Program

The origins and streams of influence affecting the emergence of cognitive–behavioral methods with children have been well-elaborated by Kendall and Braswell (1985) and Meyers and Craighead (1984). We thought it might aid the reader's understanding of the current intervention, however, if we briefly discussed the intellectual and professional streams of influence that led to the creation of this particular version of cognitive–behavioral therapy with ADHD children and their families.

As graduate students, both of us were heavily involved with research teams that achieved success in applying individually administered cognitive–behavioral techniques with subclinical populations of children with ADHD-type symptoms. One of us (L. B.) worked with Philip Kendall and colleagues at the University of Minnesota (Kendall & Wilcox, 1980; Kendall & Zupan, 1981; Kendall & Braswell, 1982b). Kendall's research group obtained positive change on a number of different measures with children referred by their teachers for displaying a lack of self-control on academic tasks and in social situations. The pretreatment scores on the Conners Hyperactivity Index and the Self-Control Rating Scale scores of these children would suggest that many, but not all, of these were displaying significant levels of difficulty. The other author (M. L. B.) had similar experiences with the Robert Schleser research group at Illinois Institute of Technology. Schleser has participated in studies examining the interaction among developmental factors, modes of delivering self-instructional training, and treatment outcome for ADHD and teacher-referred non-self-controlled children (Brown et al., 1986;

Schleser et al., 1981; Cohen & Schleser, 1984; Thackwray, Meyers, Schleser, & Cohen, 1985). While an intern, Bloomquist also worked with John Lochman in a clinical implementation of Lochman's successful cognitive–behavioral group program for conduct-disordered elementary school children (see Lochman & Curry, 1986). Thus, both of us received early, efficacy-belief building experiences with cognitive–behavioral interventions.

Then we became clinicians. It didn't take either of us long to determine that engaging in brief, individually oriented self-instructional training with an ADHD child could produce a client who was quite well-behaved in the session but whose life outside the therapy room was completely unchanged. Being good cognitive–behaviorists, we began to problem-solve about this dilemma. What could we do to amplify the potential effectiveness of these procedures? For whom would these amplified techniques be appropriate?

The inclusion of parents and teachers in the training process seemed important. As previously discussed, past attempts to include parents in cognitive–behavioral interventions have been rather limited or have failed to require any evidence of the parents' actual use of the procedures in the home environment. Given the documented interactional difficulties of parents and ADHD children, it seems crucial to involve the parents not only so they understand what the children are learning in their training but also to train them how to explicitly cue and reinforce appropriate strategy use at home. In addition, parents, like the children, need help discriminating the situations most appropriate for using problem-solving strategies from those situations that require other types of responses. Parents and teachers themselves may have certain qualities and/or attributes that could be the target of an intervention (e.g., behaviors, cognitive sets, and attitudes). Finally, we recognize that the parents and teachers of ADHD children need support to accomplish behavioral change and deserve validation of the challenge they face each day with their child or student.

As previously discussed, Abikoff (1985) has argued for greater overlap between training tasks and the demands of target or outcome tasks. Because peer relationships are such an important factor for ADHD children, the current intervention focuses heavily on addressing problems of social relating in a social context. Our program emphasizes training children in cognitive and behavioral skills focused on interpersonal relationships. In addition, children are trained and practice skills within the context of groups. Groups also permit training in solving real problems through numerous *in vivo* dilemmas that emerge by virtue of having ADHD children meet together! Therefore, group training should not only facilitate skill acquisition but should also enhance generalization to real peer problems outside of groups.

Through our clinical and research experiences, we also knew we must take into account the child's developmental level in selecting training methods and targeted skills. From our viewpoint, the developmental level of the child dictates whether the intervention is more child-focused or environmentally focused. Interventions for younger children must be more environmentally focused because the young child may not have the cognitive sophistication to benefit from direct cognitive interventions, whereas interventions for older children may be both child-focused and environmentally focused, given the older child's greater cognitive sophistication.

Our knowledge of the range of functional problems experienced by ADHD children also shapes the current program. Chapter 1 reviews the various areas of difficulty for ADHD children, including difficulties they are at risk to develop. We designed a program that would address a number of these functional difficulties and that attempts to prevent the development of other problems. Children learn a variety of skills and how to apply these skills to different problem areas. Children learn not only problem-solving and self-instruction training, but also skills in anger, effort, and emotion management. By teaching a number of skills and training skill application with a number of difficulties, it is believed that the intervention will have greater impact and demonstrate greater maintenance and generalization of positive change.

As a result of all of these concerns, we developed a general clinical intervention model that could be applied to ADHD children of different ages and with varying secondary problems. This model is detailed in Chapters 4–8. We have also developed a specific clinic and/or school-based intervention for school-age ADHD children. This specific intervention is described in the treatment manual found in Chapter 9.

Preliminary Research Support for the Current Program

The model described in this book is the product of 10 years of clinical application and the research efforts of many investigators, as well as our own research. The specific program detailed in Chapter 9 has not been empirically tested as a total intervention package, but many of the child components have been evaluated by other researchers. In our own continuing research, we have examined the effects of earlier prototypes of the child, parent/family, and teacher components appearing in Chapter 9. Thus the specific program elaborated in Chapter 9 includes modifications and additions based on the findings of ourselves and others.

Bloomquist, August, and Garfinkel (1991) examined the effects of a cognitive–behavioral therapy program with and without parent involvement, and with and without adjunctive methylphenidate, in the treatment of ADHD children. This study sought to understand if adding the parent component would be more efficacious than a cognitive–behavioral therapy program that was child-focused only, and if the combination of methylphenidate with the parent- and child-focused cognitive–behavioral therapy would produce the greatest treatment gains. All children participated in 12 cognitive–behavioral therapy group sessions in which they were trained in self-instruction and problem-solving skills. The parents of half of these children took part in a parent training component in which they were trained to prompt and reinforce children for using the cognitive–behavioral strategies in the home environment. The children received active medication or placebo throughout the 12-week experimental protocol and throughout a 6-week follow-up period.

Bloomquist et al. (1991) found that cognitive–behavioral therapy with parent involvement was associated with improved parent ratings of child behavior at posttest, but this effect was not maintained at a statistically significant level at follow-up. Methylphenidate was associated with the greatest improvements on many attention deployment tasks at posttest, with this effect maintained, but attenuated at follow-up. (Children were continued on methylphenidate at posttest and follow-up assessments.) The combination of cognitive–behavioral therapy with parent involvement and methylphenidate was significantly better than any other combination of treatments at improving parents' ratings of child behavior at posttest, but this effect was again not maintained at a statistically significant level at follow-up. There were no meaningful treatment effects on child self-report measures nor on child or parent ratings of parent–child relationship at posttest or follow-up. It appeared as though cognitive–behavioral therapy and methylphenidate affected different treatment processes. The parent- and child-involved cognitive–behavioral therapy was primarily associated with improved parent ratings of child behavior, while methylphenidate appeared to affect attention deployment.

Bloomquist, August, and Ostrander (in press) studied the effects of a multicomponent school-based cognitive–behavioral intervention for ADHD children. In the multicomponent school-based intervention, children were seen in 20 group therapy sessions in which they learned self-instruction and problem-solving skills training. Teachers participated in seven sessions. Parents participated in six sessions. Both teacher and parent programs focused on training them to prompt and reinforce children for using the strategies in the classroom and home environments, respectively. Comparison groups were a teacher only group and a waiting list control group. The teacher only group involved teachers receiving the teacher component, but children and parents were not seen. The effects of intervention were assessed at a posttest and after a 6-week follow-up period. Several feasibility issues emerged within the context of conducting the study. There was some difficulty getting parents to attend the parent sessions on a regular basis, and there were difficulties getting response measures completed by parents at posttest and follow-up periods. As a result of the incomplete parent data, analyses were not conducted on parent measures.

Bloomquist et al. (in press) found that the multicomponent cognitive–behavioral therapy was superior to the teacher only treatment and waiting list control groups in improving blind observers' ratings of children's off-task disruptive behavior in the classroom at posttest. The effects of the disruptive off-task behavior improvements were maintained at a 6-week follow-up for the multicomponent cognitive–behavioral therapy group, although between-group differences were not significant. Teachers' ratings of child behavior were not significantly changed at posttest or follow-up. There were also no effects on child self-report measures at posttest or follow-up. The authors concluded that the multicomponent cognitive–behavioral therapy intervention was minimally efficacious overall. It was difficult to change the teachers' perceptions of the children. This is similar to findings of Lochman et al. (1984) and Lochman and Curry (1986) who observed that child-focused cognitive–behavioral therapy methods improved children's actual behavior, but teachers' perceptions were unchanged.

The Bloomquist et al. (1991, in press) studies give modest preliminary support for the efficacy of the intervention. Both of the studies evaluating components of this intervention do have methodological limitations, however, which suggests the need to interpret results cautiously. In each of these studies, nonblind parent and teacher ratings were used. Fortunately, in the Bloomquist et al. (in press) study, blind observers of classroom behavior were used. In the Bloomquist et al. (1991) study, parents were a primary focus of the intervention, and teacher data were not obtained to assess generalization. Likewise, in the Bloomquist et al. (in press) study, teachers and parents were a primary focus of the intervention, but parent data were not available. The studies did not evaluate the effects of the interventions on parents or teachers themselves (e.g., beliefs, attributions, or parent/teacher–child interactions). There were also small sample sizes in both studies that could have masked potential treatment effects. The studies did not evaluate whether booster sessions would facilitate follow-up effects or evaluate the effects of the intervention over a long period of time to see whether or not competence was enhanced and if adverse outcomes were lessened.

Need for Multimodal Intervention

Considering the strengths and limitations of medication, behavioral, and cognitive–behavioral interventions, it is clear that no one form of intervention is adequate for meeting the needs of most ADHD children. From our perspective, it is also clear, however, that medication and behavioral approaches have achieved such reliable and positive effects that these two modes of treatment should be considered key elements in the intervention protocols of most ADHD children, except in those cases in which co-occurring symptoms or adverse side effects render medication inappropriate. An ideal approach to treatment might involve the initial implementation of behavioral training methods in the home and school environments. If these methods do not produce acceptable levels of functioning, then medication could be added to the regime. Unfortunately, even the use of both medication and behavioral approaches may leave some ADHD children with unmet treatment needs. In some cases, the selective use of cognitive–behavioral methods may be advised, particularly when cognitive training incorporates behavioral methods and includes parents and teachers in the training process.

Any given treatment should be viewed as only one component in a multimodal approach. Studies conducted by Satterfield, Cantwell, and Satterfield (1979) and Satterfield et al. (1987) have concluded that multimodal interventions are superior to medication only and no treatment conditions in terms of improving a long-term outcome for ADHD children. In these past investigations, multimodal intervention included individual therapy, family therapy, behavioral therapy, cognitive–behavioral therapy, psychopharmacology, and special education services. Future research is needed to clarify which ADHD children need which forms of intervention and to determine the optimum timing of such intervention.

Chapter Four

An Ecological–Developmental Model of Cognitive–Behavioral Therapy for ADHD Children and Adolescents: Overview

The remainder of the book focuses on the actual clinical practice of cognitive–behavioral therapy (CBT) with ADHD children and adolescents. In this chapter, we provide an overview of an ecological–developmental model of CBT that guides our clinical work. We, like many others, conceptualize CBT as a collaborative, goal-oriented, skills-training, directive approach to psychological treatment. Both cognitive and behavioral processes are targeted for change via cognitive and behavioral therapeutic procedures. We also advocate that therapy must address children's needs within the context of their ecology and in a manner that is developmentally appropriate.

Interventions derived from an ecological perspective intervene not only with the child, but with important environmental variables and transactions occurring between children and environments across time (Craighead, Meyers, & Wilcoxon-Craighead, 1985; Henggeler, 1982; Meyers, Cohen, & Schleser, 1989). The environment is viewed as settings within which the child exists, such as home, school, neighborhood, and culture. Within these environments, there are certain people, such as parents, siblings, teachers, and peers, who affect and are affected by the child. Subsumed under the ecological model is the notion that childhood problems result from transactions between the child and his/her environment. Transactions between the individual and his/her environment across time combine to determine the expression of behavior (Fiese & Sameroff, 1989). For example, Patterson and Bank (1989) have summarized evidence supporting the view that antisocial behavior results from transactions between parents and children over time. Initially, the child exhibits age-appropriate noncompliance, but the parents' response is ineffective in managing the child's behavior. The child's noncompliant behavior is then inadvertently reinforced. If these transactions occur repeatedly, gradually the child's behavior problems escalate, culminating in antisocial behavior in later childhood and adolescence. Similar coercive parent–child interactions have been described between ADHD children and their parents (Barkley, 1988b). In the case of ADHD, dysfunctional parent–child interaction is not seen as the original cause of the attentional difficulties, but as an important factor in the development of secondary behavioral problems. CBT, therefore, needs to modify not only how children think and behave, but also how important individuals in the children's environment think and behave, and the transactions that occur between children and individuals in the environment.

The child's developmental level needs to be considered during assessment and treatment planning. Skills vary in their developmental appropriateness. For example, it would be inappropriate to expect preschoolers to display self-controlled behavior more typical of school-age children or adolescents. Optimally, the intervention matches the developmental capabilities of the child. For example, Meyers et al. (1989) summarized a series of studies that examined the interface between a child's developmental level and interventions. Piagetian-defined preoperational children benefited from more simple, concrete interventions, such as the therapist telling a child how to solve a problem and then having the child practice the strategy. Piagetian-defined concrete operational children could take a more active, involved role in the intervention. These children responded well to interventions in which they were not told what to think, but how to think through a directed-discovery approach. The children are led to discover how to solve problems on their own. Meta-analysis of the CBT literature on childhood problems also highlighted the importance of developmental factors (Dush et al., 1989). The results of this analysis revealed a larger effect size for children over the age of 11 years than for younger children. While many factors complicate the interpretation of the specific results of the Dush et al. (1989) analysis, virtually all investigators and clinicians agree that the child's developmental status must be considered in the intervention process.

Table 4 provides a summary of the major principles of the ecological–developmental model of CBT for ADHD children and adolescents. This model is an integrated approach to intervening with multiple variables within multiple contexts by using a variety of cognitive–behavioral procedures. Problems are conceptualized and then treated within a cognitive–behavioral framework, taking into account ecological and developmental factors. Those cognitive and behavioral factors descriptive of the child, parents/family, and school (or other environments) are discerned. Cognitive–behavioral interventions are then employed to remediate these factors. A variety of interventions aimed at reeducation and/or remediation of specific cognitive and behavioral factors for the

TABLE 4
An Ecological–Developmental Model of Cognitive–Behavioral Therapy for ADHD
Children and Adolescents

I. Conceptualization of child and environment within a cognitive–behavioral framework
    A. ADHD child or adolescent
        1. Discern cognitive and behavioral difficulties.
        2. Consider the developmental context of these difficulties.
    B. Parents/family
        1. Discern cognitive and behavioral difficulties.
        2. Consider family developmental context of these difficulties.
    C. School (and other significant environments)
        1. Discern cognitive and behavioral features of staff that may be involved in child and/or parent difficulties.
    D. Consider the transactional nature of child, parent, and/or school interactions.

II. Use of cognitive and behavioral interventions
    A. With the child
        1. Reeducate child if he/she manifests inappropriate information, beliefs, or expectation and if child is mature enough for reeducation.
        2. Remediate developmentally inappropriate behaviors and cognitive processes of the child.
    B. With the parents
        1. Reeducate parents if they manifest inappropriate information, beliefs, or expectations.
        2. Remediate inappropriate parenting behaviors or cognitive processes.
    C. With the school (or other significant environment)
        1. Reeducate staff if they manifest inappropriate information, beliefs, or expectations.
        2. Remediate inappropriate staff behaviors or cognitive processes.
    D. Address destructive transactional processes among the child, parents, and school (or other significant environment).

child, parents/family, and school personnel are used. Any existing transactional problems among or between child, parents/family, and school are also targeted. The conceptualization of these problems and related specific interventions is elaborated in the remainder of this book.

Cognitive–Behavioral Conceptualization of ADHD and Coexisting Problems

Cognitive–behavioral theorists have hypothesized that certain cognitive and behavioral variables are related to certain types of childhood psychopathology (Kendall, 1985; Kendall & Siqueland, 1989). In order to conduct CBT, it is helpful to understand the hypothesized cognitive and behavioral factors that may be characteristic of ADHD and related problems. In recognition of the importance of ecological factors, the cognitive and behavioral characteristics of the parents and families of ADHD children should also be considered. There is little available research describing typical cognitive and behavioral factors of school personnel in relation to ADHD children. We hypothesize, however, that many of the cognitive and behavioral factors characteristic of parents/ families may also be characteristic of school personnel/school environments. It is recognized that cognitive and behavioral phenomena in humans rarely occur in isolation, for most phenomena involve combinations of cognitive and behavioral components, but for heuristic purposes, we shall discuss these factors separately.

Cognitive and Behavioral Factors Associated with ADHD and ADHD/Conduct-Disordered Children

We shall review research that has been conducted with both ADHD and Conduct Disorder (CD) samples, given that many children have both disorders and that ADHD children are at risk for developing CD. Cognitive and behavioral factors associated with ADHD and ADHD/CD children are summarized in Table 5. As discussed in Chapter 1, ADHD children were found to be deficient in their ability to sustain attention (Douglas, 1983). These children have difficulty with vigilance and with maintaining effort to tasks requiring sustained attention. ADHD children have also been found to have difficulties with impulsive cognitive tempo (Douglas, 1983). Impulsive children tend to make decisions very quickly and in an error-prone fashion. Another cognitive variable related to ADHD is deficiency in problem-solving skills (Tant & Douglas, 1982). Problem-solving has to do with purposeful planning and organizing of one's thoughts and behaviors to solve a problem. It involves the components of problem recognition, alternative and consequential thinking, and evaluation of the effectiveness of employed strategies. Deficits could be related to difficulty with either impersonal or interpersonal problem-solving (Kendall & Braswell, 1985).

Cognitive variables related to CD in children and adolescents have been studied extensively. Many CD children have similarities to ADHD children in terms of problems with sustained attention, impulsive cognitive tempo, and problem-solving deficiencies. The problem-solving deficits more characteristic of CD children and adolescents include generating fewer and more aggressive solutions than comparison children (Asarnow & Callan, 1985; Lochman & Lampron, 1986; Richard & Dodge, 1982). CD children were also found to have deficits in means–

TABLE 5
**Cognitive and Behavioral Factors Associated with ADHD and
ADHD/CD Children**

Cognitive
    I. Difficulties with sustained attention
   II. Impulsive cognitive tempo
  III. Deficits in problem-solving
      A. Impersonal problem-solving
      B. Interpersonal problem-solving
  IV. Deficits in means–end thinking
   V. Deficits in perspective-taking
  VI. Information processing errors
      A. Misattribution of intent
      B. Selective attention and recall
 VII. Impulsive anger
      A. Deficits in mediation of behavior, affect, and cognition
      B. Information processing errors

Behavioral
    I. Off-task behavior
   II. Noncompliance
  III. Social behavior skill deficits
  IV. Aggressive behavior
   V. Antisocial behavior

end thinking (Asarnow & Callan, 1985; Lochman & Lampron, 1986; Shure & Spivack, 1972; Spivack, Platt, & Shure, 1976). Poor means–end thinking ability suggests that CD children are deficient in the ability to think of the steps necessary to reach a goal. Perspective-taking ability was also found to be deficient in CD children and adolescents (Chandler, 1973; Chandler, Greenspan, & Barenboim, 1974; Gurucharri, Phelps, & Selman, 1984; Spivack et al., 1976). These children have difficulty understanding the thoughts, feelings, and perceptions of other individuals. CD children are more likely to make errors in how they attribute causation for others' intentions (Dodge, 1986; Dodge et al., 1984; Milich & Dodge, 1984; Nasby, Hayden, & Depaulo, 1980; Lochman, 1987). They were found to misinterpret neutral or benign interpersonal behaviors of others as indicating hostile intent. CD children and adolescents also have selective attention and recall biases (Dodge, 1986; Dodge & Frame, 1982; Dodge & Newman, 1981; Milich & Dodge, 1984). They are more likely to pay attention to and recall hostile social cues rather than neutral or positive social cues in interpersonal interactions. CD children and adolescents may have difficulties with impulsive anger, which could be related to many of the previously discussed cognitive variables (Lochman, Nelson, & Sims, 1981). Impulsive anger also seems to be related to deficits in mediation of behavior, affect, and physiological arousal, as well as errors in information processing.

As discussed in Chapter 1, children with both ADHD and CD have been found to have certain overt behavioral characteristics. These children are found to be off-task frequently, are more noncompliant, engage in higher frequencies of aggressive behavior, have social behavior skills deficits (e.g., poor eye contact, deficient communication skills, limited sharing, and limited assertiveness skills) and may engage in antisocial behavior (e.g., stealing, truancy, and drug and alcohol abuse) (Barkley, 1981, 1988a, 1989; Henker & Whalen, 1989; McMahon & Forehand, 1988; McMahon & Wells, 1989).

We do not suggest that these cognitive and behavioral factors occur only in or are caused solely by the child. Obviously, the family and other environmental/social/cultural variables strongly influence the expression of these factors in children. Nonetheless, it is helpful to think of these factors as potential targets for child intervention.

Cognitive and Behavioral Factors Associated with Family Relationship Dysfunction

There is some overlap and lack of precision when reviewing the literature describing family dysfunction from a cognitive–behavioral perspective. Some empirical studies and theoretical discussions have focused specifically on describing cognitive and behavioral factors associated with parents and families of children with ADHD and ADHD/CD. Other relevant literature describes these factors as indicative of parent and family relationship problems in general (which may or may not be associated with ADHD or ADHD/CD). We shall discuss both bodies of literature to alert therapists to potential areas of therapeutic focus.

Cognitive and behavioral factors associated with parental or familial dysfunction are summarized in Table 6. Parents of children exhibiting behavioral problems have been found to make trait attributions toward their children in an attempt to infer causation about their negative behavior (Bauer & Twentyman, 1985; Dix & Grusec, 1985; Epstein, Schlesinger, & Dryden, 1988; Sobol, Ashbourne, Earn, & Cunningham, 1989). Parents are likely to attribute the child's misbehavior to internal dispositions rather than to external factors. Parents may also engage in attributions of self-blame when a child misbehaves (Di Giuseppe, 1988). The parents attribute the child's problems to deficiencies in themselves and their parenting abilities, and these conclusions are typically followed by self-condemnation. Parents of behavior-problem children have been observed to have unrealistic beliefs about their child and themselves

TABLE 6
Cognitive and Behavioral Factors Associated with Family
Relationship Dysfunction

Parent cognitive
   I. Dysfunctional attributions
       A. Trait attributions toward child
       B. Self-blame attributions toward self
  II. Unrealistic beliefs
       A. Stable/global beliefs about child
       B. Stable/global beliefs about self
 III. Unrealistic expectations
 IV. External locus of control
  V. Perceptual bias
 VI. Impulsive anger

Family behavioral
   I. Negative reinforcement of inappropriate behavior
  II. Low rates of positive reinforcement of appropriate behavior
 III. Ineffective discipline
 IV. Poor parental monitoring of child

Family cognitive and behavioral
   I. Family problem-solving deficits
  II. Family communication deficits
 III. Family anger and conflict management deficits

(Epstein et al., 1988; Vincent Roehling & Robin, 1986). Parents may
hold stable/global beliefs about their child, such as "He will always have
problems," or stable/global beliefs about their parenting, such as "I am a
terrible parent." Parents of children exhibiting behavioral disorders may
also have unrealistic expectations for their child (Morton, Twentyman,
& Azar, 1988; Sobol et al., 1989). This may manifest itself in the parents
having age-inappropriate expectations concerning their child's capacity
for self-control. Relative to parents of nondisturbed children, parents of
behavior-disordered children have been found to manifest an external
locus of control (Campis et al., 1986; Mouton & Tuma, 1988). Parents
exhibiting an external locus of control typically feel very little
responsibility for their child's behavior and also have feelings that their
child's behavior is out of their control. Some parents of CD children may
also have a perceptual bias (Brody & Forehand, 1986; Forehand,
Lautenschlager, Faust, & Graziano, 1986; Griest, Forehand, Wells, &
McMahon, 1980; Middlebrook & Forehand, 1985). Typically, this bias is
manifested by parents who are either depressed or under significant
stress and involves the parent perceiving neutral and appropriate child
behavior as disruptive or inappropriate behavior. Currently, there is
debate about whether depressed parents actually misperceive their

child's behavior or whether they are perceiving inappropriate behavior that nondepressed parents tend to minimize (Conrad & Hammen, 1989). Nonetheless, the point is that parental perceptions of child behavior may vary depending on the emotional status of the parent. Finally, some parents may have difficulties with the inappropriate expression of anger (Di Giuseppe, 1988; Nomellini & Katz, 1983). Problems in anger management may stem from cognitive and behavioral processes related to deficits in self-monitoring and recognition of anger cues and having poor coping skills to modulate anger and respond in a more adaptive fashion to their child's behavior.

Characteristics of dysfunctional families have also been explored from a more behavioral perspective. Behaviorists have noted that negative reinforcement often shapes and maintains children's and parents' dysfunctional behavior (Gard & Berry, 1986; Patterson, 1972, 1982). Both parents and children engage in aversive behaviors toward each other as a way of controlling one another. When a parent or child gives in to the aversive behavior of the other, this negatively reinforces such behavior and increases the probability that the behavior will be repeated. Another behavioral characteristic of dysfunctional families is a low rate of positive reinforcement for appropriate behavior (Barkley, Karlsson, & Polland, 1985; Cunningham & Barkley, 1979; Ramsey & Walker, 1988). When children are engaging in appropriate or prosocial behavior, their parents oftentimes do not pay attention to them or reinforce them in more tangible ways. Parents of behavior-problem children have also been observed to be ineffective in disciplining noncompliant or disruptive behavior (Barkley, Karlsson, & Pollard, 1985; Cunningham & Barkley, 1979; Ramsey & Walker, 1988; Ramsey, Walker, Shinn, O'Neill, & Stieber, 1989). They may give vague and frequent commands to their children in an effort to gain their compliance. When the parents do not state exactly what the child is supposed to do and say the vague command repeatedly, the child is less likely to be compliant. These parents may also give too many warnings and not follow through with consequences when indicated. The family problems may also involve poor parental monitoring of the children's behavior (Patterson & Stouthamer-Loeber, 1984; Ramsey & Walker, 1988). For example, the parents do not undertake actions necessary to monitor the child's activities and whereabouts.

Dysfunctional families also display a number of cognitive–behavioral skills deficits. Family problem-solving deficits have been found to discriminate dysfunctional from functional families (Foster & Robin, 1989; Ramsey & Walker, 1988; Ramsey et al., 1989). Families exhibiting problem-solving skills difficulties are unable to generate alternative solutions or to agree on how to solve family problems. Poor communication skills have been related to parent and adolescent relationship difficulties (Alexander & Parsons, 1982; Morris, Alexander,

& Waldron, 1988; Foster & Robin, 1989). Families having difficulties with communication skills are likely to express themselves in a vague, unclear, and destructive fashion and to have poor listening skills. Many problem families exhibit high levels of conflict and have deficits in skills to control anger and resolve conflicts (Foster & Robin, 1989). Families with poor conflict-resolution skills are likely to have difficulty with problem-solving and communication because of the high level of conflict. They may also have difficulties controlling their anger when trying to work out problems.

We do not suggest that the cognitive and behavioral factors for parents and families exist independent of the child. Child variables strongly influence the expression of these factors. We do think it is meaningful, however, to discuss these issues as parent and family factors that could be targeted for intervention.

Conducting Therapy

Now that we have discussed the cognitive and behavioral characteristics of ADHD and ADHD/CD children and their families, we can proceed with an overview of interventions designed to address these problems. In this section, we shall discuss therapist elements, such as therapist style and therapist tools of the trade, that are necessary for effectively conducting CBT. Then we shall review the "how to's" of treatment, including diagnostic and treatment-related assessment, treatment planning, skills training, school consultation, termination, and follow-up. The stages of cognitive–behavioral intervention for ADHD children/adolescents and their families are summarized in Table 7.

As detailed in Table 7, there are six therapeutic stages in this model of CBT. The first stage is assessment. A diagnostic evaluation is conducted that, among other things, begins the process of determining the eventual choice of intervention methods. Treatment-related assessment is conducted to delineate the specific child, parent, and family cognitive and/or behavioral factors that need to be addressed in the intervention. The therapist considers the severity of the child's and family's dysfunction as well as the child's developmental level in determining a treatment plan. The extent to which the school will be involved is also considered. The second stage consists of preparing the child, parents, and family for change. The third stage involves actually training the child, parent, and/or family members in specific cognitive or behavioral coping skills. The fourth stage involves consulting with the school. In this stage, the school is typically involved to enhance generalization of skills originally trained in the clinic, but occasionally the school may be the training site. The fifth and sixth stages concern termination of the intervention and

TABLE 7
Stages of Cognitive–Behavioral Intervention for Children and Families

---

I. Assessment
   A. Diagnostic assessment
   B. Treatment-related assessment
   C. Treatment planning
      1. Target specific cognitions and behaviors of child and parents/families.
      2. Consider severity of child dysfunction.
      3. Consider severity of family dysfunction.
      4. Consider developmental factors.
      5. Consider extent of school involvement.
II. Preparation for change
   A. Forming a collaborative relationship
   B. Beginning to modify sources of resistance
III. Cognitive and/or behavioral skills training
   A. Child focused
   B. Parent focused
   C. Family focused
IV. School consultation
 V. Termination
VI. Follow-up

---

follow-up (booster) sessions, respectively. Efforts are made to program for generalization and maintenance of treatment effects throughout the intervention.

Characteristics of the Therapist

CBT is a collaborative, goal-oriented, skills training approach to intervention. Certain therapist characteristics are needed to conform to these therapeutic parameters. Alexander, Barton, Schiavo, and Parsons (1976) examined therapist characteristics related to best therapeutic outcome with functional family therapy. Functional family therapy is also a goal-oriented skills training approach to family therapy. Alexander et al. found that those therapists who were high in relationship skills (i.e., able to establish rapport, humor, etc.) and high in structuring skills (i.e., directive, active, etc.) achieved the best outcomes with functional family therapy. We hypothesize that similar types of therapist skills and characteristics are required for successful outcome in CBT with ADHD children.

We qualify the structuring component further by stating that therapists need to be directive in a Socratic manner. This approach entails asking questions to guide individuals to develop and apply skills to specific problem areas. It is also important for the therapist to focus on the process rather than the content of therapy, helping children and families to solve their own problems. The therapist does not tell individuals or families what to do, but rather helps them discover these things for themselves. An example of this would be an adolescent who comes to therapy stating that he/she wants to find a job. The cognitive–behavioral therapist would not focus on the content of helping the adolescent find a job. Rather, the cognitive–behavioral therapist would focus on the process necessary to facilitate the teenager finding his/her own job. This could be accomplished by introducing problem-solving skills to the client and asking him/her to use the problem-solving steps to figure out how to solve the problem of finding a job.

The cognitive–behavioral therapist may employ a variety of tools to enhance therapeutic outcome, including didactic instruction, modeling, role-playing, behavioral rehearsal, homework exercises, and contingency management to facilitate acquisition of skills. Written materials, such as charts, graphs, or logs, may be used as visual or memory aids throughout the therapy process. We shall refer to these therapeutic tools throughout the upcoming discussion of treatment.

Assessment, Treatment Planning, and Preparation for Change

It is most common to think of CBT as a therapist teaching a set of skills to a client through a specific set of procedures/techniques. It is our contention, however, that much therapeutic work needs to be done before actual skills training can take place. This section provides an overview of our procedures for assessment, treatment planning, and preparation for change. These concepts are discussed in this chapter for the sake of presenting a comprehensive overview of our treatment model, but these notions will be elaborated in Chapter 5.

Assessment and Treatment Planning

We use a three-stage process for assessment and treatment planning, including diagnostic assessment, treatment-related assessment, and treatment planning procedures. The diagnostic assessment procedures were detailed in Chapter 2. The primary purpose of this stage of the process is to determine the presence of ADHD and possible coexisting psychiatric disorders. The treatment-related assessment focuses on determining which cognitive and behavioral factors of the child, parents/family, and school should be targeted in the treatment. The cognitive and behavioral factors summarized in Tables 5 and 6 can serve as a guide for the treatment-related assessment process. Essentially, the therapist organizes the assessment material and conducts a problem-focused interview to determine the factors that need to be addressed in treatment. As discussed earlier, the parent and family factors described in Table 6 may also be typical of school personnel/school environments. The final stage is actual treatment planning. At this point, the therapist has already defined the problems, and now the task is to match specific, appropriate interventions to the defined problems, while considering ecological and developmental factors. For example, a school-age child who is found to have problem-solving deficits would probably benefit from problem-solving therapy. If it were determined that a parent was making negative trait attributions about the child's behavior, then cognitive restructuring exercises for the parent would be in order. If the assessment reveals that the family is exhibiting significant conflict, then conflict management training procedures may be indicated.

Preparation for Change

Now that diagnostic and treatment-related assessments and treatment planning have been accomplished, the therapist can focus on intervention. Before implementing the actual cognitive and behavioral skills training, however, it is necessary to set the stage to ensure that change can take place. In this regard, we agree with the thinking developed and articulated in functional family therapy by Alexander and colleagues (Alexander & Parsons, 1982; Barton & Alexander, 1981; Morris et al., 1988). In functional family therapy, concepts and strategies from systemic family therapy are blended with behavioral and CBT procedures. The functional family therapist divides an intervention into two stages. The first stage is therapy. The therapy stage has a heavy cognitive focus, with the ultimate goal of modifying family members' cognitions to reduce resistance and motivate a desire for change. This is followed by the second stage, that of education. Once the goals of the therapy stage have been accomplished, then the therapist can prescribe specific behavioral and cognitive–behavioral strategies to help the family develop skills necessary to better cope with and solve problems. Alexander and colleagues argue that if the therapy stage is not successfully completed before the education stage, then change is unlikely to occur.

Our clinical experience in practicing CBT also suggests the value of preparing the child and family for change, much as Alexander and colleagues described in the therapy stage of functional family therapy. We have modified strategies set forth by Alexander and colleagues by blending our CBT procedures with those of functional family therapy. The preparation-for-change process has two separate components: forming a collaborative relationship and dealing with resistance.

Forming a collaborative relationship with the child and family involves providing information and making decisions together. In the early stages of therapy, it is necessary to provide adequate information about ADHD and CBT. Uninformed children/adolescents and parents will be less likely to participate in therapy effectively. It is also necessary to get family input regarding the focus of therapy. The therapist should collaborate with the child/adolescent and family on treatment-related decisions. This collaboration could take the form of making decisions about which skills should be trained initially, or it involve other decisions, such as whether or not the family should pursue an evaluation for medication use, should lobby for more special education services, or should make efforts to help the child become involved in selected extracurricular activities.

Before skills training, it is often helpful to begin to modify resistance. We know that resistance is often inevitable in any type of therapy, so it makes sense to us to deal with it *a priori*. The therapist should take the time to ask questions about the family members' thoughts about themselves, other family members, and various aspects of therapy. It may be necessary to employ cognitive restructuring procedures to modify these thoughts, beliefs, and attributions. For example, if the parents hold the view that the child is "the cause of all of our problems," and the clinician has information to suggest that the parents also are contributing to the problem, it will be necessary to modify the parents' beliefs before starting a family skills training module. The receptivity of the child/adolescent and parents to the skills training modules will be greatly increased if the preparation-for-change stage is conducted satisfactorily.

Skills Training Overview

After the child and family have been prepared for change, the therapist can work with the child, parents, and family on skill development. The child skills training, parent and family skills training, and school consultation procedures are detailed in Chapters 6, 7, and 8, respectively, but the skills training modules are briefly reviewed here.

Therapy does not necessarily focus on all of the skills training modules, and the training modules do not necessarily need to be delivered in the order presented in this volume. Rather, the therapist must choose modules based on the functional assessment of the child, parents, and family. *The therapist selects only those modules that are specifically relevant to a particular ADHD or ADHD/CD child and his/her family.*

In clinical practice, some of the child, parent, and family skills training sessions may be implemented simultaneously. This could be accomplished by working with the child separately for part of a session and then working with the parents and/or family for the remainder of a session, or by seeing the child for several weeks followed by a family session. The CBT program presented in Chapter 9 is an example of how to intermix child, parent, and family sessions. The therapist conducting CBT with ADHD children and their families may elect to combine child, parent, and family components in a similar manner or modify the components to fit the constraints of his/her clinical practice. We view school consultation as an extension of the skills training process. The purpose of school consultation typically is to train school personnel to facilitate the child's use of his/her newly acquired skills in the school environment.

Child Skills Training

The cognitive–behavioral therapist can use a variety of procedures to remediate and/or change the cognitive and behavioral factors that have been implicated in children with ADHD and ADHD/CD. The cognitive–behavioral interventions for ADHD/CD children are summarized in Table 8.

Problem-solving and self-instruction training procedures are the classic interventions for treating children with these types of problems. Problem-solving training involves teaching individuals methodical strategies for solving problems (D'Zurilla & Goldfried, 1971). Self-instruction

TABLE 8
Child Skills Training for ADHD and ADHD/CD

   I. Problem-solving and self-instruction training
      A. Self-control strategies
      B. Component skills
         1. Problem recognition
         2. Solution generation
         3. Consequential thinking
         4. Anticipating obstacles
         5. Executing specific behavior
      C. Means–end problem-solving
      D. Decision-making problem-solving
  II. Interpersonal problem-solving training
 III. Anger/frustration management
 IV. Poor effort management
  V. Behavioral social skills training
 VI. Relaxation training

---

training involves training people to say problem-solving self-statements to themselves when confronted with a problem (Meichenbaum & Goodman, 1971). The primary focus is on teaching children self-control strategies via problem-solving and self-instruction training. Children are trained in a variety of component problem-solving skills, including how to recognize problems, how to generate alternative solutions, how to anticipate consequences, how to anticipate obstacles that may arise, and how to execute specific behaviors to solve problems. Problem-solving and self-instruction training can be geared toward impersonal problems (e.g., academic tasks or poor effort/off-task behavior) or interpersonal problems (e.g., difficulties interacting with peers and adults) (Kendall & Braswell, 1985).

Through interpersonal problem-solving, children learn how to use problem-solving steps to solve interpersonal dilemmas (Urbain & Savage, 1989). Perspective-taking training can be incorporated in interpersonal problem-solving to help children learn how to understand the thoughts and feeling of other individuals in the interpersonal problem-solving process.

To buttress interpersonal problem-solving training, behavioral social skills training is often employed. In behavioral social skills training, children learn to execute and increase the use of specific prosocial behaviors (Bierman & Furman, 1984; Bierman, Miller, & Stabb, 1987; Urbain & Savage, 1989). Such training typically involves the process of didactic instruction, coaching, role-playing, and application practice of specific skills, such as maintaining appropriate eye contact, playing cooperatively, and expressing feelings appropriately.

Anger/frustration management training is often used to train children to better modulate their emotional arousal (Lochman et al., 1981). Children are taught to use problem-solving and self-instruction steps geared toward management of anger/frustration, relaxation techniques, and coping self-statements to control anger/frustration. One component of anger/frustration management involves training children in situation interpretation strategies so they learn to more accurately attribute the intent of others' behaviors.

Given the fact that ADHD and ADHD/CD children are known for off-task behavior and poor effort, we also have developed modules that focus on poor effort management. Through this training, children learn to use problem-solving and self-instruction skills and coping self-statements to manage poor effort.

Finally, relaxation skills are important for ADHD and ADHD/CD children to learn. Given the fact that these children often have difficulty controlling their arousal due either to anger/frustration or to simple excessive motor activity, it is helpful for them to learn simple relaxation techniques and when and how to apply them appropriately.

Parent and Family Skills Training

The cognitive–behavioral therapist can use a variety of procedures to remediate and/or change those cognitive and behavioral factors implicated in family adjustment difficulties. Parent and family skills training modules are summarized in Tables 9 and 10.

To modify parents' thoughts and attitudes, educational and cognitive restructuring procedures are used. The therapist needs to provide accurate information to the parents about ADHD and CBT so that expectancies and beliefs might be more appropriate. Parents are also trained to recognize dysfunctional cognitions about their child and/or themselves, understand why those thoughts are dysfunctional, and replace them with more functional thoughts.

In cognitive–behavioral child management, the focus is on encouraging the child's use of productive cognitive processes. Parents are trained in a Socratic parenting method whereby they facilitate the children's use of cognitive–behavioral strategies to solve problems that occur at home. One component of this training involves helping parents learn to be better observers of their children and themselves in ongoing activities at home and, as a result, learn to identify repetitive behavioral sequences in parent–child interactions. Next, parents are educated about specific CBT skills their children are learning, without breaking

TABLE 9
Parent Skills Training

  I. Modifying parent thoughts and attitudes
     A. Education
     B. Cognitive restructuring and refocusing
 II. Cognitive–behavioral child management
     A. Child/self-observation
     B. Education of skills child is learning
     C. Prompting and reinforcing child for application of skills at home
III. Behavioral child management
     A. Child/self observation
     B. Improving parent relationship through special play time
     C. Parent self-monitoring
     D. Reinforcement
     E. Commands
     F. Time-out/removal of privileges
     G. Structuring environment
     H. Training child/adolescent in self-monitoring
     I. Behavioral contracting
     J. Monitoring

TABLE 10
Family Skills Training

   I. Family problem-solving
      A. Family interaction control strategies
      B. Component skills
         1. Problem recognition
         2. Solution generation
         3. Consequential thinking
         4. Anticipating obstacles
         5. Executing specific behaviors
  II. Family communication skills training
      A. Family self-monitoring
      B. Effective expression
      C. Effective listening
      D. Congruence
 III. Family anger/conflict management training
      A. Recognizing dysfunctional anger/conflict
      B. Family coping with anger/conflict
      C. Family problem-solving and communication

---

confidentiality of the child's disclosures. This is accomplished by simply explaining to parents what specific skills their children are learning, without going into personal issues that children may raise in therapy. Finally, the parents learn how to help the child discover when, where, and how to use CBT strategies and to reinforce appropriate application.

In behavioral child management (Forehand & McMahon, 1981; Barkley, 1987), the focus is on children's behavior. Parents learn methods to modify their children's behavior at home. Again, the first step is to help the parents learn how to better observe children and themselves to become familiar with repetitive behavioral sequences in parent–child interactions. A number of procedures can be employed to improve parent–child interactions and to facilitate the parents' behavioral child management skills. One technique involves improving parent–child relationships through special play time. Parents learn how to increase specific positive behaviors, such as praising, describing, and touching, while decreasing specific negative behaviors, such as commands, criticisms, and questions, during structured play time activities. Another skill parents can learn is self-monitoring. Parents learn to observe themselves, reduce negative interactions, and increase positive interactions, as well as increase ignoring of mild inappropriate/attention-seeking child behavior. This is accomplished through a self-monitoring exercise in which parents monitor the frequency with which they emit these behaviors, while trying to decrease negative parent behaviors and increase the positive parent behaviors. Another parenting skill involves learning how to reinforce compliance and specific appropriate behavior. To accomplish this, structured procedures are implemented whereby parents' reinforcement is contingent upon children emitting specified behaviors.

The commands that parents give a child when trying to elicit compliance can also be the focus of behavioral child management. Parents learn to recognize when they are giving ineffective commands and learn how to give firm, specific, one-step commands to gain children's compliance. Time-out/removal of privileges is another effective child management strategy that can be used by parents. Through these procedures, parents learn to attach consequences to noncompliance and specific inappropriate behavior. Structuring the home environment can also be a powerful way to manage children's behavior. To develop this skill, parents learn how to create more routines and schedules and clearly define household procedures, rules, and expectations to provide more external structure and predictability for the child. Training the children in self-monitoring can also be an effective way for parents to modify a child's behavior. Parents are instructed how to monitor and reinforce children for staying on-task. Parents may also need to learn more effective child monitoring strategies. Behavioral contracting can be a powerful tool to modify more severe maladaptive behavior of children. By employing behavioral contracting, parents and children negotiate and sign contracts specifying contingencies for problematic child behaviors.

Family problem-solving training can be a very useful skill for families to learn (Alexander & Parsons, 1982; Foster & Robin, 1989). In family problem-solving training, family members learn to focus discussions and to use a methodical step-by-step approach for solving problems that is similar to children's problem-solving training. The focus in family problem-solving, however, is on family relationships rather than on any particular child.

Another powerful technique that can positively effect family processes is family communication skills training (Alexander & Parsons, 1982; Foster & Robin, 1989). In this type of training, family members learn about dysfunctional communication patterns that may be characteristic of their family and learn specific techniques and skills for communicating in a more adaptive/functional way. In this regard, family self-monitoring is often used whereby family members learn to identify dysfunctional communication patterns on an ongoing basis. Effective expression and effective listening are emphasized in family communication skills training. Finally, congruence, which involves family members learning to communicate the same message on a verbal and nonverbal level, is also a component in communication skills training.

The final family skills training module involves family anger/conflict management training (Foster & Robin, 1989). In this type of training, family members learn to reduce anger/conflict so they are able to employ family problem-solving and communication skills. The first step is to train family members to recognize dysfunctional anger/conflict. In this regard, family members learn to identify cues that inform them that family members are too angry or out of control. The second step is to train family members to cope more effectively with anger/conflict. Family members learn to separate briefly, employ anger management strategies individually, and then reunite. Then, the final step is for family members to employ family problem-solving and communication skills training.

School Consultation

The content of school consultation is summarized in Table 11. School consultation can take a cognitive–behavioral or behavioral focus. It is helpful to first provide the school personnel with information about ADHD and CBT to begin to modify maladaptive thoughts. Although not always easy, it may be helpful to try to modify maladaptive cognitions school personnel hold about themselves and the child in a manner similar to the way parents' cognitions are modified. In cognitive–behaviorally focused school consultation, the emphasis is on giving school personnel specific strategies and skills to promote the child's use of newly acquired skills in the school environment. The first step is to explain to the school personnel specifically what skills the child learned in the clinic setting. The second step is to devise methods to help school personnel work with the child in a cognitive–behavioral manner. This typically involves devising methods to prompt, evaluate, and reward the

TABLE 11
School Consultation

    I. Modifying school personnel thoughts and feelings
       A. Education
       B. Cognitive restructuring
   II. Cognitive–behavioral school consultation
       A. Explaining child skills
       B. Devising methods to promote generalization to school environment
          1. Methods to prompt child for strategy usage
          2. Methods to evaluate child strategy usage
          3. Methods to reward strategy usage
 III. Behavioral school consultation
       A. Devising specific behavioral interventions

---

children for strategy usage in the school environment. With behavioral school consultation, the focus is on promoting behavioral child management skills similar to those discussed in parenting skills training.

Termination

Once the child, parents, and/or family members have demonstrated positive change and seem to be applying new skills appropriately and school consultation has been implemented, the therapist should consider terminating therapy. We recommend using subjective and objective means to determine if termination of therapy is warranted. Subjective assessments can be derived from the therapist's observation and by asking the child/adolescent and parents their opinion about therapeutic progress. The therapist's observations should center around whether or not he/she has observed adequate skill acquisition. Questions to the family should address their perceptions of the child's improvement in school, with peers, with the family, in the community, etc. All family members should be asked to comment about improvements in family relationships. Objective assessments can include readministering tests given during the diagnostic or functional assessment phases. If the therapist observes convergence between his/her observations, the child and parents' observations, and the objective assessments, then termination of therapy should be seriously considered.

Before actually terminating a child and/or family from therapy, the therapist should broach the topic of relapse prevention. Relapses are inevitable, especially with the chronic nature of ADHD and ADHD/CD. The therapist should review with the family how they may want to respond when relapses occur. The family members may want to review problem-solving strategies for the child, family communication skills, etc., and then attempt to employ these skills once again in a more structured fashion. The therapist and family should also discuss the specific signs and symptoms that would warrant a return to therapy.

Follow-Up

It would be naive to assume that once therapy with an ADHD or ADHD/CD child and family is complete, that the child and/or family members will never need therapy again or that therapeutic gains will necessarily be maintained. Although there are few studies evaluating the effects of booster sessions with ADHD children, there is evidence that booster sessions are helpful in maintaining treatment effects with other disorders (Whisman, 1990). Therefore, it is essential that the therapist monitor the child's and family's progress and provide booster sessions in some fashion. This can range from informal telephone contacts to scheduled follow-up or booster sessions. As discussed in the introduction, we believe that ADHD children and their families have certain treatment themes that are relevant across childhood and adolescence, and these children are also likely to present with different primary and secondary symptoms at different times. For example, a family may need help establishing a structure to support developmentally appropriate behavior at various key transition points in the child's life. Thus, this family theme remains constant, but the child's primary symptoms may vary from impulsivity and overactivity in early childhood, to oppositionality and defiance in middle childhood, to rebelliousness and demoralization in adolescence. We recommend that the therapist make the follow-up plans consistent with the unique needs and features of each child and family while remaining cognizant of overarching treatment themes that are relevant to most families of ADHD and ADHD/CD children.

Limitations of Intervention

We end this chapter by discussing our impressions of the limitations of the ecological–developmental CBT model and examine how our model fits in with other modes of intervention.

One problem is the fact that our model has not been empirically validated in its entirety. Nonetheless, this model of therapy borrows heavily from other, more empirically validated, approaches (e.g., functional family therapy, parent management training, and CBT). The model described in this chapter and elucidated in Chapters 5–8 is very much a clinical model. Our clinical experiences suggest that, in many cases, the application of this model can be quite successful in at least promoting a better adaptation to ADHD. Some of the data summarized in Chapter 3 (Bloomquist et al., 1991, in press) provide modest support for at least portions of this model, but there is clearly a need for further experimental evaluation of this model.

ADHD and ADHD/CD children are at high risk for developing low self-esteem, depression, and anxiety. The model that we describe here does not directly deal with these problems. We hypothesize that if children and families receive the type of treatment described in this model, the potentially negative effects of ADHD and ADHD/CD on self-esteem and mood will be moderated. If, however, the therapist is treating a child with significant depression or anxiety coexisting with ADHD or ADHD/CD, then other skills training procedures (e.g., cognitive restructuring, pleasant event scheduling, affective education, and systematic desensitization) should be used. While we recognize the importance of treating depression in ADHD and ADHD/CD children, it is beyond the scope of this volume to review therapeutic procedures for treating these problems. The interested reader is referred to Stark, Rouse, and Livingston (1991) for a review of CBT for childhood depression, and to Kendall et al. (1991) for a discussion of CBT applied to childhood anxiety.

Even though we believe CBT is a very appropriate treatment for many children with ADHD and ADHD/CD, other therapeutic modalities can be very helpful adjuncts to the treatment procedures described in this volume. More traditional strategic and structural family therapies may be useful in treating some ADHD and ADHD/CD children's families. Psychodynamic therapy may also be a useful adjunct to CBT, especially for ADHD and ADHD/CD youngsters who have a history of adverse or traumatic psychosocial difficulties. The reader is referred to Hoberman and Peterson (1990) for information on integrating CBT with psychodynamic therapy in the treatment of children. As detailed in earlier chapters, we are also strong supporters of traditional behavioral, pharmacological, and educational interventions for ADHD children, and, in many cases, these forms of intervention should take precedence over CBT methods. The need for multimodal approaches to treatment for these children cannot be overemphasized.

Chapter Five

Before Skills Training: Treatment-Related Assessment/Planning and Preparation for Change

As discussed in Chapter 4, much therapeutic work needs to be done before the child/adolescent and family are introduced to skills training. It is necessary for the therapist to have a thorough understanding of problems of the child/adolescent and family from a cognitive–behavioral perspective, so that the appropriate cognitive–behavioral intervention can be applied. As was also previously noted, it is necessary to prepare the child/adolescent and family for change so that they are more receptive to the skills training procedures. This chapter provides a detailed review of the rationale and procedures for conducting a treatment-related assessment, treatment planning, and preparing the child/adolescent and family for change.

Diagnostic Assessment

Specific tools for conducting a diagnostic evaluation of the ADHD child and his/her family were described in Chapter 2. The diagnostic evaluation often consists of a medical evaluation; parent and child interviews; parent and teacher ratings of the child's behavior; direct observations of the child; cognitive testing; assessments of attention, learning and impulsivity with specialized measures; child self-report measures; and an assessment of parent and family functioning. The diagnostic evaluation entails gathering information from all of these sources and looking for patterns of convergence that give evidence for a diagnosis of ADHD and/or other disorders for a given child. The diagnostic evaluation will, in a global sense, focus the therapist toward ultimate treatment issues. When a diagnosis of ADHD is made, this has certain implications for possible pharmacological treatment and will give the clinician clues as to what child, parent, and family factors to examine more closely to determine the specific foci of psychological treatments.

Treatment-Related Assessment

Whereas the purpose of the diagnostic assessment is to establish a diagnosis, the purpose of treatment-related assessment is to determine the areas to be addressed in therapy. Not all children, parents, and families exhibit every cognitive and behavioral factor previously discussed in Chapter 4. As a result, the therapist must be able to focus on the cognitive and behavioral factors most relevant for a given child and family. A treatment-related assessment can be conducted by reviewing diagnostic assessment data from the perspective of defining treatment targets and goals. In addition, information obtained through a problem-focused interview is extremely important.

Problem-Focused Interviews

When conducting a problem-focused interview with a child, the initial focus is on how the child sees his/her problems. If such information has not already emerged in the initial assessment, the interviewer asks questions about problems at home, at school, and with peers. If the child gives little information, the interviewer can ask the child what others (parents, teachers, peers, coaches, etc.) say his/her problems are. The interviewer can also ask the child about problem-solving. How does the child solve problems with homework, peers, teachers, parents, etc.? Does the child consider himself/herself to be a good problem-solver? The interviewer can ask the child if he/she has problems with anger. If such difficulties are acknowledged, the interviewer can ask questions to explore possible biases in interpreting situations or the intent of others. For example, the interviewer can ask, "Let's imagine you are walking down a crowded hallway at school and someone bumps into you. Why do you think he or she did that?" or "How would you solve that problem?" etc. Finally, it may be wise to ask the child his/her opinion of medications, if pharmacological treatment is being considered.

The interview with the parents can give information about the child, parents and family. Regarding the child, once the child's problems at home, at school, and within the family environment have been clarified and the antecedents and consequences of these problems have been discussed, the interviewer can clarify several issues of relevance for enacting cognitive–behavioral therapies. For example, the interviewer may ask the parent if the child has difficulty solving problems with peers, siblings or other significant individuals. Questions about the child's tendency to act without thinking or be aggressive may be helpful. The interviewer can also question parents to clarify the child's capacity to take the perspective of others when problem-solving.

Parents are also asked about their parenting behaviors, their perceptions of the child and themselves, and family factors that could influence the choice of treatment. The interviewer must ask the parents about their current discipline strategies, eliciting descriptions of both methods that do and do not seem to work with the target child. Particularly with adolescent clients, it is valuable to ask the parents about their child monitoring skills. Do the parents know what their children are doing and where they are doing it? Do they have rules about the child checking in with them or being in by a certain time? In two-parent households, are both parents in agreement about the rules and involved in rule enforcement? The interviewer can ask open-ended questions about the parents' expectations for the child to determine if the parents have unrealistic or developmentally inappropriate expectancies that may be creating or compounding family difficulties. Exploring the parents' beliefs about the child's future and beliefs about their ability to parent this child is also important. The parents' locus of control, at least with regard to parenting issues, can be assessed by asking general questions about how effective they are as parents and how much control they feel they have over their child's behavior. The parents' thoughts and feelings about various treatment options, including medication, can be assessed. Finally, if such information has not already been clarified in the initial diagnostic evaluation, parents must be assessed for the presence of significant psychiatric difficulties, chemical dependency, familial physical or sexual abuse, and marital discord.

The entire family should be interviewed together at some point in the treatment-related assessment process. The interviewer asks open-ended questions about what each family member perceives to be the problem, paying particular attention to how family members attribute causation for the problem. The interviewer questions how each family member thinks the family is doing in terms of problem-solving, communicating, negotiating, etc. The interviewer can also ask how close the family is generally and who is particularly close to or distant from another. Finally, the interviewer should inquire about siblings and other family members who may not be present, but may play an important role in the family's problems. The interviewer may want to ask the family to bring those family members in for subsequent interviews.

In order to organize the information emerging from the problem-focused interview, the clinician may find it helpful to complete the rating forms presented in Figures 1–4. These forms organize observations or findings about child, parent, and family cognitions and behaviors. In selected cases, the clinician might choose to have the family complete the forms, but we usually prefer to use these as tools for organizing the therapist's thinking and planning for the treatment process.

Child's name: _____

Parent's name: _____ Date: _____

Directions: Listed below are a variety of behaviors that may be descriptive of children. Drawing from information from parents, child, and any other assessments, the therapist can rate the frequency of occurrence of these difficulties in a week or the extent to which these difficulties characterize the child's general functioning. This information can then be used to formulate specific treatment targets and goals.

1	2	3	4	5
Not at all	Sometimes	Moderately often	Often	All the time

I. *Attention span*
_____ A. Can't pay attention to tasks that aren't fun and require effort for a long time.
_____ B. Has difficulty staying on task with tasks that aren't fun and require effort.

II. *Impulsive*
_____ A. Typically does not think before he/she acts and gets himself/herself into trouble.
_____ B. Typically does not think about what he/she is saying before blurting out statements.

III. *Problem-solving*
_____ A. Has difficulty solving impersonal problems (solving tasks, organizing homework, putting puzzles together, etc.)
_____ B. Has difficulty solving interpersonal problems (getting along with other people, solving problems between peers, siblings, family members, etc.).

IV. *Means–end thinking*
_____ A. Typically does not think of goals.
_____ B. Typically does not figure out the steps necessary to reach a goal.

V. *Perspective–taking*
_____ A. Usually does not think about other people's thoughts and feelings.

VI. *Information processing*
_____ A. Often misinterprets other people's behavior and assumes that they are "after him/her" or acting in a hostile manner toward him/her.
_____ B. Tends to focus on other people's aggressive or hostile behavior.

VII. *Anger*
_____ A. Has difficulty controlling his/her anger.

VIII. *Compliance*
_____ A. Typically does not listen and does not do what he/she is told by authority figures.

IX. *Social skills*
_____ A. Is typically passive in solving interpersonal problems.
_____ B. Is typically aggressive in solving interpersonal problems.
_____ C. Is not very good at specific social behaviors (eye contact, initiating conversations, listening, assertiveness, etc.)

X. *Delinquent behavior*
_____ A. Probably is using drugs/alcohol.
_____ B. Probably is getting in trouble in the community.
_____ C. Probably is getting in trouble in school.

FIGURE 1. Child Treatment Targets Form.

Child's name: _____

Parent's name: _____ Date: _____

Directions: Listed below are a variety of thoughts that parents may have about their children and themselves. The therapist or, in some cases, the parents can rate the frequency with which these thoughts seem to occur in a week or the extent to which these thoughts characterize the parents' thinking about the child/family difficulties. This information can then be used to formulate treatment targets and goals. Use a separate form for each parent in a two-parent household.

1	2	3	4	5
Not at all	Sometimes	Moderately often	Often	All the time

I. *Attributions about the child*
_____ A. This child is a brat.
_____ B. This child does it intentionally.
_____ C. This child is the cause of all the family's problems.
_____ D. This child is just trying to get attention.

II. *Attributions about self/others*
_____ A. It's my fault that this child is that way.
_____ B. If I wasn't such a poor parent this child would be better off.
_____ C. It's his/her (other parent's) fault that this child is that way.
_____ D. If he/she (other parent) wasn't such a poor parent, this child would be better off.

III. *Beliefs/expectations about the child*
_____ A. This child's future is bleak. When he/she grows up, he/she will probably be irresponsible, a criminal, high school dropout, etc.
_____ B. This child should behave like other children. I shouldn't have to teach this child how to behave.
_____ C. This child must do well in school, sports, scouts, etc. It is unacceptable if this child does not do as well in these activities as any other child.
_____ D. This child is defective. This child has many problems. This child does not fit in with other children.

IV. *Beliefs/expectations about self and/or family*
_____ A. Our family is a mess.
_____ B. I can't make mistakes in parenting this child.
_____ C. I give up. There is nothing more I can do for this child.
_____ D. I have no control over this child.. I have tried everything.

V. *Beliefs/expectations about medications*
_____ A. He/she needs medications. He/she can't function without medications.
_____ B. Medications are the answer. This child's problems will be greatly diminished or gone when he/she is on medications.

VI. *Beliefs/expectations about therapy*
_____ A. Therapy will fix or cure this child.
_____ B. My child is the focus of therapy.
_____ C. Therapy will not really help.

FIGURE 2.   Parent Cognitions Target Form.

Child's name: _____

Parent's name: _____ Date: _____

Directions: Listed below are a variety of behaviors that parents may display. The therapist or, more rarely, the parents can rate the frequency with which these behaviors occur in a week or the extent to which these behaviors seem to characterize parent–child interactions. When ratings for each parent in a two-parent household would differ, put an "M" by the rating for mother and an "F" by the rating for father.

1	2	3	4	5
Not at all	Sometimes	Moderately often	Often	All the time

I. *Problematic commands:* Telling the child what to do ineffectively.
   ____ A. Vague commands—Not specifying exactly what child is to do (shape up, knock it off, etc.).
   ____ B. Question commands—Asking a question in attempt to gain child's compliance (would you please pick up your toys?, etc.).
   ____ C. Rationale commands—Explaining why the child needs to comply (you need to ge dressed or we will be late, etc.).
   ____ D. Multiple commands—Telling the child to do too many things at once (pick up your toys, get dressed, and come to the table for lunch, etc.).
   ____ E. Frequent commands—Repeating commands to the child and not following through with consequences when parent says he/she will.
II. *Negative reinforcement:* Adult and child use aversive means to control one another; it works and is therefore reinforced. The aversive control behaviors are repeated.
   ____ A. Child—Giving in and allowing child to "get his/her way" because he/she is so difficult/belligerent.
   ____ B. Adult—Yelling, threatening, etc. until child gives in and/or complies.
III. *Low levels of positive reinforcement:*
   ____ A. Ignoring and/or not attending when child is behaving neutrally or appropriately.
IV. *Inadvertent reinforcement of problem behavior*
   ____ A. Giving child attention and accidentally reinforcing problem behavior (attention for disruptive behavior, whining, somatic complaints, moping, when child says it's too hard, etc.).
V. *Poor parental monitoring of child:*
   ____ A. Not sure what child is doing or where child is when away from home.
VI. *Ineffective discipline:*
   ____ A. Having problems controlling the child's behavior.
   ____ B. Yelling and threatening too much.
   ____ C. Being inconsistent in disciplining approaches.
VII. *Overcontrolling:*
   ____ A. Telling the child what to do most of the time.
   ____ B. Not allowing the child to solve his/her own problems.

FIGURE 3. Parent Behavior Target Form.

Child's name: _____

Parent's name: _____ Date: _____

Directions: Listed below are a variety of behaviors and interactions that family members may display. The therapist or, perhaps, family members can estimate the frequency with which these events seem to occur in the family. This information can then be used to formulate treatment targets and goals.

1	2	3	4	5
Not at all	Sometimes	Moderately often	Often	All the time

I. *Family problem-solving*
____ A. Difficulty solving family problems.
____ B. Difficulty recognizing and defining problems.
____ C. Use same solutions over and over. Don't think of new ways to solve our problems.
____ D. Don't think ahead about whether a solution might work.
____ E. May figure out a good solution, but often don't use it.

II. *Family communication*
____ A. Seldom aware of when they are having communication problems.
____ B. Express themselves in very destructive ways (put-downs, blaming, talking on and on without coming to the point, etc.)
____ C. Not good at listening to each other (poor eye contact, daydreaming, thinking about what one is going to say without listening to what the other person is saying, etc.)
____ D. Often communicate different messages on verbal and nonverbal levels (e.g., saying "I love you" in a loud screaming voice while pounding one's fist on a table).

III. *Family anger/conflict management*
____ A. Usually don't recognize when anger and conflict is becoming destructive.
____ B. Rarely know how to control anger/conflict, and it gets out of hand.
____ C. Difficulty using problem-solving and communication during family conflict.

FIGURE 4.   Family Target Form.

Treatment Planning

After the diagnostic and treatment-related assessments have been completed, the therapist's task is to integrate the data, make decisions about what problems to address, and select treatment strategies appropriate for alleviating the identified problems. The treatment planning stage is one of the most important stages of therapy. *The therapist would not use all of the skills training interventions (described in Chapters 6–8), but rather only those deemed necessary after the treatment-related assessments have been completed.*

Figure 5 outlines one method of organizing the treatment planning process. For treatment to proceed in a logical manner, the therapist must make some judgments about the general status of the child and family, such as discerning the severity of the child's ADHD and/or Conduct Disorder (CD) problems and the level of family dysfunction. This analysis of the severity of difficulty includes considering the pervasiveness of the child's or family's difficulties, with more pervasive problems requiring interventions that will involve or cut across all significant environments (e.g., home, school, and work). The therapist also considers the child's mental age and how this impacts the choice of intervention strategies. To be effective, the intervention must be able to use strategies that are within the child's or family's capacity even if these strategies are not currently within their behavioral repertoire. It is useful to challenge children and families to learn new skills, but not if these skills require prerequisite abilities that are not present. For example, for

General conceptualization of problems

I. High severity—child	_____	Low severity—child
II. High severity—family	_____	Low severity—family
III. Younger mental age	_____	Older mental age

Specific treatment targets

Child		Parent		Family
Cognitive	Behavioral	Cognitive	Behavioral	Cognitive and behavioral
1.	1.	1.	1.	1.
2.	2.	2.	2.	2.
3.	3.	3.	3.	3.
4.	4.	4.	4.	4.
5.	5.	5.	5.	5.

Specific treatment strategies

Child		Parent		Family
Cognitive	Behavioral	Cognitive	Behavioral	Cognitive and behavioral
1.	1.	1.	1.	1.
2.	2.	2.	2.	2.
3.	3.	3.	3.	3.
4.	4.	4.	4.	4.
5.	5.	5.	5.	5.

FIGURE 5. Treatment Planning.

the use of the child-focused cognitive–behavioral strategies, we argue that most children need to have attained a mental age of at least 8 years.

The next task of the therapist is to specify cognitive and behavioral targets that are relevant for the child, parent, and family. The factors summarized in Tables 5 and 6 (Chapter 4) can be used as aids in conceptualizing the child, parent, and family targets, or the therapist can complete the forms in Figures 1–4. We advise the therapist to order the cognitive and behavioral targets in terms of their salience to the child's or family's presenting complaints. Targets with a higher level of salience should be addressed earlier in the course of intervention.

The final task of the therapist is to decide which intervention strategies to use to address the child, parent, and family cognitive and behavioral targets. A general rule of thumb is that the more severe the child's dysfunction, the more severe the family's dysfunction, or the younger the child's mental age, the more behavioral the initial intervention should be. Conversely, the less severe the child's dysfunction, the less severe the family's dysfunction, and the older the child's mental age, the more cognitive *and* behavioral the initial intervention can be. Usually, longer and more intensive treatment is needed for severe child or family dysfunction. Occasionally, it may be helpful to start out with a behavioral focus and then move to a cognitive focus as the child and/or family make initial treatment gains.

The therapist then selects specific strategies to intervene with specific cognitive and behavioral targets. In Tables 12 and 13, we outline our view of currently available interventions that can be matched with various cognitive and behavior problems for children and parents/family, respectively. The therapist could use these tables to guide decision-making in the treatment planning process. For example, the therapist may have determined that an adolescent has poor problem-solving abilities, so problem-solving training would be indicated. If a preschool child is noncompliant, training parents in the use of time-out would be recommended. If parents are making dysfunctional trait attributions about the child, education and cognitive restructuring techniques with the parents would be attempted. Obviously, a child and his family may present with many treatment needs. In addition, the therapist must be flexible and able to change the course of therapy as warranted. For example, the therapist may have decided to focus initially on the child's problem-solving abilities but, after the fourth session, recognizes that the focus should shift to family conflict resolution skills.

Before embarking on a cognitive–behavioral therapy (CBT) intervention with an ADHD child and his/her family, the therapist needs to consider if this form of intervention is warranted at all. The child may have met the diagnostic criteria for ADHD or ADHD/CD, but that does not necessarily mean that CBT is indicated. Through the functional

TABLE 12
Matching Child/Adolescent Problems and Skills Training Modules

Targets	Interventions
Child cognition	
I. Difficulties with sustained attention	Poor effort management, self-monitoring training, structuring the environment
II. Impulsive cognitive tempo	Problem-solving, relaxation
III. Deficits in problem-solving	Problem-solving, interpersonal problem-solving, means–end problem-solving, decision-making problem-solving, family problem-solving
IV. Deficits in means–end thinking	Means–end problem-solving
V. Deficits in perspective-taking	Perspective-taking
VI. Information processing errors	Problem-solving (emphasize problem recognition), situation interpretation
VII. Impulsive anger	Anger management, relaxation, family conflict management
Child behavioral	
I. Off-task behavior	Poor effort management, self-monitoring training, reinforcement, structuring the environment
II. Noncompliance	Compliance training, time-outs/removal of privileges, reinforcement of compliance
III. Social behavioral skills deficits	Behavioral social skills, reinforcement (of prosocial behavior), interpersonal problem-solving
IV. Aggressive behavior	Anger/frustration management, time-out/removal of privileges, perspective-taking, behavioral contracting
V. Antisocial behavior	Perspective-taking, time-out/removal of privileges, behavioral contracting, monitoring

Note. Parent skills training in cognitive–behavioral child management will facilitate all of the above child skills training modules.

assessment and treatment planning processes, other factors in the child and family need to be evaluated to determine if CBT is indicated. If a child has a significant substance abuse problem, severe undersocialized CD, coexisting mood or anxiety disorder, severe social withdrawal or rejection, underlying organic difficulties, or psychotic symptoms, CBT alone would not be an adequate or preferred mode of treatment. If the

TABLE 13
Matching Parent/Family Problems with Specific Skills Training Modules

Targets	Interventions
Parent cognition	
I. Dysfunctional attributions	Cognitive restructuring/self-monitoring, education
II. Unrealistic beliefs	Cognitive restructuring/self-monitoring, education
III. Unrealistic expectations	Cognitive restructuring/self-monitoring, education
IV. External locus of control	Cognitive restructuring/self-monitoring, cognitive–behavioral child management, behavioral child management
V. Perceptual bias	Cognitive restructuring, education
VI. Impulsive anger	Anger/frustration management, family conflict management
Family behavioral	
I. Negative reinforcement	All behavioral management modules
II. Low rates of positive reinforcement	All behavioral management modules (particularly parent self-monitoring and reinforcement)
III. Ineffective discipline	All behavioral management modules
IV. Monitoring	All behavioral management modules (particularly monitoring)
Family cognitive and behavioral	
I. Family problem-solving deficits	All family skills training modules (particularly family problem-solving training)
II. Family communication deficits	All family skills training modules (particularly family communication skills training)
III. Family anger and conflict management deficits	All family skills training modules (particularly family anger/conflict management training)

parents manifest severe psychopathology, chemical dependency, or significant marital problems, CBT might not be indicated as the primary intervention. Additionally, if there is evidence of physical or sexual abuse in the family, CBT certainly would not be the primary therapeutic mode. In these cases, alternative psychotherapies, residential/hospital treatments, intensive school-based services, marital/family therapy, child protective services, etc. need to be considered as possible first-line therapies before CBT is attempted, or in addition to CBT.

When the treatment-related assessment and treatment planning stages are complete, the therapist should know how he/she will focus the intervention. In addition to having selected developmentally appropriate training methods and targets, the therapist and family can collaborate to decide which targets should be addressed first and which settings or environments must be involved in the treatment process.

Preparation for Change

Forming a Collaborative Relationship

One of the hallmarks of CBT is forming a collaborative relationship with the client. In the early stages of CBT with an ADHD or ADHD/CD child, we see the client as the entire family. The therapist first acts as a consultant to the family. This involves educating the family members and helping them make decisions. The therapist should explain the diagnosis of ADHD and any related difficulties. Cognitive and behavioral therapeutic approaches should also be explained. We use the "Attention-Deficit Hyperactivity Disorder" and "Cognitive–Behavioral Therapy for Children with Attention-Deficit Hyperactivity Disorder" information charts found in Appendix B to supplement our explanation of the different aspects of ADHD and CBT. The therapist should explain all treatment recommendations and the rationale behind these recommendations. Ultimately, the therapist and all family members must agree on the focus of therapy or the success of the intervention is jeopardized. The success of the intervention is facilitated by encouraging the family members to use cognitive and behavioral therapy terms while defining the problems to be addressed. We also find it helpful to verbally define a therapeutic contract delineating recommendations and expected length of therapy.

The therapist must help the family members make decisions in a number of areas unrelated to CBT. As discussed in Chapter 3, the best treatment for ADHD and ADHD/CD is a multimodal therapeutic approach that often involves medical and school-based intervention, as well as individual and family CBT. The therapist can serve as a consultant to the family to help them coordinate all of these interventions. One of the most difficult decisions a family will need to make is whether or not to pursue a trial of psychostimulant or antidepressant medication. If a physician has recommended medication, then the therapist can help the family make a decision about whether or not they can support this recommendation. In Table 14, we offer a series of questions for medical and mental health professionals that are adapted from Barkley (1981) and are designed to be used as a guide for problem-solving about the appropriateness of medication use in the case of a given individual. These questions focus attention on both child and family factors that should be considered if planning a medication trial.

Another important decision concerns whether the child should be considered for any type of special education services. Clearly this type of decision also involves the active input of the child's school staff, but the

TABLE 14
Questions Concerning the Use of Psychostimulant Medication

---

1. Has the child undergone an evaluation process that is adequate to clearly determine that he/she is manifesting ADHD? If not, medication should not be recommended until a diagnosis has been established.
2. Even if ADHD symptoms are clearly present, does the child have tics or a family history of tic disorders? If so, psychostimulants are not advised.
3. Does the child present with thought disorder or other signs of psychosis or present as highly anxious and fearful? Again, psychostimulant medication is contraindicated.
4. How old is the child? Psychostimulant treatment is rarely recommended for use with children under 4 or 5 years of age.
5. Have other interventions been given an adequate trial? If no other treatments have been attempted (for example, if the parents of a young child have not participated in any child management training courses), then medication may not be advised. Obviously, with very severe cases, it may be necessary to simultaneously initiate medication as well as other forms of intervention.
6. How severe is the child's behavior? The degree of severity can and should influence the point at which a medication trial is attempted.
7. Can the family afford the money and time required for the medication and adequate medication follow-up?
8. Are the parents able to appropriately supervise the use of the medication and guard against its abuse? If the adult(s) in the home cannot be trusted to administer the medication in accordance with the physician's orders, then its use is ill-advised.
9. What are the family's feelings and thoughts about medication usage? Parents should not be forced to carry out a treatment they believe to be wrong. If forced to do so, they may sabotage the implementation of the treatment.
10. What are the child's feelings about medication usage? It is important that children be given an adequate rationale for medication use that does not undermine their sense of control of and/or responsibility for their actions and accomplishments. As with the parents, if a child is extremely opposed to medication, he/she may sabotage its use.
11. Is there a drug-abusing adolescent or adult in the household? If so, the probability of abuse and misuse may outweigh any possible benefit to the child.
12. Does the physician have the time to monitor these medications properly? If not, then he/she may prefer to refer the family to other appropriate medical staff.

Note. Adapted from Barkley (1981) with permission from the author.

process. To illustrate this, the therapist can ask the parents to think about their child having a belief such as "I can't do math; I am no good at it." Ask the parents how such a belief would influence the child's ability and desire to want to change and learn new math skills. Have parents understand that their beliefs can get in the way too. Try to help parents develop a "possibility" belief about their children and themselves. The child and parents can learn to cope with problems and can make the best of it. The children and parents themselves may not be perfect, but they can try.

A related, but subtly different, type of cognition is the parents' or family's attributions about the cause of the problems. As discussed earlier, parents often make trait and intentional attributions about the child's behavior. They may label the child as a "brat who does these things on purpose to make us mad." They may suggest that the child has a "bad attitude." Another common attribution has to do with the parents causing the problems. They may state that they never could figure out how to parent him/her properly, and that's why the child is the way he/she is today. The mother may blame the father because he is too strict, the father may blame the mother because she is too lax, and the child may blame both parents because they keep nagging him/her. We have found it helpful to guide families away from trying to decide who is really causing the problem to a perspective of shared ownership of difficulties. The therapist should discuss specific examples of behavior and each of the family members' roles in maintaining the problem behavior. For example, if the parents report that the child didn't want to clean his/her room, the therapist should inquire as to what the mother and father did in response to this. It may be determined that the mother gave the child numerous warnings and then the father yelled at the child until he/she eventually complied. The child's behavior is only one part of the problem, with the mother and father also contributing to an overall problematic interaction. The mother gave too many warnings, and the father yelled and created an aversive interchange between the child and parent. In a similar vein, the therapist could also process interactions that emerge during the session. We believe the family will be more open to change if they are not entrapped in placing extreme blame on the child or themselves. The therapist can help the family realize the low functional value of trying to decide who caused the problem and focus more on the idea that the child and family must learn how to cope with it.

With highly defensive families, it may be helpful to move them toward a perception of shared ownership of family difficulties using techniques from functional family therapy (Alexander & Parsons, 1982), such as reframing various blaming behaviors as indicators of how deeply pained all family members are by their current difficulties or as in-

therapist can advise the parents concerning how they may wish to mak
a decision to seek (or avoid) special services. The therapist can also hel
parents contact local advocacy groups that can advise parents of thei
rights and responsibilities in this decision-making process. Additiona
school-based recommendations that could be discussed with the family
and school are presented in Chapter 8 and in Appendix C.

Beginning to Modify Resistance

Resistance is an inevitable part of therapy. People do not like to change.
Much resistance can be predicted and is a normal process in all therapy,
including CBT. Resistance can occur at any stage in the therapeutic
process and since some degree of resistance is inevitable, it makes sense
to address it via an active, preventative approach. We strongly recommend that the therapist take the time to deal with resistances before
embarking on skills training to ensure success with the skills training
intervention. We shall focus our discussion on both cognitive and behavioral manifestations of resistance.

Many different forms of resistance occur at the parental and family
levels. We have found that some resistance to treatment may arise from
the family having inadequate or mistaken information about the ADHD
diagnosis. Thus, the importance of simply providing adequate information should not be underestimated. As we discussed in the previous
section, such information should be provided early in the treatment
process.

In addition to inadequate information, parents hold beliefs, attributions, biases, or expectancies that interfere with the change process.
Cognitive restructuring (Beck, 1976) is a therapeutic tool that can be
used to modify these types of cognitions. The therapist helps the client
(in this case, the parents and family) identify maladaptive thoughts,
recognize how these thoughts are dysfunctional, and replace them with
more functional and adaptive thoughts. Reframing is a form of cognitive
restructuring that is used by therapists to change the perceived meaning
of a cognition from negative to benign or positive.

For example, parents often have negative stable/global beliefs about
their children. Parents may believe that he/she "is a problem child and
probably always will be." Parents also can have negative global/stable
beliefs about themselves as parents. The parents may believe that "we
have failed to parent our child, and we probably will continue to fail."
These comments suggest that the parents have a negative belief about
their past parenting efforts and their perceived ability to cope with the
situation in the future. To restructure these cognitions, the therapist
could point out how negative beliefs can get in the way of the change

dicators of how much concern is present within the family. We have also found it useful to illustrate shared blame through the use of hypothetical or real examples of conflicted interaction between the therapist and family, such as scheduling hassles or miscommunication about recommendations. By using examples involving himself/herself, the therapist is able to model the acceptance of his/her part in creating or maintaining a difficulty and, thus, become a coping model for the family. Therapist expressions of empathy for how painful it can be to acknowledge one's own role in a difficulty can also be extremely important in facilitating the family's move away from a blaming stance.

Expectations of CBT should also be confronted in the early stages of therapy. Therapists should discuss the notion that CBT (and other treatments, for that matter) is not a cure for ADHD and the related social, emotional, school, and behavioral problems. This type of therapy, however, offers a chance for the child and parents to learn additional coping skills for dealing with their problems in a more effective way. A goal of discussion is to help the parents and child achieve a realistic appraisal of what they can expect from participating in CBT. The therapist may find it helpful to use the analogy of chronic illness. When an individual develops diabetes, he/she and his/her family must learn how to cope with the illness, although he/she is never cured. We argue that a similar conceptualization is necessary to learn to cope with ADHD.

Although much of the early focus of the intervention is at the parental and family level, eventually the child may become the focus of therapy. Most children, and especially ADHD and ADHD/CD children, can present their own unique resistances that need to be dealt with by the therapist. A common stumbling block reflects the way in which most children enter therapy—on the insistence of their parents or teacher. This beginning leads the child to accurately attribute his/her presence in therapy to a decision made by some powerful other in his/her life. For example, the child may state, "I am here because my parents make me come here," or "I am here because you said I needed a shrink." While technically accurate, such beliefs may make it difficult for the child to take responsibility for his/her therapy. The therapist may be able to decrease the child's resistance by noting that the parents/family must also be present because improving the situation will have to be addressed as a family issue, not just a child issue. With regard to the child's role in therapy, the therapist could also state, "I don't want you to be here either. We have set up some goals and you are not achieving them. It is really up to you to cooperate and try to meet the goals. I would like to recommend to your parents that you not come to therapy as soon as you make some changes. I would like you to work me out of a job." These comments essentially tell the child that he/she does not have to shoulder all the blame but does have some responsibility for the work to be done in therapy.

Many children are resistant to taking medication. The child may believe that medication indicates he/she is a failure or defective. When medication is an important part of a child's treatment plan, we have found it helpful to reframe the taking of medication for the child. Medication for the ADHD child could be discussed as analogous to a hearing aid for the hard-of-hearing, glasses for those with impaired vision, or insulin for people with diabetes.

Behavioral resistance can also emerge early in the therapeutic process. CBT typically utilizes homework assignments. If the child and/or family members become noncompliant with homework assignments, this issue must be directly addressed. In fact, resistance to homework can be addressed in a preventative manner by the therapist stating the importance of homework and by voicing the belief that there can be no positive, meaningful change without practice of skills in the home environment. We sometimes use the analogy of an exercise and weight loss program and explain that if you do the exercises and follow a reasonable diet, the chances are great you will lose weight. If you don't, the chances are great that you won't achieve your weight loss goals. The same is true with the CBT homework exercises; if the family doesn't do them, they are choosing to minimize the chance that any meaningful change can occur. Perhaps one reason the child or family is being resistant is because interfering cognitions (e.g., beliefs and attributions) have not yet been fully addressed, and they have not yet been prepared to change. Another common factor, however, is that the homework assignments themselves are causing resistance. It is important to make sure that the child and family members fully understand the rationale and mechanics of carrying out the homework assignments. The therapist would be wise to make homework assignments very simple, explain them thoroughly, rehearse them with the child and the family, and possibly engage the child and family in role-play simulations. The therapist may also want to make telephone calls between sessions to make sure that the homework is completed. Additional procedures to address noncompliance with homework exercises will be addressed in later chapters.

While it is important to address resistances early in therapy, clearly some resistances may not emerge until later in therapy. The therapist may not be fully aware of the parents' beliefs, family members' attributions, etc. until several sessions have been conducted. It may not be until the fourth or fifth session that a therapist assigns some homework and then does not get compliance. Therefore, the therapist needs to keep these strategies to deal with resistance in mind throughout the entire therapeutic process.

Chapter Six

Child and Adolescent Skills Training

The current chapter provides a detailed description of the procedures for conducting cognitive and behavioral skills training modules for ADHD children and adolescents with Conduct Disorder (CD). We offer separate discussions of how to conduct the skills training module with school-age children (8–12 years old) and adolescents (13–18 years old), as the research literature and our clinical experience suggest the value of using different procedures with these groups. We have found that children under the age of 8 years typically benefit less from cognitive–behavioral therapy (CBT) than children age 8 years and older. We encourage the reader to review the procedures for each developmental level. For example, if the reader is primarily interested in adolescents, he/she would still need to read the sections on school-age children because this section contains introductory comments that are then elaborated and modified for working with adolescents.

We do not recommend that the therapist deliver every skills training module we describe to every child/adolescent. Rather, as discussed in Chapter 4, the therapist selects the methods relevant for use with a particular child/adolescent based on his/her functional assessment of the child.

Our discussion begins with a consideration of the merits of and procedures for conducting the child skills training modules in individual and/or group therapy sessions. We then consider the procedures involved in problem-solving and self-instruction training and how to gear application of these skills to interpersonal, poor effort, and individualized content areas. Procedures for anger/frustration management with children are described. Finally, behavioral social skills training procedures are reviewed.

As we describe the skills training modules, we present the way such training would be conducted in group therapy sessions. If the reader will be conducting only individual sessions, then he/she will have to modify accordingly. Generally, anything that is done within the context of a group can be duplicated to some degree with a role-play situation between the therapist and child in an individual session.

Individual Therapy Delivery

The numerous advantages of using group delivery over individual delivery will be explained later in the group delivery section; nonetheless, the realities and constraints of clinical practice are such that some therapists may not have the luxury of working with groups of children/adolescents. Recognizing this reality, we discuss methods that could be used in individual delivery of the child/adolescent skills modules, regardless of the specific skills training module being administered.

School-Age Children

It is, of course, necessary to begin the therapeutic process by trying to develop rapport with the child. We recommend that the therapist present himself/herself in an animated fashion and try to make the sessions as much fun as possible. When actually introducing the skills, several steps should be followed. First, the therapist should describe and model how the skills are applied. The child should then be allowed to practice the skills with the aid of either verbal or visual prompting. Finally, the child should practice the skills without any therapist prompting. For example, when training a child in self-instruction skills, the therapist models how to use the self-instruction strategies, allows the child to practice the strategies while prompting him/her, and then allows the child to practice without prompting. It is also helpful to use role-playing as a training method. For example, if a child is learning anger management skills, it is more lifelike to have the child learn how to use the skills and then practice coping with someone who is making him/her angry via role-play exercises. When some mastery is evident in the session, the child should be given homework assignments to practice skills outside the session. These homework assignments should be reviewed during the following session. The therapist would be wise to modify the delivery of the intervention to fit the needs and skills of each child. Some children progress faster than others and the therapist will need to calibrate the delivery of the skills to meet each individual child's needs. The therapist needs to allow the child to be actively involved in terms of selecting strategies, procedures and role-play exercises, etc. (Braswell, Kendall, Braith, Carey, & Vye, 1985). For example, when practicing anger management, the therapist might ask the child, "What typically makes you mad?" The child is then actively encouraged to generate scenarios that can be used in role-play exercises. We also recommend that the therapist use a "discovery" delivery approach (Schleser et al., 1983). The discovery procedure involves the therapist asking questions that lead the child to discover solutions to problems rather than presenting the child with therapist-derived strategies to be memorized.

We recommend that behavioral contingencies be used in each individual session. Kendall and Braswell (1985) discuss use of a response–cost system that involves giving the child some chips, tokens, or points at the beginning of the session that can be exchanged for a reward at the end of the session. The child loses chips for the violation of a few clearly defined rules of behavior. For example, if the child makes a mistake in implementing a strategy, is off-task, is noncompliant, etc., then he/she would lose a chip. At the end of the session, the child turns in the chips for a reward he/she has selected from a reward menu or listing of the available rewards and their chip value. The more chips the child has at the end of the session, the bigger the reward. A self-evaluation and reinforcement procedure can also be helpful. This involves telling the child at the beginning of the session that if he/she tries hard, he/she will get a reward at the end of the session. The reward may consist of a small object or an opportunity to play a game with the therapist. We often use the "How Hard I Tried" chart, which is found in Appendix B. This chart has descriptions of how hard a child might try, ranging from 1 (didn't try at all) to 5 (tried very hard). If the child receives a mutually agreed on rating of 3, 4, or 5, the child would be able to get the reward at the end of the session.

Adolescents

Most of the concepts discussed above are applicable in working with adolescents; however, some modifications of the procedures are needed. It is less important to have a game-like atmosphere in conducting the session with an adolescent. Furthermore, we find more success when the contingencies are more informal. For example, based on our experience, we do not recommend using response–cost with an adolescent. An informal use of the self-evaluation reinforcement procedure appears to be more fruitful. We have implemented such a procedure by telling the adolescent client that if he/she tries hard during the session, then he/she will be able to get a can of soda or perhaps go play pool or foosball. At the end of the session, we ask the adolescent to evaluate how much effort he/she exerted in the session and, if both the therapist and adolescent agree there was reasonable effort displayed, the reward is administered.

Group Therapy Delivery

Delivering the child skills modules within the context of group sessions has several advantages over individual sessions. Group delivery has the potential to enhance skill acquisition and generalization. Group sessions more closely approximate real life peer relationship situations. ADHD and ADHD/CD children are well-known for having peer group relationship problems. What better place for them to practice using their skills than in the context of interacting with others? The group sessions also have the advantage of providing more realistic role-play situations. Several children can be involved in each role-play, rather than a child role-playing with an adult therapist. Finally, and most importantly, group process can be used as a training task. Those readers who have spent any amount of time in a room with six to eight ADHD or ADHD/CD children can attest to the rich opportunities for the children to practice using their new skills! Many situations arise involving interpersonal conflict, negative thoughts, poor effort, and anger/frustration problems that can become learning opportunities by having children actually solve their problems *in vivo*.

School-Age Children

Groups should be limited to six to eight children. We strongly recommend using two therapists for the groups because the group leader is required to conduct multiple simultaneous activities, including maintaining some degree of order in a very active group.

As mentioned above, the group process is extremely important in helping children learn skills. When problems emerge, the therapist can prompt the children to use their strategies and then reinforce them for proper application. For example, if a therapist notices that one child is repeatedly kicking the chair of another child, the therapist might comment to that child, "This might be a good time to use a plan" (i.e., problem-solving strategy). The child doing the kicking is then given an opportunity to use a plan. The therapist helps a child through the problem-solving process as needed. The child is given points for using the plans (points are discussed later). Every task the group faces together, such as deciding on group rules, how to take turns, etc., can be presented as a problem to be solved by the group. In other words, plans can be used for the individual child to solve a problem or for the group as a whole. When conducting this type of group, therapists are continuously going back and forth between teaching content of the session and problem-solving about what is happening in the group.

The use of behavioral contingencies is essential to running a group with six to eight ADHD children; in fact, the group could quickly dissolve into chaos without a contingency management system. In our groups, one therapist is in charge of maintaining the contingency management system throughout the entire group. This is a very difficult, yet extremely important function. We use the "Group Points" chart found in Appendix B. The children receive points for positive behaviors (e.g., staying on task, listening, talking, etc.) and for actually using the skills being trained in the session. Shaping is emphasized through the use of the contingency system. For example, if a child is not talking very much, but then does choose to talk, the therapist tells the child, "You get a point for talking; keep up the good work!" The therapist who is keeping track of the points should keep track of each child and shape specific behaviors according to the child's needs. To enhance compliance with completing homework charts, we often give extra points to children for completing and bringing in charts to the session. We also take points away for mild verbal and physical aggression, disruptive behavior, and oppositional behavior. The group therapist will first ask a child to use a strategy to change his/her behavior, but if he/she does not comply, then points are taken away. Children are told that they will get a "strike" when exhibiting extremely disruptive or aggressive behavior. If a child acquires three strikes, he/she is removed from the group for that day, or if the child's parents are meeting in a simultaneous group, the child must meet with his/her parents to create a plan for how he/she can manage more appropriately in group. At the end of the session, the therapist tallies the points and whoever earns the most is designated "Kid for the Day." The Kid for the Day gets to choose the game or activity that all group members will engage in for the last 10 to 15 minutes of group. We have found this contingency system to be surprisingly effective in managing difficult behavior in an active group.

A comment is necessary regarding group therapist style. The group therapist should act as a facilitator, not as a controller, in the group. The idea is for the children to be as responsible as possible for solving their own problems in group. This requires the therapist to have a relaxed style, in which external control is somewhat limited. The therapist will allow children to kick each others' chairs, look out the window, and call someone a name. Instead of responding with "Stop that," "Don't do that," etc., the therapist will respond with "I bet you could use a plan to solve that problem right now," or "Perhaps you should try anger management right now." Also, when and if children raise objections about features of group, such as the point system, the therapists should encourage the group to actively problem-solve about these issues and be prepared to modify group procedures in accord with such problem-solving. Obviously, the therapist should have input in this process and may need to clearly hold to some absolutes about the group structure, but within certain limits, child-initiated modification of the group should be viewed as positive. For example, in one of our groups, several members became frustrated because the same child won the Kid for the Day honors several weeks in a row and this child always selected the same reward activity. We helped the group define this problem, and they produced the extremely reasonable solution of letting the Kid for the Day select his/her two favorite activity choices. The rest of the group would then vote to select the single activity to be used that week.

Adolescents

The procedures used for running a group with adolescents are subtly different from the procedures used with school-age children. We recommend that the group be limited to six to eight adolescents and that two therapists be involved in these groups. Again, group process should be capitalized on with adolescents. The therapist should act as a facilitator, not a director, of the group process. Problems will emerge between adolescents, and these can be used as in-session training tasks. A process whereby adolescents offer support to each other should be fostered.

It has been our experience that formal contingency management systems are unnecessary in adolescent groups. Adolescents seem to view such systems as childish and this creates resistance. Fortunately, the overall rate of inappropriate behaviors is generally less in the adolescent groups than in the younger children's groups. Rather than a point system, we recommend that the last 15–20 minutes of the group be used for playing games such as basketball, pool, football, or video games. This usually gets the adolescents motivated to attend group. We make the entire group's participation in this type of activity at the end of the session contingent upon active and appropriate participation by all group members. If all group members do not participate appropriately in group, then no one gets to participate in the rewarding activity. To facilitate completion of homework charts (homework charts are discussed later), we sometimes make the reward activity contingent on adolescents completing and bringing in the charts. It typically does not take long for the group to exert some positive influence on recalcitrant group members so they can participate in the fun activity at the end of the next session.

While not emitting as many inappropriate behaviors in group, adolescents may be more resistant than younger children. We recommend using group process as a way of dealing with resistant adolescents. The group can support, encourage, and confront other adolescents to reduce the resistance of certain group members. Also, if one individual is resistant, then it is the responsibility of the entire group to help this person become less resistant, if they would like to play the games at the end of the session. Finally, if these procedures are ineffective in dealing with an adolescent's resistance, it may be necessary to involve his/her parents. Sometimes it is helpful for the adolescent to work out a contract with his/her parents, specifying certain kinds of rewards to be earned if he/she participates appropriately and specifying certain kinds of restrictions or privileges to be lost if he/she does not participate appropriately. The therapist would obviously have to provide feedback to the parents about the adolescent's group behavior to ensure that this type of behavioral contract would be successful. The group can also provide significant support for each adolescent member. Adolescents will share issues related to low self-esteem, demoralization, school problems, interpersonal problems, and difficulties getting along with members of their family. The therapist should facilitate an atmosphere that allows the adolescent to express these issues in the presence of other adolescents who can listen and offer support. Not only will the adolescents will benefit from expressing these issues, but they will also find some comfort in realizing that other adolescents with ADHD or ADHD/CD are struggling with similar problems. If a problem-solving atmosphere permeates the group, then other adolescents will offer constructive feedback and potential solutions for the adolescent expressing himself/ herself. This type of supportive mechanism can be very powerful in positively influencing the adolescent with ADHD or ADHD/CD.

Problem-Solving and Self-Instruction Training

Problem-solving and self-instruction training skills are designed to remediate deficits in sustained attention, impulse control, problem-solving, and means–end thinking abilities. In essence, children are trained to think before they act. Problem-solving and self-instruction training are, however, much more elaborate than that simple summary phrase might imply. Children are not only learning to think before they act, they are also learning to recognize when problems exist, produce alternative solutions, think of consequences, anticipate obstacles, and use strategies to control their behavior. In our clinical work, we train children to say a five-step problem-solving strategy to themselves through self-instruction training. The five steps are:

1. Stop! What is the problem?
2. What are some plans?
3. What is the best plan?
4. Do the plan.
5. Did the plan work?

The problem-solving strategy is eventually internalized by having children instruct themselves in this manner while solving a wide range of problems (see also the Training Parents in Cognitive–Behavioral Child

Management module in Chapter 7). Although having children self-instruct is facilitative, it is also necessary to train them in the component skills of problem recognition, alternative and consequential thinking, and anticipating and coping with obstacles, and actually executing specific behaviors. After children have learned how to use problem-solving and the self-instruction steps, specific exercises are used to help them learn component skills.

We then train children to apply self-instructions with real life problems. We do not assume that because children learned these skills they will automatically apply them to relevant content areas. For school-age children, we find the relevant content areas are interpersonal conflicts and situations involving poor effort behavior. For adolescents, these problems include those just listed plus coping with peer pressure, addressing family relationship difficulties, planning for vocational and career goals, and making decisions about drug use and sexual behavior. For some of the content areas, additional skills training modules are used to augment training (e.g., perspective-taking training for interpersonal problem-solving). The therapist can train the child to apply the skills to any content/problem area important for a given child.

Our experience suggests that approximately six to eight sessions are needed for school-age children and adolescents to acquire the capacity to use these problem-solving and self-instruction methods. More sessions may be needed to adequately address all the different content areas and other issues impacting the lives of children/adolescents in the group.

School-Age Children

The first task is to introduce children to the problem-solving/self-instruction steps. The therapist should explain what the steps are and the purpose of each step. Using the example of the five-step sequence previously described, Step 1 (Stop! What is the problem?) is designed to help children recognize when a problem exists. Step 2 (What are some plans?) directs children to generate possible alternatives to problems. Step 3 (What is the best plan?) reminds children to think of the consequences of each alternative and then select the best alternative. Step 4 (Do the plan.) has to do with children actually applying a strategy. Finally, Step 5 (Did the plan work?) requires children to evaluate whether or not a strategy worked, because if it did not, then a new strategy would need to be used.

It is helpful for the therapist to first model how to apply each step. This is best accomplished through role-playing in which the therapist acts as a child, and a child acts as someone else in the problem. The child and therapist act out a situation and then the therapist verbalizes using a plan (i.e., the five-step problem-solving strategy). For example, the therapist might say:

> "In this situation, you are sitting behind me in class and you are kicking my chair. OK, start kicking my chair. *(The child pretends to kick the chair.)* **Stop! What is the problem?** The problem is that he is kicking my chair and I am getting mad. **What are some plans?** I could turn around and kick his chair, I could tell the teacher, or I could ignore him. **What is the best plan?** If I turn around and kick him, he might get really mad at me or just keep kicking me. If I tell the teacher, he might stop kicking me, but he might call me a tattletale. If I ignore him, he may stop kicking me. I think I'll try ignoring him. **Do the plan.** OK, now I need to ignore him because that was my best plan. *(The therapist models ignoring while the child kicks his chair.)* **Did my plan work?** Yes, it did. I thought about it; came up with some plans; did the best one, which was to ignore him; and he stopped kicking my chair."

After this modeling example, the children would be required to use plans in role-playing exercises. The therapist can prompt the children verbally if they are unable to come up with the steps. It is best to train children using a variety of role-play situations involving interpersonal and off-task/poor effort problems. In group, children can go through the steps to solve actual problems emerging in the group session. We recommend doing as many role-play exercises and processing as many group problems as needed for children to gradually acquire a working knowledge of the steps. While the early examples employ stilted, deliberate elaborations of the steps, the eventual goal is to have the children use strategies in a more automatic fashion.

After the children have demonstrated at least basic mastery of the problem-solving process (usually after four or five sessions), the therapist can implement "short plans." With short plans, children are required to state what the problem is and what they are going to do about it. The therapist can require less overt verbalization of the steps as the children demonstrate their understanding of the process.

Problem Recognition

Learning to recognize the existence of a problem is a key component of problem-solving training. Problem recognition skills training is designed to help children comprehend the signals (cues) that tell them that a problem exists. The more we do CBT with these children, the more we are struck by the fact that problem recognition is often the most important skill these children need to learn. One could train a parrot to state a certain number of problem-solving steps, but training when to engage in such a series of steps is really the key to the process. Hinshaw and Erhardt (1991) also discuss the importance of developing the child's capacity to monitor and evaluate his/her own behavior. Training in problem recognition skills begins didactically and then leads to role-play exercises. The didactic component involves explaining what signals are. A traffic light analogy is used. Children are asked what they would do if they were driving down the road and a traffic light turned yellow and then red. The therapist explains that the traffic light is a signal that tells someone that something needs to be done, namely putting on the brakes in the car. Children are trained to recognize signals from the environment that tell them of a problem. The therapist trains children to recognize external signals, such as facial expressions (e.g., frowns and smiles) and body postures (e.g., crossed arms on another individual, raised fists, and loud tone of voice), and how to read "sticky situations" (e.g., recognizing when children are teasing and recognizing when someone's feelings are hurt). Once the group members seem to understand the meaning of external or environmental signals, the therapist can move on to a discussion of how to recognize internal or personal signals, such as feelings (e.g., sadness and anger), thoughts (e.g., angry thoughts and sad thoughts), and body signals (e.g., tense muscles, rapid heart rate, and sweating). The group leader helps the children recognize their individual affective, cognitive, and physiological cues by having them recall highly emotional experiences and explain what they were feeling and thinking. Group members can also give feedback about various signals they have observed each other display.

One exercise we have used to help children acquire problem recognition skills is problem recognition charades. Children are asked to generate examples of different types of problems that occur at home, at school, and with friends. The therapist writes down the children's examples on separate slips of paper and explains that some children will work together to act out the problems they draw from the container, while other children in the group try to recognize the problem being acted out. Once they have identified the problem, the children are instructed to discuss the external and internal signals that told them what the problem was.

The following is an example of a problem recognition charades exercise. Two children have just role-played walking down the hall, when one child suddenly pushes the other:

THERAPIST: Can anyone recognize what the problem is?
CHILD 1: He is mad.
THERAPIST: Does anyone else recognize what the problem is?
CHILD 2: He pushed him and that made him mad.

THERAPIST: What were the signals that led you to figure out what the problem was?

CHILD 1: He looked mad; his face had a frown [facial expression signal].

CHILD 2: He pushed him [sticky situation signal].

THERAPIST: Can anyone else think of any other signals?

CHILD 3: I bet he was feeling mad inside and his heart rate went up and his muscles got tense [body signal].

THERAPIST: That's very good. *(To the children who were acting out the problem):* Did they recognize the problem correctly?

This exercise can be used repeatedly until the children are more adept at problem recognition. The leaders can then be attentive to reinforcing the children's use of good problem recognition skills, both with themselves and others, during ongoing group activities.

Solution Generation and Consequential Thinking

Another essential concept in problem-solving/self-instruction skills training is that of solution generation and consequential thinking. It is necessary to explain to children that when a problem exists, it is helpful to generate as many alternative solutions or choices as possible, and then learn to think ahead about what would happen if they employed each of the alternative solutions. To facilitate this process, we use an alternative solution and consequential thinking exercise. Children are asked to generate a potential problem. They are then asked to think of as many solutions as possible for that particular problem. The therapist writes down all the alternative solutions the children generate (see example below) before discussing any consequences. The therapist does not judge any of the alternative solutions stated. The children may state many very inappropriate alternative solutions, but at this point the purpose is to brainstorm rather than censure comments. On occasion, a child may attempt to capture the attention of the group by offering particularly bizarre or inappropriate alternative solutions. We have found it most effective to not let ourselves or other group members get sidetracked by reacting to such outlandish suggestions, but rather to respond to extreme alternative solutions by stating, "That's one idea. What's another plan?" In other words, continue to calmly insist on the group's capacity to come up with additional solutions.

After the children appear comfortable with the notion of generating alternative solutions for a problem, the therapist can then direct them to discuss evaluating the consequences for each of the possible alternative solutions. Discussion of consequences involves encouraging children to think ahead to emotional and behavioral consequences for themselves and others. While the children may quickly recognize the consequences for others, they are likely to need encouragement to think about how selecting a particular choice will make them feel about themselves. The therapist writes down all the anticipated consequences (see example below) for a given solution. After the group has stated all the possible consequences for each of the alternative solutions, the children are allowed to decide or vote on which is the best solution.

The following is an example of an alternative solution and consequential thinking exercise completed by a therapist and a group of children. The therapist has written alternative solutions and consequences on the board following discussion of a problem of what to do if someone pushes you:

Alternative solutions	*Consequences*
1. Push him back.	• He'd push me back.
	• We'd both get madder.
	• I'd get in trouble from the teacher.
	• I might feel good about pushing him but bad about getting into trouble.
2. Tell the teacher.	• He'd call me a tattletale.
	• The teacher would punish him.
	• The teacher would tell me to handle it myself.
	• Sometimes it might feel OK to get the teacher's help. Other times I might feel like a baby.
3. Ignore him.	• He'd keep pushing.
	• He might get bored and stop pushing me.
	• He would walk away.
	• I might feel in control or "cool" if I could ignore him.

Anticipating Obstacles

In addition to being able to select the best alternative solution, effective problem-solving requires being able to anticipate obstacles and generate backup plans. The therapist can lead the group in a discussion of how even our best plans do not always work. The goal of this discussion is to lead the children toward the view that when a plan doesn't work, it is a signal that a new plan is needed—not a signal to blow up or give up on the problem-solving process. We find it easy to introduce the concepts of obstacles and backup plans by using examples from sporting events. For example, we might discuss how a pro quarterback calls a certain play in the huddle, but when the team is at the line of scrimmage, he must read the defense and decide if he should change the plan and call an audible to his players. This particular example usually works very well with 10-

to 12-year- old boys who then go on to discuss how the team could probably win more games if they did a better job of anticipating obstacles and using backup plans. The therapist should try to select introductory examples that are consistent with the expressed activity or career interests of the group. Once the concepts of anticipating obstacles and using backup plans are understood, the therapist can then shift the discussion to applying these concepts with commonly occurring interpersonal problem situations. We have the children role-play situations in which they use a plan that did not work, necessitating use of another plan. Example role-plays include situations such as the following:

- Sibling conflict in which your brother or sister is unwilling to work out a cooperative arrangement.
- A playground situation where you are attempting to play a certain game, but then you realize that you do not have enough people for the game.
- You want to prepare a certain snack or food item and begin to do so, but then realize that you do not have all the ingredients necessary for preparing that particular dish.

As the leader has the children practice these skills via role-plays, he/she should keep in mind the implicit goal of helping children reframe plans that do not work as cues to recognizing existing obstacles and producing new plans.

Executing Specific Behavior

Effective problem-solving involves the use of specific behaviors once a plan has been chosen. The task at this stage of the problem-solving process is to put the thought into action. We have found that even after the children have learned the cognitive part of problem-solving (i.e., coming up with a plan), that does not guarantee that they will then be able to emit the behavioral part of the problem-solving process (executing the specific behaviors). Therefore, it is essential to train children in this important skill. Training children in the skill of executing specific behavior requires fewer cognitive and more behavioral procedures. The therapist employs didactic instruction, modeling, coaching and role-play exercises to increase specific behaviors in children's repertoires. Specific behaviors that might be addressed include ignoring, expressing feelings appropriately, assertiveness, cooperation/sharing, complying with adults' requests, listening, taking turns, staying on-task, and finishing assignments at school. The therapist should tailor the behaviors to be practiced to each child and his/her specific needs.

A common example of a specific behavior that ADHD children may need to practice is ignoring behavior. To begin, the therapist explains what ignoring is. The explanation might be not paying attention to and avoiding other people or situations that are problematic. The therapist then models how ignoring might involve turning away, avoiding eye contact, walking away, etc. Next, the therapist engages the children in role-play exercises in which they actually apply ignoring. The therapist coaches the children in proper execution of those specific behaviors. For example, the therapist may have the children role-play a situation in which one child is sitting in class and the child behind him/her is throwing paper clips at him/her. The therapist can devise several role-play situations focused specifically on ignoring. It may be helpful to frame ignoring as a way to appear to keep one's cool in a tough situation.

Fading Problem-Solving and Self-Instruction Training

The eventual goal is to help children internalize the newly acquired skills. Like learning to play the piano, one must concentrate and go through all the steps at first, but the process becomes more automatic with continued mastery. In a similar way, it is not necessary to have children go through every step once they begin to master the process. Once the children display mastery over the five-step problem-solving/self-instruction procedures, the therapist can work with the children to fade out the use of the five steps.

To accomplish this fading procedure, we have children start to use short plans. The therapist will need to assess each child's mastery of the procedures to decide when to implement short plans. Short plans entail the children stating what the problem is and then deciding and implementing the best solution.

Application to Interpersonal Problems

Interpersonal problem-solving is an extremely important skill for ADHD and ADHD/CD children to learn, given their propensity for peer relationship difficulties. We usually allow approximately four sessions to learn specific applications of interpersonal problem-solving.

We augment interpersonal problem-solving with training in perspective-taking training. This involves training children to recognize others' thoughts and feelings, and the effect they have on others. One way to accomplish this is to engage children in perspective-taking role-play exercises. Children are asked to generate possible interpersonal situations for role-playing. Examples are two children picking on another child and a child arguing with a parent or teacher. Children then take turns role-playing these situations. The therapist asks the children to stop in the middle of their role-plays and discuss how they are thinking and feeling, and how they think the other person in the role-play is thinking and feeling. The therapist then asks the children to switch roles and once again engage in the same role-play. The therapist again asks the children to stop in the middle of the role-plays and describe their thoughts and feelings, and the thoughts and feelings of the other person in the role-play. We recommend repeating this exercise until the children appear to be accurately identifying the perspectives of others in the practice situations.

Once the children have acquired perspective-taking skills, we move to problem recognition for interpersonal problems. The therapist engages the children in problem recognition charades exercises in which they are required to recognize other people's perspectives (i.e., their thoughts and feelings). To accomplish this, the therapist has children role-play a variety of interpersonal problem situations within the context of problem recognition charades (see previous discussion of problem recognitions charades). The content of the role-play exercises would center around interpersonal problem situations in which two of the children act out various interpersonal problem scenarios. The other children act as observers to identify the perspective of each individual and the interpersonal problem situation. The task is for the children to discuss signals that indicate what the other person is thinking and feeling. The therapist can conduct as many exercises incorporating perspective-taking as necessary for each individual to grasp the concepts.

After problem recognition skills have been developed, the children can then proceed to learn how to solve interpersonal problems, taking into account other people's perspectives. This is accomplished by having children learn how to use "everybody happy plans," in which they choose solutions to problems that take into account everyone's perspectives. The children role-play interpersonal problem-solving situations and then think out loud about various solutions, while considering how everyone would think and feel if a given solution was used in that situation. The ultimate goal is to select solutions that would make the most people happy in that particular problem situation. After a plan has been selected by the people doing the role-playing, the therapist asks the other children in the group if they think that everyone would be happy with that solution in that particular interpersonal problem situation. It may not be possible to come up with a solution that would make everybody happy in specific interpersonal problems, but at least the children try to make as many people happy as possible.

(See the Behavioral Social Skills Training module later in this chapter.)

Application to Poor Effort Problems

Another example of a specific relevant content area for application of problem-solving and self-instruction training is poor effort/off-task behavior. Poor effort management is important for ADHD and ADHD/CD children to learn, given the problems they typically have in this area. We find that it is usually necessary to employ at least three sessions for children to learn the specific application of problem-solving and self-instruction to poor effort content.

The first step in poor effort management is learning to recognize poor effort. The therapist explains to the child that poor effort is when a person is off-task, feels like giving up, doesn't try hard, etc. The therapist then describes the specific signals that tell the individual he/she is exhibiting poor effort. Signals might include children's feelings, thoughts, and behaviors. The objective is to get children to be more familiar with and able to recognize these phenomena as they relate to poor effort. Common examples of feelings associated with poor effort include frustration, boredom, and anger. The therapist explains what these feelings are and generates some discussion about other feelings children have had when they are exhibiting poor effort. Common thinking signals that should be explained include put-down thoughts about themselves (e.g., "I am no good."), frustration thoughts (e.g., "I hate math."), and give up thoughts (e.g., "Forget it, I give up."). Specific off-task behavior signals related to poor effort include staring off into space, doing one activity when you are supposed to do another, and/or getting distracted. The therapist engages the children in discussion to help them specify which of these feelings, thoughts, and behaviors are typical for themselves. This discussion is followed by problem recognition charades focusing on poor effort signals. In this case, the charades exercise involves having the children verbalize their thoughts while acting out situations in which they are giving up or putting in poor effort. The other group members attempt to recognize feelings, thoughts, and behavior signals related to poor effort.

After children have mastered recognition of poor effort signals, they need to learn how to cope with poor effort. To accomplish this, we typically have children learn how to use "try harder" plans in which they choose solutions to help them maintain their effort and get back on task. Children are engaged in role-play exercises about poor effort problems such as being frustrated or bored with work at school or home. In the role-plays, children display inappropriate behavior, recognize the signals, and practice using a specific self-statement or coping strategy to maintain effort. Coping self-statements include language such as "I am not going to give up," "I will do the best I can," "I'll give it my best shot," etc. Coping behavioral strategies might include having the child learn to remove or minimize environmental distractions, having him/her break down a long task into more manageable chunks, and/or rewarding himself/herself for task completion with a more desirable activity.

(See the Training Parents in Cognitive–Behavioral Child Management module in Chapter 7.)

Application to Individualized Content/Problem Areas

The therapist can adapt the problem-solving and self-instruction training to any content/problem area unique to a given child, including difficulties with compliance with adults, negative self-deprecating thinking/self-statements, displaying "poor sport" behavior, and coping with peer pressure. Obviously, the possibilities are endless. With each content/problem area, the training procedures should help the child (1) define the problems, (2) recognize signals related to the problems, and (3) practice thinking of and implementing solutions to the problems.

Adolescents

The language and methods we use when training adolescents in problem-solving and self-instruction skills are slightly different from those used with school-age children. The content of the program still focuses on helping the client develop self-control through problem-solving processes. Plans are not typically emphasized with adolescents because they often perceive this to be childish. Rather, the therapist should tell the adolescents that the primary purpose of the group is to learn problem-solving skills and to talk with each other (i.e., obtain support). Problem-solving should be introduced early in the group, and the concept should be stressed throughout the entire intervention. We give adolescents the "Problem-Solving Skills" chart found in Appendix B. This chart explains five-step, means–end, and decision-making problem-solving procedures. These skills are reviewed in depth and then referred to throughout normal group discussion as adolescents work on their problems.

As with school-age children, we train the five-step problem-solving process, but with adolescents we explain that this type of problem-solving is most useful with immediate problem situations. For example, adolescents may use the five-step problem-solving sequence if they are faced with an argument with a peer, have some problems complying with a parent's request, or have difficulty staying on-task in class.

Another type of problem-solving emphasized with adolescents is means–end problem-solving (Spivack & Shure, 1974; Shure & Spivack,

1978). This type of problem-solving entails setting a goal (end) and identifying steps (means) necessary to reach the goal. Means–end problem-solving is useful for long-term goal attainment and decision-making about important issues for adolescents. For example, an adolescent who wants to obtain a job (end) would find it useful to articulate the steps (means) to obtain a job. If thinking from a means–end problem-solving perspective, he/she would realize that it is necessary to take steps such as filling out applications, buying a new interview outfit, going out on job interviews, and completing a resume to obtain a job. Adolescents could also use means–end problem-solving for other major goals, such as trying to reestablish their parents' trust and trying to do better with homework.

A final type of problem-solving that is emphasized with adolescents is decision-making problem-solving. Teenagers are often faced with very difficult and important decisions. Long-term prognosis data suggests that ADHD and ADHD/CD adolescents may not be very good at making these decisions. We have had some success in training adolescents to write down pros and cons for a given decision that must be made. We further instruct the adolescents to assign a weight to each pro and con according to how important that factor is in their judgment. If the level of importance is low, then the adolescent would write down a one or a two for that factor. If a factor is of midrange importance, he/she would rate it a three. Most important factors would be rated a four or five. The adolescent then adds up the numbers on each side to see which choice attains a higher score, with the higher score indicating the preferred choice.

The traditional, means–end and decision-making problem-solving strategies can be reviewed and applied for the duration of the intervention to discuss any problems and decisions facing the adolescents. Common issues in our adolescent groups include problems with academic performance, peer group relationships, peer pressure, family relationships, vocational and career planning, drug use, and sexuality.

Problem Recognition

As with younger ADHD children, adolescents with ADHD can benefit from exercises that enhance their problem recognition skills. They need help recognizing the signals that identify a problem and then knowing when and how to use a strategy to solve the problem. Teenagers can be trained to monitor events, thoughts, feelings, and physiological cues that lend themselves to identifying and/or articulating the types of problems they are having. Role-play exercises can be used in the therapy sessions in which the adolescents act out various problem situations, followed by a description of the cues to be identified. As the teenagers process events that occur in group and significant real life events, the therapist can direct them to think about the signals that told them of the problem.

Solution Generation and Consequential Thinking

Alternative solutions and consequential thinking exercises can also benefit the ADHD adolescent. We recommend using the problem-solving and self-instruction training exercises described earlier in the section on school-age children. The therapist may want to be less formal by simply having adolescents think about alternative solutions and consequences as they discuss various problems and issues raised during the normal course of group therapy. Group process can also be used to facilitate acquisition of alternative solutions and consequential thinking skills. For example, if one adolescent brings up a problem, such as how to improve a relationship with a parent, the other adolescents could be asked to help by generating alternative solutions and thinking of consequences that may be applicable to the group member having the original problem.

Anticipating Obstacles

Learning to anticipate obstacles is an important skill for ADHD adolescents. Teaching adolescents this skill is usually accomplished through didactic discussion and through ongoing problem-solving within the context of group discussion. Therapists should take the time to explain that effective problem-solving also involves thinking ahead about how to handle a problem if the original solution doesn't work. For example, the adolescent may want to negotiate with his/her parents about changing his/her curfew to a later time on weekends. The adolescent may take the time in group to discuss this issue, obtain input from other adolescents about alternative solutions, think about the consequences of trying alternative solutions, and decide on a very good plan. That does not mean, however, that the plan will work. The parents may not change the adolescent's curfew. The therapist should sensitize group members to the fact that original plans oftentimes do not work, but that does not mean that adolescents should become frustrated or discouraged and make impulsive choices.

When adolescents are employing problem-solving strategies outside of the group and bring in examples, the issue of anticipating obstacles arises naturally. As in the curfew example, the adolescent may try the plan and come back and tell the group that it did not work. Then the group can problem-solve with the adolescent about alternative ways to accomplish the same goal or may counsel him/her not to try to obtain that goal at the current time.

Executing Specific Behavior

As with school-age children, the therapist cannot assume that an adolescent who has thought up a good solution has the skills to execute his/her plan. We typically use less structured training than with school-age children but still focus on helping adolescents develop the ability to execute specific behaviors. During the course of group discussion of plans, we prompt the clients to detail how they will carry out the plan. We often elicit other group members' input when defining how a plan will be implemented. Occasionally, we also role-play how the plan will be enacted. For example, if an adolescent plans to negotiate with his/her parents to change his/her curfew, we prompt him/her to think of when and where to negotiate, as well as what to say to the parents. Role-playing the negotiating process with parents then enhances the client's ability to implement the plan.

Fading Problem-Solving and Self-Instruction Training

The goal of abbreviating the problem-solving and self-instructional process is the same for adolescents as for school-age children. Again, we shorten the process only after mastery of the overall problem-solving/ self-instruction skills has been observed. We are less structured with adolescents and do not use the term "short plans." We do, however, introduce the notion of solving problems by defining what the problem is and deciding and implementing the best solution.

Application to Interpersonal Problems

We also stress perspective-taking skills with adolescents because of the crucial role of these skills in interpersonal problem-solving. We have found that adolescents will cooperate with and enjoy the perspective-taking exercise as previously described in the school-age children's section. In addition, we employ self-monitoring procedures, such as having adolescents fill out the "How I Affect Others" chart found in Appendix B. This chart requires adolescents to monitor positive and negative actions they emit each day and how these actions make other people think and feel. The therapist asks adolescents to bring these completed charts back to group for general discussion. Processing group events can also facilitate acquisition of perspective-taking skills. If one group member says something disrespectful to another group member or the therapist, the speaker could be asked to reflect on how his/her remarks may have affected the other person. We use group process by asking others to give their perspective on the impact of the other group members' words or actions.

As with school-age children, adolescents need to develop the skills of creating solutions to interpersonal problems that satisfy not only themselves but also other individuals. In teaching the application of "everybody happy" plans with teens, the therapist can be less structured and didactic than with school-age children but still focus on the concept of choosing solutions that consider the thoughts and feelings of all involved. Formal role-play exercises may be helpful in this regard, but adolescents also seem to benefit from processing group interactions and interpersonal problems occurring outside of the group. When problems arise in the group, the therapist can prompt the clients to produce solutions that are the most satisfying for all group members. When adolescents bring in examples from outside of group, the therapist can maintain an emphasis on producing solutions that will make the most people happy. Problems that are common for this type of discussion involve interactions with peers, as well as with adults such as parents and teachers. Oftentimes, adolescents do not take into account the thoughts and feelings of adults in their lives and, as a result, they sabotage their own problem-solving efforts and do not reach the goals that are meaningful to them. The therapist can help adolescents tune into the fact that if they take into account the thoughts and feelings of these adults, they are more likely to get what they want as well.

(See the Behavioral Social Skills Training module later in this chapter.)

Application to Poor Effort

Many of the procedures discussed in the section on school-age children for poor effort management are directly applicable in working with adolescents. Adolescents typically frown on structured role-play exercises regarding poor effort management, although they do participate more in verbal discussions of these issues. Many adolescents will be able to identify that they have poor effort problems, but they may benefit from discussions of the specific signals that indicate the presence of such difficulties. The therapist can engage the group in a discussion about identifying and monitoring these poor effort signals on an ongoing basis. Therapists may also want to discuss and model application of "try harder" coping self-statements to better manage their effort and off-task behavior. With an adolescent group, it is particularly important to emphasize that these effort regulation methods are strategies they can use to control themselves rather than strategies others can use to control them. It may also be helpful to discuss these concepts with examples of particular interest to group members as well as with the obvious examples of managing effort directed towards academic tasks. For example, initially discussing effort management when trying to perfect athletic abilities, solve a problem with one's car, or develop a unique skill, like juggling, may meet with less resistance than discussions initially addressing how to maintain concentration with homework.

Application to Individualized Content/Problem Areas

As with school-age children, the therapist can adapt and focus the problem-solving and self-instruction training to any content/problem area unique to a given adolescent. Similar content/problem areas as listed with school-age children could be the focus or other content/problem areas more typical of teens could be selected, such as peer pressure, sexuality, drugs, and vocational/career choices.

Bringing It All Together for Adolescents

We employ the "Using Problem-Solving" chart found in Appendix B to facilitate the adolescents' use of problem-solving skills outside of the group. The adolescents are required to monitor real life events/problems and how they did or did not use a problem-solving strategy. They indicate what the problem was, what the signal was that informed them of a problem, what type of problem-solving strategy they used or could have used, and how well it did or could have worked. We ask adolescents to bring these charts to group each week to aid their review of the week's application of problem-solving.

(See also the Training Parents in Cognitive–Behavioral Child Management and Family Problem-Solving Training modules in Chapter 7.)

Anger/Frustration Management

Anger/frustration management training is designed to remediate deficits in problem-solving, information processing errors related to misattribution of intent, and selective attention to aggressive cues. Such training also teaches children coping skills to modulate cognitive, affective, and physiological processes associated with anger/frustration. Anger/frustration management training builds on skills learned in problem-solving and self-instruction training. We recommend that problem-solving and self-instruction training be conducted before introducing a child to anger/frustration management. Our approach to anger/frustration management incorporates the stress inoculation training procedures of Novaco (1978) and Lochman et al. (1981). Children learn skills related to recognizing when they are angry/frustrated, interpreting situations more accurately when angry, coping with anger, and effectively solving problems that made them angry in the first place. Similar skills are used for training school-age children and adolescents, although the training procedures are somewhat more complex with adolescents. Our experience suggests that most school-aged children and adolescents require a minimum of four to six sessions to acquire at least a basic understanding of anger management skills.

School-Age Children

The first skill addressed is recognizing when one is angry/frustrated. This is introduced through didactic presentation and discussion. The therapist explains to children that everyone gets angry/frustrated, but how one handles anger/frustration can be a problem in and of itself. It is further explained that anger/frustration has a "body part" (physiological) and a "thinking part" (cognitive). The therapist asks children to list and discuss common body (physiological) and thinking (cognitive) signals that tell them they are angry or frustrated. Common body and thinking signals identified by children are listed below:

Body signals
- Breathing rate increased
- Heart rate increased
- Sweating increased
- Face color flushed
- Muscle tension increased
- Voice tone raised

Thinking signals
- "I hate myself."
- "I feel like hurting myself."
- "I hate him/her."
- "I am going to hit him/her."
- "I hate doing math."
- "I would like to burn down the school building."
- "I am dumb."
- "I can't do anything right."

Problem recognition charades can be used to help children enhance their skills for identifying the physiological and cognitive signals associated with anger and frustration. This can be accomplished by having children act out situations in which they become angry/frustrated. The actor is asked to verbalize thoughts while acting. The observers take turns recognizing the body and thinking signals as previously discussed.

Situation interpretation training, a form of cognitive restructuring, can be helpful for those children who tend to get angry very impulsively. This training process is designed to help children examine how they interpret others' actions. First, the therapist educates children about the tendency to jump to conclusions that some children have when they become angry. Next, it is explained that some people jump to conclusions or think something without enough evidence to support it, such as assuming that other people are after them or are trying to hurt them. The concept of hypothesis testing is then introduced. For example, if a child bumps another child in the hallway, the child who is being bumped could generate a number of alternatives to explain why the other child bumped him. Alternatives might include "He is out to get me," "He slipped and accidentally bumped me," "Someone may have bumped him, which caused him to bump me," etc. The children practice not jumping to conclusions and trying to determine which one of the alternatives makes the most sense. This can be accomplished by thinking about the alternatives and trying to come up with evidence to support each alternative. For example, the therapist could train children to say to themselves: "What are the signs that the child pushed me on purpose?" "What are the signs that the child may have accidentally slipped or was pushed by someone else?" Role-play exercises in which children act out various ambiguous scenarios while overtly verbalizing various alternative explanations for the other's actions can help make this process clear for the children. All members of the group can be encouraged to participate in generating alternatives and weighing the evidence for the alternatives.

One way to present the concepts associated with situation interpretation training in a game-like fashion is to play the Kids Court game.* This involves role-playing ambiguous provocation situations and then acting out a trial. The child plays both the prosecuting and defense attorneys. The therapist is the judge and other group members are the jury. The child takes turns presenting the evidence that each of his/her "clients" (i.e., the different alternative explanations) is correct. The judge and jury weigh the evidence and, through a lively discussion, arrive at a verdict.

Relaxation training is another component of anger/frustration management. We have found it very difficult to engage ADHD children in lengthy relaxation training exercises. Rather, we recommend techniques that can be quickly enacted and require active responding on the part of the child. The "robot/rag doll" technique described by Kendall and Braswell (1985) is an example of one type of relaxation technique that has been successfully applied with this population. This technique simply requires children to tense up all their muscles and become stiff like a robot, hold the tension for 10–15 seconds, and then release their muscles like a rag doll and hold this relaxed state for 30 seconds. Another workable technique involves having the children focus on their heart rate. The children are taught how to count their heart rate while resting for approximately 30 seconds and then write down their rate. The

*We are indebted to Deborah Anderson for this suggestion.

children then run in place or jump around for 1 or 2 minutes. (Needless to say, they like this part!) At the end of this period, they record their heart rate again. Finally, the children are asked to rest while using slow, deep breathing for 1 minute and then take their heart rates a third time. Explain that you want to see who can get his/her heart rate closest to his/her original resting rate. Adding this small element of competition seems to make the process of relaxing and using slow, deep breathing more salient to the group members. Later, children are asked to apply these relaxation skills during stress inoculation training.

As previously stated, the stress inoculation training we use is adapted from Novaco (1978). Novaco describes four phases of problem confrontation; however, it is our experience that presenting all four phases is confusing for many school-age children. We recommend focusing on the "preparing for the situation" and "coping with arousal in the situation" phases (Novaco, 1978). Children learn to identify these two phases and use "cool-down plans" (i.e., coping self-statements) to regulate physiological and cognitive aspects of anger and frustration during these phases.

Preparing for the situation involves thinking ahead to situations that may make a person angry/frustrated and using coping self-statements to remain cool. This phase is relevant to situations that can be anticipated, such as preparing for contact with someone who is very likely to be provocative or preparing for a situation in which the child knows he/she may feel frustrated. Examples of possible self-statements would be:

- "I can handle this."
- "I just need to remind myself to take deep breaths and stay relaxed."
- "If I keep my cool, I won't get in trouble."
- "He/she may try to make me mad, but I'll control my feelings. I don't want to lose it."

Coping with the situation requires an individual to recognize that he/she is already mad and must try to cool down by using coping self-statements. Examples of self-statements to use in this phase would be:

- "I'm getting really mad; I need to stay cool."
- "Take it easy."
- "Chill out."
- "Time to take some deep breaths because I'm getting too upset."
- "I'm getting really tense; I need to relax."
- "I'm getting mad; I won't let him/her get to me."

After children have mastered recognizing when they are getting angry and using coping self-statements, it is beneficial to engage them in a series of role-play exercises in which they are gradually introduced to more and more stressful situations to practice using their newly acquired skills. At first, the therapist asks children to practice cool-down plans when confronted with mild feelings of anger or irritation, such as those that arise when doing a difficult math problem. Children also learn to employ the strategies when confronted with moderately stressful situations. An example of a moderately stressful situation would be when a child is walking down the hallway and someone calls him/her a name. Finally, children practice their anger/frustration management skills when confronted with very stressful situations. Examples of very stressful situations would be three or four children teasing one child, or perhaps a teacher accusing a child of stealing when the child did not. These role-plays should occur over three to four sessions as children acquire the skills necessary to cope with these increasingly stressful situations.

Adolescents

The procedures described for school-age children can be applied to adolescents with some modifications. We recommend using more didactic discussion to help adolescents understand the various components of anger/frustration. One point to focus on with adolescents is that anger is one response to difficult situations. The therapist helps the adolescents understand, however, that anger can interfere with their ability to do their best thinking and can lead them to choose responses that could make the problem worse in the long run. The issue is not getting rid of anger but rather being able to keep one's anger at a level that leads to productive rather than destructive choices. Adolescents can also participate in role-play exercises such as those described for the school-age children. Role-play exercises designed to facilitate problem recognition, situation interpretation, and use of coping self-statements are applicable with adolescents. One pragmatic note of caution, however, is to not use the term "cool-down plan." In our experience, it seems many adolescents find this childish, and use of the term can cause resistance. We have found it more helpful to use the actual term "coping self-statements" when discussing how to control anger with adolescents. Adolescents are also able to employ more elaborate relaxation training whereby they learn to relax specific muscle groups throughout the body.

We have found that adolescents can benefit from a self-monitoring exercise related to anger. With teens, we often employ the "When I Get

Angry" self-monitoring chart found in Appendix B. The purpose of this chart is to help the client become more aware of cognitive, physiological, and behavioral processes associated with anger. The therapist engages the adolescents in a didactic discussion and demonstration of how to use this chart. Group members are then asked to fill out the chart between sessions as a homework assignment. The clients are to keep track of events that make them angry, how their body felt during those events, and their automatic angry thoughts during the events. They are also required to rate the intensity of how angry or frustrated they became when confronted with the event. The idea is for them to bring back these charts to the sessions, discuss them, and become more aware of recurring patterns, such as what events typically make them angry, what their thoughts typically are, and how their bodies typically react.

The self-monitoring exercises can then be followed by exercises designed to facilitate adolescents using anger coping strategies outside of the session. The "Anger Combat Chart," found in Appendix B, is one method of structuring the adolescents' use of their skills outside the session. Adolescents are to record the events that make them angry or frustrated, how they use coping self-statements to modulate physiological and cognitive processes, and use of alternative methods (e.g., problem-solving) to handle the events. They are also required to keep track of the effectiveness of their alternative methods. Adolescents bring these charts back to group and discuss them thoroughly. The goal is for them to become aware of the most effective way(s) for them to cope with anger and frustration.

(See also the Training Parents in Cognitive–Behavioral Child Management and Family Anger and Conflict Management Skill Training modules in Chapter 7.)

Behavioral Social Skills Training

Behavioral social skills training is designed to teach ADHD children to execute specific prosocial and adaptive social behaviors. Social skills training includes both cognitive and behavioral components. Cognitive components have already been discussed and include problem-solving, self-instruction, perspective training, anger management training, and skills in inhibiting aggressive impulses. The behavioral component of social skills training typically involves facilitating children's abilities to execute specific behaviors such as maintaining eye contact, initiating and maintaining conversations, sharing/cooperation, complimenting, expressing feelings, and assertiveness. One cannot assume that behavioral skills will follow from the cognitive skills without specific training.

ADHD children typically have a limited repertoire of prosocial and adaptive social behaviors. Therefore, a combination of cognitive and behavioral approaches to improving social skills may ultimately be the best intervention. Behavioral social skills training is typically accomplished by first identifying the social behavior deficiencies of each child. The therapist then attempts to increase these social behaviors through both formal and informal behavioral methods.

The formal behavioral methods include didactic instruction, modeling, role-playing, application practice, and feedback regarding specific behaviors. Didactic instruction involves explaining precisely what a specific social behavior is. Modeling usually involves the therapist or a peer demonstrating how to execute a behavior. Role-playing involves engaging children in role-play exercises in which they practice using these specific behaviors. Application practice involves using these specific behaviors outside of role-play situations but when group is in session or practicing behaviors outside of the session. Feedback involves both the child giving himself/herself feedback about how well he/she is improving on executing specific behaviors and/or getting feedback from other group members or the therapist.

A more informal method to increase specific prosocial and adaptive social behaviors in children involves using group process. During group therapy, children give each other feedback about their behavior. This may entail negative feedback, such as identifying maladaptive social behaviors, as well as feedback regarding when the child is emitting prosocial and adaptive social behaviors in group.

The number of sessions necessary to accomplish training of a few key social behaviors will vary with the needs of the group and the limitations of the treatment context. In the program detailed in Chapter 9, we describe how to train specific social behaviors in the context of training cognitive processes. We model, practice, and reinforce the use of certain behaviors, such as maintaining eye contact, during the course of group discussions and role-plays. Alternative modes of delivery would include structuring specific sessions to focus on the training of select behaviors or having children participate in a social skills training group before participating in a cognitive–behavioral intervention. The latter alternative is particularly appropriate for ADHD children with extreme social behavior deficits.

As is evident from this discussion, we feel that behavioral social skills training is best delivered within the context of group therapy because of the rich opportunity for using group process and group feedback. If the therapist is able to conduct only individual sessions, then he/she must rely on structured role-playing exercises and *in vivo* practice, perhaps with the child receiving feedback from other informed adults, such as parents or teachers.

School-Age Children

When working with school-age children, the therapist needs to be very concrete in the delivery of behavioral social skills training. The therapist can emphasize the formal delivery methods discussed previously and concentrate on shaping specific social behaviors with school-age children. Such shaping can be accomplished by noticing, commenting, and reinforcing the children when they emit specific adaptive social behaviors. The feedback mechanism can be more structured. The therapist may want to have children give each other feedback and set goals at the beginning of the group. This might entail each group member setting personal goals to work on for the duration of the group. At the end of the session, the group can review how well each child met his or her goal.

Adolescents

Many of the procedures described in working with school-age children are applicable in working with adolescents. The advantage of working with adolescents on behavioral social skills is that the group process and feedback mechanisms can be capitalized on to a greater extent. The therapist needs to create an atmosphere that permits group members to give each other feedback about specific social behaviors. The therapist can model giving and receiving feedback and prompt group members to give each other feedback periodically. For example, Frank (a group member) may be disrupting the group and the therapist could ask, "How is Frank coming across to all of you today? Can you give him some specific feedback about his behavior?" or "I feel tired today and I feel like I'm not showing you that I do really want to be leading group today. How am I coming across to you?" The therapist's job is then to help the peers be very specific about giving the problematic group member or group leader feedback about his/her behavior. For example, if an adolescent says, "Frank, you are bugging me," the therapist asks that adolescent to state exactly what he/she means. The adolescents need to be prompted to give specific feedback about alternative behaviors. For example, one adolescent may give Frank feedback that he needs to listen more. The therapist would ask the adolescents to define exactly what listening is. This may include specific behaviors such as maintaining eye contact, nodding one's head, etc. The procedure of setting goals at the beginning of group and evaluating whether or not these goals are met at the end of group can also be used with adolescents.

(See the Problem-Solving and Self-Instruction Training—Application to Interpersonal Problems section earlier in the chapter.)

Conducting Child-Focused CBT within the Ecological Context

For organizational purposes, this chapter presented only child-focused therapeutic procedures. It is mandatory, in our opinion, to change the environment to accommodate the child's use of these skills outside of the treatment context. Therefore, it is essential to involve parents and teachers in the training process. In subsequent chapters, we describe the particular methods we use to involve parents, family members, and school personnel in the treatment process. If a clinician's setting does not afford the luxury of conducting both elaborate child group training and parent and teacher training, we urge the clinician to devote treatment sessions to training the entire family in the skills that match their particular needs. In this way, at least some aspects of the child's extratherapy environment can be impacted.

(See the Training Parents in Cognitive–Behavioral Child Management module in Chapter 7.)

Chapter Seven

Parent and Family Skills Training

This chapter provides specific details for conducting parent and family skills training. The discussion first centers around changing dysfunctional cognitions and attitudes that parents may have about their children and about themselves as parents. Next, we present a model of cognitive–behavioral child management that involves training parents to work with children to facilitate the child's use of cognitive strategies at home. Then we discuss behavioral child management strategies, including training parents in techniques to decrease negative or inappropriate child behaviors and increase positive or appropriate behaviors. Finally, we address how to conduct family skills training, which may include teaching the family important skills to improve family problem-solving, communication, and conflict management. Where relevant, we consider how these approaches are best implemented with children of different ages. We want to reiterate that not all of the parent/family skills training modules should be used with each child/family. The therapist determines which modules to apply based on the functional assessment.

Individual, Group, and Family Therapy Delivery

The first decision the therapist must make is whether or not to deliver the parent skills training modules within the context of individual (i.e., one parent or one set of parents at a time) or group therapy. There are advantages and disadvantages to both individual and group therapy delivery methods. By working with parents individually, the therapist can shape and focus the intervention specifically to meet the unique needs of each individual child and family. A major advantage of group delivery is that parents can obtain significant support from each other and are sometimes more receptive to trying ideas offered by other parents rather than by "experts." Indeed, many parents completing our parent group sessions have commented that the support they obtained from each other was as valuable, if not more valuable, than the actual skills training they received. The group setting provides a place for parents to share their trials and tribulations as they struggle with the parenting challenges presented by very difficult children. Through a group, parents find they are not alone in the difficulties that they experience. In addition, we believe parents need education about the common features of ADHD children, and this educational function is more efficiently conducted in a group context. A disadvantage, however, of working with groups is that the therapist cannot completely tailor the information and skills presented to the specific needs of each individual parent and family. The therapist must offer a more generic parent skills training program.

When the focus is on family skills training, then, obviously, family therapy is indicated, at least in part. It may be possible to introduce family skills training to groups of parents. To actually work on family skills, however, it is important to involve the entire family in family therapy sessions.

We often combine group parent training with individual parent or family sessions. In this way, we can capitalize on the advantages of both methods. Such a combination training can be accomplished by having parents complete the formal parent group training procedures (see the Parent Component—Group Process/Support section in Chapter 9, for example) and participate in individual or family sessions on a periodic basis, so the therapist can individualize the program.

Modifying Parents' Thoughts and Attitudes

As discussed in Chapter 4, there are a variety of dysfunctional attributions, beliefs, expectancies, and biases characteristic of parents experiencing parent/child relationship difficulties. Some of these cognitions should be modified in the preparation-for-change stage of therapy as discussed in Chapter 4. Parental cognitions can also be a direct target of intervention. It is very important to reduce these dysfunctional cognitions because of the deleterious effects they have on children, parents, and parent–child relationships. Whereas in the preparation-for-change stage the primary focus is on reframing activities of the therapist, in the skills training phase of therapy the therapist can be more directive in teaching parents specific cognitive restructuring skills. This is accomplished by teaching the parents to identify maladaptive cognitions, recognize their dysfunctional nature, and replace them with more functional cognitions. Cognitive restructuring can also be augmented by engaging parents in self-monitoring exercises. The self-monitoring exercises serve to systematize the cognitive restructuring process and help parents learn to use the procedures outside of therapy. These procedures are appropriate for parents of children at any age.

The first stage in modifying parents' thoughts and attitudes is education. We typically review the "Adult Self-Evaluation of Thoughts Form" found in Appendix B with parents. This form is identical to the "Parent Cognitions Target Form" (Figure 2, Chapter 5) but is designed to be completed by the parents rather than by the therapist. The therapist asks parents to fill out and rate each item on the form, urging the parents to be as candid as possible. This form gives both the therapist and parents information about the types and frequency of problematic thoughts the parents have. It is necessary to preface this discussion with definitions of attributions and beliefs and with the provision of reassurance about how natural and common it is for parents of ADHD children to have such thoughts. Once the parents have indicated the type and frequency of attributions and beliefs they typically have about their child, the therapist can use this information as an educational tool. We recommend a Socratic approach to discussing these issues with parents. This is accomplished by asking questions rather than making statements. Examples of questions to ask parents include: "What is the problem with these thoughts?" "What influence would these thoughts have on your relationship with your child?" "How would these thoughts influence the way you behave toward your child?" and "What messages would the child receive as a result of your behavior?"

Once dysfunctional thoughts have been recognized, the next step is to help the parents restructure their thinking in a more adaptive manner. This process can be facilitated by reviewing the "Adaptive Attributions and Beliefs Regarding ADHD" chart found in Appendix B with parents. Listed on this chart are a variety of counters (i.e., adaptive thoughts) that parents can use to replace any problematic thoughts identified in the self-evaluation process. Again, the therapist can ask similar questions in a Socratic manner. These questions might include: "What is the advantage of having these thoughts?" "How would these thoughts influence the parent/child relationship?" "How would these thoughts influence your behavior toward your child?" and "What messages would your behavior send to your child?" The two charts are designed to be used together. For example, thought IA of the "Adult Self-Evaluation of Thoughts Form" can be countered with thought IA on the "Adaptive Attributions and Beliefs Regarding ADHD" chart, and so on.

To solidify the modification of the parents' thoughts and attitudes, it is helpful to employ self-monitoring exercises. This would involve filling out the "Adult Self-Evaluation of Thoughts Form" on either a daily or weekly basis. Some parents will not complete the form outside of the therapy session but still can be asked to complete the form at the beginning of each therapy session. The task is to have the parents reflect on how they have thought about their children during the time since the last session. The goal is to have them reduce the problematic attributions and beliefs they have about their children.

Another form of cognitive restructuring involves changing the focus of parents' thinking away from their child's weaknesses to their child's strengths. We have found that many parents dwell on the deficiencies or weaknesses of their ADHD child. For example, parents focus on their child's difficulties with school or are concerned that their child never finishes anything or is a poor sport in baseball. We often frame these problems as issues that may never be cured or go away. We educate parents about the possible consequences of always focusing on these issues with their child. To balance the impact of these "failures" on their child's self-esteem, it is necessary to focus on their child's strengths. To facilitate this process, we have parents complete the "Inventory for Child's Strengths and Weaknesses" chart found in Appendix B. We ask parents to ponder whether or not the so-called weaknesses are modifiable or whether they will go away. Most parents can be made to realize that these weaknesses need to be accepted because they likely will not change. To continue to focus on weaknesses could adversely affect the child or parent–child relationship. The therapist also explains to parents that another purpose of this chart is to focus their attention on their child's strengths. The parents are encouraged to hereafter notice and reinforce their child when exhibiting his/her strengths. The parents can help the child with his/her weaknesses (e.g., employ cognitive–behavioral or behavioral child management) but not dwell or focus on these issues in other daily interactions.

Training Parents in Cognitive–Behavioral Child Management

Cognitive–behavioral child management training is designed to facilitate generalization and maintenance of the child's cognitive–behavioral therapy. It also involves helping parents learn more functional ways to interact with their child. Cognitive–behavioral child management cannot be accomplished until the child or family has received some initial training in cognitive–behavioral methods. The parents' job is to then work with their child in such a manner that he/she will continue to show therapy-related gains in the home environment. Parents essentially learn how to conduct cognitive–behavioral therapy with their children. To accomplish this, it is necessary to modify the home environment to accommodate to the child's skill usage, change parent–child interaction patterns, and train parents how to prompt and reinforce children for using cognitive strategies. We usually require four to six sessions working with parents, with some sessions involving children, to accomplish this therapeutic task.

School-Age Children

The first step in cognitive–behavioral child management is to train parents to be better observers of themselves and their child. The goal is for parents to learn how to identify and react differently to typical behavioral interaction sequences that are characteristic of themselves and their child. This is accomplished by introducing them to the concepts of antecedents and consequences of behavior. Parents are introduced to the "Child Observation Chart" found in Appendix B. The therapist explains to the parents that the purpose of the "Child Observation Chart" is to train them to be better observers of their children and themselves. The chart is designed to help parents recognize the sequence of events involved in their child's problem behavior, including their response to the child's behavior.

Parents are asked to identify two general problem behaviors that are common for their child. These general problem behaviors usually fall into the categories of noncompliance, interpersonal problems, and off-task/poor effort behavior. Therapists need to help parents think up specific examples of behaviors that fall into each of these general categories. Some examples are:

1. *Noncompliance:* Not minding when they are told, refusing to do homework, talking back when told to do something.
2. *Interpersonal problems:* Arguing, hitting, not taking turns, not sharing, butting into conversations, losing temper.
3. *Off-task/poor effort behavior:* Not completing a task due to being distracted, not listening to parents because of poor attention, starting a project and not finishing it, giving up.

Using these examples, the therapist discusses, models, and engages parents in role-play exercises demonstrating how to complete the "Child Observation Chart" in a step-by-step fashion. Parents are told to identify the problem behavior first, then the antecedents, followed by the consequences. It is usually very difficult for parents to grasp these concepts. The therapist needs to make the discussion as concrete as possible and have the parents describe specific examples they anticipate will be occurring at home.

During the next session, parents are asked to discuss their completed "Child Observation Charts." A very important goal is for parents to recognize the events/situations that precede and often trigger problem behavior and to recognize how they and their child typically respond after the problem behavior. It is especially helpful for the parents to understand what things happen just before a problem behavior is exhibited, because it is during the antecedent stage that they would be able to most successfully use the cognitive–behavioral child management strategies. Specifically, parents are told that they could prompt their child to use a plan during the antecedent stage of the problem behavior sequence. The therapist stresses the notion that it is usually more effective to intervene early in the problem behavior sequence before the child and/or parents become emotionally upset, angry, frustrated, etc. By looking at the "Child Observation Chart" data, parents are able to become aware of typical antecedents.

Another goal of using the "Child Observation Chart" is to help parents recognize helpful and unhelpful ways they respond to the child's behavior during the consequence stage of the problem behavior sequence. The idea of inadvertent reinforcement of the problem behavior is discussed. Parents typically bring in examples, such as doing tasks for children or simply not doing anything in response to the child's problem behavior. With these examples, parents can be made aware that their responses may serve to reinforce the problem behavior of the child. Parents are also told that they can respond to the child's behavior by prompting him/her to use a plan in the consequence stage of the problem behavior sequence.

After the parents are more aware of the problematic behavioral interaction sequences characteristic of their child and themselves, they can then begin to employ cognitive–behavioral child management strategies. We train parents to prompt and reinforce children for using cognitive strategies and to be appropriate models of the use of cognitive strategies. It is important to keep in mind that in our program, we train the children in cognitive self-control strategies, and it is up to the parents to provide an atmosphere that will enhance generalization and maintenance. We employ the "Stop, Think, and Use a Plan Chart" and "Tally for Using Plans (Weekly or Daily)" chart found in Appendix B as guides to help parents work within a cognitive–behavioral framework at home. These charts are designed to enable the parents to monitor and structure when they prompt and reinforce their child for using cognitive strategies. The therapist needs to discuss the procedures of how to use the "Stop, Think, and Use a Plan Chart" in detail. This usually entails a didactic discussion, modeling how to use the chart, and having the parents do some role-play practice of how to employ the charts with their child. The exact sequence for using the chart is: (1) the child has a problem behavior; (2) the parent asks the child if he/she could use a plan; (3) the child employs the plan; and (4) the child and parents discuss, mutually agree, and then record the child's performance on the "Stop, Think, and Use a Plan Chart."

Typically, children are not internally motivated to use plans at home. Just as external reinforcement is required in the children's training group, we work with the parents to establish incentives for skill use at home. The parents learn to reinforce cognitive behavior in addition to overt behavior. The focus is on whether or not a child uses the strategy, not just his/her final action. To facilitate this process, it is necessary to discuss in detail the procedures for using the "Tally for Using Plans (Weekly or Daily)" chart found in Appendix B. Parents need to understand that their child may not be motivated to use plans on his/her own, and therefore it is crucial to reinforce the child for using plans. The weekly tally chart encourages the parent to reward their child for the quality of his/her plan-making and not for the quantity of the plans used. The therapist explains that in order to emphasize quality, children are reinforced for obtaining ratings of 3 and 4 when they are using a plan at home. Depending on the reinforcement needs of the child, some are reinforced weekly and others daily.

An ultimate goal of this form of training is for children to initiate plan use. Thus, if the child comes up with the idea to use plans more frequently than the adult(s) around him/her, the child will receive additional reinforcement, as is indicated on the "Tally for Using Plans (Weekly or Daily)" chart.

It is crucial to discuss the rewards parents will use with their children. This discussion should occur before the parents actually use the charts at home. To facilitate this process, therapists should discuss the "Reinforcement Ideas" chart found in Appendix B. Parents need to choose a reinforcer that is both motivating to the child and realistic for the parents. The parents should discuss this reinforcer with the child before using any of the charts at home to make sure that the reward is indeed motivating for the child. Ideally, the parents and child can jointly create a reward menu from which the child can later select his/her reward. By providing variety and novelty in the choice of rewards, the reinforcement system will have a greater and more long-lasting impact on the child's behavior.

After the child has demonstrated some mastery of the problem-solving and self-instruction steps and the parent is very familiar with procedures involving the "Stop, Think, and Use a Plan Chart" and "Tally for Using Plans (Weekly or Daily)" chart, then the family can be given homework assignments to begin applying these procedures at home. It will be necessary for the family to try these procedures and come back to group to review successes and failures with the therapist for at least several sessions. During these review sessions, it is crucial for parents to discuss difficulties they have had applying the procedures at home. The therapist should make it clear to the parents that discussing implementation failures is as important or even more important than discussing implementation successes, for unsuccessful implementations communicate more information about how the methods will need to be tailored to their individual family. The primary purposes of the discussions are to identify problems in implementation and think of solutions. Typical difficulties that arise involve parents not understanding the procedures and/or children responding in a resistant fashion to the parents' attempts to prompt them to use plans at home. Sometimes the problem lies with the parents' failure to use the procedures at all.

There are several methods a therapist can employ to help parents solve the problems they are having implementing these procedures at home. The therapist can help the parents brainstorm alternative solutions for any particular problem they are having. Another method the therapist can employ is to review concepts. Typically, parents have not stressed to the child that they can earn rewards for using plans at home. The notion of antecedents can also be raised by the therapist again. The therapist should emphasize that catching the child in the antecedent phase of the problem behavior sequence and prompting the child to use plans at that stage will usually be the most successful. Finally, it may be helpful for the therapist to once again use modeling and role-playing to review the procedures. The therapist should go through the guidelines for the "Stop, Think, and Use a Plan Chart" and "Tally for Using Plans (Weekly or Daily)" chart in a step-by-step fashion, making the procedures as concrete as possible.

The next concept we recommend addressing is how parents can model plan use for their children. The therapist should emphasize to the parents that modeling is a powerful tool for teaching their children how to use these strategies. The therapist should ask the parents to first model how to use the plans for "neutral" problems. This may involve the parents stating the five problem-solving steps out loud while solving dilemmas such as what to fix for dinner, how to make sure that a parent can get themselves up early in the morning, etc. Eventually, parents can model how to use the five-step problem-solving plan to solve difficult problems too. This may involve the parents stating the five problem-solving steps out loud while solving interpersonal problems, problems at work, etc.

Adolescents

Parents can aid adolescents in generalizing and maintaining their newly acquired cognitive–behavioral skills in the home environment. Similar procedures as described for school-age children would be used, but typically in a less formal manner. Parents of adolescents can benefit from previously discussed exercises related to the "Child Observation Chart." This can be followed by methods to facilitate the adolescent's use of problem-solving strategies at home. Adolescents often do not seem as responsive to charts completed by their parents for which they can earn external reinforcers. We recommend familiarizing the parents with the skills that the adolescents are learning without divulging confidential information about specific problems that the adolescent is having.

As with the school-age children, the parents of adolescents can be helped to develop skills that will facilitate the adolescent's use of problem-solving methods at home. The therapist familiarizes the parents with five-step, means–end, and decision-making problem-solving strategies by providing them with the "Problem-Solving Skills" chart in Appendix B. The therapist should then assist the parents in adopting a Socratic parenting style that will accommodate the adolescent using these skills at home. It is helpful for parents to develop an interaction style in which they do not solve problems for their adolescent or automatically provide limits and consequences for problem behavior. Rather, it is more helpful if the parents require the adolescent to solve his/her own problems. For example, if the adolescent is having difficulty getting along with his/her younger brother, the parent may ask him or her to use a five-step problem-solving strategy to solve this problem. Another example would be if the adolescent wants to buy a new motorcycle, the parent may encourage him/her to use means–end problem-solving to determine how to accomplish this goal. If the adolescent wants to make a decision about whether or not to get a part-time job while going to school, the parent could encourage the adolescent to use decision-making problem-solving to address this issue. The parents learn that the focus is less on providing ideas or consequences and more on helping the adolescent discover his/her own strategies for successful problem-solving.

(See also the Family Problem-Solving Training module later in this chapter.)

Training Parents in Behavioral Child Management

Behavioral child management is designed to address problems related to child noncompliance (Barkley, 1987; Forehand & McMahon, 1981) and the coercive family process (Patterson, 1972, 1982; Patterson & Bank, 1989). These problems include the issues of negative reinforcement, low rates of positive reinforcement, vague and frequent parental commands and poor monitoring of the child's behavior outside of the home. With behavioral child management training, the parents are the focus of the intervention, and the children are seen only within the context of working with the parents. Parents learn to implement behavioral child management strategies that are based on operant behavioral principles. Many behavioral child management programs have been developed for children exhibiting ADHD, ADHD/CD, CD, and oppositional defiant behavioral disorder, and we shall review the basic components of these programs (e.g., Barkley, 1987; Forehand & McMahon, 1981; Gard & Berry, 1986; Marlowe, Reid, Patterson, Weinrot, & Bank, cited in McMahon & Wells, 1989; Patterson et al., 1975). Parents learn skills related to improving commands, administering reinforcement for specific appropriate and prosocial behaviors, ignoring inappropriate behaviors, and administering consequences for inappropriate or antisocial behavior. The therapist uses direct instruction, modeling, role-play procedures, and homework assignments to facilitate the parents' acquisition of these skills. Each specific skill in this section will typically require two to four sessions of training. Research suggests that these approaches can be very powerful in reducing specific problem behaviors in ADHD and ADHD/CD children (see reviews by Barkley, 1989; McMahon & Wells, 1989). We shall review procedures that are useful in working with preschool, school-age, and adolescent clients.

Preschool and School-Age Children

Popular programs for working with preschool and school-age children have many common characteristics. Therefore, we shall review components that are similar and have been found to be effective in working with both of these age groups. Gard and Berry (1986) suggest that there are five basic skill components involved in behavioral child management. These five skills include (1) increasing general positive interactions between child and parent, (2) parents using reinforcement procedures to increase specific positive child behaviors, (3) parents using ignoring to decrease mild negative/oppositional child behavior, (4) parents giving clear and consistent commands to their children, and (5) parents using consequences to reduce inappropriate and noncompliant child behavior.

We have found it profitable to educate parents about problematic parent behavior in terms of child behavior management. To facilitate this process, we may review with parents the "Adult Self-Evaluation of Behavior Form" presented in Appendix B. The parents are instructed to rate each of the items in terms of its frequency as it occurs over the average 1-week period. We ask the parents to be as open and honest as possible while they are filling out this form. This form serves both an educative and a self-evaluative purpose for the parents. After the parents have completed the form, the therapist engages them in a discussion about the implications of these types of behaviors in parent–child relationships. Again, this is best conducted with a Socratic approach to discussion, whereby the therapist asks the parents questions. Questions that can be asked include: "What is the problem with these parent behaviors?", "What influence would these parent behaviors have on parent-child relationship?", "What messages would these parent behaviors send to the child?", and "Do you find yourself repeating these parent behaviors even though they don't work?"

After parents have become more familiar with problematic behaviors on their part, it is helpful to familiarize them with more adaptive parent behaviors in child management. This can be facilitated by giving the parents the "Adaptive Behavioral Interchanges between Adults and Children" chart found in Appendix B. This chart provides information about adaptive parent behaviors that can be developed to replace many of the maladaptive behaviors previously described. It may be helpful for the therapist to explain all of these different types of behaviors to the parents. Again, the therapist can ask similar types of questions about these more adaptive kinds of behaviors. Example questions are: "How would these parent behaviors work?", "What influence would these parent behaviors have on the parent–child relationship?", and "What messages would these parent behaviors send to the child?"

Once the parents have become more familiar with maladaptive and adaptive parent behaviors, it can be helpful to get their input on how to focus the child-management skills training. The therapist can guide the parents in discussing the areas they want to work on and goals they want to set. Getting input from the parents about the focus of the behavioral child management can facilitate their being more open to learning the skills.

It is helpful to improve parents' ability to observe themselves and their children in terms of repetitive negative interaction behavior sequences. We employ the "Child Observation Chart" and related procedures for this purpose. The reader is referred to the previous discussion about this procedure in the section Training Parents in Cognitive–Behavioral Child Management.

One method that has been used to increase positive interactions between the parent and child is the "child's game" (Forehand & McMahon, 1981). The parents are taught special play techniques to use with their child within the context of the child's game (i.e., free play). Parents are instructed to choose dolls, houses, trucks, and/or blocks (not games) and then engage in free play with their child. Parents are taught to increase the amounts of praising, describing, and touching behaviors they emit, and decrease the frequency of commands, questions, and criticisms they emit, during the child's game. The therapist first instructs the parents in the specific behaviors, followed by modeling how it would look to play with a child in this manner. Parents then role-play how they would engage in this type of play with their child. Home use of these procedures is assigned once the parents demonstrate mastery of these special play techniques in the clinic setting. When we use this type of approach, we typically ask parents to set aside 10 minutes per day and to engage in the child's game at home. We have developed the "Practice Positive Parenting through Special Play Time" chart, found in Appendix B, to structure this activity and better ensure that the parents will follow through and comply with practicing these skills at home. Parents are required to bring these charts back to each session. This chart is employed for as many weeks as necessary until the parents demonstrate proficiency with the skills and are applying them at home.

We have found that parents have a hard time breaking habits and are not aware of recurrent negative patterns of response to their children. It appears to be difficult for some parents to attend to neutral and positive behavior instead of attending only to negative behavior in their children. We have developed a self-monitoring chart for parents to use to help change their behavior. The "Practice Positive Attention and Reinforcement" chart is found in Appendix B. To use this chart, parents keep track of purposeful attending/praising behaviors, frequency of negative behavior, and ignoring of mild negative/inappropriate behavior in their child. Purposeful attending and praising is defined as noticing, commenting, touching, and praising of the child's neutral, appropriate, compliant, and prosocial behavior. Negative behavior is defined as nagging, yelling, hitting, and ignoring appropriate behavior. Ignoring mild negative behavior is defined as not noticing or paying attention to any of the child's mild inappropriate and attention-seeking behavior. The therapist instructs, models, and engages parents in role-play exercises so that they understand and demonstrate proficiency with this system. Parents are instructed to employ this chart between sessions and to bring this chart to every session for review and discussion with the therapist. The chart is discontinued when the parents are showing increased frequency of purposeful attending and praising behavior, decreased negative behavior, and increased ignoring behavior.

Reinforcement strategies can be used to increase appropriate and prosocial behavior of children. The first task is to define a target child behavior to be increased by reinforcement. One method to accomplish this is to define the target behavior as a behavior that is incompatible with a problem behavior. For example, a behavior incompatible with noncompliance is compliance. Because noncompliance is a frequent problem, we have developed a procedure to reinforce compliance directly. We operationalize compliance as "listening and obeying." We employ the "Listen and Obey" chart found in Appendix B to facilitate reinforcement of compliance behavior. Parents are instructed to prompt their child with the words "listen and obey" when they want them to comply with a command. Parents are allowed to remind children that they can get rewarded for listening and obeying. If the child does listen and obey, a smiling face is drawn in the "yes" column for that day. If the child does not listen and obey, a frowning face is drawn in the "no" column for that day and the parent is instructed to use time-out (to be discussed later). At the end of the day or week, depending on the needs of the child, the parent adds up the smiling and frowning faces. If there are more smiling faces than frowning faces, the child would get a predetermined reward. The therapist uses instruction, modeling, and role-play practice exercises to facilitate the parents' acquisition of the skill needed to use the "Listen and Obey" chart. The parents are required to use the "Listen and Obey" chart between sessions and to bring this chart into each session for discussion with the therapist. The chart is employed for as long as is necessary for the child to increase the frequency of listening and obeying behaviors.

Another reinforcement strategy involves targeting specific recurring problematic behaviors. The therapist helps parents define what these recurring problem behaviors are, specify the child behaviors incompatible with these problematic behaviors, and then reinforce incompatible behavior. As a way of structuring this type of procedure, we employ the "Reinforcement of Specific Behavior" chart found in Appendix B. To use this procedure, the therapist begins by helping the parents identify four specific problematic behaviors and then operationalize how the child would behave if he/she was not exhibiting these problem behaviors. Examples of problematic behaviors and their incompatible alternatives include dawdling in the morning versus brushing teeth, getting dressed, and being ready for school by 7:30 A.M.; failing to complete homework in a timely way versus completing homework between 4:00 and 5:00 P.M.; and staying up too late versus being in bed by 8:30 P.M. Parents keep track of the frequency with which the child completes the specified behaviors in the manner defined on the chart, and then administers contingent reinforcement on either a daily or weekly basis, depending on the individual child. Again, the therapist employs instruction, modeling, role-playing, and homework assignments as a means of facilitating the parents' acquisition of these skills. This particular chart can be employed until the frequency of the specific appropriate behaviors has increased to a specified criterion level.

Giving clear and effective commands is one very important skill that parents need to learn in behavioral child management. This is especially important when working with the parents to increase their child's compliance. Many parents give one or all of the following types of poor commands: vague commands, chains of commands, question-type commands, or rationale-type commands. A vague command is such that it does not state exactly what the child is required to do (e.g., "Shape up."). A chain of commands involves the parent giving the child too many things to do at one time (e.g., "Clean up your room, take out the garbage, and set the table for dinner."). A question-type command is when a parent asks the child to do something in the context of a question (e.g., "Would you please pick up the toys?"). A rationale-type command involves the parent asking the child to do something and following that with a rationale for why the child should do it (e.g., "You need to get dressed now because we have to go to the doctor's appointment at 1:00 P.M., and if you don't get dressed soon, we'll be late."). The therapist's task is to educate the parents about the negative effects of these poor commands on the child's compliance. There are too many loopholes for the child so that he/she is not required to comply with those types of commands. For example, if a parent asks a questiontype command, the parent should be prepared for the child to answer, "No." Parents are instructed to give clear, one-step commands in ten words or less as an alternative to these problematic commands. These one-step commands are designed to tell the child exactly what he/she is supposed to do and do not allow loopholes for noncompliance. Examples of these types of commands are "Clean up your room," and "Come inside the house for dinner now." Again, the therapist modeling and engaging parents in role-playing on how to give effective commands is helpful. Procedures for parents to follow when their child is still noncompliant with the one-step command will be discussed next.

Time-out is probably one of the most important behavioral child management skills that a therapist can teach parents. Time-out is especially effective for noncompliance in children. The "Time-Out" chart in Appendix B can be given to parents to summarize the procedures. The way we practice time-out involves a four-step procedure. These steps are: (1) give a one-step command for compliance; (2) give a warning; (3) administer time-out; and (4) ask for compliance again. We have already reviewed procedures for giving a clear one-step command. The parent should give a warning if the prompting to listen and obey the command did not gain the child's compliance. A warning is an if–then statement. For example, if a child is refusing to clean up his toys, the parent may give the following warning: "*If* you don't clean up your room, *then* you will have to go to time-out." If the child does not comply within 5 seconds after the warning, the parent administers time-out. Typically, time-out consists of putting the child into a situation where he/she cannot receive any reinforcement. This may include having the child sit on a chair or in a room with nothing in it. We recommend that the child be placed in time-out for 1 minute for each year of age. After time-out, the child is required to comply with the original command. If the child is again noncompliant, then the entire procedure would be repeated. It is extremely important to inform parents that their consistency in administering the time-out in this fashion is the key to its success. Some children take longer than other children, but every child will eventually comply with this type of procedure. The parents should be prepared to spend a great deal of time enforcing this procedure when they first begin to use it, especially if they have very noncompliant children. Parents should continue these procedures indefinitely.

An environmental intervention that has utility with ADHD and ADHD/CD children is providing a structured and scheduled environment. As has been discussed previously, many of these children appear to lack internal self-control skills. Therefore, providing a structured, scheduled, predictable environment will help the child function more adequately even if he/she has deficits in self-control. The therapist may want to assess the family in terms of everyday operations, schedules, and procedures at home. The therapist may find that family members lead hectic and chaotic lives. There may be little predictability in their structure, procedures, or schedules. While this may not be a problem for many children, the therapist should determine if this unpredictability is adding to the difficulties of a given ADHD or ADHD/CD child. If it is affecting the child, the therapist may want to help parents develop daily schedules, predictable rules and discipline methods, etc.

In addition to establishing predictable rules and schedules, parents can also be trained to take a more active role in structuring certain activities or times of the day that are reliably problematic for their child. This positive structuring has been implied in our earlier discussion of the use of the "Reinforcement of Specific Behavior" chart. The process detailed via this chart can be used to establish a structure/schedule for predictably difficult moments of the day, such as getting ready for school in the morning or getting ready for bed at night (or at nap time for young children).

Parents can also help their child better structure himself/herself by using behavioral self-control procedures during certain specified times or activities. As discussed in Chapter 3, while behavioral self-control methods have more commonly been used in classroom settings, we have found it useful to train some parents in the use of these methods to address certain home situations that are analogous to the classroom situations for which these methods were developed. More specifically, these methods can provide a helpful means of increasing the ADHD child's on-task behavior while completing homework. We encourage parents to make being on-task during homework part of the daily or weekly reward system they are implementing with their child. The parent can explain to the child that he/she will be more successful at being on-task (and therefore earn more points or smiling faces), if he/she has a way to monitor on-task behavior. The parent can then introduce the "Am I On-Task?" chart presented in Figure 6. The child is told that when he/she hears a certain sound, such as a tone played on an audiotape or a beeper on a digital clock, he/she is to mark whether or not he/she is paying attention to his/her work. Ideally, the child should hear a tone or beep every 45–90 seconds. If the child has been on-task a certain percentage of the rating intervals, then he/she can earn points, etc. An example of a self-monitoring point chart is also presented in Table 15. This chart depicts a reinforcement schedule for being on-task 60%–100% of the interval. The specific percentages to be reinforced must be tailored to the capacities of the individual child. For some extremely inattentive children, parents may need to begin by reinforcing being on-task 50% of the intervals and then slowly work up to being on-task a greater percentage of the time. The parents can then explain to the child that it is important for him/her to be honest about being on-task versus off-task and that the parent will conduct "accuracy checks" in which the child can earn extra points for being honest, whether or not he/she is on- or off-task. Ideally, we like to introduce this procedure during a joint session with the parents and child so the therapist can model the explanation and use of the procedures directly with the child. It is our sense that parents have responded positively to this procedure because getting their child to complete his/her homework has previously been such a difficult task, and the parent must typically help the child with this activity at a point in the day when even children receiving medication treatment are not under the effects of the medication.

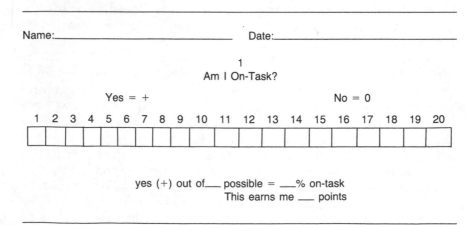

FIGURE 6.   Record form for monitoring attention to task.

TABLE 15
Samples of Performance Standards for Self-Evaluation of On-Task Behavior

Less than 60%	=	0 points	
60%–69% on-task	=	1 point	This means at least 12 of 20
			18 of 30
			24 of 40
70%–79% on-task	=	2 points	This means at least 14 of 20
			21 of 30
			28 of 40
80–89% on task	=	3 points	This means at least 16 of 20
			24 of 30
			32 of 40
90%–99% on-task	=	4 points	This means at least 18 of 20
			27 of 30
			36 of 40
100% on-task	=	5 points	This means 20 of 20
			30 of 30
			40 of 40

Adolescents

Behavioral child management procedures applied to adolescents still primarily focus on the parents, but the adolescents may be involved to a greater extent than preschool and school-age children. Many of the procedures described earlier for working with preschool and school-age children are applicable to parents working with adolescents within a behavioral framework. Procedures such as "Practice Positive Attention and Reinforcement," "Reinforcement of Specific Behavior," and structuring the environment may be useful. Several other behavioral techniques are unique to working with adolescents.

As when working with preschool and school-age children, it is important to increase the positive interactions that occur between parents and adolescents. It is frequently the case that parents and adolescents find themselves wallowing in a quagmire of negative interactions with each other. To help this problem, at least in part, it can be useful to make specific plans for increasing the frequency and quality of interactions between parents and adolescents. One way to facilitate this is to have the parents and adolescents use the "Positive Activity and Interaction Schedule for Parents and Adolescents" found in Appendix B. This chart will structure how the parents and adolescents specifically attempt to increase their positive interactions with each other. It is similar to the child's game in its ultimate aim, but the focus and procedures are more relevant for adolescents. The chart structures a five-step process for improving parent–adolescent interactions. It is very important that both the parent and the adolescent equally contribute input to completing this five-step process. Step 1 involves the parent and adolescent listing several activities that they enjoy doing together that can be accomplished in about 30 minutes. Step 2 involves scheduling at least two times, preferably more if feasible, in which the parent and adolescent will engage in these activities for at least 30 minutes over 1 week. Make sure that they specify the day, date and time. Step 3 involves the parent listing specific behaviors that he/she will try to emit more frequently when engaged in the scheduled interaction with the adolescent (e.g., listening, praising, or paraphrasing). It is crucial to get the adolescent's feedback and input about specific behaviors that he/she would like his/her parent to emit more of towards him/her during the activity times. Step 4 is the same except it involves the adolescent coming up with specific behaviors that he/she will try to emit more of while interacting with his/her parent (e.g., talking, eye contact, or expressing feelings). Likewise, it is important that the parent give the adolescent feedback and suggestions about specific behaviors that he/she would like to see more of from their adolescent during the activity times. Step 5 involves the parent and adolescent writing down comments about how the activity and interaction time went. The comments should focus on their general thoughts and feelings, as well as how satisfied they were with the specific interaction.

We have found a procedure involving removal of privileges for noncompliance to be effective with adolescents. This procedure is similar to, but different from, the time-out procedure used with preschool and school-age children. Instead of restricting the adolescent to a chair or to an isolated room, the adolescent loses privileges when he/she does not comply. We use the "Removing Privileges for Noncompliance" chart found in Appendix B when working with parents trying to gain the compliance of older children and adolescents. There are four steps in compliance training with adolescents. The first step is to give a clear, concise, one-step command. The second step is to give a clear warning in the form of an if–then statement. The third step is to remove one of the adolescents' privileges (e.g., television, car driving privileges, or allowance) until compliance is gained. The fourth step is to return the privilege once compliance is gained. For example, if an adolescent refuses to do the dishes, the parent will give the adolescent a warning and then follow through by removing driving privileges until the adolescent does the dishes. Parents are advised to avoid arguing with the adolescent or getting into power struggles. They are instructed to let their actions do their talking by following through with the removal of the privilege until the adolescent complies.

Typically, both parents and teens can identify specific behaviors exhibited by the other that are unacceptable to them. For example, parents may complain that they continuously have to tell their adolescent to do chores on a daily basis. Adolescents may complain that they have to put up with a lot of nagging from their parents. Behavioral contracting can be one effective method for dealing with this type of problem. We employ the "Daily Behavior Contract" chart found in Appendix B as an aid to contracting. When completing this chart, the first task is to specify those behaviors that are required of the adolescent. The second task is to specify those privileges that will be earned if the adolescent meets the expectation or lost if the adolescent does not follow through with emitting the specific behaviors that are described in the contract. The goal is to make more desirable daily activities contingent on the completion of less desirable daily activities. For example, the contract may specify that the adolescent is to get up and be ready for school at 7:00 A.M. each morning. The adolescent earns extra driving privileges for the day if he/she is up and ready at the specified time or loses driving privileges all together for the day if he/she does not fulfill the behavioral expectation. Parents are instructed to avoid nagging the adolescent if he/she does not comply but to follow through with granting or removing specific privileges. It is important that everyone sign the daily contract. The daily contract should be employed between sessions, and the parents and adolescent should bring the contract in to each session so that it can be reviewed with the therapist. Some parents have admitted having so much difficulty refraining from nagging their child/ adolescent that they found it helpful to prepare a daily contract for themselves concerning this behavior. For example, one father agreed to make himself earn his morning coffee by refraining from nagging his teenage son about getting up and getting ready in the mornings, with the mother agreeing to monitor the father's actions. While it is frightening for many parents to let go of nagging behavior and let their actions do the talking, most admit to being very pleased with both the observed changes in the child's behavior and the improved affective tone in the family that emerges when the nagging stops.

Another form of contracting involves parents monitoring their adolescent's behavior. A "Monitoring Contract," such as the one found in Appendix B, can be applied with adolescents who are getting into frequent trouble at school and/or in the community and are breaking rules at home. This strategy is often employed when adolescents are out of control and very difficult to manage. The first step is to help parents identify troublesome behaviors that they have observed or suspect their adolescent is exhibiting. The parents then devise systems for monitoring the adolescent's behavior. For example, parents may want to monitor school-related behaviors or problems by making daily telephone calls to the school or by asking teachers to send home daily written reports. The parents may monitor the adolescent's behavior in the community by requiring him/her to call home each hour to report where he/she is. The parents may require that the adolescent state specifically where he/she will be and then follow through by checking up on the adolescent's whereabouts. The parents may want to specify rules for the home, such as specific times that the adolescent is required to come home at night or which friends can be in the house. If monitoring reveals that the adolescent is engaging in unacceptable behavior or is not meeting behavioral expectations, then a previously specified consequence is administered. The contract should be signed by all parties involved and should be reviewed at each session until the adolescent's behavior improves.

As discussed in the section on school-age children, parents can also have adolescents engage in self-monitoring activities while completing homework. With some adolescents, their attentional capacities may have developed to the point that it is possible for them to monitor work completion rather than attention-to-task.

Family Problem-Solving Training

Family problem-solving training is designed to facilitate adaptive family functioning and may also have an indirect effect on children's internalization of problem-solving skills. Procedures for family problem-solving training closely parallel procedures for the child problem-solving training with the obvious exception that all family members are involved instead of the individual child. Essentially, family members learn to effectively solve problems and negotiate with each other in a more adaptive manner. Similar to what the children are learning, families also learn how to define problems, generate alternatives, think of the consequences of their alternatives and pick the best one, implement that particular strategy, and check to see whether or not that strategy worked. Typically, two to six sessions are necessary to train family problem-solving.

We use the same five-step problem-solving process with families as we do with individual children. With families, the specific language is changed to incorporate the words "we," "us," and "our." The five steps are:

1. Stop! What is the problem we are having?
2. What are some plans we can use?
3. What is the best plan we could use?
4. Let us do the plan.
5. Did our plan work?

When family members have problems, they are instructed to use these steps as a way of structuring and focusing their discussion. This type of training can be conducted after the children have learned problem-solving skills training by themselves, or family problem-solving skills training could be conducted without the child going through his/her individual program. With families exhibiting mild to moderate problem-solving deficits, problem-solving training alone may be sufficient. With those families exhibiting severe problem-solving deficits, communication skills and anger/conflict management training may be necessary prior to engaging in problem-solving training.

School-Age Children

We recommend that school-age children receive their own training in problem-solving (see the Problem-Solving and Self-Instruction Training module in Chapter 6) before involving them in family problem-solving training. This will facilitate their ability to work with parents in family problem-solving. We use the term "family plans" to refer to family problem-solving with school-age children and their families. To facilitate the process of using family plans, we employ the "Stop, Think, and Use a Plan Chart" along with the "Guidelines for Collaborative Plans" and "Family Problem-Solving" information sheets found in Appendix B. It is necessary to engage the parents in a discussion of how they might use family plans. They should be able to identify common problems that occur at home involving the family. Examples of problems appropriate for family plans range from deciding where to go out for dinner to arguing or negotiating about how late a child may stay outside. Situations involving arguing and negotiating are the most common and most appropriate for using family plans. The therapist helps the family learn to use family plans and reinforce the child for appropriate participation. The best way to accomplish this is for the child to receive credit on the "Stop, Think, and Use a Plan Chart" and "Tally for Using Plans (Weekly or Daily)" chart (see the Training Parents in Cognitive–Behavioral Child Management module earlier in this chapter) for participating in family plans. The therapist will need to employ didactic presentation, modeling, and role-play exercises to facilitate acquisition of the parents' and child's abilities to use family plans. During training role-plays, it is often helpful to have family members switch roles, so that children and parents have an opportunity to view the process from each other's perspective. Switching roles can also help resistant and/or uncertain family members become more engaged in the problem-solving process.

A common issue presented by parents in regard to using these family plans concerns how to involve untrained siblings. The therapist can work with the parents to help them determine whether or not siblings are appropriate for using family plans. Siblings need to be capable of cooperating with the process and understanding the concepts. If the parents feel that the siblings meet these criteria, they should try to include them in the process of creating family plans. If the siblings are too young for participating in the process, they can still be included or affected by family plans, but they don't have full input into the creation of plans.

Adolescents

Family problem-solving training for families with adolescents is somewhat more sophisticated than the training for families with school-age children. It may not be necessary for the adolescent to receive his/her own training in problem-solving before being able to participate in family problem-solving. In working with adolescents, the parents will be prompting the adolescent to a lesser degree than with a school-age child, and the adolescent will actually be more involved in the problem-solving process. The same five steps are used with adolescents as were used with school-age children. We refer to these steps as family problem-solving, rather than family plans as we did with school-age children. We have adapted our model for working with adolescents and families for problem-solving skills training from the work of Robin and Foster (1989).

We give family members copies of the "Family Problem-Solving" chart found in Appendix B. The family problem-solving steps should be introduced to the family through didactic discussion. If the family exhibits a very high level of conflict, it may also be helpful to engage them in role-play exercises to practice the five-step problem-solving process initially with contrived problems. Otherwise, the best way to facilitate the family's acquisition of these skills is to use the five-step problem-solving process to discuss actual family issues in the sessions. When topics of dispute arise, the therapist focuses on the problem-solving process with the family, rather than the content of what the family is discussing. The following is an example of how the therapist might work with the family in a family problem-solving context:

ADOLESCENT: I'd like to drive the car more often than I do now.
FATHER: No way, you can't even go to school every day, so I'm not going to let you drive the car more.
THERAPIST: This might be a good time for your family to use family problem-solving strategies.

FATHER: OK, I'll give it a try.

ADOLESCENT: I'll try, too.

THERAPIST: What is the first step?

MOTHER: What is the problem?

THERAPIST: That's right. What is the problem your family is having? How do each of you see the problem?

ADOLESCENT: I want to use the car more often.

FATHER: You want to use the car more often, and I want you to be more responsible.

THERAPIST: What is the problem?

ADOLESCENT: We want something from each other.

THERAPIST: Do you all agree on that?

FATHER: Yes.

MOTHER: I guess.

THERAPIST: What is the next step in family problem-solving?

MOTHER: Think up some alternative solutions. Think up some plans.

ADOLESCENT: You give me more car privileges, and I'll go to school every day.

FATHER: How about if you go to school first on a more regular basis, and then we'll let you use the car more often.

MOTHER: I agree with your father. Why don't you try to go to school every day for a week, and then we'll let you use the car more on the weekend.

THERAPIST: You have all said some options. What is the next step?

FATHER: We need to decide which is the best plan.

ADOLESCENT: I'll go to school every day for a week, and then you give me one more night of driving privileges. OK?

FATHER: Okay, let's try that.

THERAPIST *(To the mother)*: Do you agree?

MOTHER: Yes, I agree.

THERAPIST: Now what are you supposed to do in the family problem-solving process?

ADOLESCENT: We'll do the plan.

THERAPIST: OK, you try that for this week and let me know how it goes next week when you come in for your next session.

After the family has demonstrated some mastery of family problem-solving in the sessions, the therapist could give them homework assignments to try these procedures at home. Oftentimes it is best to recommend that the family use these strategies to solve neutral problems at home initially before using them to solve more difficult problems. An example of a potentially more neutral problem would be using the family problem-solving steps to figure out what to prepare for dinner or what activity to select for a family outing. After successfully using the methods with neutral issues, the family could use family problem-solving skills to solve more difficult problems. During each subsequent session, the therapist explores whether or not the family has had success in employing these problem-solving steps at home.

Family Communication Skills Training

Family communication skills training is designed to promote adaptive family functioning. Communication skills deficits are a common difficulty of troubled families. Certainly, families with ADHD or ADHD/CD children can manifest such problems. Communication problems include vague/ambiguous statements, blaming, getting off-topic, dominating conversation, put-downs and destructive verbalizations, interrupting, poor listening and poor eye contact, and incongruent verbal and nonverbal messages. Communication skills training involves helping family members realize their destructive communication patterns and learn new skills. The therapist trying to facilitate communication skills training with families will need to provide them with feedback about their communication patterns, instructions on how to change these patterns, and modeling of ways to change these patterns. The therapist then works with the family to apply new skills in and out of the sessions (Robin & Foster, 1989). The communication skills training procedures that we shall describe have been adapted from Alexander and Parsons (1982) and Robin and Foster (1989). Based on our clinical experience, we recommend that this form of intervention be used primarily with families who have older school-age children or adolescents. Therefore, when describing family communication skills training, we shall not make distinctions between procedures for different age groups. Typically, at least two to six sessions are needed to train family communications skills.

The first step in family communication skills training is to educate the family about communication skills and give them feedback about their communication patterns. The therapist will interpret communication patterns that he/she has observed in the family and present a rationale for why these communication patterns need to change. The therapist should explain that the family needs to learn constructive and effective ways to say what they want and need, and to hear what others want and need. Without effective and constructive communication, families cannot negotiate and solve their problems. Therapists can facilitate this process by giving family members the "Communication Skills" chart found in Appendix B. The therapist needs to review all of the "do's" and "don't's" on the "Communication Skills" chart with the family. It is helpful to ask the family to evaluate themselves based on the information on the chart and see if they can pinpoint and agree on repetitive communication problems (i.e., don'ts) they have. The therapist can also give his/her feedback to the family about what he/she has observed of their communication style. Together the therapist and family members should set goals to increase specific communication skills (i.e., dos) they would like to improve.

The second stage in family communication skills training is for the therapist to model the use of the selected skills and then have the family practice those skills. For example, the family members may have decided to work on being brief and direct in their communications. The therapist could raise a topic with the family such as an adolescent getting homework done each day. The therapist could model the "sermon" style of communicating: "It's important that you get good grades. This has a lot to do with what happens to you for the rest of your life. Your whole future rests on whether or not you do well at this time in your life at school. When I was your age, I didn't take school seriously and I had to struggle. . . ." The therapist would then model how this same communication could be done by being brief and direct: "I want you to get your homework done each night by 9:00 P.M." The therapist could also model other skills such as those related to active listening. Poor listening would be modeled by sitting back in a chair, crossing the arms, and looking away. The therapist could then model active listening by sitting forward, keeping the arms to the side, and engaging in good eye contact. The family members could then take turns practicing these skills in the session, with the therapist acting as a coach.

After specific skills have been addressed, the therapist helps the family use these skills as they discuss various issues in the family sessions. The therapist focuses on the process of communication and not on the content of what the family is trying to communicate. The therapist acts as a coach to the family members by giving them feedback when they are exhibiting poor communication and by redirecting them to use more effective communication skills that they have already practiced. It may be helpful to videotape family discussions in the session and play them back as a direct form of feedback.

The following is a sample dialogue summarizing many of these points. The topic being discussed in this particular family session is what time the adolescent should come in on school nights:

ADOLESCENT: I want to stay out later because everyone else does.

MOTHER *(To the adolescent)*: Your father and I don't care what other people do. If we did what other people do, our family would be in worse shape than it is. It is important to get a good night's sleep. It affects your performance the next day, and your grades will decline. When I was your age, I had to be in by 7:00 P.M. . . .

ADOLESCENT: *(Looking out the window.)*

THERAPIST: I want to stop you at this point and have you notice how each of you is communicating. Are you falling into some of those old communication patterns we discussed previously? What do you think?

MOTHER: I guess I was sermonizing again. I was going on and on.

THERAPIST *(To the adolescent)*: What do you think is going on?

ADOLESCENT: Yep, she was sermonizing.

THERAPIST: What were you doing?

ADOLESCENT: I guess I was tuning her out and not listening.

THERAPIST: What are you both going to do to communicate more effectively?

MOTHER: I'll try to be brief and to the point.

THERAPIST *(To the adolescent)*: What about you?

ADOLESCENT: I'll try to do more active listening.

THERAPIST: OK, let's try this discussion again. This time try the communication strategies you just described.

MOTHER: I want you to keep coming in at the same time as you have been because in my judgment that is what is best for you.

ADOLESCENT *(Looking at his mother)*: Can't we work out a deal?

After the family has demonstrated some mastery over communication skills in the sessions, then they should be given homework assignments to use these skills outside of the sessions. It is effective to recommend that family members post the "Communication Skills" charts at strategic places in the house (i.e., refrigerators, bulletin boards, etc.) to increase awareness of communication issues. An effective homework assignment is to instruct the family members to set aside specific times during the week to have family meetings to practice their skills. The number of family meetings to be scheduled should be individualized to meet the needs of each family. The family is instructed to sit down with the "Communication Skills" charts in hand and try to talk about various issues. Families should first try to use these skills while talking about more benign or neutral problems and then later try to use them with more important or affect-laden difficulties.

Family Anger and Conflict Management Skill Training

Family problem-solving and communication skills are crucial for healthy family functioning. These skills can be applied to family problems with and without conflict. Occasionally, however, families present with so much conflict and anger that they cannot effectively employ the family problem-solving and communication skills. For such families, it may be important to add a training component addressing anger and conflict management. Foster and Robin (1989) state that adding an anger management component to family problem and communication skills training has not yet proven itself to be efficacious, primarily because it has not been researched extensively. They further argue, however, that adding an anger management component may help some individual families whose anger is so high that it is interfering with problem-solving and communication skills training.

For working with such families, we shall describe procedures that have been adapted from Novaco's (1978) work with anger management for adults and that of Nomellini and Katz (1983) on anger management for parents. We divide anger and conflict management for families into three stages: recognizing anger/conflict, coping with anger/conflict, and employing problem-solving and communication skills. The "Family Anger and Conflict Management" chart found in Appendix B can be given to family members to facilitate training and summarize the major steps in the process. Again, we shall gear the discussion of these procedures toward families who have older school-age children and adolescents.

The first stage in family anger and conflict management skills training is to educate family members about anger and conflict. Much of that education will involve explanation of physiological, cognitive, and behavioral aspects to anger/conflict for each individual in the family. The goal is for family members to recognize signals that tell them they are having an anger/conflict problem. This can be accomplished by educating family members about body signals, thinking signals, and actions of self/others signals. The therapist should instruct family members to generate many examples of these types of signals. It is preferable for the therapist to keep track of the signals and prompt the family when necessary. Signals listed and discussed might include:

Body signals	*Thinking signals*	*Actions of self/others signals*
Breathing rate increased	"He's making me mad."	Raised voice
Heart rate increased	"I hate him."	Facial expressions
Sweating increased	"I wish he were dead."	Body postures
Face color flushed	"I'm going to hit her."	Put-down verbalizations
Muscle tension increased	"I wish she would move out of the house."	Interrupting
Voice tone raised		

The next stage of family anger/conflict management skill training is to work with family members to cope better with anger. This can be accomplished by setting a standard procedure whereby one of the family members can call a time-out once he/she recognizes high levels of destructive anger and conflict. It is crucial to make sure that all family members agree *a priori* that it is OK for one family member to call this time-out. The family is then instructed to separate for 5 or 10 minutes (or some agreed upon time acceptable to all family members) to individually practice coping with anger. Family members can cope with anger by employing deep breathing, muscle relaxation, and coping self-statements (e.g., "I'm not going to let him get to me," and "I'm going to try to stay calm," and "I'm going to try to think of constructive ways to get my point across to her."). The family members should reunite after they have time to cope with their anger and then try to employ family problem-solving and communications skills. It may be necessary for the therapist to model some of the anger coping strategies for the family such as deep breathing, relaxation of muscles, and the use of coping self-statements. It is always helpful to have the family members take some time to practice using these skills before they actually employ them to real anger/conflict situations.

The therapist should ask the family to practice the entire sequence of skills within the context of family sessions. The therapist may present contrived conflictual situations and/or prompt the family to use the skills to solve real conflictual situations emerging during the sessions. The therapist's task is to process with the family all the stages of family anger/conflict management skill training. The therapist asks the family members to employ the anger/conflict recognition skills, separate for 5–10 minutes and practice coping skills, and then come back together to use problem-solving and communication skills. Occasionally, it may be necessary for the therapist to actually stop the session, instruct everyone to walk out of the room, and then have them come back in 5 minutes to use the family problem-solving skills and communication. It will be necessary for the therapist to monitor the family's use of these anger/conflict management strategies at home, perhaps by having them audiotape a home discussion of a highly conflicted topic. Special attention should be paid to recurring obstacles to effective skill use. The therapist can help the family problem-solve around such obstacles and can also help the family recognize and celebrate successful attempts at anger management and conflict resolution.

Chapter Eight

School Consultation and School-Based Intervention

In this chapter, we shall discuss various methods for helping the ADHD child implement problem-solving skills in the school environment. First, we shall consider issues in consulting with the parents and school on the appropriateness of the child's current educational setting and plan. The discussion will then focus on methods a consultant can use to enhance transfer of the skills trained in clinic-based cognitive–behavioral therapy (CBT) intervention to the school setting. Finally, we shall describe different models for conducting intervention within the school environment.

Consultation Regarding the Child's School Setting and Educational Plan

As indicated in the introduction, most experts on ADHD children are in agreement that establishing an appropriate educational plan must be considered a primary treatment goal. Obviously, the mental health professional does not have final decision-making power in determining a child's educational setting or curriculum. Rather, the mental health professional can act as a consultant to the child's parents and possibly the child's school in offering an informed opinion about the extent to which the current educational setting is meeting the child's needs. Throughout the professional's contact with the child, he/she must be considering how observations and findings from evaluations and therapeutic contacts reflect on the child's educational needs.

In order to have an informed opinion, the consultant must take responsibility for obtaining the information he/she needs. In Chapter 2, we discussed the importance of obtaining information directly from the child's teacher and other relevant educational personnel. In this way, the professional does not have to depend solely upon the parents' perceptions of the teacher's viewpoint. This can be particularly important in situations that seem affected by chronic misunderstandings between the parent and teacher. By establishing direct communication with both parties, the professional can experience how easy or difficult it is to communicate with each source. For example, the consultant could find the educator to be extremely difficult to communicate with and very closed to input regarding the child or might discover the educator can be more communicative and open regarding the child with a third party than with the parents, suggesting a possible parent–teacher personality conflict. Once communication has been established, the consultant can review with the parents and educator(s) how the child's educational needs have been assessed, the methods of remediation or intervention that have been attempted, and the degree of success achieved by these past or current attempts. Such a review may indicate that current interventions are producing realistic progress or may suggest the need for greater levels of service or some other modification of the educational environment.

While different states, and even different school districts within the same state, use various labels for their more intensive educational services, most locales provide special services under two broad labels: services for children with emotional or behavioral problems and services for children with specific learning disabilities. Within each of these categories, there are different levels of service, ranging from simple monitoring of the child, to specialized support for the classroom teacher, to time spent in specialized classroom settings. Some ADHD children with more extreme behavioral difficulties and/or the coexistence of another psychiatric disorder or learning disability may qualify for such specialized services. The majority of ADHD children, however, do not qualify for special education services under current criteria.

Fortunately, there are many modifications of the mainstream classroom environment that seem to benefit the ADHD child. The reader is referred to Appendix C for a listing of possible classroom modifications and techniques. The specific methods used must be selected with regard to the individual child, not with regard to the general category of ADHD children. With that said, however, we offer some generic comments about what seems to work best with most ADHD children. ADHD children appear to achieve most successfully in classroom environments that are well-structured and predictable in terms of expectations for work and behavior, that clearly reinforce appropriate behavior and have consequences for inappropriate behavior, that break up periods of individual work time with short, focused, multisensory lesson presentations requiring the student's active involvement, and that are taught by firm but nurturant teachers who are accepting of individual differences in their students' learning styles. While all these factors are very important, we would recommend that the consultant give priority to the issues of establishing clear expectations and behavioral rewards and consequences if these features are not present in the child's current classroom environment. The reader is referred to a number of articles and books providing additional suggestions for specific classroom interventions (Barkley, 1981; Braswell, Bloomquist, & Pedersen, 1991; Kelley, 1990; O'Brien & Obrzut, 1986; Ryan et al., 1986; Zentall, 1989).

The mental health professional can offer guidance to the school regarding the particular educational modifications that would seem most likely to benefit a particular ADHD child in his/her current classroom environment. If such modifications are not possible, the therapist can then problem-solve with the parents and child about other educational options. Finding the perfect educational environment may be an impossible goal in some locations, but the therapist can work with the parents and school to maximize the impact of the available resources.

Cognitive–Behavioral School Consultation

In this section, we shall describe how one might implement school consultation that occurs in conjunction with having the child and family participate in a form of cognitive–behavioral intervention, as described in Chapters 4–7. This mode of consultation tends to focus on the child's social behavior in the school environment and general academic behavior issues such as work completion. We would like to note, however, that there is a rapidly growing literature that addresses how cognitive–behavioral approaches can be incorporated into strategies for addressing specific academic content areas such as mathematics, reading, spelling, and written language. Discussion of these academic applications is beyond the scope of this volume, but the interested reader is referred to Hughes and Hall (1989) and Ryan, et al. (1986) for more thorough discussions of the application of cognitive–behavioral methods with specific academic subjects.

We recommend that the therapist provide CBT consultation to school personnel (teachers, counselors, school psychologists, social workers, principals, etc.) to enhance long-term maintenance of treatment effects and transfer of the therapy-trained skills to the school environment. It is not necessary to inform school personnel of every skill a child has learned (e.g., anger/frustration management, perspective-taking, and family communication). Our experience suggests that helping school personnel promote the child's use of a few specific strategies or skills in the academic setting is particularly fruitful. Depending on the child's needs in the school setting, the clinician might choose to emphasize interpersonal problem-solving, anger/conflict management, or effort management. It is crucial not only to plan and model how the child can use these skills in the school but also to establish a clear method of reinforcing the child for appropriate skills use. In this way, the school's task is defined in a manner that is more likely to be accomplished.

In a similar vein, it is also wise to help the school develop plans that address problematic issues in a stepwise manner rather than taking on all problems simultaneously. For example, if the school would like to address poor work completion, the consultant could encourage the application of problem-solving strategies (or any other methods for that matter) in a subject-by-subject approach. Targeting specific subjects (or behaviors) in turn is more likely to produce success and may lead to greater sensitivity in recognizing the factors associated with difficulty in each specific area. For example, poor work completion in one subject may be the result of poor time management, while in other subject areas it may be the result of poor time management, poor task comprehension, poor motivation, and/or poorly developed prerequisite skills.

Several suggestions are offered concerning the logistics of cognitive–behaviorally oriented school consultation. Barring a crisis situation, the school consultation should not take place until after the child has completed at least some segments of therapy successfully. This means that the child should have demonstrated proficiency in the use of some skills in the sessions in clinic and at home before attempting to use these skills at school. Often, it is necessary to arrange a school conference involving the teacher, parents, and other relevant school personnel. Preferably, there should be at least one face-to-face session and some type of follow-up with the school. It may be more successful if several meetings can be arranged. If only one face-to-face meeting is feasible, it is recommended that the consultant have at least telephone follow-up contact with school personnel or help the school and parents establish some system for monitoring school intervention efforts over the long term. It may be helpful for the consultant to bring the charts the child completed through the process of therapy in order to make the trained skills more understandable for the school staff.

The process of school consultation is extremely important. The consultant should not approach school personnel as "the expert" who knows all about how to intervene with ADHD children. Understandably, this approach could cause resistance from school personnel. The consultant should simply review what the child has learned. The charts can be used to emphasize points about the program and the child's accomplishments. The consultant should then take the stance of being part of a team and work with the team in determining which procedures are most relevant for the school environment and how these procedures should be implemented in the school context.

Obviously, school personnel vary in terms of opportunity and enthusiasm for use of these types of procedures. Some teachers want to implement all program procedures and charts, while others are reluctant to use any of the methods. To help the acceptance of these procedures, the consultant should emphasize that school personnel are not directly involved in training the child to use these skills, as the child has already learned them through therapy. Rather, the role of school personnel is to assist the child in recognizing when to use his/her new skills in the school environment. To emphasize this point, we have found it helpful to include the child in all or part of the school meeting so that he/she can demonstrate the use of the problem-solving skills when addressing concerns of school personnel, such as poor work completion, misplacement of completed work, or inappropriate behaviors. Having the school staff actually observe the child's ability to use such coping methods seems to increase their willingness to foster the use of these methods in the classroom, perhaps because such a display makes it clear that they will only need to prompt, not teach, these skills.

If school personnel bring up a number of reasons why they cannot attempt to use the procedures, it can be quite impactful if the consultant approaches these issues as problems to be solved using the problem-solving steps. For example, one common objection raised by some school personnel is that attempting to use the methods with one child in a large classroom will take up too much of the teacher's time. In response to this, the consultant can acknowledge that this is a serious concern and then analyze the problems using the five-step problem-solving sequence. We have commonly found that on closer examination teachers are willing to admit that, often, having no system for coping with the child's behavior may actually take more time away from direct instruction due to the need to repeatedly deal with that child's off-task or inappropriate behaviors. The consultant should also be aware of cognitions (e.g., beliefs and expectancies) that school personnel may hold that are similar to those described for parents in Chapters 4 and 5. It may be helpful to use some of the cognitive restructuring principles outlined previously for parents with school personnel. Perhaps a subtle goal of the consultation is to move school personnel toward a problem-solving or coping orientation in relation to the child and away from a sense of hopelessness or overly negative attributions regarding the child.

School-Age Children

CBT school consultation for school-age children needs to focus on helping school personnel develop concrete methods to work with the child at school. We try to help school personnel develop methods to

TABLE 16
Methods to Prompt Child, Evaluate Plan-Making, and Reward Plan-Making in the Schools

Methods to prompt child
1. School personnel could prompt the child verbally by informing the child that "this may be a good time to use a plan." School personnel should not tell the child what a good plan is, but rather help the child discover the best plan on his/her own.
2. School personnel may prompt the child to use plans with a visual hand signal. This is sometimes preferable if a child has stated that he/she prefers not to be singled out for having to use a plan when other children in the class are not doing so. The teacher and the child could pick some type of hand signal to cue the child to use a plan.
3. School personnel could give the child a card with the five steps written on it. This card could be at the child's desk, on the bulletin board, or in some other place visibly accessible to the child as a reminder of how to use plans.
4. The child can simply tell school personnel when he/she has used a plan to solve a specific problem.

Methods to evaluate plan-making
1. School personnel and the child could complete the "Stop, Think, and Use a Plan Chart," found in Appendix B, in a manner similar to that used by the parents and the child at home.
2. School personnel may make a global evaluation hourly or at the end of the day. This could entail stating either that the child did a good job or that the child could show improvement in using plans at school. To assist in evaluation, a copy of the four-point rating scale could be posted in the classroom or on the child's desk.

Methods to reward plan-making
1. School personnel and the child could follow the same procedures used with the "Tally for Using Plans (Weekly or Daily)" chart (in Appendix B) in the manner that the parents and child do at home.
2. Many children are already being rewarded at school for appropriate behavior. The existing system could be modified to include being rewarded for making plans. For example, many children receive smiling faces and a signature from a teacher on a card if they have had a good hour. This could be modified somewhat so the child could also receive a smiling face and a signature on a card for using plans in an appropriate manner on an hourly or daily basis.
3. Tangible rewards, activities, or privileges could be awarded by the teacher on an hourly, daily, and/or weekly basis.
4. Rewards could be administered by parents, providing that teachers communicate with the parents on the child's progress in making plans at school.

prompt the child to use a plan (i.e., five-step problem-solving sequence), evaluate the child's use of the plan, and reinforce the child for using the plan. A number of alternatives for reaching these goals are presented in Table 16.

Ask school personnel to identify at least two general target problems the child routinely has at school. Point out that school staff should try to catch the child having these problems and prompt him/her to use plans to solve them. Since verbalizing elaborate versions of the problem-solving process in the classroom can be somewhat cumbersome for the child and school personnel, it is suggested that short plans be used at school. By the time the child is asked to start using plans at school, he/she is likely to be pretty adept at the short-plan procedure. If the teacher prompts the child to use a plan and the child pauses and then demonstrates altered behavior, then the child should receive credit for using a plan.

A final and very important point to emphasize with school personnel is that they will need to alter their interaction style with the child. Oftentimes school personnel and other adults dealing with the child respond to the problem behavior of the child by setting limits and providing consequences for the child. To some extent, that would change using these procedures. The teachers would not respond automatically with limits or consequences. Rather, the teacher would need to prompt the child to use a plan. If the child exhibited positive behavior change, then he/she should not receive any limits or consequences. If the child's behavior did not improve, then the teacher could set limits and consequences. Thus, the sequence would be: (1) child problem behavior observed, (2) prompt child to use a plan, and (3) consequence of limits administered to child if behavior did not improve.

Adolescents

Many of the comments discussed above for school-age children are relevant to working with adolescents; however, we view the practice of CBT-oriented school consultation with adolescents as being more informal than the procedures used with school-age children. A major goal of the CBT school consultation component with adolescents is to familiarize school personnel with problem-solving procedures that adolescents have learned through therapy. The consultant may find it beneficial to provide school personnel with the "Problem-Solving Skills" chart found in Appendix B as a way of familiarizing them with the skills to which the adolescent has been exposed. The consultant should explain the meaning and use of traditional, means–end, and decision-making problem-solving skills.

The consultant can then encourage school personnel to develop methods and ways of interacting with the adolescent to accommodate his/her use of these new problem-solving skills at school. As with school-age children, school personnel are encouraged to focus less on limits and consequences with the adolescent and more on allowing the adolescent to be responsible for his/her own problems. The school personnel can help the adolescent discover solutions to problems. For example, if the adolescent hasn't completed his/her homework, the teacher may want to encourage the student to figure out what to do about this situation (traditional problem-solving). If an adolescent says he/she wants to obtain improved grades, the teacher may encourage the adolescent to figure out how he/she intends to accomplish this goal (means–end problem-solving). If the teen is trying to make a decision, such as whether or not to join the football team, given a heavy class schedule, the teacher may want to encourage the student to think about the pros and cons of each alternative (decision-making problem-solving).

The consultant should help school personnel understand that, by changing their interaction styles and facilitating adolescents' use of problem-solving, this will ultimately help the adolescent internalize these procedures. This is not to suggest that adolescents should be given free rein and always be given second chances. If an adolescent is taking advantage of this system, then naturally the school personnel would want to provide appropriate limits or consequences for that student.

Monitoring Consultation

The consultation is complete once school personnel, parents, and the consultant agree that some type of strategy has been created to facilitate plan use by the child at school. As part of any strategy, it is important to have a mechanism for monitoring its success. This could take the form of the teacher sending notes or plan forms home for the parent's signature or some other mode of regular communication among teachers, parents, and the child. Planning a follow-up meeting to review evidence of the success or failure of the agreed-upon strategy is extremely important. The consultant should be available to school personnel or the parents if any problems emerge or if they have any questions when attempting to implement these strategies.

Models for School-Based Interventions

In addition to implementing traditional clinic-based treatment, we have had the opportunity to conduct cognitive–behavioral interventions with

ADHD children in the elementary school environment. Before discussing different models for school-based intervention, it is relevant to note that such interventions offer several potential advantages and disadvantages relative to clinic-based services.

The chief advantage of school-based intervention is that the training environment is the same as one of the major target environments for skills use. With school personnel serving as trainers, the mere presence of these individuals can cue the child to use his/her new coping skills. Fellow group members can also become stimuli that aid the generalization of problem-solving skills from group therapy to the classroom, lunchroom, and playground. Given their greater involvement with school-based treatment, school staff may also be more likely to prompt skill use than is the case when they are asked to do so by an outside consultant.

Another advantage concerns the cost of intervention. Generally speaking, school-based services are provided without direct cost to the child's family. Thus, limited finances and/or inadequate insurance coverage do not prevent a child from receiving needed services. The absence of direct cost to the family also makes it easier to conduct interventions of greater length and breadth of content. As illustrated in the intervention manual in Chapter 9, when conducting clinic-based treatment, we employ a 14-session core program that addresses general problem-solving, interpersonal problem-solving, anger/frustration management, and behavioral social skills. This program length represents a compromise between the content we would like to cover and the pragmatic limitations of time and money that most families face. With school-based interventions, there are still limitations in how much parental involvement can be expected, but it is certainly possible to have more than 14 contacts with the child. For example, the school-based application includes content for 18 child sessions. The 18-session program has the same content as the 14-session program, but also provides additional training in management of poor effort and negative thoughts and feelings.

Considering the disadvantages of school-based programs, if a child is referred to an intervention program at the recommendation of school staff rather than his/her parents, the parents may be less motivated to work toward change and harder to involve in the treatment process. Even if the parents do become involved, they may feel uncomfortable disclosing relevant but sensitive family information to a therapist who is perceived as an agent of the school.

In light of these pros and cons, one might hypothesize that an ADHD child whose primary difficulties are at school would be well-served by a school-based program. A child whose behavior is problematic in many environments or who has obvious family difficulties would require clinic-based intervention in addition to appropriate school services.

With these general considerations in mind, we shall describe three models of school-based treatment that vary in terms of the role of various school personnel and the number of treatment components involved. Our experience has been in the implementation of these models in elementary, rather than secondary, school settings. As we have previously discussed, we recommend that this type of intervention be used with children who have attained a mental age of 8 years. Readers interested in the use of cognitive–behavioral interventions in junior high and high school settings are referred to the work of Feindler and Ecton (1986) and Sarason and Sarason (1981).

Focused School-Based Intervention

One method of program intervention involves having the school psychologist, counselor, or social worker conduct child groups and meet with teachers to help them learn to prompt and reinforce the children's use of newly trained skills in the classroom. Felton, Kia, Swanson, and Bloomquist (1987) developed such a program for use with behavior-disordered students. The program content emphasized the use of self-instruction and problem-solving skills to cope with interpersonal difficulties. Children were seen in groups of six to eight for a total of eight 60-minute sessions. Teachers for the children receiving treatment participated in four 45- to 60-minute inservice/supervision sessions. Felton et al. (1988) found the treated group improved in cognitive problem-solving abilities and perceptions of self-control relative to a waiting list control group, but teacher ratings of behavior and number of referrals to a "behavior room" did not improve as a result of intervention. The authors concluded that the intervention may have been too brief to produce significant change in the children's classroom behavior.

Classroom-Based Intervention

In certain educational settings, such as resource rooms or self-contained classrooms, it may be possible to have the teacher implement a cognitive–behavioral group program in the classroom. Braswell (1988) developed a teacher-delivered program for children exhibiting learning, attentional and behavioral problems. Teachers trained children in self-monitoring, problem-solving/self-instruction, and management of anger/frustration with both interpersonal and academic difficulties. The curriculum included twenty-four 45- to 60-minute classroom sessions that were conducted over a 12-week period. Teachers received 12 hours of initial training, involving didactic presentations, modeling, and role-playing, and participated in weekly supervision for the duration of the intervention period. Braswell and August (1989) conducted behavioral observations indicating that the teachers did reliably implement key elements of the program content. Teachers rated children participating in the program as exhibiting improved behavior. Interestingly, children in the experimental classrooms did not rate themselves as improved on several self-report measures of mood and self-esteem, but children in the control classrooms reported both decreases in self-esteem and increases in depressive symptomatology over the course of the intervention and follow-up periods. Braswell and August (1989) hypothesized that some element of the intervention may have helped the children in the experimental group maintain their initially positive self-perspectives, even when challenged by the demands of the school year.

Comprehensive School-Based Intervention

With adequate personnel, it is possible for school staff to intervene with the home as well as school environment. Bloomquist and Braswell (1989) developed a school-based intervention for 8- to 12-year-old ADHD children with child, teacher, and parent components. The elements of this intervention are detailed in the manual presented in Chapter 9. The major content areas for the children include training skills for problem-solving/self-instruction and coping with anger/frustration, poor effort, and negative self-talk. Separately, parents and teachers receive information about ADHD as well as training in behavioral and cognitive–behavioral child management skills. Parents and teachers are also asked to consider their thoughts and beliefs about these children so that maladaptive cognitions can be recognized and transformed into more adaptive ways of thinking. Importantly, the intervention is conducted on a school-wide basis. *All* children are exposed to elements of the CBT program in the classroom; however, only the identified children received the child group and parent training components. In this way, the entire school environment can be prepared to accommodate the child without children being singled out in the classroom. Bloomquist et al. (in press) evaluated the implementation of such a program and the results are detailed in Chapter 3. This program is also the current subject of an extensive school-based research program designed to explore the long-term impact of such intervention efforts.

Conclusion

Whether the clinician's school contact involves offering advice about the appropriateness of the child's current education plan, helping teachers prompt and reinforce therapy-trained skills, or conducting an in-school training program, we hope we have made it clear that the clinician has an obligation to contact the child's school staff and do what is necessary to help the school environment become as responsive as possible to the needs of the particular child. Obviously, parents must grant permission for such contact to occur. If parents are reluctant to allow the clinician to communicate with the school, while abiding by the parents' wishes, the clinician should try to educate the parents regarding the value of a comprehensive, team approach for addressing their child's difficulties.

Chapter Nine

Cognitive–Behavioral Intervention for School-Age Children: Treatment Manual

This manual is designed for the purpose of conducting cognitive–behavioral therapy with school-age children (ages 8–12 years) who have ADHD with or without Conduct Disorder (CD). Although not intended for adolescents, parts of the manual can be adapted for use with 13- to 17-year-old clients. The manual contains separate child, parent/family, and school components. These components can be applied working from either a school or clinic setting. Much of the content of this treatment manual has been evaluated in two studies cited in Chapter 3 (Bloomquist et al., 1991, in press). It is important to note, however, that the current form of the manual is the product of revisions based on our previous research studies and clinical experience. Thus, the particular combination of components in this manual is only now undergoing empirical testing.

The outpatient clinic model of program delivery is summarized in Table 17. This model consists of child and parent/family training components and individualized school consultation. The intervention occurs over 14 weeks. Children are seen in groups and are trained in basic problem-solving and self-instruction skills and the application of problem-solving and self-instruction skills to interpersonal problems, anger management, and behavioral social skills. Parents receive support and education through parent groups. They also receive training in the modification of any dysfunctional thoughts and attitudes and in the application of cognitive–behavioral child management and behavioral child management skills. Three family sessions are conducted to further individualize the methods for each family situation. School consultation

TABLE 17
Clinic Model of Cognitive–Behavioral Therapy for ADHD School-Age Children

Week	Child component	Parent component	Family component
1	Introduction		
2	Problem Recognition I (Eye Contact)		
3	Problem Recognition II (Eye Contact)	Introduction	
4	Alternatives, Solutions, and Consequential Thinking (Expressing Feelings Appropriately)	Group Process/Support	
5	Evaluating Outcomes and Using Backup Plans (Expressing Feelings Appropriately)	Examine Parent Cognitions and Behaviors	
6	Interpersonal Problem-Solving I (Sharing/Cooperation)	Child-Focused CBT I	
7	Interpersonal Problem-Solving II (Sharing/Cooperation)		
8			Child-Focused CBT at Home
9	Anger/Frustration Management I (Ignoring)	Collaborative CBT I	
10	Anger/Frustration Management II (Ignoring)	Collaborative CBT II	
11			Collaborative CBT at Home
12	Program Review I	Behavioral Child Management I	
13	Program Review II	Behavioral Child Management II and Program Review	
14			Program Review

TABLE 18
School Model of Cognitive–Behavioral Therapy for ADHD School-Age Children

Week	Child component	Parent component	Teacher component
1	Introduction		
2	Problem Recognition I (Eye Contact)	Introduction	Introduction
3	Problem Recognition II (Eye Contact)		
4	Alternatives, Solutions, and Consequential Thinking (Expressing Feelings Appropriately)	Group Process/Support (Examine Parents' Expectations for Program)	Group Process/ Support (Examine Teachers' Expectations for Program)
5	Evaluating Outcomes and Using Backup Plans (Expressing Feelings Appropriately)		
6	Review	Examine Parent Cognitions and Behaviors	Examine Teacher Cognitions and Behaviors
7	Interpersonal Problem-Solving I (Sharing/ Cooperation)		
8	Interpersonal Problem-Solving II (Sharing/ Cooperation)	Child-Focused CBT I	Child-Focused CBT I
9	Anger/Frustration Management I (Ignoring)		
10	Anger/Frustration Management II (Ignoring)	Child-Focused CBT II	Child-Focused CBT II
11	Anger/Frustration Management III (Assertiveness)		
12	Review	Collaborative CBT I	Collaborative CBT I
13	Poor Effort Management I		
14	Poor Effort Management II	Collaborative CBT II	Collaborative CBT II
15	Negative Thoughts and Feelings Management I		
16	Negative Thoughts and Feelings Management II	Behavioral Child Management I	Behavioral Child Management I
17	Program Review I		
18	Program Review II	Behavioral Child Management II and Program Review	Behavioral Child Management II and Program Review

typically occurs after the family has completed the program, and the nature of this consultation varies with each child's needs and school situation.

The school model of cognitive–behavioral therapy (CBT) is summarized in Table 18. This model consists of child, parent, and teacher components. The intervention is delivered at school over 18 weeks. The child component is similar to that conducted in the clinic setting but also includes additional sessions focused on management of poor effort and negative thoughts and feelings. The procedures for training management of negative thoughts and feelings have yet to receive empirical investigation by our research team, so these methods must be considered highly experimental. The parent component is essentially the same as that delivered in the clinic, although there are typically no family therapy sessions. In our experience, we have found it difficult to have the staff necessary to deliver family therapy sessions in the schools, but if a particular school did have that capability, then the family therapy sessions could be integrated into the school-based model. Teachers are also heavily involved in the school-based model, learning information and skills similar to those learned by the parents.

The manual presents the child, parent/family, and school components separately. It is up to the practitioner to select the sessions that he/she believes to be useful for his/her particular setting. But while we encourage clinicians to tailor the content to the needs and constraints of their settings, we strongly urge all consumers of this material to make efforts to have their selected content address child, parent/family, and school aspects of the ADHD child's treatment needs.

Child Component

Procedural Overview

Children receive their training in groups. The group format allows children to learn and practice the concepts being learned in a peer context. Theoretically, this will increase the probability of skills generalization by increasing the similarity between the training and target environments. The child groups are limited to six to eight children. We strongly recommend that two therapists be used for the groups because the therapists will be required to do many simultaneous activities, including maintaining some degree of order in a very active group. We have structured the group sessions to last 90 minutes. The sessions could be shortened, but additional weeks would be necessary to cover all of the content.

It is important to follow the sessions in the sequence listed because the content of each session builds on the content of previous sessions. The therapists need to periodically assess whether children are acquiring initially presented skills before moving on to subsequently presented skills. It may be necessary to spend an extra session on a particular skill area.

The group process is extremely important in helping the children learn the skills. While the groups are in progress, many problems typically emerge related to interpersonal problems, compliance, staying on-task, etc. These problems should be used as training tasks for using plans (i.e., five-step self-instruction strategy) in the group. The therapist can prompt the children to use plans and reward them for correct plan use. For example, if a therapist notices one child is repeatedly kicking the chair of another child, the therapist might comment to the child, "This may be a good time to use a plan." The child doing the kicking is given an opportunity to use a plan. The therapist helps the child through the problem-solving process, as needed. As we shall be discussing in greater detail, the child is given points for using the plan. Every task the group faces together, such as deciding on group rules or who checks in first, can be presented as a problem for the group to use a plan. In other words, plans can be used for the individual child to solve a problem or for the group as a whole. The therapists are continuously moving back and forth between the formal content of the sessions and the process of addressing problems in the group. Whenever possible, the therapists should help children discover solutions to their own problems. The therapists should avoid telling children what to do to solve problems. It may be helpful to review Chapter 5 and see examples of how to work with group process.

In addition to training children in cognitive problem-solving, a few specific behavioral social skills are addressed in the course of treatment. Based on our clinical experiences with ADHD children, we have selected the following skills as training targets: maintaining appropriate eye contact, sharing, ignoring, expressing feelings appropriately, and responding assertively. Specific training activities are used to train children in these behavioral skills.

The therapists need to establish a routine group format for conducting each session. We have identified six stages for the average group, including:

1. *Check-In* (10 minutes). Inquire how each child's week has gone and review homework assignments.

2. *Set Social Behavior Goals* (10 minutes). After check-in, the therapists should designate the social behavior goal to work on for the session. In earlier sessions, the behaviors to work on are generated by the therapists (e.g., eye contact, expressing feelings, sharing/cooperation, ignoring, assertiveness). In later sessions, the children can generate their own ideas about other behaviors. The therapists' task is to describe and model the behaviors. The children will then practice the behaviors and receive points for the remainder of group when they emit them.

3. *Introduce New Skill(s)* (45 minutes). The therapist presents each skill through didactic instruction, modeling, and role-play practice. Although skills are introduced each session, adequate time must be allowed for using problem-solving methods to address ongoing group interactions.

4. *Relaxation* (5 minutes). Simple muscle tension relaxation exercises are used at the end of each group.

5. *Review and Feedback* (10 minutes). Each child reviews the skills learned in group, gives feedback about the behavior of other children, and discusses whether or not he/she met the social behavior goal during the group.

6. *Kid for the Day and Activity* (10 minutes). At the end of each group, points are totaled. The child with the most points is Kid for the Day and gets to select the free play activity for that day. The last 5–10 minutes of the group are spent in this activity.

The use of behavioral contingencies is essential to running a group with six to eight ADHD children. One therapist is in charge of maintaining the contingency management system throughout the entire group. This is a very difficult, yet extremely important function in the group. We recommend using the "Group Points" chart found in Appendix B. One group therapist will give points to each child in the group when he/she uses a plan and for specific, appropriate behaviors (including emitting the social behavior goal for that session). Whenever a child uses a plan, the group therapist will note whose idea it was to use the plan (child or other) and administer points. If the child uses a plan when prompted by a therapist, he/she receives one point. If he/she uses a plan without being reminded, he/she receives two points. The group therapist also keeps track of other behaviors on the chart. For example, the group therapist gives one point every time a child is on-task, talks appropriately, listens appropriately, displays targeted social behaviors, etc. Any behavior the therapist wants to strengthen can be reinforced. If a child is not talking very much, but then does begin to speak, the therapist can tell the child, "You get a point for talking—keep up the good work!" The therapist administering the points can keep track of each child and shape specific behaviors accordingly. The children can lose one point for mild verbal and physical aggression, disruptive behavior, or oppositional behavior. The group therapist first asks the child to use a plan, but if he/she does not comply, then points are taken away. The children can receive a "strike" if they engage in extremely disruptive or aggressive behavior. If a child acquires three strikes, he/she is removed from the group and, in the clinic model, must meet with his/her parents to problem-solve about the difficult behavior and make a plan for what he/she must do to better manage himself/herself in group. In the school model, after three strikes, the child must return to the classroom. At the end of group, the therapist totals up the points for all of the children. The child who has the most points is designated as the Kid for the Day. The Kid for the Day then gets to choose the activity that all of the group members will engage in for the last 5–10 minutes of group. We have found it helpful to offer three or four choices of activities each week and vary the choices across different weeks so the children do not become bored with a specific activity.

As discussed in Chapter 6, the group therapist should act as a facilitator, not as a controller, in the group. When inappropriate behavior occurs, instead of responding with, "Stop that," "Don't do that," etc., the therapist will respond with, "I bet you could use a plan to solve that problem," or ask the children if they see an opportunity for someone to use a plan. The goal is to create an environment that maximizes the children's opportunities to use plans to solve their own problems. The therapists must also be open to letting the children problem-solve about aspects of group or the contingency system that they find troubling. If a child raises a specific objection, like "He's always Kid for the Day. That's not fair!" the therapist labels this situation as a problem to be solved and encourages the children to create a plan to address their concerns.

Introduction
Clinic Model—Week 1; School Model—Week 1

Objectives

1. Introduce the children to the program.
2. Establish group rules and introduce contingencies.
3. Begin training in problem-solving and self-instruction methods.
4. Begin instruction in the use of simple relaxation techniques.

Procedures

1. *Introduce the Program.* The leader can use a narrative, such as the following, to introduce the program:

> "Over the next few weeks, we shall be spending about 2 hours each week learning some special ways you can talk yourself through difficult situations, such as academic, school, and people problems. Do any of you ever talk to yourself or know someone who talks to himself/herself?"

The leader can then encourage the children to provide examples and, in addition, share personal examples of situations in which he/she has used self-talk. The leader's examples should include situations in which self-talk was used to problem-solve or cope with a new and/or difficult situation, such as learning to drive a car, learning a new dance step, learning to fix a household appliance, etc. It is preferable, in this introductory phase, to refrain from using academic examples unless these are presented by the children. Once a number of examples have been presented, the leader can state:

> "So . . . Does talking to yourself mean you're crazy or is it always a bad thing to do? . . . Of course not! In a moment, I'm going to teach you a special way we shall use to talk ourselves through a problem and we'll practice using it, but before we do that, I wanted to get you thinking about another thing."

2. *Establish Group Rules.* The leader should now help the group establish their rules or guidelines. The leader can make this transition by a statement such as the following:

> "We need some special rules for what we can do and cannot do during our group. Let's come up with some group guidelines that will help us get along well. What do you think would be good rules or guidelines?"

The leader can now list the suggestions that the children provide on the board. If a child offers a rule that is formulated in negative wording, such as "No hitting," the instructor can accept this response, but also ask the child to think of a positive way to say what kids should be doing, such as "Use words to tell us if you are mad," or "Respect other people's space." It is recommended that the therapist write down the group's do's and don't's on a large sheet of posterboard that can be kept in clear view of the group at all times. It is likely that you will need to add guidelines that relate to confidentiality, such as "What's said in group stays in group," or "No gossiping outside of group about other people's problems."

3. *Explain Contingencies.* The therapists need to explain the group contingencies early in the initial group. Explain that the "Group Points" chart (see Appendix B) is completed by one of the therapists throughout each group for each child. Explain the chart in great detail so that the children understand they will earn points for following the rules, displaying targeted social skills, and problem-solving. Tell the group about the possibility of losing points for mild disruptive behavior and for acquiring strikes when they engage in extremely disruptive or aggressive behavior. Explain that if the child acquires three strikes, he/she is removed from the group and must return to his/her classroom or, if meeting in a clinical setting, he/she must leave group briefly to problem-solve with his/her parents about how to be more appropriate in group.

Explain to the children that, at the end of each group, the points will be totaled and the group member having the largest number of points will be designated the Kid for the Day. The Kid for the Day has earned the privilege of selecting the activity that the group will engage in for the final 5–10 minutes of the session.

4. *Problem-Solving and Self-Instruction Training.* The group leader is now ready to provide more specific training in the use of problem-solving and self-instruction methods. He/she could say something like:

> "Now we're ready to go back to what I explained at the beginning of our group. I have a special way of talking myself through tough situations and I want to share it with you. As I talk about the things I say to myself, I'm going to write them down on this sheet of posterboard. We'll call these steps the plan. As I talk about the things I say to myself and what they mean, I want you to think about the words you would use if you were going to try to say the same thing to yourself. We can use different words that mean the same thing and the words you might like to use may be different from the ones I pick. You can follow along with the sheet of paper I gave each of you. As we talk about each statement or step, I'm going to ask you to write things down on your plan sheet."

The therapist then leads the children through an explanation of the following five-step process:

1. Stop! What is the problem?
2. What are some plans?
3. What is the best plan?
4. Do the plan.
5. Did the plan work?

The following "dialogue" is offered as an example:

> "First, can we solve a problem if we don't know what it is? . . . Of course
> not, so the first thing I tell myself to do is to stop and figure out what
> the problem is. So I'm going to write: STOP! WHAT IS THE PROBLEM?"

The leader can then explain that after he/she has figured out what the
problem is, he/she is ready for the next step: WHAT ARE SOME PLANS? As
the therapist writes this down, he/she can explain what is meant by the
word "plans" and ask the children why it is a good idea to come up with
more than one plan. . . . After the process has been completed for all five
steps, ask the children to say the steps out loud.

   5. *Practice in Problem-Solving and Self-Instructions.* The therapist now
provides an example of how the five steps can be used to solve simple
daily dilemmas that *don't* involve interpersonal or emotionally laden
conflicts, such as not having enough desks in the classroom, not having
the materials needed to do a science project, or having a light bulb burn
out. Work through the steps as a group, writing down the group definition of the problem and the various alternatives on the blackboard. Be
sure negative as well as positive alternatives are included, as well as
alternatives that basically reflect inaction or passivity. At this stage, it is
preferable to work through a small number of problem situations in an
exhaustive manner, rather than to attempt to work through many problems in a more superficial manner.

   6. *Relaxation.* The therapists have the children meet in a small circle
on the floor. One therapist then asks if any of the children know some
simple ways to help their bodies relax. If the children offer any appropriate suggestions, use them. If not, provide the children with a brief
explanation of tension/release type exercises. This can be accomplished
by having the children imagine that they are robots and by having them
make their bodies stiff for a period of 5–10 seconds. Then have them
imagine that they are rag dolls and have them make their limbs and neck
floppy and relaxed. Repeat the tension/release sequence two or three
times. Once the children appear to be somewhat relaxed, let them know
you want them to help you come up with a signal you can give the group
(e.g., a hand signal or verbal prompt), or the group members can give
themselves, when they are becoming too tense and agitated. Let them
know they can earn points by helping themselves relax whenever the
relaxation signal is given. Finally, use the relaxation time to ask them
what they thought about the group. Encourage them to share specifics
about what they liked and disliked.

   7. *Designate Kid for the Day and Activity.* One of the therapists will total
the points for each child and indicate which child has earned the honor
of "Kid for the Day." That child can then select a group activity that

occurs for the last 10 minutes of the session. Group activities may include board games, art activities, or more physical games, such as tag or balloon volleyball. When possible, we find it helpful for the children to play a game in small teams, so they can continue to practice prosocial behaviors. Some groups are very eager to play games such as Twenty Questions, I Spy, or Sports Trivia. We have the group divide into two teams and reinforce cooperative and reflective behavior by explaining that each team must agree on the questions or answers to be offered, and blurted-out comments count against the team. After the group activity, the group leaders should remind the children to use plans at home and school between group sessions.

Problem Recognition I
Clinic Model—Week 2; School Model—Week 2

Objectives

1. Help children recognize external cues regarding the existence of a problem.
2. Model and reinforce appropriate eye contact.

Procedures

1. *Check-In.* Children are told that they will have an opportunity to check in about activities occurring over the past week, with special emphasis on opportunities in which they could have used a plan or did, in fact, use a plan. Children are given points for each example that indicates they used plans during the week. In some groups, it may be necessary to limit the number of examples each child can describe so that the check-in does not use up all the group time. In other groups, there may not be a concern about too many examples! Some children may make up their plans when they come to group, and it will be obvious to the therapists. We generally let the children do this because it allows them to think about how they may have applied the plans during the week. However, if a child is a habitual plan make-up artist, then we may talk to the child after the group and ask him/her to start using real plans on his/her own during the week.

2. *Set Social Behavior Goal.* Explain that each week the entire group will also be working on a common social behavior goal and that children can earn points for exhibiting the targeted behavior. Ask the children if any of them know what eye contact means. Elaborate on the children's explanations and model both appropriate and inappropriate eye contact. Have each child give an example of appropriate eye contact.

Be sure each child is awarded a point for an appropriate response. Then explain that at certain points during the group, the leaders will give points to all group members maintaining appropriate eye contact.

3. *Review Problem-Solving and Self-Instructions.* To review the steps learned in Session 1, turn the plan poster prepared in Session 1 away from the children and ask them, "What is the first thing we need to do to solve a problem?" When a child responds with the first step or a close approximation, ask another child why it is important to do that step first. If no one is able to state the first step or explain why it is important to do it first, ask the group a forced choice question, such as "Can we solve a problem if we are rushing around, or do we need to stop and think?" Then ask, "Can we solve a problem if we don't know what it is?" Through this highly structured questioning, you can lead them to discover the first step. Repeat this process for each of the remaining steps. At first, try more general questioning to elicit responses, but if the children cannot respond, then formulate more structured versions of the questions.

4. *Explain the Importance of Problem Recognition.* Explain that the group will be learning more about the different parts of the problem-solving process. Let them know that over the next three sessions the group will be spending time thinking about how a person even recognizes that a problem, dilemma, or difficulty exists. Emphasize to the children that this component may be the most important element of any type of problem-solving because if a person fails to even recognize that a problem exists, there isn't much that he/she can do about it. If the children seem to have some understanding of what the term "problem recognition" means, then you may wish to ask them about what they think the consequences would be for failing to recognize different types of problems or difficulties that arise. You may wish to use a non-people-oriented example to get across this point. For example, ask the group what would happen if a person failed to notice that the gas gauge on his/her car was pointing at empty. Ask the children what would happen if a person who was driving a car did not know what a red light or a stop sign meant.

Then ask the group what kinds of problems can happen if you fail to correctly read interpersonal cues or signals. For example, maybe you have a friend that you can tease on some days and he/she thinks it is funny, but if you tease him/her on other days or at other times, he/she gets mad. Try to elicit other examples of the consequences of failing to read interpersonal cues. If this task is too hard for the group, do not try to force the discussion. The leader can make attempts to discuss this concept later in the session when the children are role-playing.

5. *Discussion of External Signals.* Tell the children that you want to

discuss signals that come from our external environment and that tell us that a problem might be present. Ask the children what a signal is. Then have all the children in the group attempt to give you examples of various types of signals that we receive from our external environment. After the children have given you easily recognizable signals, such as stoplights and stop signs, you can encourage them to think about very real, but slightly more subtle, signals that we take for granted, such as: "What does it mean or what is it telling us when we see a big, dark thundercloud coming our way? . . . What would happen if we didn't recognize this signal?" Ask the children to give other examples of signals and what they mean. The group leader should write these down on the board.

6. *Discussion of Signals from People.* Explain to the children that other people are an important part of our external environment and that people are constantly sending us signals. Tell them that you are going to have them think about and show each other some different types of signals that we send each other. Start with asking the children to think about a *facial expression* that shows other people how they are feeling. Have the children go around the room displaying an expression of their choice and have the other children guess what this expression is communicating. If the children seem reluctant to engage in this task, you might ask them to display what their teachers' or a parents' faces look like when they are getting angry. This example usually gets children readily involved in this task.

After all the children have presented one or two examples of facial expressions, then ask them to think about the cues we get just from seeing someone else's *body posture* or stance. Give them a moment to think about this and then have them each model for the other children an example of a body stance or posture that communicates a relatively clear meaning. Again, have the other children guess what meaning is being communicated.

After the children have discussed body posture, present the concept that we can communicate just with our *tone of voice*. Model examples of different tones of voice that you frequently use and ask the children to identify the different meanings that are inherent in these different tones of voice. Then have each of them develop an example and model their examples for the group, with the group guessing the meaning or implications of each particular tone of voice.

Finally, summarize for the group that not only do humans send each other cues through facial expressions, body posture, and tone of voice, we have *words* with specific meanings to send each other messages. Ask the children to think of examples of words that we use with each other that are meant to be specific signals, such as: "Stop!" or "Don't touch!" or "Fire!" Ask the children for examples of words they hear from adults and other children and what they mean in terms of problem recognition.

Ask the children to review and give examples of signals from people. Try to help them include examples that represent facial expressions, posture, tone of voice, and words. The group leader should write these examples on the board.

7. *Discussion of Internal Signals.* If the group easily grasps the notion of external environmental and interpersonal cues and there is time remaining in group, the leaders can introduce the concept of internal cues as presented in the next session.

8. *Relaxation.*

9. *Review and Feedback.* Ask the children to give each other feedback about their behavior for the session. Focus this discussion on both positive and negative behaviors children observed in each other. Ask the group members to give each other feedback about whether or not they met the social behavior goal set at the beginning of the group. Although negative feedback is permitted, the group leaders must help the children learn to express this in constructive rather than destructive ways.

10. *Kid for the Day and Activity.*

Problem Recognition II
Clinic Model—Week 3; School Model—Week 3

Objectives

1. Help children recognize internal cues regarding the existence of a problem.

2. Practice problem recognition skills.

3. Model and reinforce appropriate eye contact.

Procedures

1. *Check-In.*

2. *Set Social Behavior Goal.* Remind children that they will continue to receive reinforcement for displaying appropriate eye contact. If the group struggled with this behavior in the last session, have all group members model examples of appropriate eye contact. If the children were able to display good eye contact in the previous session, then it is not necessary to engage them in this additional modeling.

3. *Discussion of Internal Signals.* Review notion of external cues and then explain to the children that signals can also come from within us and these are known as internal signals. For example, ask the children what it means when their stomach growls—it means they are hungry.

Ask the children what it means if their nose is running and they feel like they are aching all over—it means they probably have a cold. Explain to the children that we will be talking about three different types of internal signals. These three types of signals are thought, feeling, and body signals. *Thought* signals are those signals that come from our internal thoughts. Ask the children what the thought "I hate math" means in terms of a problem. Ask the children to generate as many thought signals that may be representative of different types of problems as they can. The therapist should write down these thought signals on the board or on a posterboard.

The discussion centers next around *feeling* signals. Spend some time discussing what different types of feelings are. It may be helpful to have a feelings chart available in the group to facilitate this discussion. The therapist should discuss with the children what some of the basic feelings are, such as anger, sadness, happiness, and fright. The therapist may also want to lead the children to discuss a variety of feelings other than those. Next ask the children to generate as many feelings as they can and what they might signal. For example, if someone feels angry, what type of problems might be associated with this feeling?

Next discuss *body* signals. Explain to the children that there are a variety of signals coming from our bodies, such as tense muscles, accelerated heart rate, sweating, or a "queasy feeling in your stomach." Ask the group to generate as many examples of body signals as they can and ask them what types of problems might be associated with these different types of body signals. The therapist should write down their examples on the board.

4. *Problem Recognition Charades.* For this exercise, the children are asked to generate examples of different types of problems that can occur at home, at school, and with friends. The therapist writes down the children's examples on separate slips of paper. Explain to the children that they will work together to act out the problems they draw from a container. The children should be instructed to demonstrate overt behaviors and, if appropriate, say their thoughts out loud. The other children are to recognize the problem being acted out. Once they identify the problem, they should discuss how they recognized it and what the signals were that told them what kind of problem it was. To begin, the therapists should act out the first problem to model how to do the role-plays. The therapists may wish to determine some random method of assigning role-playing partners so that the children have an opportunity to interact with all other group members. Be sure all group members have an opportunity to participate in several role-plays. The reader is referred to Chapter 6 for a specific example of the use of problem recognition charades.

5. *Relaxation.*
6. *Review and Feedback.*
7. *Kid for the Day and Activity.*

Alternatives, Solutions, and Consequential Thinking
Clinic Model—Week 4; School Model—Week 4

Objectives

1. Introduce the concept of alternative solution generation or brainstorming.
2. Introduce the concept of consequential thinking.
3. Model and reinforce appropriate expression of feelings.

Procedures

The children have now begun to understand the concept of signals as part of problem recognition. From this point on, when children use plans in the group, they should be asked periodically to identify the signal that told them that they had a problem. In other words, the children will be required to state the signal and then go through the five-step self-instruction process to receive points. By repeating this process for the remaining sessions, the children will solidify their understanding and use of problem recognition.

1. *Check-In.*
2. *Set Social Behavior Goal.* Explain that today the whole group will be working on how to express feelings appropriately. Ask the group if any of them have seen someone else show their feelings in a way that made the situation even worse. If the group is unable to think of examples, the therapist could model an example of a child having a tantrum or reacting in some other inappropriate manner. Be sure the example makes it clear that the inappropriate expression of feelings did not help the child achieve what he/she wanted.

Then ask the group what they think would have been a more appropriate way to express the feelings modeled in that example. The therapist can explain and model the specific use of "I statements" when expressing feelings, encouraging the group to say "I feel _____ when you _____" versus "You made me _____." It may be helpful to prepare a large sign that states "I feel _____ when you _____," and have the group refer to this sign when they are unsure of how to express themselves. Emphasize that feelings are not bad; in fact, they are very important signals to ourselves and others. Rather, it is how we express or show the feelings that can help us or get us into trouble. Then have every group member model the appropriate verbal expression of angry feelings using an example such as what you could say if someone else has just cut in line in front of you. Have each child use an "I statement" but otherwise let them individualize their responses.

Tell the children that they will receive points for the appropriate expression of feelings during group role-plays, discussions, and problem-solving about group dilemmas. Obviously, this is a challenging skill for children and adults, so the group leaders will need to reinforce successive approximations of the ideal forms of expression of feelings.

3. *Generating Alternatives.* Introduce the concept of alternative solution generation. Ask the children if they have noticed, when you have had them engage in the problem-solving process, what you have them do at Step 2. Guide them in recognizing that you have already been asking them to practice generating a number of choices, solutions, or alternatives for any given problem situation. Explain the value of being able to think of more than one solution for a given problem situation.

Explain to them that being able to think of more than one solution is an important skill for people in business, not just for children who are trying to solve problems. Tell them that when business people do this, they often talk about it as brainstorming. Describe how one must be willing to have an open mind and be creative about the ideas he/she comes up with in order to do successful brainstorming. In addition, while brainstorming, it is important to refrain from judging the quality of any particular choice. Explain that you will be describing some ways to evaluate the quality of a particular choice in a moment, but that during brainstorming or the phase of generating alternatives, it is important to not be judgmental with yourself or with others.

4. *Brainstorming Exercise.* In order to engage the children in alternative generation, it is often helpful to start with an absurd or silly problem. For example, you might ask them how someone could turn rocks into gold or how you can make a cat fly. In other words, you want to use an example that will "tickle their fancy" and help them be more creative in the choices they generate. After they have completed this fanciful example, you might have them engage in the same process with a more practical question, such as, "What would be some of the different ways you could arrange the chairs in the group room or classroom?" The therapist should write down the alternatives generated.

5. *Thinking of Consequences.* After the children seem to understand the process of brainstorming, you can then explain that once you have been able to generate a number of choices, it is then valuable to look at the consequences of each choice. Let them know that each choice is likely to have many consequences and that consequences can be both behavioral and emotional. To put this in simpler language, explain that each choice usually leads to certain events that happen and certain

emotions that you feel. Also discuss how there are consequences not just for the individual making the choice, but for all others involved in the situation.

6. *Consequential Thinking Exercise.* Using the alternatives generated in the brainstorming exercise, ask the children to think of several consequences for each alternative. The therapists should write down the anticipated consequences, and the children should be given an opportunity to decide the best final solution to the problem. Sometimes we allow the children to vote to decide the best solution. Lead the children through several such exercises. Be sure to reinforce children for expressing feelings appropriately throughout this discussion. The reader is referred to Chapter 6 for additional discussion of this process of introducing alternatives and consequential thinking.

7. *Relaxation.*

8. *Review and Feedback.* Be sure to reinforce the appropriate expression of feelings during feedback giving.

9. *Kid for the Day and Activity.*

Evaluating Outcomes and Using Backup Plans
Clinic Model—Week 5; School Model—Week 5

Objectives

1. Introduce concept of evaluating the outcome of a plan.
2. Introduce concept of creating and using backup plans.
3. Model and reinforce appropriate expression of feelings.

Procedures

1. *Check-In.*

2. *Set Social Behavior Goal.* Ask all group members to continue to practice the appropriate expression of feelings. If necessary, have each group member again model the appropriate expression of some type of negative affect in response to a hypothetical situation.

3. *Evaluating Outcomes.* Engage the children in a discussion regarding how we know a particular plan did or did not work. Ask them how they can tell when they are satisfied with a particular choice or outcome. Explain that determining whether or not they are pleased with a particular outcome will require them to be sensitive to their own feelings. Ask the children to describe what their feelings are like when they are not pleased with a particular outcome. Then explain that while some plans affect only their feelings, some plans or problems may involve

other people. Ask them how they can tell if someone else is pleased with a particular choice or outcome.

The discussion of evaluating outcomes might also involve a review of signals, but in a different context. Have the children think of internal and external signals that might tell them if a plan worked or did not work. For example, if they choose a plan and their teacher frowns at them, what does it mean?

4. *Using Backup Plans.* The above discussion leads naturally into the presentation of the notion that sometimes one's first plan or strategy for solving a problem may not be effective at all, no matter how carefully thought out that choice was. This lack of effectiveness can occur for a number of reasons, such as lack of cooperation on the part of the other people involved in the situation or from a change of circumstances that had not previously been anticipated.

To provide an example, the instructor can use a sports analogy. For example, a quarterback may call a certain play in the huddle. However, when the team gets up to the line of scrimmage and is about to start the play, he/she may look at the setup for the defense of the other team and realize that the play he/she had called back in the huddle would never work. In that situation, the quarterback has to be a very flexible problem-solver and has to have a backup plan that he/she can call on at the last minute. Ask the children what would happen if the quarterback became too frustrated or just gave up when his/her first plan did not work. Ask the children for examples of other situations that require a backup plan. Emphasize that if one's first plan does not work, that is a signal that more problem-solving is needed.

5. *Role-Playing the Use of Backup Plans.* Now ask the children to come up with role-play situations in which their first choice or attempt at problem-solving is not successful and they are required to try other strategies. Ask the children to give special attention to what the character would be thinking and saying to himself/herself when he/she realizes that the first plan is not going to work.

For children who are having difficulty thinking of an example of such a situation, some samples might include:

- A sibling conflict in which your brother or sister is unwilling to work out a cooperative arrangement.
- A playground situation where you are attempting to play a certain game, but then you realize that you do not have enough people for the game.
- You want to prepare a certain snack or food item and begin to do so, but then realize that you do not have all the ingredients necessary for preparing that particular dish.

- A girl is bugging you at school. You decide to ignore her, but she keeps bugging you.

Allow each child to present his/her role-play, including as many other actors or actresses as is appropriate. Assign coaches to help the main characters problem-solve about how to cope with this situation. The children should practice trying a plan, and if it does not work, then using another plan.

    6. *Relaxation.*
    7. *Review and Feedback.*
    8. *Kid for the Day and Activity.*

Review
School Model Only—Week 6

Objectives

    1. Review concepts presented in Sessions 1–5.
    2. Review specific behavioral skills associated with appropriate eye contact and expression of feelings.

Procedures

    1. *Check-In.*
    2. *Set Social Behavior Goal.* Ask children to practice eye contact and expressing feelings.
    3. *Explain the Purpose of the Group.* Explain that the children have learned a great deal of new information over the past few sessions and that today's session will focus on reviewing that information. The therapist can also use this session to catch up with any material that could not be presented in the preceding sessions.
    4. *Lead Discussion of Concepts.* Ask what the children remember having learned. Try to lead them to discover all the key concepts learned. (The therapist may want to refer to the objectives of previous sessions to be sure all relevant material has been reviewed.) Also review the specifics of appropriate eye contact and expression of feelings, particularly the latter.
    5. *Create and Enact Role-Plays.* Have the children create and act out role-play situations, if necessary, to practice previously learned concepts and skills.
    6. *Relaxation.*
    7. *Review and Feedback.*
    8. *Kid for the Day and Activity.*

Interpersonal Problem-Solving I
Clinic Model—Week 6; School Model—Week 7

Objectives

1. Help the children recognize and define interpersonal conflicts.
2. Introduce the concept of being able to take the perspective of another person.
3. Model and reinforce sharing/cooperative behavior.

Procedures

1. *Check-In.*
2. *Set Social Behavior Goal.* After selecting individual goals, explain that the entire group will be working on how to share or act cooperatively. Ask the group what cooperation means. Then ask group members to recall any experiences they have had when someone did not share with them. Discuss how this made them feel. It may be helpful if the therapist models some examples of cooperative behavior. Have all group members model examples of cooperative and/or sharing behavior. Remind the children they can earn points for showing cooperative behavior with each other during group.
3. *Define Interpersonal Problems.* Explain to the children that they will be learning how to use plans to solve problems that occur between people. Ask the group if they know what you mean when you refer to interpersonal problems. Ask for examples from the group. After the group has offered several examples, the leader can note that these examples all reflect the common theme of people having different opinions about, or perceptions of, the same problem or event.
4. *Explain Perspective-Taking.* Then ask the group if one person's perception of a situation is automatically better than anyone else's perception. Help them work toward the recognition that, while people disagree in their view of a specific situation, each perspective is valid. To illustrate this point, give a sports example, such as an umpire in a baseball game calling a runner out at home base, while the runner thinks he/she was safe. Both people may be stating their honest opinion, but they have different perspectives on the situation. Then ask if that makes one person bad and the other person good. Try to help the children recognize that it is not a question of good and bad, but rather a question of having different perceptions of the same event.

Then explain that to fully understand a situation, it is important to be able to understand the perspective of the other people in the situation. Tell the group that a phrase the group will be using as a reminder to take another's perspective will be *"Put yourself in the other guy's shoes."*

Ask the children to tell you what this phrase means. Ask each child, so you can be sure no one is taking this phrase too literally. Help the children understand that others may *think* and *feel* a certain way in any interpersonal situation. For example, if one child calls another child a name, how would it make that child *think* and *feel*?

The therapist should be prepared to present pictures from magazines or cards from the Toward Affective Development program (Dupont, Gardner, & Brody, 1974) that depict interpersonal problem situations. The therapist should pick pictures and cards that display a wide range of interpersonal situations, such as arguing, cooperating, picking on others, and playing games together. The therapist then shows these pictures to the group members and engages them in a discussion about what it would be like to be in "the other guy's shoes." Ask the children to describe how they think the characters in the pictures are thinking and feeling in each of the interpersonal situations depicted.

5. *Perspective-Taking Role-Play Exercises.* Have the children generate possible interpersonal situations that they can role-play. An example would be two children picking on one other child. Another example would be arguing with a parent or teacher. Have the children generate as many scenarios as possible. Next have the children take turns role-playing these situations. The therapist will ask the children to stop in the middle of their role-plays and discuss how they are thinking and feeling, and how they think the other person in the role-play is thinking and feeling. The therapist will then ask the children to switch roles and engage again in the role-play. Once again, the therapist will ask the children to stop in the middle of their role-plays and describe their own thoughts and feelings, and the thoughts and feelings of the other person in the role-play. Have the children engage in this particular exercise for as many times as possible for most of the remainder of the group.

6. *Introduce the "Stop, Think, and Use a Plan Chart."* * Explain that, beginning after this session, the children can use the "Stop, Think, and Use a Plan" charts at home with their parents (and school, if applicable, with school model). Explain to the children that their parents (teachers) know about plans and are going to ask them to use plans at home. When they use the chart, they need to write down what the problem was, whose idea it was to use the plan, and how well the plan was used, based on the four-point rating scale at the bottom of the chart. Explain that the child and parent will complete the charts together.

It is very important to stress to the children that they will get reinforcement for completing the charts. Explain to the children that if they bring their charts into the group each session, they will receive

---

*Clinic model only. School model introduces this material in its Child Session 8.

points automatically at the beginning of the group. Explain further that their parents will be working to provide them with reinforcement at home for using the charts.

7. *Relaxation.*

8. *Review and Feedback.*

9. *Kid for the Day and Activity.*

Interpersonal Problem-Solving II
Clinic Model—Week 7; School Model—Week 8

Objectives

1. Apply problem recognition skills with interpersonal problems.

2. Practice taking the perspective of another and using plans to solve interpersonal problems.

3. Model and reinforce sharing/cooperative behavior.

Procedures

1. *Check-In.*

2. *Set Social Behavior Goal.* Remind the children that the entire group is continuing to work on the display of sharing/cooperative behavior.

3. *Problem Recognition Charades—Incorporate Perspective-Taking.* Have the children generate a list of several different examples of interpersonal conflicts and situations that may occur between two people. Assign dyads to act out each situation, and have the other children act as observers to help each character consider the other's perspective. The task is for the children to discuss signals that indicate what the other guy is thinking and feeling. Review the discussion of signals from previous sessions as the concepts relate to perspective-taking. Be sure each child participates in at least two role-plays.

4. *Introduce "Everybody Happy" Plans and Conduct Role-Play Exercises.* Have the group generate several examples of interpersonal problems that involve three or more different perspectives. Examples would include picking teams for baseball, taking turns, sharing, and children picking on another child. Then assign role-play teams and have them select the situation to be role-played. During these role-plays, have each character verbalize his/her own perspective and the perspective of each of the other characters. Through the recognition of everybody's perspectives, help them come up with "everybody happy" plans. In other words, have them use a plan and recognize whether using the plan

would result in everyone being happy. After a plan is selected, ask the children if everyone would be happy. If such a positive resolution is not possible in all cases, engage the group in a discussion regarding how some situations do not permit an "everybody happy" plan, so one must try to think of the best possible plan. It is important to emphasize alternative solution generation to maximize the possibility of coming up with everybody happy plans. Role-play as many different interpersonal situations as possible.

  5. *Introduce "Stop, Think, and Use a Plan Chart."* * See Procedure 6 in previous session.

  6. *Relaxation.*

  7. *Review and Feedback.*

  8. *Kid for the Day and Activity.*

Anger/Frustration Management I
Clinic Model—Week 9; School Model—Week 9
(Family Session Occurred in Week 8
of Clinic Program)

Objectives

  1. Introduce the view that strong emotional reactions can become problems in themselves.

  2. Educate the children about the affective, physiological, and cognitive aspects of emotions.

  3. Help the children begin to be aware of physiological and cognitive signals related to anger/frustration.

  4. Practice coping with anger/frustration via coping self-statements.

  5. Model and reinforce appropriate use of ignoring behavior.

Procedures

  1. *Check-In.*

  2. *Set Social Behavior Goals.* Explain that in some situations it is helpful to know how to ignore the irritating behavior of others. Ask the group to identify circumstances in which it might be useful to be able to ignore others. If the group has difficulty with this, the leader could offer examples such as when a sibling or classmate is trying to bug the child (perhaps in an effort to get him/her into trouble), when there is an irritating noise occurring while the child is trying to work, or when the child is out walking or riding his/her bike and strangers call names or

---

*School model only.

whistle at him/her. In the last example, ignoring strangers could even be framed or explained as a safety skill when accompanied by seeking out a helpful adult. Ask the children what they have to do or what they could say to themselves in order to ignore someone or something effectively. Encourage group members to come up with self-statements that fit the situations described above, such as "I need to keep doing my work," "Don't look at him. He's just trying to bug me," or "Keep going. Don't talk to these guys because they could be dangerous." Then have each group member practice using ignoring skills while another group member tries to bug him/her in a very mild way. Remind the children that they will receive points for the use of ignoring when appropriate circumstances arise in group. Note that if they are really doing a good job using ignoring, the leaders may not notice so it is all right in today's group for the children to let the leaders know when they are using ignoring skills to cope with a situation.

3. *Present Concept of Strong Emotions as Potential Problems.* Explain that there are times when having strong feelings is very normal and very appropriate. Ask the children for examples. If they are unsure, offer examples, such as feeling extreme sadness if something happens to someone you love or feeling extremely scared when you are in a dangerous situation. In these situations, strong feelings are natural. Then explain that sometimes people experience strong feelings when these feelings do not really fit the situation. Present an example, such as a child who throws a fit over something his/her sibling has done and, because he/she is so hysterical, the parent will not let him/her do some desirable activity. Help the children come up with examples of similar situations that occur in both the home and school environments. Continue the discussion to the point that the children seem to grasp the view that while some problem usually triggers the strong feelings, it is the overreaction to the original difficulty that becomes the major problem to be solved. Ask the children to think of examples of situations in which the child would have been in a better situation or "gotten off easier" if he/she had not overreacted. The leader can give personal examples of situations in which the same has been true for him/her.

4. *Discuss Components of Strong Feelings.* After the children seem to understand the concept presented in Procedure 3, explain that strong feelings have several parts or components. Explain the physiological and cognitive components in language such as, "There is the *body* part, which is how our body is reacting to the event, and there is the *thinking* part, which is what we are saying to ourselves in our heads about the event." Write the words *body* and *thinking* on a blackboard or posterboard. Discuss an example of what would be happening with the specific components of a particular strong feeling. Anger is usually the easiest example for the children to understand. Engage the group in the discus-

sion by asking them to identify how their bodies could be reacting, and what their thoughts might be when angry.

5. *List and Describe Common Physiological Signals.* Explain that in today's session the group will focus on understanding more about common body signals of arousal. Ask the children to help you list common body (physiological) signals. After a signal is named, write it on the board and have one or two children demonstrate or model this signal, if that is possible. Signals listed and discussed might include:

    a.   *Change in breathing rate*: rates increase with arousal.

    b.   *Change in heart rate*: rates increase with arousal.

    c.   *Change in sweating*: more sweating associated with greater arousal.

    d.   *Change in face color*: for some, face becomes flushed with arousal; for others, face becomes more pale with arousal (particularly if associated with shock).

    e.   *Change in muscle tension*: for some, increased muscle tension is experienced, especially in shoulders, neck, and jaw areas.

    f.   *Change in voice quality*: for some, voice becomes more broken, while others display increased loudness.

If the children express other appropriate examples, include these in the listing.

6. *Identify Individuals' Physiological Signals.* After various physiological changes have been identified and described, explain that it is important for a person to recognize and become sensitive to his/her own particular ways of reacting to stressors. Then engage the group in a discussion about what each child thinks are his/her particular bodily reactions or cues. The therapist will need to monitor the accuracy and appropriateness of responses. After discussing this issue, have each child write down the two, three, or four signals that he/she is most likely to show. The therapist may need to influence this process by pointing out that virtually every human being experiences breathing and/or heart rate changes in response to stressors.

7. *List and Describe Common Anger Thinking Signals.* Explain that certain thoughts are also usually associated with anger/frustration. Ask the children to list common anger thinking signals. After an anger thinking signal is named, write it on the board. Signals listed and discussed might include:

    a.   *Angry thoughts toward self*
- "I hate myself."
- "I feel like hurting myself."

 b. *Angry thoughts toward others*
  • "I hate him/her."
  • "I'm going to hit him/her."
  • "I wish he/she was dead."
 c. *Angry thoughts toward tasks/places*
  • "I hate doing math."
  • "I'd like to burn down the school building."

If the children express other appropriate examples, include these in the listing.

 8. *Identify Individuals' Anger Thinking Signals.* After various thoughts have been described, explain the importance of children understanding the thoughts they most often have when angry/frustrated. Have the children write down the two, three, or four typical thoughts they think they usually have in response to anger/frustration.

 9. *Problem Recognition Charades—Anger/Frustration Signals.* Have the children act out situations in which they became angry/frustrated. The actors should also state what their thoughts are while acting. The observers should take turns recognizing the physiological and cognitive signals discussed earlier.

 10. *Introduce Collaborative Plans for Home (School).** Explain to the children that plans can be used to solve problems with someone else. Define collaboration and how plans can be used with parents (teachers) in a collaborative fashion. Inform the children that they and their parents (also teachers in school model) will begin using collaborative plans at home (school) to work out problems between people. Spend some time role-playing, if necessary, so that the children understand how collaborative plans work. Explain how the "Stop, Think, and Use a Plan Chart" will be used for collaborative plans.

 11. *Relaxation.*

 12. *Review and Feedback.*

 13. *Kid for the Day and Activity.*

Anger/Frustration Management II
Clinic and School Models—Week 10

Objectives

 1. Help the children recognize at least two different phases of problem confrontation.

---

*Clinic model only. School model introduces this material in its Child Session 12.

2. Help the children use coping self-statements (e.g., cool-down plans) to aid their coping with physiological and cognitive aspects of strong feelings.

3. Model and reinforce the appropriate use of ignoring behavior.

Procedures

1. *Check-In.*

2. *Set Social Behavior Goal.* Remind the children that they can continue to earn points for the appropriate use of ignoring behavior.

3. *Explain Phases of Confrontation and Using Cool-Down Plans.* The idea of thinking about different phases of problem confrontation and using cool-down plans for each phase, as is presented here, has been adapted from Novaco (1978). To make the concepts more age appropriate, we emphasize only two of the four stages described by Novaco. We recommend focusing on the "preparing for the situation" and "coping with arousal in the situation" phases (Novaco, 1978). The children can learn to identify these two phases and use cool-down plans (i.e., coping self-statements) to regulate physiological and cognitive aspects of strong emotions. Once they have cooled down, they can then employ regular plans to solve any problems that may have made them feel angry/frustrated. As described by Novaco (1978), the phases include:

a. *Preparing for the tough situation.* This phase involves what to say to yourself in anticipation of a stressful event or confrontation that is likely to create strong feelings. This phase isn't always relevant, since many stressful events happen without notice, but it may be appropriate for situations such as anticipating a test or confrontation with an unpleasant person.

Self-talk at this phase can emphasize a number of aspects of the situation, such as the need to stay relaxed, the need to not take things personally, the need to trust your own ability to manage the situation, or the need to stick to the issues being discussed. For some people, it may be helpful to remind themselves of the consequences of losing control of their emotions. These goals could be met through phrases such as:

- "I can handle this. I just need to remind myself to take deep breaths and stay relaxed."
- "Just listen to what he/she has to say and take your time to answer."
- "If I keep my cool, I won't get into trouble."
- "He/she may try to make me mad, but I control my feelings. I don't want to lose it."

After presenting this phase, the leader should ask the children for examples of situations in which they would have some time to prepare for the stressful or tough situations. Include academic and interpersonal examples. Then ask them to come up with a list of things children could say to themselves to get ready for the tough situations. The children may need help understanding that the comments should be geared toward decreasing arousal ("I need to breathe deeply and stay cool."), instead of increasing arousal ("That guy is such a jerk. I want to punch him out!").

b. *Coping with arousal.* This phase concerns what you say to yourself when you can tell you're starting to get upset. This phase involves the hard work of really trying to keep your cool. Examples of self-statements would be:

- "Take it easy."
- "Stay cool."
- "Chill out."
- "Time to take deep breaths."
- "I'm getting tense. Relax my neck and shoulders."
- "Keep listening and keep your cool. I'll get my turn to talk."
- "If I lose it now, he/she will have gotten control of me. Hang in there."
- "I won't let him/her get to me."

Repeat the process of discussion and identification of situations (preferably real life examples) where such self-talk can be used. *Important:* The child should practice using a cool-down plan followed by a regular plan.

The group leader must determine the degree of anger that the current group will be able to tolerate in conducting the following role-plays. The initial situations used for practicing anger management skills should be irritating enough to present a mild challenge to the children but not so irritating as to overwhelm them and decrease the likelihood of successful skills application. As a result of time limitations, we include practice with only mild and moderately stressful situations in the clinic model of the program. If the clinician is able to include an extra session, and the group is able to tolerate it, we do recommend practicing skills use with more significantly stressful analogue situations as are described in Week 11 of the school model.

4. *Practicing Skills with Mildly Stressful Situations.* Ask the children to do role-play exercises employing the techniques with situations that generate mildly uncomfortable feelings. Have each child come up with examples that involve feelings of mild anger or irritation. Select situations that involve some anticipation so each phase of problem confrontation can be addressed. Examples of mildly provocative situations, including some anticipation, might be as follows:

- You want to ask your parents to let you go visit a friend, but you don't think they'll let you, and when you ask, they do say, "No."
- You ask your parent to fix a certain food for dinner and he/she says that might not be possible. When dinner is ready, your requested food wasn't prepared.
- You ask your little brother/sister to return a toy he/she has borrowed from you by a certain time, but he/she doesn't do it.

Other examples that involve less anticipation include:

- Your parent doesn't cook what you want for supper.
- Your friends ask you to play outfield, when you want to play pitcher.
- Your brother/sister is standing right by the door to your room but he/she won't shut the door when you ask him/her to.

5. *Practicing Skills with Moderately Stressful Situations.* Ask the children to now identify situations that make them moderately angry. Examples of moderately anger-provoking situations might include when a child calls you a name, or your brother/sister takes your favorite toy without asking. Help the children identify role-playing partners. Allow them some time to discuss their respective role-plays. While they are engaging in this discussion, let the group know that you are very serious about helping them learn to cope with strong feelings and, as a result, you recommend that they really work hard to pretend that what they are role-playing is really happening to them. Explain that you will not allow anyone to really hit or harm another; however, it is OK for them to use realistic name-calling or realistic language in their role-play. Then assign each role-play team a coach who will help the primary actor engage in coping self-talk during the role-play. Challenge the main character to really use the coping self-statements in a meaningful way if he/she seems to be using the statements in a more superficial manner.

Let each dyad present their role-play situation in turn. If, during the role-play, one of the actors really seems to be close to losing emotional control, stop the role-play and engage the entire group in problem-solving about what that person can do to help himself/herself to feel better.

With some groups, it may be necessary to emphasize that each child is working on something that is hard for him/her, so that child needs the respectful attention and involvement of the group. Additional kidding, teasing, or put-downs that are not a part of the formal role-play will require additional time for problem-solving and may be penalized.

6. *Review the Process.* Following the completion of the role-play exercises, engage the whole group in a discussion about how it felt for them to be involved in these role-plays. Also ask them to think more generally about how being able to cope with these difficult situations would make a person feel about himself/herself.

7. *Identify Situations for Using Cool-Down Plans.* Have each child select a target situation in which to apply his/her cool-down plans and relaxation skills. These should be situations in which the child knows from previous experience that he/she is likely to get angry.

8. *Relaxation.*

9. *Review and Feedback.*

10. *Kid for the Day and Activity.*

Anger/Frustration Management III
School Model Only—Week 11

Objectives

1. Practice use of anger coping skills with stressful analogue situations.

2. Explain distinctions among and between aggressive, passive and assertive responses to difficult situations.

Procedures

1. *Check-In.*

2. *Set Social Behavior Goal.* Explain that the children will be able to earn extra points for acting in an assertive way when dealing with a tough situation rather than acting in a passive or aggressive way. Ask the group what it means to respond too aggressively to a situation. Then ask them to describe what it means to be too passive or "wimpy" in a situation. Finally, ask them if there's some other way to respond that's neither too aggressive nor too wimpy. Explain that this other way or middle choice is called being *assertive*. It may be helpful to prepare a chart with the visual aid depicted below:

Response:	**AGGRESSIVE**	**ASSERTIVE**	passive
Thinking of:	(Me Only)	Myself and Others	(Others Only)

The leader can discuss how an assertive response considers both one's own feelings and the feelings of others in the situation. The leader can also explain that being assertive involves using some of the specific behaviors the group has already been practicing, such as maintaining eye contact and expressing feelings appropriately.

The group leaders can then model aggressive, passive, and assertive responses to dealing with a situation such as asking a classmate to return a pencil he/she has borrowed from you or telling a sibling that you want some time alone in your room without being bothered. Ideally, the leaders should act out responses to these situations and have the children guess whether a particular response is aggressive, passive, or assertive. The leaders can then have each child think of and verbalize an assertive response to a troubling situation he/she experienced in the last week. Then remind the group members they can earn extra points for displaying assertive behavior in role-play situations or in response to real dilemmas arising in group.

3. *Practicing Skills with Very Stressful Situations.* Explain to the children that you want to use the whole group to do some continued practice of using coping skills in difficult situations. It is recommended that the therapist provide the situations for this purpose, possibly selecting from two or three of the more difficult situations that the children have presented in the previous session and making some variations in these scenes so as to accommodate most of the group in the role-plays. Allow the main character in a given role-play, who is the one expected to engage in appropriate self-talk, to select a coach to help him/her remember when to use his/her relaxation skills and self-talk.

Common choices for role-play scenarios include:

- Name-calling in which three or four children are ganging up on one child.
- A group play situation in which one person ends up being rejected.
- A classroom situation in which other children are spreading rumors that are untrue about another child.
- A situation in which the teacher accuses a child of doing something, such as taking someone else's possession, when the child did not actually do that.

Make sure that each child in a group gets to be either a main character in a role-play or a coach in a role-play. Encourage the children to imagine that they are really in the situation being acted out. Encourage them to have the feelings that they think they would really experience in such a situation.

When each role-play nears its end, regardless of the specific outcome, ask all of the actors or actresses in the role-play to freeze. Once they have stopped their motion, ask each of them to think about what their character thinks about himself/herself at that particular moment. For example, ask the child who has just coped with the situation of being called names how he/she is feeling about himself/herself now that he/she has coped with that situation. In addition, ask the people who were name callers how they are feeling about themselves at that particular point. Have the children unfreeze and use cool-down plans to cope with the stress.

4. *Review the Process.* As discussed in the last session, process any residual feelings created by the role-plays by having the children express feelings appropriately and use cool-down plans. Provide praise and encouragement to the children for working so hard at keeping their cool in tough situations.

5. *Identify Situations for Using Cool-Down Plans.* Repeat Procedure 7 in the previous session.

6. *Relaxation.*

7. *Review and Feedback.*

8. *Kid for the Day and Activity.*

Review
School Model Only—Week 12

Objectives

1. Review material introduced in Sessions 7–11.
2. Introduce use of collaborative plans.

Procedures

1. *Repeat Review Process Described in the Review Session, Week 6.* Emphasize the use of assertive responses in role-plays, reviewing the major elements of interpersonal problem-solving and anger/frustration management.

2. *Introduce Collaborative Plans for Home (School).* See Procedure 10 in Anger/Frustration Management I.

Poor Effort Management I
School Model Only—Week 13

Objectives

1. Introduce the view that effort is a key ingredient in facing difficult problem situations.
2. Help the children to recognize poor effort.

Procedures

    1. *Check-In.*

    2. *Set Social Behavior Goal.* Continue to emphasize that children can earn points for displaying good eye contact, appropriate expression of feelings, sharing/cooperative behavior, appropriate use of ignoring, and assertive responses.

    3. *Explain Effort.* Ask the group what the word *effort* means. Be sure the group has the understanding that effort is *how hard one is trying* to do something. Ask them what's good and bad about effort. If the children have trouble with this discussion, the leader can ask something like, "How do you feel when you are playing a baseball game and it seems like the other children on your team aren't really trying to play very well?" or "How do you feel when you ask your mom or dad to help you with your homework but it seems like they aren't trying to help very much?" The point is to get the children to recognize moments or situations in which they are frustrated by *someone else's* lack of effort. Then ask how it makes them feel when their team is trying very hard or a parent is working hard to help them.

    Also discuss how people vary in their need to exert effort in specific subjects. For example, some children have an easy time with reading and don't have to exert a lot of effort, but they may have to try harder to learn mathematics facts. Other people are just the opposite. Also bring different domains of activity into the discussion, such as having an easy or difficult time with sports, with musical activities, or with making friends.

    4. *List and Discuss Common Feeling Signals about Poor Effort.* Explain that certain feelings are usually associated with poor effort. Ask the children to list and discuss these feelings. The group leader should write and define these on the board. Feeling signals listed and discussed should include frustration, boredom, and anger.

    5. *List and Discuss Common Thinking Signals about Poor Effort.* Explain that certain thoughts are associated with poor effort. List and discuss these with the children. Thought signals listed and discussed should include:

    a. *Put-down thoughts about self*
        • "I'm no good at this."
        • "I'm dumb."
    b. *Frustration thoughts*
        • "I hate math."
        • "I'm so mad about this project."
    c. *Give-up thoughts*
        • "Forget it. I'm sick of this stuff."
        • "I'd rather go play."
        • "I give up."

6. *List and Discuss Common Off-Task Behavior Signals about Poor Effort.*
Explain that certain off-task behaviors are associated with poor effort.
List and discuss these with the children. Off-task behavior signals listed
and discussed should include:

    a. Staring into space.
    b. Doing one activity when you are supposed to be doing another.
    c. Getting distracted.
    d. Other: The children should be able to come up with numerous
       examples of their own off-task behavior.

7. *Individualizing Feeling, Thinking, and Off-Task Behavior Signals.* Ask
the children to identify the feeling, thinking, and off-task behavior
signals they usually experience when they want to give up.

8. *Problem Recognition Charades—Poor Effort Signals.* Have the children act out situations in which they are giving up or putting in poor
effort. The actors should state their thoughts while acting their parts.
The observers should take turns recognizing feeling, thinking, and
off-task behavior signals.

9. *Relaxation.*

10. *Review and Feedback.*

11. *Kid for the Day and Activity.*

Poor Effort Management II
School Model Only—Week 14

Objectives

1. Practice recognizing self-dialogue associated with lack of effort.
2. Practice using try harder plans.

Procedures

1. *Check-In.*

2. *Set Social Behavior Goal.* Remind the children that they can earn
points for emitting all previously learned social behaviors.

3. *Practice Using Try Harder Plans.* Ask the children to think of a
situation that has happened to them in the last 2 weeks that would have
been improved by having an effort plan. Examples might include becoming frustrated with work at school and engaging in inappropriate
behavior, becoming frustrated with homework and refusing to complete
it, and becoming frustrated with trying to do a household chore that
seems too hard.

Have each child describe what happened and push him/her to re-construct what he/she might have been saying to himself/herself. Then have the group problem-solve about appropriate try harder plans. Role-play the try harder plan the group creates for each child. If a situation involves a child or parent interacting with a child who is frustrated, have the character who is playing the adult speculate about what the adult's internal dialogue might be at key points in the interaction and have the group help the adult character improve his/her internal dialogue (use try harder plans, too), if necessary.

Self-statements associated with a try harder plan might include:

- "Don't think about the whole assignment. Just focus on each prob-lem as I get to it."
- "I'm not going to give up."
- "I'll just do the best I can."
- "All I can do is try."
- "I'll give it my best shot."
- "It's OK if I don't do it perfectly."

Do as many role-plays involving try harder plans as possible. *Impor-tant:* The child practicing using a try harder plan may want to follow this with a regular plan, if appropriate to the situation.

4. *Relaxation.*

5. *Review and Feedback.*

6. *Kid for the Day and Activity.*

Negative Thoughts and Feelings Management I
School Model Only—Week 15

Objectives

1. Introduce the children to the concept of negative thoughts and their relationship to negative feelings.

2. Help the children to develop the skill to recognize negative thoughts.

Procedures

1. *Check-In.*

2. *Set Social Behavior Goal.*

3. *Explain the Relationship between Negative Thoughts and Negative Feel-ings.* Explain that sometimes children are negative thinkers. At these times, children tend to say negative things to themselves inside and, as a

result of this, have negative feelings. For example, ask the children what someone might feel like if they think, "I'm no good." Help the children understand that individuals who think this way have a lot of negative feelings, such as sadness, anger, and depression. Ask the children what someone would feel like if they thought, "I'm a nice person." Help the children understand that the individual thinking this type of thought would have a more positive feeling, such as happiness or pride. Explain to the children that we want them to develop the skill to recognize when they are doing negative thinking and to change their thinking to be more positive.

4. *Thinking/Feeling Connection Exercise.* Write down on the board examples of negative self-deprecating and positive self-building thoughts. Then ask the children to generate possible feelings that may go along with the negative and positive thoughts. Try to come up with at least five to ten examples to facilitate this discussion.

5. *List and Describe Common Negative Thinking Signals.* Ask the children to list common negative thinking signals. After a negative thinking signal is named, write it on the board. Signals listed and discussed might include:

a. *Self-put-down thoughts*
- "I'm dumb."
- "I can't do anything right."
- "No one likes me."

b. *Too difficult*
- "I can't do it; it's too hard."
- "Forget it! I'm not going to try."

6. *Individualize Negative Thinking Signals to Each Child.* The therapist may want to first self-disclose some of his/her typical negative thoughts he/she has about himself/herself. This will facilitate the children's self-disclosure and will help the children recognize that many people think negatively on occasion. Then ask the children about the negative self-statements they use on a routine basis. Try to facilitate an open discussion of this issue.

7. *Problem Recognition Charades/Negative Thinking Signals.* Have the children act out situations while stating their thoughts out loud. Situations could involve events occurring at home, at school, with their peers, while doing homework, etc. The observers should take turns recognizing the negative thought signals, as discussed earlier, and they should also try to describe what kinds of feeling states might go along with the particular thoughts. The therapist should try to engage the children in as many problem recognition charades/negative thinking signals exercises as is possible for the session.

8. *Relaxation.*
9. *Review and Feedback.*
10. *Kid for the Day and Activity.*

Negative Thoughts and Feelings Management II
School Model Only—Week 16

Typically, cognitive restructuring exercises are used to help individuals change negative thinking patterns. Cognitive restructuring often involves the steps of (1) identifying and monitoring negative thoughts, (2) understanding the irrational and dysfunctional components of negative thoughts, and (3) using more adaptive thoughts to replace the irrational/dysfunction thoughts.

This intervention, however, is geared to 8- to 12-year-olds, and it is not thought that the majority of children in this age group can benefit from the complex and more abstract thinking process of understanding the roots of their irrational/dysfunctional thoughts. Therefore, the objective in this session is simply to get the children to (1) recognize and identify their negative thinking, and (2) use new, more adaptive self-statements to replace the negative ones. The goal is not to prevent children from experiencing negative feelings when appropriate, but to minimize the negative effects of irrational or catastrophizing self-statements.

Objectives

1. Continue practicing negative thinking recognition.
2. Practice using be-fair-to-yourself plans.

Procedures

1. *Check-In.*
2. *Set Social Behavior Goal.*
3. *Explain Be-Fair-to-Yourself Plans (i.e., Adaptive Self-Statements).* Explain to the children that the idea for today's session is to help them learn how to replace negative thinking with more helpful thinking. This will be accomplished by first recognizing when they are saying negative things themselves and then using be-fair-to-yourself plans to replace them. The therapist should write down on the board a list of negative thoughts and have the children generate alternative be-fair-to-yourself thoughts that they could use to replace those negative ones. Below is a list of examples:

Negative thoughts	*Be-fair-to-yourself thoughts*
"I'm no good at math."	"This is hard for me, but I can still try as hard as I can."
"I hate myself."	"I'm mad right now, but I'm OK; I'm just having a bad day."
"I hate myself."	"I'm not the best at school, but I am a good baseball player. Each person is good and bad at some things."
"No one likes me."	"I'm sad that Billy doesn't want to play with me, but a lot of people like me, including my friend Tom, my mother and father, and my teacher."

4. *Role-Play Discussions.* Have the children role-play situations that occur at school, at home, with their peers, while studying homework, etc., that are negative in tone, and have them state out loud their negative thinking. Have them practice recognizing their negative thoughts and then replacing those negative thoughts with adaptive thinking plans. The other group members can serve as coaches to facilitate each child using positive thinking plans in this exercise. *Important:* The child practicing a be-fair-to-yourself plan may want to follow this with a regular plan, if appropriate.

5. *Relaxation.*

6. *Review and Feedback.*

7. *Kid for the Day and Activity.*

Program Review I
Clinic Model—Week 12; School Model—Week 17

Objectives

1. Review all concepts presented in this training program.
2. Provide additional real life practice in group problem-solving.

Procedures

1. *Check-In.*

2. *Set Social Behavior Goal.*

3. *Review Program Concepts.* Ask the group what they remember about the different kinds of plans they have learned to make. Help them remember the following:

a. *Five-step problem-solving process*
   • How to recognize problems
   • How to brainstorm

- How to evaluate consequences and outcomes
- How to make backup plans, if necessary
- How to execute specific plans (i.e., adaptive behaviors)

b. *Use of problem-solving with interpersonal problems*
- Role of *putting yourself in the other guy's shoes*
- Perspective taking
- Everybody happy plans

c. *Coping with strong feelings/keeping your cool*
- Recognizing body and thinking signals
- Cool-down plans
- Relaxation skills

d. *Coping with poor effort (school model only)*
- Recognizing poor effort feelings, thinking, and off-task behavior
- Try harder plans

e. *Coping with negative thinking and feelings (school model only)*
- Recognizing negative thinking signals
- Be fair to yourself plans

4. *Practice via "Movie" Scripts.* The group leaders explain that the children are now ready to begin to create their own scripts for a plan movie (with the option of possibly showing the movie to their parents and/or teachers, if the therapists choose). In order to accomplish this goal, it may be helpful to have the group split into two small subgroups. Each group leader can then help those three to four children create a script about a problem-solving situation that is particularly relevant for each child. The child should be the "star" of his/her movie and select several "guest stars" to play different parts. We recommend that each child develop a no-plan script in which he/she does not use a plan to solve the problem and a plan script in which a plan is used. If they choose to do so, the children can develop scripts where they incorporate everybody is happy, cool-down, be fair to yourself, and poor effort plans into their script. The therapists should write down the scripts and act as the "directors" in the movie-making process. Therapists can use the "Plan Movie Script" chart in Appendix B. (See the example of how the chart is completed.)

After each child has had an opportunity to generate a script, the group can then reconvene and practice, if time permits. The movies are designed to help the children practice while maintaining their interest. This activity also allows the children to observe the contrast between not using and then using a plan to solve problems. The act of creating scripts may also create many new opportunities for problem-solving within group. The leaders should encourage the children to problem-solve as dilemmas arise, such as one child feeling left out because he is not a "guest star" or another child attempting to dominate each scene in which he appears.

    5. *Relaxation.*

    6. *Review and Feedback.*

    7. *Kid for the Day and Activity.*

Program Review II
Clinic Model—Week 13; School Model—Week 18

Objective

    1. Assist the children in reviewing and appreciating their accomplishments over the past sessions.

Procedures

    1. *Check-In.*

    2. *Set Social Behavior Goal.*

    3. *Film Each Child's Plan Movie.* The group leaders may want to divide the group again in order to provide the children with more opportunities to rehearse their movies and make any modifications they desire. The group then reconvenes and each child's problem situation is role-played and videotaped. As was the case with preparing the scripts, the process of videotaping the movies will undoubtedly create new opportunities for plan-making. Help the children make plans about what should be appropriate behavior "on the set" or "in the studio audience," etc.

    4. *Show Plan Movies.* The plan movie videotapes are then presented and discussed. The discussion should focus on verbally reinforcing the children for their effort and how the plans were used in the movie. Typically, we stop between each child's movie for applause and discussion. (The therapists may want to invite the parents and/or teacher to see the plan movies.)

    5. *Relaxation.*

    6. *Review and Feedback.*

    7. *Kid for the Day and Activity.*

    8. *Say Goodbyes.* Allow 5–10 minutes at the end for the children and the therapists to say goodbye and discuss the aspects of group that they liked and those they disliked. Ask for their suggestions on how to improve the group.

Parent Component

Procedural Overview

In the nine parent group sessions, participants receive education about ADHD, examine and change dysfunctional attributions/beliefs, and are trained in cognitive–behavioral child management, family problem-solving skills (e.g., collaborative plans), and traditional behavioral child management skills. The skills the parents learn closely parallel what the teachers are learning to do with the child when applying the school model.

Another purpose of the parent group sessions is to provide ongoing support for the parents, who are struggling with very difficult children. In addition, the parents often find it trying to learn and apply the skills they are being trained to use in the groups. To accomplish this supportive function, the group facilitates general discussion among parents in each session.

Each parent group is led by one therapist. Groups are convened weekly with the clinic model and biweekly with the school model. The sessions last $1\frac{1}{2}$ hours. In the clinic application, it is convenient to hold the parent group at the same time the children's groups meet. The format consists of didactic presentations and discussion. The content of each group builds from previous sessions and coincides with skills the children are learning. The therapist models difficult-to-grasp concepts and procedures and encourages parents to do role-playing when necessary to ensure acquisition of skills.

Introduction
Clinic Model—Week 3; School Model—Week 2

Objectives

    1. Review information about ADHD and the program.
    2. Set positive, but realistic, expectations for the program.

Procedures

    1. *Introductions.* Instruct parents to introduce themselves and to identify their child who is participating in the program. It is sometimes helpful to have parents write their names and the names and ages of other members of their immediate family on a piece of paper that can be easily seen by the other group members.

2. *Education about ADHD.* Introduce and discuss the chart entitled "Attention-Deficit Hyperactivity Disorder" found in Appendix B. Review and discuss each of the concepts on the chart.

3. *Medical Information.* Much of the session focuses on education regarding medical aspects of ADHD. The therapist can focus primarily on medication issues if this is of great concern to parents. This presentation should include a thorough discussion of the purposes and possible side effects of the medications. In some settings, it may be possible to have an experienced physician provide the medical information and lead discussions of medication issues.

4. *Education about CBT.* Introduce and discuss the chart entitled "Cognitive–Behavioral Therapy for Children with Attention-Deficit Hyperactivity Disorder" found in Appendix B. Review and discuss each of the concepts on the chart. Emphasize that parent involvement is very important for success of the program.

5. *Expectations for the Program.* Discuss the notion that this program is not a cure for ADHD and related social, school, and behavioral problems. The program does offer, however, a chance for parents to participate and learn additional coping skills that they can use to deal with their children on an ongoing basis. A goal of this part of the session is to help the parents achieve a very realistic appraisal of what they can expect from participating in this program.

6. *Review Upcoming Sessions.* Inform the parents about the upcoming sessions. The parents should also know that they will be assigned homework in future sessions. Tell parents that each family will be asked to complete various charts regarding the homework and to bring them in each week.

Group Process/Support
Clinic Model—Week 4; School Model—Week 4

Objectives

1. Establish routine check-in at the beginning of group.
2. Establish group guidelines.
3. Establish group cohesion.
4. Examine feelings of loss.

Procedures

1. *Check-In.* Establish a routine check-in period at the beginning of the session. The routine check-in essentially entails the parents report-

ing and describing issues or concerns about their children that have occurred since the previous session. When possible, the therapist should focus the check-in on discussion of implementing various therapeutic strategies and techniques at home and the success or lack of success the parents are having.

2. *Establish Group Guidelines.* The leaders can explain that all groups seem to function more effectively with some guidelines. Ask the parents what guidelines they would like to have operating for their group. The leaders can explain that a common guideline concerns confidentiality, with confidentiality being a legal and ethical requirement for the leaders but an issue of courtesy for fellow group members. Other guidelines that we have found helpful in our past groups with parents include: "Give support and ideas, not judgments," "Share the time," and "Take responsibility to ask for more time/support when you need it." If many of the parents have not had previous group therapy experiences (which is often the case), it may be difficult for them to come up with clear guidelines initially. The leaders can "jump start" the group's thinking on this issue by asking them to identify behaviors of others that they have observed and disliked in previous social or work experiences. The leaders can then ask the group to help in shaping these don't's or negative behaviors into a list of do's for the group.

3. *Establish Group Cohesion.* To establish group cohesion, have the parents participate in a discussion of "war stories." The overall aim is to facilitate a discussion of common problems, concerns, frustrations, etc. that parents have had as they have struggled to raise their children. We have found this to be a powerful way to establish group cohesion. Usually parents have no trouble bringing up example after example of difficulties with which they and other group members have struggled. Parents typically comment that they no longer feel alone, and it is helpful to find out other parents' struggles with similar issues. We recommend that approximately 30 minutes be used for this purpose. It is also important to encourage parents to tell "war stories" and other related difficulties that they have been having throughout the course of all of the parent group sessions.

4. *Examine Feelings of Loss.* It is usually helpful for the therapists to raise the issue of feelings of loss about having ADHD children. Parents should be informed that parents of ADHD children often feel a sense of loss because they realize that they do not have a perfect child. Parents realize that they will be coping with the problem of ADHD for years to come. Through this discussion, parents are educated about typical stages of mourning, including (1) disbelief, (2) anger, and (3) working through. It may not be essential to go through all the details of these stages, but to simply review with the parents how they may have felt or currently are feeling a sense of loss. Try to facilitate a discussion of the importance of

eventually working through these feelings. This type of discussion is oftentimes affectively laden and will bring out many feelings in parents. Encourage an active discussion and interchange between parents regarding the issue of loss. The therapist's role at this stage is to facilitate the discussion and provide support when necessary.

Examine Parent Cognitions and Behaviors
Clinic Model—Week 5; School Model—Week 6

Objectives

1. Examine and begin to modify attributions/beliefs of parents about themselves and their child.
2. Examine and begin to modify typical behavioral interchanges between parents and children.
3. Focus on children's strengths and weaknesses.

Procedures

In this session, the parents are asked to complete several charts. These charts are designed to facilitate education of parents and modification of their cognitions and behaviors.

1. *Examine Common Parental Attributions/Beliefs.* Pass out the "Adult Self-Evaluation of Thoughts Form" found in Appendix B. Ask the parents to complete the form, urging them to be very open and honest. Thoroughly discuss the chart and parents' unique responses. It may be necessary to explain the concepts of attributions and beliefs to the parents before engaging in this discussion. Review each of the attributions and beliefs in as much detail as necessary. Ask parents to discuss the problematic or dysfunctional aspects of those particular attributions or beliefs where a high score was obtained (e.g., 3 or above). Ask the parents in what way these attributions or beliefs would interfere with their ability to work with their child. Ask the parents how these attributions and beliefs would influence their behavior toward their child and what types of messages would be communicated to their child by their behavior. Use the discussion of these forms as an opportunity to educate parents.

2. *Review Adaptive Attributions and Beliefs Regarding ADHD.* Pass out the "Adaptive Attributions and Beliefs Regarding ADHD" chart found in Appendix B. Explain to the parents that the purpose of this chart is to help them think of new ways to look at (think about) these children and their problems. The idea is to broaden their view of ADHD children. Suggest that these thoughts could be used to counter those thoughts

they view as dysfunctional as identified in the previous parent self-evaluation form. Review each attribution and belief on the chart. Ask the parents in what way these new attributions and beliefs would positively affect their ADHD child. Ask the parents how these new attributions and beliefs would facilitate their abilities to work with their child. Ask the parents how these attributions and beliefs would influence their behavior toward their child and what messages these behaviors would communicate to their child.

3. *Examine Common Parent–Child Behavioral Interchanges.* Pass out the "Adult Self-Evaluation of Behavior Form" found in Appendix B. Ask the parents to complete this form. Prompt them to think about these common behavioral interchanges as they may relate to themselves and their ADHD child. Ask the parents to be very open and honest, and discuss some of their typical behavioral interchanges with the group. Thoroughly review the form and the parents' unique responses. Discuss each of the common behavioral interchanges in as much detail as necessary. Ask parents to discuss what could be problematic or dysfunctional about those particular behaviors that occur frequently. Ask the parents in what way these behaviors interfere with their ability to work with their child. Ask the parents what type of messages would be communicated to their child if these types of behavioral interactions were typical. Use the discussion of this form as an opportunity to educate the parents.

4. *Review Adaptive Behavioral Interchanges between Adults and Children.* Pass out the "Adaptive Behavioral Interchanges between Adults and Children" chart found in Appendix B. Explain to the parents that the purpose of this chart is to help them think of new ways to respond to their child's behavior. Inform the parents that many of the skills on this chart will be addressed in remaining parent sessions. Review each of the adaptive behaviors on the chart. Ask the parents in what way these adaptive behaviors would more positively affect their ADHD child and their ability to work with their child. Ask the parents what messages would be communicated to their child if they engaged in these adaptive parent–child interactions.

5. *Self-Monitoring.* Explain to the parents that one goal of the intervention is to change parents' maladaptive attributions/beliefs and parent–child behavioral interchanges. To accomplish this, we ask the parents to self-monitor by completing the parent self-evaluation forms once a week for the remainder of the program. Parents can complete the chart before or at group each week. Another goal is to monitor their own progress as they go through the program.

6. *Focusing on Children's Strengths.* Explain to the parents that ADHD children have many weaknesses in the areas that are traditionally called upon to function successfully at school and in other areas. These children have weaknesses in the ability to stay on-task, get their work done,

and handle emotions and social situations appropriately. Explain to the parents that in many respects, no matter what we do in terms of interventions, these children will continue to have some problems in these areas. To lessen the impact of these "failures" on the child's overall self-esteem, it is necessary to focus on their strengths.

Pass out the chart entitled "Inventory for Child's Strengths and Weaknesses" found in Appendix B. Explain to the parents that the purpose of this chart is to focus their attention on their child's individual strengths. The idea is to write down all the child's weaknesses and strengths they can identify. Following this effort, encourage the parents to notice and reinforce the child for exhibiting his/her strength behaviors.

Child-Focused CBT I
Clinic Model—Week 6; School Model—Week 8

Objectives

1. Introduce alternative ways for parents to handle their child's problem behavior that are based on cognitive–behavioral skills. Introduce the "Stop, Think, and Use a Plan Chart" and "Tally for Using Plans (Weekly or Daily)" Chart found in Appendix B. A goal for this session will be to train parents to facilitate their child's use of self-instruction skills at home.

Procedures

1. *Check-In.* Conduct check-in as before, but also add a self-monitoring component. Each week, ask the parents to complete the two parent self-evaluation forms previously discussed. Ask parents to complete these forms to reflect their thoughts and behavior for the period of time between sessions. Approximately 10 minutes each week should be devoted to the parent self-evaluation forms. Use this opportunity to continue educating parents about these concepts. It may be helpful to review the adaptive thoughts and behavior forms, too.

2. *Review Problem-Solving Steps.* Pass out the "Five-Step Problem-Solving" chart found in Appendix B. Review each of the five steps with the parents. Explain that Step 1 is geared toward problem recognition, Step 2 is geared toward solution generation, Step 3 is geared toward consequential thinking, Step 4 is geared toward implementing a plan, and Step 5 is geared toward reviewing the success of having used a plan. Explain that you would like them to start using this type of problem-solving process at home with their child. Explain to the parents that

when their child is having a problem of any kind, they could ask the child to use these steps in an effort to solve his/her own problems.

The parents should also be encouraged to model using these steps. This can be accomplished by having the parents say the steps out loud to themselves when they are trying to figure out what to do at home. For example, if a parent is trying to figure out what to make for dinner that night, he/she could use the strategies, stating them out loud so that the child can observe the parent using them.

Explain to the parents how to prompt the child to use a plan. The therapist could provide some verbal examples of dialogues that might be used at home when trying to get a child to use the plans. The following is one example:

When a Child Is Refusing to Do His/Her Homework

PARENT: This might be a good time to use a plan.
CHILD: I don't want to use a plan.
PARENT: Remember, if you use a plan, you can earn some rewards.
CHILD: Well, OK! I'll try one.
PARENT: OK, what is the first step?
CHILD: Well, I have to ask myself, "Stop! What is the problem?" The problem is that I don't want to do my homework and you want me to.
PARENT: Good! Why don't you see if you can do the rest of the problem-solving steps now?
CHILD: OK, the next step is that I need to figure out: "What are some plans?" Well, I could just ignore you, or I could do my homework like you said, or I could try to work on a deal where I have fun now and do homework later. The next step is: "What is the best plan?" Well, if I ignore you, I'll probably get in trouble. If I do my homework, I wouldn't get in trouble, but I wouldn't be able to do what I want to do right now. If we work out a deal, maybe then we'd both be happy. OK, I think the best plan is to try to work out a deal. Next I have to: "Do the plan." So now I'll try to work out a deal.
PARENT: That's good! And what will be the last step?
CHILD: Well, the last step would be to see if my plan worked.

The therapist should bring up more examples of what the dialogue might sound like when a child is confronted with a different type of problem and the parent is trying to work with him/her to use the problem-solving steps.

3. *Introduce Charts for Home Use of Plans.* Introduce the "Stop, Think, and Use a Plan Chart" and "Guidelines for Using the Stop, Think, and Use a Plan Chart" found in Appendix B. Discuss the guidelines and example for the "Stop, Think, and Use a Plan Chart" in detail. The therapist should first model a demonstration of how to use the charts. Ask a parent volunteer to act out a child engaging in some problem behavior, while the therapist acts out the parent responding and using

plans and the chart. Follow the sequence provided in the guidelines very carefully, so the parents will have correct modeling of how to use the chart. Have parents divide into dyads and role-play how to use the chart with problems/situations they think may arise with their children. The therapist should walk around the room coaching the parent dyads on the appropriate way to use these procedures. Tell parents their children are being familiarized with the charts in their groups.

Pass out the "Tally for Using Plans (Weekly or Daily)" and the "Guidelines for Using Tally for Using Plans (Weekly or Daily)" charts found in Appendix B. Discuss the guidelines and example for the "Tally for Using Plans (Weekly or Daily)" chart (see Appendix B). Be sure parents understand that children are to be rewarded to increase their motivation to use plans in their home. Also, parents need to understand that the children are to be rewarded for the quality of their plan-making, not for the quantity of plans that are used. Explain that in order to emphasize quality, children are rewarded for obtaining ratings of three and four when they are using plans at home. Another goal is for children to eventually initiate plans themselves. Thus, if the child comes up with the idea to use plans more frequently than the adults around him/her, the child will receive additional reinforcement.

Encourage parents to discuss with their children which rewards they want to receive. This discussion should occur before actually using the charts at home. Encourage parents to set aside at least 30 minutes with their child to discuss all of this at home before starting. Discuss appropriate reinforcers the parents can give their children for using plans. Hand out the "Reinforcement Ideas" chart found in Appendix B. Help parents choose reinforcers that are motivating to the child and realistic for the parents. Explain the importance of having an array of possible reinforcers, given the ADHD child's tendency to satiate to any one reward. Encourage parents to discuss the reinforcers with the child before using the plans at home.

4. *Homework.* Ask the parents to use the system and bring the "Stop, Think, and Use a Plan Chart" and the "Tally for Using Plans (Weekly or Daily)" chart to the parent groups each week.

Child-Focused CBT II
Clinic Model—Week 7; School Model—Week 10

Objectives

1. Review the "Stop, Think, and Use a Plan Chart." Have parents identify problems and potential solutions to the difficulties that arose in the implementation of the plans/procedures at home.

2. Discuss with parents the concept of modeling problem-solving behavior at home.

Procedures

1. *Check-In.*

2. *Review Use of Plans at Home.* Have each parent discuss any difficulty applying the procedures at home. The primary purposes of the discussion are to identify problems in implementation and think of solutions. The typical difficulties that arise involve parents not understanding the procedures and/or the children responding in a resistant fashion to parents' attempts to cue them to use plans at home. Sometimes the problem lies with the parents' failure to use the procedures at home. There are several methods a therapist can employ to help parents solve the problems they are having in implementing these procedures at home. The first method involves using group process. The therapist should encourage other group members to engage in a discussion with the parents who are having difficulties and brainstorm alternative solutions for the problems. Another method the therapist can employ is to review the concepts. Typically, parents have not stressed to their child that they can earn rewards for using plans at home. Finally, it may be helpful for the therapist to once again use modeling and role-playing to review the procedures. The therapist could go through the guidelines for the "Stop, Think and Use a Plan Chart" and the "Tally for Using Plans (Weekly and Daily)" chart in a step-by-step fashion, making the procedures as concrete as possible. This part of the session should take at least 1 hour.

3. *Parents' Modeling of Self-Instruction.* Emphasize that parents' modeling for their children is a powerful tool for teaching children to use plans. We suggest having parents initially model "neutral" ways of using plans. This may involve the parents stating the five problem-solving steps out loud while solving problems such as what to fix for dinner or how to make sure a parent can get themselves up earlier in the morning. Parents can also model how to use plans to solve difficult problems too. This may involve the parents stating the five problem-solving steps out loud while solving interpersonal problems, on-task problems, etc.

4. *Homework.* Continue using child-focused CBT at home.

Collaborative CBT I
Clinic Model—Week 9; School Model—Week 12

Objective

1. Introduce collaborative problem-solving (i.e., parent–child plans or family problem-solving).

Procedures

1. *Introduce the Concept of Collaborative Plans.* Explain to parents that they can use plans to solve problems with their child. Also, explain that using collaborative plans provides valuable modeling for the child. In this context, however, the child is learning these procedures to solve family-oriented problems. Inform parents that using collaborative plans can also reduce children's resistance to using plans in general.

Pass out the "Stop, Think, and Use a Plan Chart: Collaborative Plan Example" and the "Guidelines for Collaborative Plans" found in Appendix B. Engage the parents in a discussion of when they might use collaborative plans. They should be able to identify common problems that occur at home involving the family. Examples of problems appropriate for collaborative plans range from deciding where to go out for dinner to arguing or negotiating about how late the children may stay outside. Situations involving arguing and negotiating are the most common and most appropriate for using collaborative plans. To make this information very clear, the therapists may again want to use modeling and role-playing with the parents. The therapist may also need to work with the parents to determine whether or not the siblings are appropriate for inclusion in family plans.

2. *Understanding the Distinction between Child-Focused and Collaborative Plans.* Help parents understand that they now have a larger repertoire of ways to handle their child's problem behavior. Specifically, the parents now can (1) prompt children to use a plan or (2) use collaborative plans. Engage the parents in a discussion of problems and situations that are appropriately addressed by these two procedures.

3. *Homework.* Continue to employ child-focused and also begin using collaborative CBT at home.

Collaborative CBT II
Clinic Model—Week 10; School Model—Week 14

Objective

1. Continue to review and problem-solve about implementing child-focused and collaborative CBT methods at home.

Procedures

1. *Check-In.*
2. *Review Child-Focused and Collaborative CBT Methods at Home.* The therapist should use most of the session to review the concepts and procedures that have been learned in previous sessions. The therapist should focus the discussion primarily on how well the parents have used

the collaborative CBT methods at home. The therapist should be aware that there tends to be significant variability in how well the parents are grasping the concepts and/or complying with using the procedures at home. It may be necessary to use modeling and role-play exercises to emphasize certain points.

3. *Homework.* Continue to employ child-focused and/or collaborative CBT methods at home.

Behavioral Child Management I
Clinic Model—Week 12; School Model—Week 16

Objective

1. Introduce behavioral child management strategies.

Procedures

1. *Check-In.*

2. *Introduce Behavioral Child Management Strategies.* Explain to parents that child-focused and collaborative plans are not always effective, particularly when the child or the parents are too upset to use a plan. Also explain that one of the goals of this program is to increase parents' repertoire of skills. Pass out the "Time-Out" chart found in Appendix B. Explain the procedures of time-out in enough detail so that all parents understand. See the handout for a guide on how to explain the procedures to the parents. Time-out is a very complicated procedure for parents to understand completely. The therapist would be wise to spend a majority of the time discussing time-out. Oftentimes, parents will report that they have used time-out and it has not been successful. Upon closer review with the parents, it can be determined that parents were using time-out in an inappropriate or ineffective manner. It is necessary for the therapist to take the time to model and engage the parents in role-play exercises about implementing time-out with their children.

3. *Understanding the Distinction between Child-Focused Plans, Collaborative Plans, and Behavioral Child Management Strategies.* Help the parents make the distinction that they now have an even larger repertoire of ways to handle their child's behavior problems. Specifically, the parents can now (1) prompt the child to use a plan, (2) use collaborative plans, or (3) use behavioral child management strategies. The main· point to emphasize is that parents will want to use these strategies sequentially. If a child is having behavioral difficulties, we recommend using either a child or collaborative plan, but, if that is not successful, then a time-out procedure would be in order. Engage the parents in a

discussion of problems and situations that can be addressed by these three strategies.

4. *Homework.* Ask the parents to continue to employ child-focused and collaborative CBT methods, but also to use time-out procedures when appropriate at home.

Behavioral Child Management II and Program Review
Clinic Model—Week 13; School Model—Week 18

Objectives

1. Review concepts related to time-out.
2. Introduce other alternative behavioral child management methods.
3. Review all concepts addressed in program.

Procedures

1. *Check-In.*
2. *Review Time-Out.* The therapist should ask the parents to review their use of time-out with their children. The therapist should ask the parents to give specific examples of when they used time-out with their children and take note as to whether or not time-out has been implemented appropriately. If time-out has not been implemented appropriately, the therapist should take the time to model and role-play correct implementation of time-out.
3. *Introduce Alternative Behavioral Methods.* Pass out the "Reinforcement of Specific Behavior" and "Daily Behavior Contract" charts found in Appendix B. Review these charts in enough detail so that the parents can adequately understand how each of the charts is used. The "Reinforcement of Specific Behavior" chart can be used to increase specific behaviors on a daily basis. The "Daily Behavior Contract" chart can also be used to increase specific behaviors. The focus is somewhat different with this chart in that the parent is granting or removing privileges when specified behaviors are or are not emitted by the child.
4. *Review All Strategies.* Discuss and review all the concepts that have been learned previously in the program. Again, the therapist can use discussion, modeling, and role-playing to communicate these points in a very concrete manner.
5. *Fading Reinforcement.* Eventually the child will not need or profit from reinforcement for using CBT strategies. Parents cannot realistically follow through with the reinforcement system indefinitely. Discuss

with the parents the need to "fade out" the reinforcements (i.e., stop using the "Stop, Think, and Use a Plan Chart" and the "Tally for Using Plans (Weekly or Daily)" chart). The parents will need to evaluate the progress their child has made to determine when to fade out the reinforcement. When their child appears to use plans spontaneously, or at least is cooperative with his/her parents in using them, they should consider stopping the reinforcement system. This fading process might involve moving from weekly to biweekly and then triweekly rewards prior to stopping the formal reinforcements. Forewarn the parents that there may be relapses, and the reinforcement procedure could be reinstated periodically for short periods of time. Another option is to stop reinforcing plan use for issues that have become more routinely handled in an appropriate way but continuing a formal system of reinforcement to address problems with which the child or family continues to struggle.

6. *Plan for Follow-Up (Optional).** Explain to the parents that the intervention should not be expected to cure the child of ADHD. It will be necessary to have follow-up sessions in the future. Explain the booster session format (outlined in the last section of this chapter) to the parents. If applicable, make arrangements to meet again with the parents and/or family.

Family Component (Clinic Model Only)

Procedural Overview

The primary purpose of the three family sessions is to tailor the intervention to meet the unique needs of each family. During these sessions all previous concepts/procedures are reviewed; no new material is introduced. The therapist also problem-solves with the family to think of solutions to any difficulties that may have come up while they were implementing the concepts/procedures at home. The family therapy sessions provide an excellent opportunity to deal with resistance or poor follow-through with the procedures/concepts. If the therapist perceives the family as not attempting to implement the procedures, this perception should be shared and discussed. It is important to frame the family's noncompliance as a dilemma to be understood and solved rather than as a failing on the part of the parents and/or child. (See Chapter 4 for ideas on how to deal with resistance.)

---

*School model only.

Child-Focused CBT at Home
Clinic Model Only—Week 8

Objective

1. All concepts and procedures for child-focused plans are reviewed.

Procedures

1. *Before-Session Evaluation.* It is preferable for the family to meet with one therapist from the parent group and one therapist from the child group, but if this is not possible, one therapist could easily meet with the family. To maximize the potential impact of the family sessions, it is recommended that the therapists meet before the family session to make an overall assessment of the child and the family, and to think of areas that need to be addressed in the family session. The therapists should evaluate the child in terms of his/her ability to implement the procedures in the group and his/her reports of how he/she is implementing the procedures at home. The therapists should also evaluate the parents in terms of their understanding of the major concepts and their ability to implement these procedures at home.

2. *Check-In.* The family is asked how the week has gone and any questions they may have from the previous weeks are answered.

3. *Review Implementation of Child-Focused CBT at Home.* The "Stop, Think, and Use a Plan Chart" and the "Tally for Using Plans (Weekly or Daily)" chart for that week are reviewed in detail. The family is asked if they have any questions or concerns about implementing these procedures at home. The therapist should spend most of the time reviewing problems the family might be having regarding implementation of plans at home. The therapists will want to facilitate an interchange between the parents and the child as they discuss these issues. It may be useful for the family to engage in role-playing.

4. *Review Common Problems.* There are typical problems that emerge initially with the implementation of plans at home:

a. *Understanding.* Parents and children occasionally do not understand the concepts involved in implementing procedures. To remediate this, the therapist may want to review all the charts and have the parent and child role-play implementation of the strategies.

b. *Resistance.* Occasionally children are resistant to using plans at home. Help the parents understand that they need to emphasize to the child that they can earn a reward for using the plans at home. Help the parents see that the children may not be intrinsically motivated at this time, but if the external motivation (i.e., reinforcement) is significant, the child may be more amenable to using the strategies. Tell the parents that eventually the reinforcement system will be faded out.

c. *Reinforcement.* Sometimes parents select a reinforcer that is either not motivating or is not realistic. Review the idea that reinforcement has to be something that the child will work for, but also has to be realistic in terms of the parents being able to give the child the reward. Spend as much time as necessary discussing this very important reinforcement issue. Parents may also need to consider planning reinforcement for themselves for implementing the procedures.

Collaborative CBT at Home
Clinic Model Only—Week 11

Objectives

1. Child-focused and collaborative CBT methods are reviewed.
2. Appropriate siblings are incorporated into collaborative plans.

Procedures

1. *Before-Session Evaluation.*
2. *Check-In.*
3. *Review Implementation of Child-Focused and Collaborative Plans.* The "Stop, Think, and Use a Plan Chart" and the "Tally for Using Plans (Weekly or Daily)" chart for that week are reviewed. The family is asked if they have any questions or concerns regarding implementing the child-focused and collaborative plans at home. Parents may need specific encouragement and practice with identifying opportunities for using collaborative plans. The therapist will want to use thorough discussion, modeling, and, possibly, role-playing exercises to review how to implement these procedures at home. The therapist will again want to facilitate interchange between the parents and the child as they discuss these issues.
4. *Involve Siblings.* It is helpful to discuss sibling involvement. Siblings can be active participants in collaborative plans. Parents may even decide to use the "Stop, Think, and Use a Plan Chart" and the "Tally for Using Plans (Weekly or Daily)" chart for siblings, too.

Program Review
Clinic Model Only—Week 14

Objectives

1. Review major concepts/skills acquired during program involvement.
2. Obtain the family's view of their progress.
3. Engage in disposition planning with the family.

Procedures

1. *Before-Session Evaluation.*
2. *Check-In.*
3. *Review All Concepts/Procedures.* This session should focus extensively on reviewing all concepts and procedures. The therapist and the family will need to review, discuss, model, and engage in role-playing, if necessary, to make sure that concepts and procedures are understood and are being used correctly.

4. *Review Progress.* The family is asked about their perceptions of their progress through the program. The therapist will also want to give the family feedback on his/her evaluation of the families' progress. The therapist should ask the family to anticipate any problems that may arise in the future and to plan ahead how they might handle these issues in terms of implementing the procedures at home.

5. *Discuss Future Recommendations.* Any future recommendations for the family are discussed. It is recommended that the family be engaged in at least one follow-up session, 4–6 weeks after completion of the program. In addition, it is also recommended that the therapist and the parents participate in a school conference at the child's school to determine if the school may be able to use these procedures in the school environment. The therapist may also want to recommend other types of intervention, including family therapy, social skills training, individual therapy, or medication treatment for the child. The therapist should communicate quite clearly that he/she is available to work with the family after they have completed the program.

Teacher Component (School Model Only)

Procedural Overview

The primary purpose of the teacher component is to enhance transfer of the skills the children have learned through the program to the classroom environment and to aid in long-term maintenance of program gains. The teacher component is designed to be used by all teachers and related school personnel in a particular school. We strongly recommend that *all* children in the school be exposed to the program. Ideally, efforts should be made to incorporate problem-solving into the normal fabric of everyday school life in each classroom. If all children are involved, then no one needs to feel singled out or different if someone at school asks him/her to use a plan. Teachers, principals, counselors, school psychologists, and other personnel who have contact with the children throughout the school day should be involved as much as possible. Each classroom should be equipped with a large posterboard sign with the five problem-solving steps. The teachers and other school personnel can refer to this sign when discussing the program and use of the strategies with children in the classroom. By involving the entire school system and by having these signs in each classroom, the children will be exposed to the treatment strategies through a variety of sources throughout the school day. The teachers and other relevant school personnel will also have access to the "Stop, Think, and Use a Plan Chart," which will be discussed later in this section.

The content of the teacher component parallels the content of the parent component. There is relatively less emphasis on teachers obtaining support through the meetings; sessions are education-oriented rather than therapy-oriented. The primary focus is on modifying teachers' cognitions and behaviors related to ADHD children and training the teachers in skills that will facilitate them working with the children within a CBT framework. The program is arranged so that teachers attend nine biweekly, 1-hour sessions. This can be modified to meet the unique needs of a given school.

Introduction
School Model—Week 2

Objectives

    1. Review information about ADHD and the intervention program.
    2. Set positive, but realistic, expectations for the program.

Procedures

1. *Introductions.* The consultant introduces himself/herself, as well as faculty members and school personnel who have been involved in developing the program for that particular school or district. It is very important to include principals and other individuals with positions of authority in the school system, demonstrating to the teachers that the program is endorsed and backed by those individuals. If possible, have those important authority figures present for at least a few minutes, discussing how they are excited about the program and would encourage all teachers to participate actively.

2. *Forming a Collaborative Relationship.* Explain to the teachers that your role as the consultant is to present ideas. Your role is not to tell them what to do or to evaluate them in any way. Explain that the ideas to be presented are not absolute but are modifiable. It is preferable that the teachers give lots of input into the procedures and adapt them to make

them work for their unique classrooms. Explain that the overall format of these sessions will be for them to work together and make decisions together about the specific aspects of the program. Encourage an open discussion about pros and cons of the strategies and the teachers' feelings regarding the ideas presented. Encourage the teachers to ask questions and engage in discussion. It is very important to develop rapport and a sense of collaboration and cooperation in working with the teachers.

3. *Education about ADHD.* Introduce and discuss the chart entitled "Attention-Deficit Hyperactivity Disorder" found in Appendix B. Review and discuss each of the concepts on the chart.

4. *Medical Information.* Much of the session will focus on education regarding medical aspects of ADHD. The consultant can focus primarily on medication issues. This presentation should include a thorough discussion of the purposes and possible side effects of the medications. The lecture and discussion should take approximately 30 minutes. If medical personnel are available to participate in this discussion, their involvement should be encouraged.

5. *Education about CBT.* Introduce and discuss the chart entitled "Cognitive–Behavioral Therapy for Children with Attention-Deficit Hyperactivity Disorder" found in Appendix B. Review and discuss each of the concepts on the chart. Emphasize that teacher involvement is very important for success of the program.

6. *Overview of the Program.* Inform the teachers that the program consists of the children participating in 18 group therapy sessions and the parents and teachers participating in nine training sessions. Explain that the children will be learning how to use problem-solving and self-instruction skills and then will learn to apply these skills to four broad content areas: (1) interpersonal problems, (2) management of anger/ frustration, (3) management of poor effort, and (4) management of negative thoughts and feelings. Tell the teachers that they will be involved in prompting and reinforcing the children for using self-instruction and problem-solving skills to cope with these four content areas in the classroom situation. Inform the teachers that the program has been streamlined as much as possible to help accommodate their working with the child, in recognition of their busy and hectic schedules.

7. *Expectations for the Program.* Discuss the notion that this program is not a cure for ADHD and related social, school and behavioral problems. The program does offer, however, a chance for the teachers to participate and try to learn additional coping skills that they can use to deal with these children on an ongoing basis. A goal of this part of the session would be to help the teachers achieve a very realistic appraisal of what they can expect from participating in this program.

Group Process/Support
School Model—Week 4

Objectives

1. Establish routine check-in at the beginning of group.
2. Establish group guidelines.
3. Establish group cohesion.

Procedures

1. *Check-In.* Establish a routine check-in period at the beginning of the session. The routine check-in essentially entails the teachers reporting about the activities of their ADHD students and themselves that have occurred since the last session. When possible, the consultant should focus the check-in on discussion of implementing various therapeutic strategies and techniques at school and the success or lack of success the teachers are having.

2. *Review Material from Previous Session; Focus on Teachers' Views of the Program.* Ask the teachers if they have any questions left over from the previous session. It may be helpful to review information about ADHD and the contents of the program. Importantly, it may be especially necessary to spend time focusing on teachers' beliefs and perceptions about this program. Many teachers have ideas about how to deal with these children that are rather deeply ingrained. They may be somewhat skeptical about the program or they may view it as too cumbersome or difficult to implement in the classroom. The consultant would be wise to spend as much time as possible openly discussing these issues. Ask the teachers if they feel the program would be too difficult to do in the classroom. Ask the teachers how this program may or may not mesh well with ideas and procedures that they already use in the classroom. Attempt to lead the group to recognize that these children take time to deal with whether or not one has a special system, so there may be some advantage to establishing a routine method of working with them rather than against them. The consultant will want to spend as much time as possible reviewing how this program interfaces with the teachers' ideas of how to handle ADHD children in the classroom. If this issue is not dealt with sufficiently at the beginning of the intervention, it could create a fair amount of resistance as the program evolves.

3. *Establish Group Cohesion.* To establish group cohesion, have the teachers participate in a discussion of classroom-related "war stories." The overall aim is to facilitate a discussion of common problems, concerns and frustrations that teachers have had as they struggle to teach ADHD children. We have found this to be a powerful way to establish

group cohesion. Usually teachers have no trouble bringing up examples. It is also important to encourage teachers to tell "war stories" and other related difficulties that they have been having throughout the course of all of the teacher sessions.

Examine Teachers' Cognitions and Behaviors
School Model—Week 6

Objectives

1. Examine and begin to modify attributions/beliefs of teachers about themselves and ADHD children.

2. Examine and begin to modify typical behavioral interchanges between teachers and ADHD children.

3. Focus on children's strengths and weaknesses.

Procedures

In this session, the teachers will be asked to complete several charts. These charts are designed to facilitate education of teachers and to begin modification of their cognitions and behaviors.

1. *Examine Common Attributions/Beliefs Regarding ADHD Children.* Pass out the "Adult Self-Evaluation of Thoughts Form" found in Appendix B. Ask the teachers to complete the measure in an open and honest manner and discuss some of their attributions and beliefs regarding ADHD children with the group. Thoroughly discuss the measure and teachers' unique responses. It may be necessary to explain the concepts of attributions and beliefs to the teachers before engaging in this discussion. Review each of the common attributions and beliefs in as much detail as necessary. Ask the teachers to discern the problematic or dysfunctional aspects of those particular attributions or beliefs where a high score was obtained (e.g., three or above). Ask the teachers in what way these attributions or beliefs would interfere with their ability to work with ADHD children. Ask the teachers how these attributions and beliefs would influence their behavior toward ADHD children and what types of messages would be communicated to these children by their behavior.

2. *Review Adaptive Attributions and Beliefs Regarding ADHD.* Pass out the "Adaptive Attributions and Beliefs Regarding ADHD" chart found in Appendix B. Explain to the teachers that the purpose of this chart is to help them develop new ways to think about these children and their problems. The idea is to broaden their view of ADHD children. Suggest that these thoughts could be used to counter those thoughts they viewed as dysfunctional in the previous teacher self-evaluation form. Review

each attribution and belief and ask the teachers how these new attributions and beliefs would positively affect their work with ADHD children. Ask the teachers how these new attributions and beliefs would facilitate their ability to work with these children. Ask the teachers how these attributions and beliefs influence their behavior toward ADHD children and what messages these behaviors would communicate to the child.

3. *Examine Common Teacher–Child Behavioral Interchanges.* Pass out the "Adult Self-Evaluation of Behavior Form" found in Appendix B. Ask the teachers to complete this form and then discuss some of their typical behavioral interchanges with these children. Review the form thoroughly. Discuss each of the common behavioral interchanges in as much detail as necessary. Ask the teachers what is problematic or dysfunctional about those behaviors where a high score was obtained (e.g., 3 or above). Ask the teachers in what way these behaviors interfere with their ability to work with ADHD children. Ask the teachers what type of messages would be communicated to ADHD children if these types of behavioral interactions were typical. Use the discussion of the form as an opportunity to educate teachers.

4. *Review Adaptive Behavioral Interchanges between Adults and Children.* Pass out the "Adaptive Behavioral Interchanges between Adults and Children" chart found in Appendix B. Explain to the teachers that the purpose of this chart is to help them think of new ways to behave and different ways of solving behavioral problems with ADHD children. Inform the teachers that many of the skills on this chart will be addressed in remaining teacher sessions. Review each of the adaptive behaviors on the chart. Ask the teachers how these new adaptive behaviors would more positively affect ADHD children and their ability to work with these children. Ask the teachers what new messages would be communicated to ADHD children if they engaged in these adaptive teacher–child interactions.

5. *Self-Monitoring (Optional).* The self-monitoring exercise involves teachers monitoring their thoughts and behavioral interchanges with ADHD children on an ongoing basis. As with the parent component, the self-monitoring component with teachers would involve them completing self-monitoring charts on a weekly basis. We have found through our experience, however, that teachers are sometimes resistant to this because it involves extra work on their part, when they are already extremely busy professionals. Therefore, we make the self-monitoring component an option for teachers.

The following suggestions are offered if the consultant elects to use the self-monitoring component with the teachers. Explain to the teachers that one goal of the intervention is to change the teachers' maladaptive attributions/beliefs and teacher–child behavioral interchanges. To accomplish this, we ask the teachers to self-monitor by completing the teacher self-evaluation forms once a week for the remainder of the program. Teachers can complete the chart before or at the teacher session. Another goal is to monitor their own progress as they go through the program.

Child-Focused CBT I
School Model—Week 8

Objective

1. Introduce alternative ways for teachers to handle ADHD children's problem behavior that are based on cognitive–behavioral skills. Introduce the "Stop, Think and Use a Plan Chart" and "Tally for Using Plans (Weekly or Daily)" chart found in Appendix B. A goal for this session is to train teachers to facilitate ADHD children's use of self-instruction skills at school.

Procedures

1. *Check-In.* Conduct check-in as before. If the consultant elects to use the self-monitoring component, then it should be incorporated in the check-in routine. Each week, the teachers would complete the two teacher self-evaluation forms discussed previously. Ask teachers to complete these forms to reflect their thoughts and behaviors for the period between sessions. Approximately 10 minutes each week should be devoted to these teacher self-evaluation forms. Use the opportunity to continue educating teachers about these concepts. It may be helpful to review the adaptive thoughts and behavior charts, too. Focus on whether or not the responses on the measures are going in the right direction.

2. *Review Problem-Solving Steps.* Pass out the "Five-Step Problem-Solving" chart found in Appendix B. Review each of the five steps with the teachers. Explain that Step 1 is geared toward problem recognition, Step 2 is geared toward solution generation, Step 3 is geared toward consequential thinking, Step 4 is geared toward implementing a plan, and Step 5 is geared toward reviewing the success of having used a plan. Explain that you would like them to start using this type of problem-solving process at school with *all* children in their classroom. Explain to the teachers that when any child is having a problem of any kind, they could ask the child to use these steps in an effort to solve his/her own problems.

Ask the teachers to spend a minimum of *two 30-minute intervals over the next 2 weeks* explaining these concepts to their classes. Emphasize that it is important for the teachers to explain these steps in as much detail as is necessary for all the children in the classroom to understand. The teacher may want to model and/or engage some of the students in role-play exercises to help them understand how to use these procedures appropriately. The teachers could provide a chart with the five-step plan on it and ask the children to look at it while they are explaining the steps and when using the procedures in the classroom in a formal way.

The teachers should also be encouraged to say the steps out loud when they are trying to solve common dilemmas or issues in the classroom. For example, if the teacher is trying to figure out how to present a certain concept to the class, he/she could use the strategies, stating them out loud so that the entire class can observe.

Explain how teachers can prompt the children to use plans in the classroom. The consultant could provide some verbal examples of dialogues that might be used in the classroom when trying to get a child to use the plans. The following is one example:

When a Child Is Refusing to Do His/Her Schoolwork

TEACHER: This might be a good time to use a plan.
CHILD: I don't want to use a plan.
TEACHER: Remember, if you use a plan, you can earn some rewards.
CHILD: Well, OK! I'll try one.
TEACHER: OK, what is the first step?
CHILD: Well, I have to ask myself, "Stop! What is the problem?" The problem is that I don't want to do my schoolwork and you want me to.
TEACHER: Good! Why don't you see if you can do the rest of the problem-solving steps now?
CHILD: OK, the next step is that I need to figure out: "What are some plans?" Well, I could just ignore you, or I could do my schoolwork like you said, or I could try to work on a deal where I have fun now and do schoolwork later. The next step is: "What is the best plan?" Well, if I ignore you, I'll probably get in trouble. If I do my schoolwork, I wouldn't get in trouble. OK, I think the best plan is to try to do my schoolwork now. Next I have to: "Do the plan." So now I'll go do my schoolwork.
TEACHER: That's good! And what will be the last step?
CHILD: Well, the last step would be to see if my plan worked.

The consultant should bring up several examples of what the dialogue might sound like when a child is confronted with different types of problems and the teacher is trying to work with him/her to use the problem-solving steps.

3. *Introduce "Stop, Think, and Use a Plan Chart."* Introduce the "Stop, Think, and Use a Plan Chart" found in Appendix B. Discuss the guidelines and the example of the "Stop, Think, and Use a Plan Chart" in detail. The consultant should first model how to use the chart. Ask a

teacher volunteer to act out a child engaging in some problem behavior, while the consultant acts out a teacher responding and using plans and the chart. (If possible, the consultant could prepare a videotape of a teacher using the strategies with a child in the classroom.) Follow the sequence detailed in the guidelines very carefully, so the teachers will have correct modeling of how to use the charts and procedures. Have teachers divide into dyads and role-play how to use the chart with problems/situations they think may arise in the classroom. The consultant should walk around the room coaching the teacher dyads on the appropriate way to use these procedures.

4. *Methods to Prompt the Child to Use the Plans in the Classroom.* Explain to the teachers that it may be difficult to verbally prompt the child to use the plans in the classroom, given the constraints of a busy classroom and the problems with identifying the child as having to use a plan. Teachers should consider a variety of alternative methods for prompting the child, including:

a. Teachers could prompt the child verbally by informing the child that "this may be a good time to use a plan."

b. Teachers could prompt the child to use a plan with a visual hand signal. The teacher could pick some type of hand signal or cue that the child and he/she have agreed on beforehand to signal the child to use a plan.

c. The child can simply tell the teacher that he/she has used a plan to solve a specific problem and then describe how that was accomplished.

5. *Methods to Evaluate Plan-Making.* It may also be difficult for the teacher to evaluate the child's quality of using plans on the "Stop, Think, and Use a Plan Chart" every time the child has used a plan. Again, several alternatives should be considered about how to complete the charts, including:

a. Filling out the "Stop, Think, and Use a Plan Chart" after every plan the child uses in the classroom, much as parents do with difficulties at home.

b. Completing the "Stop, Think, and Use a Plan Chart" without directly consulting the child until the end of some designated time period, like at the end of the morning or at the end of the entire day. But at some point in the day, the teacher needs to give the child some verbal feedback and review the chart to provide him/her with an idea of how well he/she is using plans.

c. Having the children take complete responsibility for completing the "Stop, Think, and Use a Plan Chart," without prompting them about using the chart. This would entail the child potentially carrying the chart around with him/her and, when a plan is used, asking the teacher for feedback in completing the chart. This has the advantage of placing the responsibility more on the child and less on the busy teacher. There is also a disadvantage in that these children may forget or not be assertive enough to ask the teacher for feedback. Before teachers elect to use this option, they should carefully consider these advantages and disadvantages.

6. *Methods to Reward Plan-Making.* Initially, children will need some sort of extrinsic reinforcement to become motivated and enthusiastic about using plans in the classroom. Teachers are very busy and may or may not be able to provide this type of reinforcement for the child. The following are some suggested ideas that could be used to reinforce children for applying these strategies in the classroom, including:

a. The teacher elects to reinforce the child in some fashion for using plans in the classroom, either verbally, with the awarding of special privileges, or with something more tangible (e.g., stickers, tokens, or small toys).

b. The teacher communicates in some fashion with the child's parents about the child's use of plans in the classroom. The parents then reward the child for using the strategies in the classroom.

c. The teacher communicates in some fashion with the child's group therapist about how the child is using plans in the classroom. The group therapist then rewards the child in some fashion for using plans in the classroom.

7. *Using Short Plans.* Using plans at school can be somewhat cumbersome for the child and teacher. It is suggested that short plans be used at school. Plans can be abbreviated so that if the teacher prompts the child to use a plan, and the child pauses and then demonstrates altered behavior, the child receives credit for having used a plan. Also, if the child does want to state the steps, he/she could just simply state what the problem is and what he/she is going to do about it. If the child prefers to use all five steps, that is OK too.

8. *Changing Interaction Style with the Child.* A final and very important point to emphasize with the teachers is that they will need to alter their interaction style with the child. Oftentimes, teachers and other school personnel find themselves dealing with the child by responding to the problem behavior in a manner such as setting limits or providing consequences to the child. To some extent, that would change when using these procedures. The teachers would not respond automatically with limits or consequences. Rather, the teacher would need to prompt the child to use a plan. If the child exhibited positive behavior change, then he/she would not receive any limits or consequences and would receive reinforcement for using a good plan. If the child does not use a plan, then the teacher would set limits and/or provide consequences. Thus, the sequence would be: (1) observe child problem behavior, (2) prompt the child to use a plan, and (3) impose consequences or limits for the child, if behavior does not improve.

9. *Homework for Teachers.* For the next 2-week period, have the teachers engage their entire classrooms in at least two 30-minute discussions, or a series of discussions, about problem-solving and its application in the classroom. Also ask the teachers to begin using the "Stop, Think, and Use a Plan Chart" and CBT procedures with specific students in the classroom.

Child-Focused CBT II
School Model—Week 10

Objectives

1. Review the "Stop, Think, and Use a Plan Chart." Have teachers identify problems and potential solutions to difficulties arising in the implementation of the plans/procedures in the classroom.
2. Discuss with teachers the concept of modeling problem-solving behavior at school.

Procedures

1. *Check-In.*
2. *Review Use of Plans at School.* Have each teacher discuss any difficulty applying the procedures at school. The primary purposes of the discussion are to identify problems in implementation and think of solutions. The typical difficulties that arise involve teachers not understanding the procedures and/or the children responding in a resistant fashion to teachers' attempts to cue them to use plans at school. Sometimes the problem lies with the teachers' failure to use the procedures at all. There are several methods a therapist can employ to help teachers solve the problems they are having in implementing these procedures in the classroom. The first method involves using group process. The consultant should have group members engage in a discussion and brainstorm alternative solutions for the implementation of problems. Another method the therapist can employ is to review the concepts. Typically, teachers have not stressed to the children that they can earn rewards for using plans at school. Finally, it may be helpful for the consultant to once again use modeling and role-playing to review the procedures.
3. *Modeling Plan Use in the Classroom.* After any teachers having implementation problems have had an opportunity to problem-solve about these difficulties, the consultant can then direct the discussion toward the identification of opportunities for teachers to model the use of these strategies in the classroom. Help each teacher pinpoint several

little issues or dilemmas that occur each week and role-play how he/she could state the problem-solving steps aloud when solving these problems. Examples might include the teacher needing to select a better place to keep keys or some other frequently misplaced object, deciding which children get to perform certain valued duties, or deciding how the class could earn bonus points in a particular subject area. Explain that helping the children understand that this problem-solving process is useful for everyone can really help decrease any resistance on the part of certain children.

4. *Homework.* Continue using child-focused CBT at school.

Collaborative CBT I
School Model—Week 12

Objective

1. Introduce collaborative problem-solving (i.e., teacher–child plans).

Procedures

1. *Introduce the Concept of Collaborative Plans.* Explain to teachers that they can use plans to solve problems with a child. Also, explain that using collaborative plans provides valuable modeling for the child. In this context, however, the child is learning these procedures to solve problems with his/her teacher. Inform the teachers that using collaborative plans can also reduce children's resistance to using plans in general.

Pass out the "Stop, Think, and Use a Plan Chart: Collaborative Plan Example" and the "Guidelines for Collaborative Plans" found in Appendix B. Engage the teachers in a discussion of when they might use collaborative plans. Examples of when to use collaborative plans in the classroom are deciding what to do for an activity in the classroom, deciding how a child might work on his/her homework, and deciding how a child might try to get along better with one of his or her peers. Situations involving arguing and negotiating are also very useful in terms of using collaborative plans. To make the points very clear, the consultant may again want to use modeling and role-play exercises.

2. *Understanding the Distinction between Child-Focused and Collaborative Plans.* Help the teachers understand that they now have a larger repertoire of ways to handle ADHD children's problem behaviors. Specifically, the teachers now can (1) prompt children to use a plan or (2) use collaborative plans. Engage the teachers in a discussion of the most

appropriate school problems and situations for using these two procedures.

3. *Homework.* Continue to employ child-focused CBT and also begin using collaborative CBT in the classroom.

Collaborative CBT II
School Model—Week 14

Objective

1. Continue to review and problem-solve about implementing child-focused and collaborative CBT methods in the classroom.

Procedures

1. *Check-In.*
2. *Review Child-Focused and Collaborative CBT Methods at School.* The consultant should use most of the session to review the concepts and procedures previously presented. The consultant should focus the discussion primarily on how well the teachers have used the collaborative CBT methods. The consultant should be aware that there tends to be significant variability in how well the teachers are grasping the concepts and/or complying with using the procedures. Continue to review and problem-solve about implementing the procedures at school. It may be necessary to use modeling and role-play exercises to emphasize certain points.
3. *Homework.* Continue to employ child-focused and/or collaborative CBT methods in the classroom.

Behavioral Child Management I
School Model—Week 16

Objective

1. Introduce behavioral child management strategies.

Procedures

1. *Check-In.*
2. *Introduce Behavioral Child Management Strategies.* Explain to the teachers that child-focused and collaborative plans are not always effective, particularly when the child or the teachers are too upset to use a

plan. Also explain that one of the goals of this program is to increase teachers' repertoire of skills. Pass out the "Time-Out" information sheet found in Appendix B. Explain the procedures for time-out in great detail. See the handout for guidance on how to explain the procedures to the teachers. Time-out is a very complicated procedure for teachers to understand completely, so the consultant would be wise to spend a significant amount of time discussing it. Oftentimes, teachers will report that they have used time-out and it has not been successful. On closer review with the teachers, it can be determined that teachers were using time-out in an inappropriate or ineffective manner. It is necessary for the consultant to take the time to model and engage the teachers in role-play exercises about implementing time-out with children in the classroom.

    3. *Understanding the Distinction between Child-Focused Plans, Collaborative Plans, and Behavioral Child Management Strategies.* Help the teachers make the distinction that they now have an even larger repertoire of ways to handle ADHD children's behavior problems. Specifically, the teachers can now (1) prompt the child to use a plan, (2) use collaborative plans, (3) use behavioral child management strategies. The main point to emphasize is that teachers will want to use these strategies sequentially. If a child is having behavioral difficulties, we recommend using either a child or collaborative plan but, if that is not successful, then a time-out procedure would be in order. Engage the teachers in a discussion of which classroom problems and situations are most appropriately addressed by these three procedures.

    4. *Homework.* Ask the teachers to continue to employ child-focused and collaborative CBT methods but also to use time-out procedures when appropriate in the classroom.

Behavioral Child Management II and Program Review
School Model—Week 18

Objectives

    1. Review concepts related to time-out.
    2. Introduce other alternative behavioral child management methods.
    3. Review all concepts addressed in program.

Procedures

    1. *Check-In.*
    2. *Review Time-Out.* The consultant should ask the teachers to review their use of time-out with children in the classroom. The consultant

should ask the teachers to give specific examples of when they used time-out with children and take note as to whether or not time-out has been implemented appropriately. If time-out has not been implemented appropriately, the consultant should take the time to model and role-play correct implementation of time-out.

3. *Introduce Alternative Behavioral Methods.* Pass out the "Reinforcement of Specific Behavior" and "Daily Behavior Contract" charts (found in Appendix B). Review these charts thoroughly. The "Reinforcement of Specific Behavior" chart can be used to increase specific behavior on a daily basis. The "Daily Behavior Contract" chart can also be used to increase specific behaviors. The focus is somewhat different with this chart in that the teacher is removing privileges when specified behaviors are not emitted by the child. Explain that these alternative behavioral methods would not be used for the entire classroom, only for selected children.

4. *Review All Strategies.* Discuss and review all the concepts that have been learned previously in the program. Again, the consultant can use discussion, modeling, and role-playing to communicate these points in a very concrete manner.

5. *Fading Reinforcement.* Depending on the needs of the children in each classroom, the teacher may be able to fade reinforcement for plan-making. The consultant can work with each teacher to decide when and how such fading should be employed for a particular classroom. In some situations, the teachers could discontinue providing reinforcement for problem-solving about matters that are now handled in a more routine manner but continue to reinforce the use of systematic problem-solving with newly emerging difficulties. Reinforcement could also be faded over time, with children moving from daily, to twice a week, to weekly rewards, etc.

6. *Plan for Follow-Up (Optional).* Explain to the teachers that the intervention should not be expected to cure the child of ADHD. It will be necessary to have follow-up sessions in the future. Explain the booster session format (outlined in the last section of chapter) to the teachers. If applicable, make arrangements to meet again with the teachers in the future.

Booster Component (School Model Only)

Previous efforts employing CBT with impulsive and ADHD children have failed in terms of achieving long-term maintenance of treatment effects. ADHD is a long-term problem that will need periodic treatment. Treatment programs trying to instill self-control skills in ADHD children must allow a sufficient amount of time for children to consolidate these abilities.

Booster sessions include modules for the child, parents, and teachers. The purpose of these booster sessions is to review and consolidate previously learned skills. No new skills should be introduced during the booster phase. The booster phase could take place at any time, but perhaps the best time would be the year following the initial training.

Procedures

Child Component. Children should be seen for eight sessions in both the fall and spring of the next academic year. The procedures for running the group would be identical to those of the intervention phase. The sessions should be devoted to reviewing, role-playing, and discussing content areas from the previous year. We recommend that Sessions 1 and 2 be devoted to reviewing problem-solving and self-instruction methods; Sessions 3 and 4 should cover anger/frustration management; Sessions 5 and 6 should review management of poor effort; and Sessions 7 and 8 should concentrate on management of negative thinking and feelings. This sequence of sessions could be used in the fall and repeated again in the spring.

Parent Component. The parents should be seen for three 2-hour review meetings during the first, third, and eighth week of the child's booster phase. These sessions focus on child-focused CBT, collaborative CBT, and behavioral child management skills. The purpose of these sessions is to review last year's program and to problem-solve about implementing the procedures this year. Modeling, role-play exercises, and discussion are used to review various strategies and techniques to facilitate maintenance of skills. Three open-format sessions of 2 hours can be held with parents in the spring to review similar procedures/ concepts.

Teacher Component. The teachers should be seen for three 1-hour review meetings during the first, third, and eighth weeks of the child booster phase. These sessions focus on child-focused CBT, collaborative CBT, and behavioral child management skills. As with the parents, the purpose of these sessions is to review last year's program and problem-solve about implementing the procedures this year. Modeling, role-play exercises, and discussion are used to review various strategies and techniques to facilitate maintenance of skills. Again, as with parents, three open-format sessions of approximately 1–2 hours each can be held with the teachers in the spring, reviewing similar concepts.

Epilogue: Future Directions in Understanding, Assessing, and Treating ADHD

Thorough consideration of any topic tends to raise more questions than are answered. Clearly, ADHD is a topic with many remaining questions concerning the nature of the disorder, assessment methods, and treatment options. In this final segment, we highlight continuing questions that face those who wish to understand and treat this condition.

Exploration of the Nature of the Disorder

As discussed in the first chapter, there is high agreement among professionals about the basic symptoms of ADHD; however, there are continuing debate and uncertainty about the extent to which all children manifesting attentional difficulties should be considered as manifesting subtypes of the same disorder. The revised third edition of the *Diagnostic and Statistical Manual of Mental Disorders* (DSM-III-R) addressed this concern by eliminating the category of Attention Deficit Disorder without Hyperactivity but adding the category of undifferentiated Attention-Deficit Hyperactivity Disorder. Professional rumblings within both clinical and research-oriented circles suggest that many in the field do not view the DSM-III-R solution as a satisfactory resolution of this issue. The committee established to develop the DSM-IV criteria for childhood disorders for the fourth edition of the *Diagnostic and Statistical Manual* has documented its awareness of these concerns (Shaffer et al., 1989), but it remains to be seen how this awareness will be translated into the formal diagnostic criteria of DSM-IV.

In a related vein, much research is needed to clarify the relationships among ADHD and the other forms of psychopathology. There is a high degree of overlap between ADHD and the other disruptive behavior disorders—Oppositional Defiant Disorder and Conduct Disorder. As noted by Barkley, Costello, and Spitzer (1989), coexisting diagnoses within the disruptive behavior disorders category is the rule rather than the exception, with currently available data suggesting that the manifestation of two of these conditions, particularly ADHD and Conduct Disorder, is predictive of particularly negative long-term outcomes. Unfortunately, our lack of knowledge is not limited to the area of the disruptive behavior disorders. We have a great deal to understand about the similarities between ADHD and the early manifestations of mood disorders, particularly Bipolar Disorder. The links between ADHD-type symptoms, especially concentration problems and impulsivity, and anxiety disorders also deserves greater attention. There is a growing body of research addressing the relationship between ADHD and learning disabilities, but further efforts are clearly needed if we are to clarify either of these diagnostic entities.

Over the past decade, progress has been made in attempting to delineate some of the major causal factors or pathways that result in ADHD symptomatology. However, future research efforts addressing causal factors will need to go further in clarifying the extent to which certain preexisting biological and/or environmental conditions are necessary or sufficient causes of ADHD and are specific to ADHD versus characteristic of, for example, children manifesting different types of disruptive behavioral disorders or learning disabilities.

Both those attempting to treat ADHD children and the families of these children will benefit from an even greater understanding of how family factors impact the child and are impacted by the child. In the Introduction, we highlighted the clinical impressions of Ziegler and Holden (1988) that ADHD children appear to make the most positive adjustment in families in which they are expected to function with normal children, in which efforts at compensation are reinforced, and in which no member of the family assumes inordinate levels of blame for the child's difficulties. This observation is consistent with our clinical experience, yet we must caution that this view awaits empirical validation. The work of Jacobvitz and Sroufe (1987) discussed in Chapter 1 raises interesting questions about how early patterns of maternal interaction may predispose some children toward a more overactive style, but this observation requires replication. Of equal interest are questions about how the experience of raising a difficult child shapes the parents' beliefs about their caregiving capacities, which, in turn, shape the types of parenting behaviors they emit.

Developing Adequate Assessment Methods

Clarification of the nature of the specific cognitive dysfunction of ADHD children will, in large part, depend on the findings of research examining causal factors; however, our understanding of the cognitive, as well as affective and behavioral, dysfunctions of these children is also hampered by limitations in our assessment instruments. The problems with commonly used behavior rating scales, particularly the Conners scales, were addressed in Chapter 2. Newer scales have been proposed to replace older problematic measures, but these new scales have yet to receive the research attention afforded the older measures, so final conclusions cannot yet be drawn about the extent to which these newer measurse represent a real improvement.

While several measures have been proposed, the field continues to await the development of a clinic or laboratory-based assessment tool that is as sensitive to treatment effects and/or medication dosage changes as behavioral observations in the classroom environment. Developing a measure that is sensitive to attentional dysfunction but is not vulnerable to other forms of neurocognitive difficulty or learning disabilities seems to be a particular challenge to the creativity of test developers.

Currently, there are no valid and reliable child self-report measures of ADHD symptomatology. Clearly, ADHD researchers are not alone, for many domains of child psychopathology are without adequate self-report measures, and the whole area of child self-report is plagued with both methodological and conceptual difficulties. But ADHD investigators could follow the lead provided by those examining the phenomenon of childhood depression. Over the past decade, those researching depression in children have developed and validated a number of self-report inventories and structured interview formats that are now providing both researchers and clinicians with the means of more adequately assessing the child's perceptions of his/her symptoms.

In addition to concerns about developing adequate assessments of ADHD symptomatology, there is also a tremendous need for tools developed to measure the hypothesized effects of different treatment approaches. In keeping with our interest in cognitive–behavioral interventions, we are particularly concerned about the shortage of adequately validated, widely accepted tools for assessing the targets of change in cognitive–behavioral interventions with children. Advance in this domain of intervention is somewhat limited by, for example, the dearth of widely accepted measures of children's interpersonal problem-solving capacities. While there are many measures of this phenomenon, there are few with broad acceptance and use. The development of such measures does seem possible, as illustrated by the area of locus-of-control research in which two or three child measures have become widely accepted and have demonstrated some degree of predictive validity.

Borrowing again from the area of childhood depression, there has been significant research interest in establishing attributional style measures of relevance for identifying children experiencing or at risk for depression. Dodge and colleagues have made gains in delineating at least some of the attributional processes associated with children who exhibit a tendency toward aggressive behavior (Dodge, 1986; Dodge & Frame, 1982; Dodge & Newman, 1981). As repeatedly urged by Whalen and Henker (1987), understanding of ADHD children would be advanced by directing more effort toward understanding their attributional processes. Developing tools to accomplish this goal will also be necessary if cognitive–behaviorists are to continue to advance their conceptualizations of childhood psychopathology, such as Kendall's (1985, 1989) hypothesized deficiencies-versus-distortions theory of childhood difficulties. This view holds that certain types of psychopathology, such as depression and anxiety, are best conceptualized as the result of cognitive *distortions*. Other types of difficulties, such as ADHD, may reflect cognitive *deficiencies*. While interesting and significant in terms of its treatment implications, such a conceptualization cannot be validated without tools to measure the hypothesized deficiencies and distortions across a broad range of childhood difficulties.

Treatment Considerations

Medication

Despite the tremendous research attention that has been focused on the use of psychostimulant medications with ADHD children, a number of highly significant questions remain. Psychostimulants produce reliable short-term behavioral and attentional improvements, and there are emerging data that suggest that certain types of learning may also be improved, yet clear long-term academic benefits have not been demonstrated. In fact, the long-term behavioral benefits of psychostimulant treatment also remain to be demonstrated. Thus, greater understanding is needed of the mechanism by which psychostimulants produce short-term benefit but fail to yield long-term gains. The extent to which psychostimulants actually promote the display of prosocial behavior (versus simply suppressing antisocial behavior) also requires greater elucidation.

Given their relatively recent use as treatments for ADHD, there is a great need for more research on antidepressant medications. In particular, the durability of behavioral improvements achieved with antidepressants needs further examination. Great practical value would be derived from additional information that would allow clinicians to make intelligent decisions about which cases should first receive a trial of antidepressants versus psychostimulants.

Psychotherapeutic Interventions

Both behavioral and cognitive–behavioral interventions continue to face the challenge of how to achieve greater maintenance and generalization of treatment effects. To meet this challenge, clinicians and researchers may have to move beyond paradigms dominated by circumscribed, time-limited interventions to approaches that more appropriately address the pervasive, chronic nature of the behavioral difficulties and secondary problems associated with disorders such as ADHD. Fortunately, virtually all major figures in this domain of childhood psychopathology recognize the need for multimodal and developmentally appropriate forms of intervention for ADHD children. Massive professional education efforts are needed for this perspective to reach the myriad of teachers, physicians, and mental health professionals that provide services for these children.

Certainly, future developments in treatment approaches will necessarily be guided by emerging knowledge concerning the nature of the disorder. More specifically, a clearer understanding of the causal factors of ADHD should logically lead to ever more precise and appropriate treatment regimes. Greater understanding of causal factors can also lead to more constructive efforts at primary and secondary prevention. For example, our growing knowledge of the prenatal impact of maternal alcohol consumption has led to educational efforts directed at preventing fetal alcohol syndrome. In other cases in which genetics or prenatal or perinatal trauma could be determined as the primary cause, efforts might be most appropriately directed at helping the child and family cope with the primary symptoms of the disorder (inattention and impulsivity) in a manner designed to minimize the emergence of common secondary symptoms (learning difficulties, conduct problems, and demoralization). Increasingly, many child intervention efforts are also guided by the recognition of the need to promote competence enhancement (August, Anderson, & Bloomquist, in press). Research efforts of the current authors, Gerald August, and Rick Ostrander to implement a school-based training program that actively includes the parents and teachers of the ADHD child, as well as intervening directly with the child, may represent one step toward the goals of decreasing secondary symptoms and enhancing competence. Other investigators are also now rising to the challenge of creating appropriately comprehensive intervention approaches. Thus, the next decade should yield much more specific information about which particular combinations of treatment will yield the most positive results for which ADHD children.

Suggested Readings on ADHD

Barkley, R. A. (1981). *Hyperactive children: A handbook for diagnosis and treatment.* New York: Guilford.

Barkley, R. A. (1990). *Attention-deficit hyperactivity disorder: A handbook for diagnosis and treatment.* New York: Guilford.

Breen, M. J., & Altepeter, T. S. (1990). *Disruptive behavior disorders in children.* New York: Guilford.

Cantwell, D. (1975). *The hyperactive child.* New York: Spectrum.

Ross, D. M., & Ross, S. A. (1982). *Hyperactivity: Theory, research and action* (2nd ed.). New York: Wiley.

Weiss, G., & Hechtman, L. T. (1986). *Hyperactive children grown up.* New York: Guilford.

Wender, P. H. (1987). *The hyperactive child, adolescent and adult: ADD through the lifespan.* New York: Oxford University Press.

Charts for
Cognitive–Behavioral Therapy

The reader is encouraged to reproduce and modify the following charts to make them better suited to specific clinical needs. We recommend enlarging each chart prior to giving it to clients.

Attention-Deficit Hyperactivity Disorder

PRIMARY SYMPTOMS
1. Attention difficulties
2. Impulsivity
3. Hyperactivity
4. Excitability

SECONDARY SYMPTOMS
1. Poor school achievement and/or learning disabilities
2. Physical and verbal aggression
3. Low self-esteem
4. Poor peer relationships

COGNITIVE DEFICITS

Inability to sustain attention and to inhibit impulsive responding on tasks or in social situations that require focused, reflective, self-directed effort.

PREVALENCE

Individual symptoms, such as overactivity or attention problems, are relatively common, but the full syndrome occurs in 1–10% of school-age children. (Different statistics are found in different studies.)

DEVELOPMENTAL SHIFTS IN SYMPTOMS
1. *Infancy:* These children may have a history of prenatal and perinatal difficulties. As infants, they are more likely to have been active, restless, and irregular in their sleeping and eating patterns, although this is not always the case.
2. *Preschool years:* As toddlers and preschoolers, these children are even more active and exploratory than is typical for this developmental stage. They may be less responsive to common disciplinary methods relative to other children and more likely to engage in dangerous behaviors as a result of their impulsivity.
3. *Early school years:* Difficulties in attention and concentration become more noticeable as the child enters school and is expected to display greater self-regulation. These children appear to lack the capacity to modulate their attention processes and activity level to match the demands of the environment. Specific learning disabilities, if present, and peer difficulties may begin to emerge and contribute to the development of low self-esteem.
4. *Adolescence:* During teenage years, attention difficulties, impulsivity, and excitability are likely to continue, but hyperactivity may decline. The secondary problems mentioned previously may become more pronounced.
5. *Adulthood:* Current research indicates that attention difficulties continue into adulthood. Other emotional and behavioral difficulties may also be present.

THEORIES OF CAUSATION
1. *Biological viewpoints:* Neurological and/or biochemical processes may be involved.
2. *Environmental viewpoints:* Dysfunctional families and/or school environments may contribute to children's inattention and overactivity.

TREATMENT APPROACHES
1. *Biological—medication:* Medication improves attention and reduces impulsivity.
2. *Dietary treatments:* Regulating diet may have some limited effect on attention and activity level.
3. *Behavioral interventions:* Environmental contingencies are used to externally control children's behavior.
4. *Cognitive–behavioral interventions:* Children develop internal self-regulatory abilities to control their own behavior.
5. *Educational interventions:* Children receive school-based interventions for learning and/ or emotional/behavioral problems.

Cognitive–Behavioral Therapy for Children with Attention-Deficit Hyperactivity Disorder

PROBLEM-SOLVING AND SELF-INSTRUCTION TRAINING
Training children to talk to themselves (internally) to guide and mediate their behavior in a problem-solving manner. Children say these steps to themselves:

1. Stop! What is the problem?
2. What are some plans?
3. What is the best plan?
4. Do the plan.
5. Did the plan work?

    A. *Problem recognition:* Training children to understand and recognize what different types of problems are and what they do that causes problems.
    B. *Solution generation:* Training children to generate more than one possible solution to a problem.
    C. *Consequential thinking:* Training children to anticipate the consequences of their behavior.
    D. *Anticipating obstacles:* Training children to think of new plans if they encounter obstacles.
    E. *Executing specific behavior:* Training children to increase behavioral skills repertoire.

INTERPERSONAL PROBLEM-SOLVING
Training children to use self-instruction, perspective-taking, and situation interpretation strategies to improve interpersonal relationships with other children and adults.

BEHAVIORAL SOCIAL SKILLS TRAINING
Training children to execute specific adaptive social behaviors.

ANGER/FRUSTRATION MANAGEMENT
Training children to use relaxation, coping self-statements and self-instruction strategies to control anger/frustration.

RELAXATION TRAINING
Training children in arousal reduction through simple relaxation techniques.

PARENT AND TEACHER CONSULTATION
Training parents and teachers in cognitive–behavioral child management, parent/teacher–child problem-solving, and behavioral management techniques.

APPLICATION TO OPTIONAL CONTENT AREAS:

POOR EFFORT MANAGEMENT
Training children to use self-instruction and coping self-statements strategies to manage poor effort behavior.

NEGATIVE THOUGHTS AND FEELINGS MANAGEMENT
Training children to recognize and evaluate overly self-critical thoughts and to use more adaptive self-statements.

How Hard I Tried

1
Didn't try
at all

2
Tried a little

3
Tried OK

4
Tried hard

5
Tried very
hard

Group Points

Date: _____

Child's name	Points earned (1 point for positive behavior and for using plans when reminded, 2 points for using plans without being reminded)	Points lost (for mild disruptive behavior)	Strikes (circle)	Total points (sum of points earned minus points lost)
1.			1 2 3	
2.			1 2 3	
3.			1 2 3	
4.			1 2 3	
5.			1 2 3	
6.			1 2 3	
7.			1 2 3	
8.			1 2 3	

Five-Step Problem-Solving

1. STOP! WHAT IS THE PROBLEM?

2. WHAT ARE SOME PLANS?

3. WHAT IS THE BEST PLAN?

4. DO THE PLAN.

5. DID THE PLAN WORK?

Problem-Solving Skills

FIVE-STEP PROBLEM-SOLVING
1. Stop! What is the problem?
2. What are some plans?
3. What is the best plan?
4. Do the plan.
5. Did my plan work?

MEANS–END PROBLEM-SOLVING
1. What is my goal?
2. What steps do I need to take to reach my goal?
    A.
    B.
    C.
    D.
3. Did my plan work? Did I reach my goal?

DECISION-MAKING PROBLEM-SOLVING
1. State decision to be made very clearly.
2. List pros and cons.
3. Weight each pro and con with a number (1–5):
    A. Not too important—1 or 2
    B. Sort of important—3
    C. Very important—4 or 5
4. Add up numbers for pros and cons separately.
5. The choice achieving the highest weighting should be the one selected.

How I Affect Others: Example

Directions: Try to write at least one example of a positive and a negative thing you did each day. It's OK if you don't remember to write it down right away, but try to write it down that day. Please provide the information asked for in each column.

Date	Positive or negative behaviors I did. (Write what you did that was positive or negative that affected others.)	How I affected others. (Write what you think other people thought and felt as a result of what you did.)
2/16	Did dishes when mom asked.	She thought I was nice and was happy.
2/17	Shoved Sam on the bus.	He probably thought I was a jerk. He was mad and sad.

How I Affect Others

Directions: Try to write at least one example of a positive and a negative thing you did each day. It's OK if you don't remember to write it down right away, but try to write it down that day. Please provide the information asked for in each column.

Date	Positive or negative behaviors I did. (Write what you did that was positive or negative that affected others.)	How I affected others. (Write what you think other people thought and felt as a result of what you did.)

Using Problem-Solving: Example

Directions: This chart can be filled out immediately after, or a long time after, having a problem. You can fill out the chart regarding how you did use, or could have used, a problem-solving strategy. Please provide the information asked for in each column.

Date	Problem (State exactly what the problem was.)	Problem signal (What told you there was a problem? How did you figure it out?)	How did you solve problem? (e.g., 5-step, means—end, or decision-making strategy—What did you do?)	How well did it work? (1—didn't work at all, to 10—worked extremely well)
7/17	My sister turned the channel when I was watching TV.	I felt mad inside.	I used a 5-step plan and decided to ignore her.	6
7/18	Trying to decide if I should take an algebra class	I felt confused.	I used a decision-making plan and decided not to take the class this semester.	9

Using Problem-Solving

Directions: This chart can be filled out immediately after, or a long time after, having a problem. You can fill out the chart regarding how you did use, or could have used, a problem-solving strategy. Please provide the information asked for in each column.

Date	Problem (State exactly what the problem was.)	Problem signal (What told you there was a problem? How did you figure it out?)	How did you solve problem? (e.g., 5-step, means—end, or decision-making strategy—What did you do?)	How well did it work? (1—didn't work at all, to 10—worked extremely well)

When I Get Angry: Example

Directions: Fill out this chart whenever you get angry. It's OK if you don't remember to write it down right away when you're angry, but try to fill it out that day. Please provide the information asked for in each column.

Date	Event (What happened to make you mad?)	How did your body feel? (Describe breathing, muscles tensing, heart rate, etc.)	What were your thoughts? (What did you say to yourself inside?)	What did you do? (What actions did you take when you were mad?)	Anger rating (1—not very angry, to 10—out of control with rage)
1/16	Joe called me a name.	Tense muscles.	I want to punch him.	I called him a name back.	7
1/17	Mom told me to be home early.	Tense muscles, heart pounding.	She's crazy; she just wants to give me a hard time. No way!	I told her to forget it and walked out. I slammed the door.	9

When I Get Angry

Directions: Fill out this chart whenever you get angry. It's OK if you don't remember to write it down right away when you're angry, but try to fill it out that day. Please provide the information asked for in each column.

Date	Event (What happened to make you mad?)	How did your body feel? (Describe breathing, muscles tensing, heart rate, etc.)	What were your thoughts? (What did you say to yourself inside?)	What did you do? (What actions did you take when you were mad	Anger rating (1—not very angry) to 10—out of control with rage)

Anger Combat Chart: Example

Directions: Fill out this chart whenever you get angry and try to control it. It's OK if you don't remember to write it down right away when you cope with your anger, but try to fill it out that day. Please provide the information asked for in each column.

Date	Event (What happened to make you mad?)	Coping self-statements (What did you say to yourself to cope and reduce anger?)	Plan of action (What did you do to solve the problem? Did you relax, negotiate, walk away, etc.?)	Rating of effectiveness (1—didn't work, to 10—worked very well)
1/16	Joe called me a name.	I'm not gonna let him get to me. I'll try to stay cool.	Walked away.	9
1/17	Mom told me to be home early.	I'm not gonna let her get to me. I'll try to relax. I should try to work it out with her.	We negotiated. I told her my point of view.	6

Anger Combat Chart

Directions: Fill out this chart whenever you get angry and try to control it. It's OK if you don't remember to write it down right away when you cope with your anger, but try to fill it out that day. Please provide the information asked for in each column.

Date	Event (What happened to make you mad?)	Coping self-statements (What did you say to yourself to cope and reduce anger?)	Plan of action (What did you do to solve the problem? Did you relax, negotiate, walk away, etc.?)	Rating of effectiveness (1—didn't work, to 10—worked very well)

Inventory for Child's Strengths and Weaknesses

Directions: The purpose of this chart is to focus the adult on the child's strengths. Simply write down all the child's strengths and weaknesses in the columns below. From this point onward, the adult may want to notice, attend to, and reinforce the child for his/her strengths. The adult may want to downplay and minimize when the child is exhibiting failure through one of his/her weaknesses. Many of these weaknesses will never change. It may be more helpful to promote the child's strengths.

Strengths	*Weaknesses*
1.	1.
2.	2.
3.	3.
4.	4.
5.	5.
6.	6.
7.	7.
8.	8.
9.	9.
10.	10.

Guidelines for the Child Observation Chart

1. The parent(s) should identify two general target behaviors that are very frequent and the most problematic for them to deal with concerning their child. The parent(s) should then monitor the child's and their own behaviors through the use of this chart in regard to these two general target behaviors. The parent(s) should be aware of when the general target behavior occurs and then should complete the chart.

2. The chart is completed by filling out the behavior first, the antecedent second, and the consequences third. For example, if a child has a problem with arguing, his/her parent(s) might write this down as a general target behavior to be observed. Next time the child argues, the parents would write down what he/she was arguing about (i.e., behavior), what child and parent behavior occurred prior to the arguing (antecedent), and how the child's and parents' behaviors could be described after the problem behavior occurred (i.e., consequence).

Child Observation Chart: Example

General target behavior	A. Antecedent What were the preceding events that triggered the behavior? Describe how the child and parent(s) behaved.	B. Behavior Describe specifically what the child did that was a problem for him/her or the parent(s).	C. Consequences Describe what happened after the behavior. Describe how the child and parent(s) responded.
1. Procrastinating	I asked him several times to do his homework. He said he would do it soon.	He was watching television. Bedtime was approaching and he still hadn't done his homework.	I got mad and eventually had to shut the television off to make him do the homework. He pouted.
2. Arguing	I asked him to do the dishes several times. He said it was his sister's turn.	He, his sister, and I argued about who should do the dishes.	I yelled at him until he did the dishes. He pouted.

311

Child Observation Chart

General target behavior	A. Antecedent What were the preceding events that triggered the behavior? Describe how the child and parent(s) behaved.	B. Behavior Describe specifically what the child did that was a problem for him/her or the parent(s).	C. Consequences Describe what happened after the behavior. Describe how the child and parent(s) responded.
1.			
2.			

Guidelines for Using Stop, Think, and Use a Plan Chart

1. The parent(s) prompt the child to use a plan, by stating, "This would be a good time to use a plan." The parent(s) should not tell the child what the problem is or any step in the five-step problem-solving sequence. The parent(s) should try to help the child to discover the five steps to the best of his/her ability. Occasionally, a parent has to help a child out, if he/she is having some difficulty with the steps. It may be necessary to remind the child that he/she can earn a reward for using a good plan. If a child is judged to be belligerent or resistant to using a plan, then the parent would want to discontinue prompting the child and use some other means of child management.

2. The child verbalizes out loud the five problem-solving steps. The child should be required to come up with a plan and then employ the plan to solve the problem. In the beginning, the child should be required to verbalize all five steps out loud, although in later weeks it may only be necessary to state what the problem is and what the solution is (i.e., a short plan).

3. The parent(s) and child complete the "Stop, Think, and Use a Plan Chart." The parent(s) or child can write on the chart. The child should be required to state what the problem was and identify whose idea it was to use the plan. Then the parent(s) and child should, together, rate how well the child used the plan on a scale of 1–4, on the bottom of the chart.

Stop, Think, and Use a Plan Chart: Example

Name: _____

Date: _____

On this chart, write what the problem was and whose idea it was to use a plan. Then rate how well the plan was used.

	Procrastinating about homework.	Arguing about taking garbage out.	Arguing with sister about which program to watch.
What was the problem?			
Whose idea was it to use a plan?	Dad	Mom	Child
How well was the plan used? Rate it 1, 2, 3, or 4.	3	1	4

Rating scale

1	2	3	4
Didn't use plan at all for problem	Tried a little, but didn't really work	Tried hard and used a plan, but for less than 1 minute	Tried real hard and used a plan for 1 minute or more

314

Stop, Think, and Use a Plan Chart

Name: _____

Date: _____

On this chart, write what the problem was and whose idea it was to use a plan. Then rate how well the plan was used.

What was the problem?		
Whose idea was it to use a plan?		
How well was the plan used? Rate it 1, 2, 3, or 4.		

Rating scale

1	2	3	4
Didn't use plan at all for problem	Tried a little, but didn't really work	Tried hard and used a plan, but for less than 1 minute	Tried real hard and used a plan for 1 minute or more

Guidelines for Using Tally for Using Plans (Weekly or Daily) Chart

1. Before starting to use plans at home, be sure to meet with the child to identify what rewards will be given for using plans. Make sure the child understands that he/she can earn rewards for using plans and for thinking of using plans on his/her own. The reward should be motivating to the child and acceptable to the parent(s).

2. The parent(s) should determine if the child will be rewarded weekly or daily. Some children cannot wait an entire week for a reward. Set aside one specific time each week (or day) to review plans for the previous week (day). For example, a parent and child may want to meet every Friday night to evaluate plans for that week (or every day at bedtime).

3. Review the "Stop, Think, and Use a Plan Charts" for the previous week (day). The child could have used only one plan or many plans for that week (day). Remember that the child is rewarded for the quality of the plans that he/she makes, and not for the quantity of plans that he/she makes. Follow the directions on the chart. Add up all the 1 and 2 plan ratings, and then add up all the 3 and 4 plan ratings. If there are more 3 and 4 ratings of plans, then the child should receive a reward. Next, add up whose idea it was to use the plans. Add up other people's ideas and the child's ideas. If there are more of the child's ideas, then the child gets to select a bonus reward.

4. If the child did well, be sure to praise him/her, give him/her the reward, and decide which rewards will be used for the next week (day). If the child did not do very well, be sure to remind the child that he/she can earn rewards for using plans the next week (day).

Tally for Using Plans (Weekly or Daily): Example

Name: _____

Date: _____

Add up all the 1 and 2 plan ratings and then add up all the 3 and 4 plan ratings.

Total plan ratings of 1 and 2 _____1_____ Total plan ratings of 3 and 4 _____2_____

If there are more 3 and 4 plan ratings, then the child gets to select a reward.

Next add up whose idea it was to use the plans. Add up other people's ideas and the child's ideas.

Total other people's ideas _____2_____ Total child's ideas _____1_____

If there are more of the child's ideas, then the child gets to select a bonus reward.

Plan reward   Stay up late to watch videos Friday night.

Bonus reward   Snacks while I watch videos Friday night.

Tally for Using Plans (Weekly or Daily)

Name: _____

Date: _____

Add up all the 1 and 2 plan ratings and then add up all the 3 and 4 plan ratings.

Total plan ratings of 1 and 2 _____   Total plan ratings of 3 and 4 _____

If there are more 3 and 4 plan ratings, then the child gets to select a reward.

Next add up whose idea it was to use the plans. Add up other people's ideas and the child's ideas.

Total other people's ideas _____   Total child's ideas _____

If there are more of the child's ideas, then the child gets to select a bonus reward.

Plan reward _____

Bonus reward _____

Reinforcement Ideas

1. Favorite dessert
2. Favorite meal
3. Special snack
4. Small toys
5. Sports equipment
6. Records/tapes
7. Rent special videos
8. Furnishings for room
9. Attention
10. Praise
11. Post work in school or at home
12. Special privileges
13. Private times
14. Special TV privileges
15. Stay up late
16. Have a friend over for dinner or for overnight
17. Special time with one parent
18. Go to a movie
19. Go to a concert
20. Go on a special trip
21. Attend a sporting event
22. Camping
23. Traveling
24. Party
25. Tokens for general exchange

Note: Make sure the reward is motivating for the child and is realistic for the parent(s) to give to the child.

Adult Self-Evaluation of Thoughts Form

Child's name: _____

Parent's name: _____ Date: _____

Directions: Listed below are a variety of thoughts that parents may have about their children and themselves. Read each thought and indicate how frequently that thought typically occurs for you over an average week. Ask the person giving you the form to clarify any questions you don't understand. Add up all the numbers for a total score.

1	2	3	4	5
Not at all	Sometimes	Moderately often	Often	All the time

I. *Attributions about the child*
_____ A. This child is a brat.
_____ B. This child does it intentionally.
_____ C. This child is the cause of all the family's problems.
_____ D. This child is just trying to get attention.

II. *Attributions about self/others*
_____ A. It's my fault that this child is that way.
_____ B. If I wasn't such a poor parent, this child would be better off.
_____ C. It's his/her (other parent's fault) that this child is that way.
_____ D. If he/she (other parent) wasn't such a poor parent, this child would be better off.

III. *Beliefs/expectations about the child*
_____ A. This child's future is bleak. When he/she grows up, he/she will probably be irresponsible, a criminal, high school dropout, etc.
_____ B. This child should behave like other children. I shouldn't have to teach this child how to behave.
_____ C. This child must do well in school, sports, scouts, etc. It is unacceptable if this child does not do as well in these activities as any other child.
_____ D. This child is defective. This child has many problems. This child does not fit in with other children.

IV. *Beliefs/expectations about self and/or family*
_____ A. Our family is a mess.
_____ B. I can't make mistakes in parenting this child.
_____ C. I give up. There is nothing more I can do for this child.
_____ D. I have no control over this child. I have tried everything.

V. *Beliefs/expectations about medications*
_____ A. He/she needs medications. He/she can't function without medications.
_____ B. Medications are the answer. This child's problems will be greatly diminished or gone when he/she is on medications.

VI. *Beliefs/expectations about therapy*
_____ A. Therapy will fix or cure this child.
_____ B. My child is the focus of therapy.
_____ C. Therapy will not really help.

Adaptive Attributions and Beliefs Regarding ADHD

Attributions

I. Trait attribution: counters

    A. Many problems are out of this child's control.

    B. It doesn't matter whose fault it is. What matters are solutions to the problems.

    C. It's not just this child. I also play a role in the problem.

II. Self-blame attribution: counters

    A. It's not just my fault; this child plays a role too.

    B. It doesn't matter whose fault it is. What matters are solutions to the problems.

Beliefs/expectations

I. About the child: counters

    A. I'm being irrational. I have no proof that this child will continue to have problems. I need to wait until the future.

    B. My belief that I have no control over this child might contribute to the problem. Many things are in my control. This belief gives me an excuse not to control this child.

    C. I can't expect this child to behave. This child needs to be taught how to behave more appropriately.

    D. I need to accept this child for whoever he/she is. It's OK if this child is not great at school. I need to focus on this child's strengths and not on his/her weaknesses.

    E. I need to focus on my child's strengths and not on his/her weaknesses or failures.

II. About self/family (classroom): counters

    A. We all have a part in the problem. It's not just this child.

    B. I'm going to make mistakes. It's natural to make mistakes. This child is more challenging than others.

    C. I have to parent (teach) this child now or later. I have no choice not to parent (teach) this child now. I need to think of new ways to parent (teach) this child. If I don't parent (teach) this child now, things might get worse.

III. About medications: counters

    A. Medications may be one component of this child's intervention, not the answer.

    B. Medications with therapy and other interventions work best.

    C. I have to help this child so that he/she does not attribute his/her improvements only to the medications, rather than to other factors in his/her control.

IV. About therapy: counters

    A. No one can fix or cure this child, but we can learn better how to adapt to the problems.

    B. The therapist will guide us to learn how to better cope with our problems.

    C. I will need to be equally involved in the therapy. I need to change, too.

Adult Self-Evaluation of Behavior Form

Child's name: _____

Parent's name: _____ Date: _____

Directions: Listed below are a variety of behaviors that parents and children may engage in. Read each behavior and indicate how frequently that behavior typically occurs for you and/or your child over an average week. Ask the person giving you the form to clarify any questions you don't understand. Add up all the numbers for a total score.

1	2	3	4	5
Not at all	Sometimes	Moderately often	Often	All the time

I. *Problematic commands:* Telling the child what to do ineffectively.
- ____ A. Vague commands—Not specifying exactly what child is to do (shape up, knock it off, etc.).
- ____ B. Question commands—Asking a question in attempt to gain child's compliance (would you please pick up your toys?, etc.).
- ____ C. Rationale commands—Explaining why the child needs to comply (you need to get dressed or we will be late, etc.).
- ____ D. Multiple commands—Telling the child to do too many things at once (pick up your toys, get dressed, and come to the table for lunch, etc.).
- ____ E. Frequent commands—Repeating commands to the child and not following through with consequences when parent says he/she will.

II. *Negative reinforcement:* Adult and child use aversive means to control one another; it works and is therefore reinforced. The aversive control behaviors are repeated.
- ____ A. Child—Giving in and allowing child to "get his/her way" because he/she is so difficult/belligerent.
- ____ B. Adult—Yelling, threatening, etc. until child gives in and/or complies.

III. *Low levels of positive reinforcement:*
- ____ A. Ignoring and/or not attending when child is behaving neutrally or appropriately.

IV. *Inadvertent reinforcement of problem behavior:*
- ____ A. Giving child attention and accidentally reinforcing problem behavior (attention for disruptive behavior, whining, somatic complaints, moping, when child says it's too hard, etc.).

V. *Poor parental monitoring of child:*
- ____ A. Not sure what child is doing or where child is when away from home.

VI. *Ineffective discipline:*
- ____ A. Having problems controlling the child's behavior.
- ____ B. Yelling and threatening too much.
- ____ C. Being inconsistent in disciplining approaches.

VII. *Overcontrolling:*
- ____ A. Telling the child what to do most of the time.
- ____ B. Not allowing the child to solve his/her own problems.

Adaptive Behavioral Interchanges between Adults and Children

I. *Commands:* Specific, one-step, ten words or less (pick up that shirt, get dressed now, etc.).

II. *Positive reinforcement:* Pay attention to and reinforce neutral and positive behavior.

III. *Ignoring:* Don't pay attention to mild attention-seeking behavior (e.g., whining, pouting, etc.).

IV. *Don't give in:* Don't allow child to get his/her way by escalating his/her aversive behavior.

V. *Socratic parenting/teaching:* Help children use problem-solving (i.e., plans) to solve their own problems and learn self-control. Use problem-solving with the child in a collaborative way (together). Model problem-solving for the child.

VI. *Effective discipline:* Use time-out, reinforcement procedures, behavioral contracts, and contingencies for child management.

VII. *Monitoring:* Develop specific rules and regulations about what child can do and where child can be. Check up on child and provide consequences if rules and regulations are violated.

Practice Positive Parenting through Special Play Time: Example

Directions: Each parent should set aside 10 minutes per day to interact with his/her child for special play time. Occasionally a parent may be too busy to do the special play time on a given day. Tell your child, "It's time for the special play time." Help your child select several favorite toys. Go to a special place in your home and play. The parent should practice describing, praising, and touching. Try to avoid questions, commands, and criticisms. Keep track on this form of when you did the special play time. Write comments about how it went. Comments should focus on your thoughts about your progress with describing, praising, and touching and your observations of how your child reacted.

	Mon.	Tues.	Wed.	Thurs.	Fri.	Sat.	Sun.
Did the child's game (yes/no)	Yes	Yes	No	Yes	No	Yes	Yes
Comments about special play time	He seemed confused by my behavior. I had a hard time increasing describing, praising, and touching.	He liked it. I still had a hard time increasing those positive behaviors.	Forgot.	He liked it. He seems to think it is special. I'm still asking too many questions.	Too busy.	He liked it. I'm getting better at increasing positive behaviors.	He liked it. He smiled a lot. I'm improving the positive behaviors, too.

324

Practice Positive Parenting through Special Play Time

Directions: Each parent should set aside 10 minutes per day to interact with his/her child for special play time. Occasionally a parent may be too busy to do the special play time on a given day. Tell your child, "It's time for the special play time." Help your child select several favorite toys. Go to a special place in your home and play. The parent should practice describing, praising, and touching. Try to avoid questions, commands, and criticisms. Keep track on this form of when you did the special play time. Write comments about how it went. Comments should focus on your thoughts about your progress with describing, praising, and touching and your observations of how your child reacted.

	Mon.	Tues.	Wed.	Thurs.	Fri.	Sat.	Sun.
Did the child's game (yes/no)							
Comments about special play time							

Practice Positive Attention and Reinforcement: Example

Directions: Each parent will try to increase positive attention and reinforcement of the child (praising, touching, interacting, talking, smiling, etc.), decrease negative interactions (criticisms, unnecessary commands, unnecessary questions, etc.), and increase ignoring of mild behavioral problems. The parent(s) will keep track of frequency of positive attention and reinforcement, negative interactions, and ignoring behaviors for themselves.

	Mon.	Tues.	Wed.	Thurs.	Fri.	Sat.	Sun.
Frequency of positive attention and reinforcement	✗✗✗✗✗	✗✗✗	✗				
Frequency of negative interactions	✗✗	✗✗✗	✗✗✗✗				
Frequency of ignoring	✗✗✗✗✗		✗✗				

Practice Positive Attention and Reinforcement

Directions: Each parent will try to increase positive attention and reinforcement of the child (praising, touching, interacting, talking, smiling, etc.), decrease negative interactions (criticisms, unnecessary commands, unnecessary questions, etc.), and increase ignoring of mild behavioral problems. The parent(s) will keep track of frequency of positive attention and reinforcement, negative interactions, and ignoring behaviors for themselves.

	Mon.	Tues.	Wed.	Thurs.	Fri.	Sat.	Sun.
Frequency of positive attention and reinforcement							
Frequency of negative interactions							
Frequency of ignoring							

Reinforcement of Specific Behavior: Example

Directions: Put a smiling face in the box if the behavior was completed. Put a frowning face in the box if the behavior was not completed. Always praise your child each time he/she gets a smiling face. Administer reinforcement on a daily or weekly basis as indicated below. Some children can wait a week to get rewarded, while other can't. The parent(s) should determine and inform the child whether he/she will get rewarded weekly or daily.

Name: _____   Week: _____

Behavior	Mon.	Tues.	Wed.	Thurs.	Fri.	Sat.	Sun.
Up and dressed at 7 A.M.	☺	☺	☺	☺	☺		
Homework before TV in afternoon	☹	☹	☹	☺	☺		
Take dog out for a walk	☹	☺	☺	☺	☺		
In bed by 9 P.M. with lights out	☺	☺	☹	☺	☺		

Total smiling faces	2	3	2	4	4		

Reward:

Daily	Weekly
1–2 smiling faces = extra bedtime story	5–14 smiling faces = special time with parent
3 smiling faces = special snack	15–21 smiling faces = new audio tape
4 smiling faces = special time with parent	22–28 smiling faces = go to football game

Reinforcement of Specific Behavior

Directions: Put a smiling face in the box in the box if the behavior was completed. Put a frowning face in the box if the behavior was not completed. Always praise your child each time he/she gets a smiling face. Administer reinforcement on a daily or weekly basis as indicated below. Some children can wait a week to get rewarded, while other can't. The parent(s) should determine and inform the child whether he/she will get rewarded weekly or daily.

Name: _____   Week: _____

Behavior	Mon.	Tues.	Wed.	Thurs.	Fri.	Sat.	Sun.
Total smiling faces							

Reward:

Daily

1–2 smiling faces =
3 smiling faces =
4 smiling faces =

Weekly

5–14 smiling faces =
15–21 smiling faces =
22–28 smiling faces =

329

Listen and Obey: Example

Directions: When your child is noncompliant, ask him/her to listen and obey. If he/she does listen and obey, put a smiling face in the yes column; if not, put a frowning face in the no column. At the end of the day, add up the smiling faces and the frowning faces. If there are more smiling faces, put a smiling face in the big box below. If there are more frowning faces, put a frowning face in the big box below. At the end of the week (or day), add up the smiling faces and the frowning faces in the big boxes.

Mon. Yes No	Tues. Yes No	Wed. Yes No	Thurs. Yes No	Fri. Yes No	Sat. Yes No	Sun. Yes No

Are there more smiling faces or frowning faces today?

If using a daily reward, give the child a reward if a smiling face appears in the big box. The reward is Fifteen minutes special time with mom.

If using a weekly reward, add up the total smiling faces at the end of the week; if there are more smiling faces than frowning faces, the child gets a reward. The reward is Go to movie with dad.

Listen and Obey

Directions: When your child is noncompliant, ask him/her to listen and obey. If he/she does listen and obey, put a smiling face in the yes column; if not, put a frowning face in the no column. At the end of the day, add up the smiling faces and the frowning faces. If there are more smiling faces, put a smiling face in the big box below. If there are more frowning faces, put a frowning face in the big box below. At the end of the week (or day), add up the smiling faces and the frowning faces in the big boxes.

Mon. Yes No	Tues. Yes No	Wed. Yes No	Thurs. Yes No	Fri. Yes No	Sat. Yes No	Sun. Yes No

Are there more smiling faces or frowning faces today?

If using a daily reward, give the child a reward if a smiling face appears in the big box. The reward is _____ .

If using a weekly reward, add up the total smiling faces at the end of the week; if there are more smiling faces than frowning faces, the child gets a reward. The reward is _____ .

Time-Out

1. *Make a request of the child.* Be sure that the request is short and clear regarding exactly what is expected of the child. Do not ask a question, make a suggestion, or plead when something is requested. It may be helpful to prompt the child to listen and obey. (See "Listen and Obey" chart.)

2. *Give a warning.* If the child does not follow through with the request, then the child should be given a warning. A warning is an *if–then* statement. The warning should be stated clearly and concisely. For example, "*If* you don't (request), *then* you will have to sit in the chair for time-out."

3. *Time-out.* If after 5–10 seconds, the child does not comply, then immediately put the child in the designated time-out place. The child is required to sit quietly in his/her chair. It may be helpful to set a timer for 2–5 minutes (the parent(s) should judge what is an adequate time length and use the same time length for every time-out). If the child leaves the chair or acts in any disruptive manner, the parent(s) should warn him/her that the timer will be set back until he/she can sit in the chair quietly. If this does not work, the parent(s) may have to use a consequence such as taking away a future privilege. For example, if the child doesn't sit in the chair, he/she has to go to bed 30 minutes earlier. If the child is able to sit quietly, then set the timer again for the designated time period.

4. *After time-out.* Ask the child to comply with the request. If the child is still noncompliant or resistant, then repeat the above steps.

Positive Activity and Interaction Schedule for Parents and Adolescents

Directions: The parent and adolescent should complete each step together. Both should give equal input and effort to make sure each step is accomplished. It may be helpful to review communication skills before using this procedure.

Step 1:   List as many activities as possible that the parent and adolescent enjoy doing together that can be accomplished in 30 minutes or less.

_____   _____   _____

_____   _____   _____

Step 2:   Schedule two or more 30-minute periods per week when the parent and adolescent will engage in one or more of the above activities together. (Indicate day, date, and time.)

_____   _____   _____

_____   _____   _____

Step 3:   Parent lists specific positive behaviors he/she will try to do more of during the activity (listening, praising, giving feedback, hugs, etc.). (Get input from the adolescent.)

_____   _____   _____

_____   _____   _____

Step 4:   Adolescent lists specific positive behaviors he/she will try to do more of during the activity (talking, eye contact, expressing feelings, discussing events at school, etc.). (Get input from the parent.)

_____   _____   _____

_____   _____   _____

Step 5:   Parent and adolescent write down comments about their perceptions of each activity period. Both should write down observations and feelings about themselves and the other. (Use the back of this form if necessary.)

Activity time 1:   _____

_____

Activity time 2:   _____

_____

Removing Privileges for Noncompliance

1. *Make a request of the child/adolescent:* Be sure that the request is short and clear regarding exactly what is expected of the child/adolescent. Do not ask a question, make a suggestion, or plead when something is requested.

2. *Give a warning:* If the child/adolescent does not follow through with the request, then the child/adolescent should be given a warning. A warning is an *if–then* statement. The warning should be stated clearly and concisely. For example, "*If* you don't (request), *then* you will (lose a privilege)." Loss of privileges may include restriction of TV time, access to the telephone, going outside, driving privileges.

3. *Loss of privilege:*
   A. *Option 1:* The child/adolescent is told that the privilege is lost until he/she is compliant with the original command.
   B. *Option 2:* The child/adolescent is told the privilege is lost for a specified period of time (e.g., 24 hours).

   The parent(s) should try to avoid power struggles if the child/adolescent becomes upset or belligerent at the loss of the privilege. If the child/adolescent does not comply with the loss of privilege, then the child/adolescent should be told that eventually he/she will have to comply with the loss of privilege, whether it be at the current time or later. Further, the child/adolescent should be told that further privileges can be revoked if he/she is noncompliant with the original loss of privilege.

4. *After compliance:* Once the child has complied with the original command, then the lost privilege is returned to the child/adolescent.

Guidelines for Using Daily Behavior Contract

1. The parent(s) and child/adolescent discuss and specify problems that seem to occur regularly. Examples include the child/adolescent not completing chores or homework, problems getting up on time, tardiness or truancy at school, fighting with siblings, and swearing.

2. The parent(s) and child/adolescent discuss and specify extra privileges the child/ adolescent would like to earn and specific privileges the child/adolescent could lose for a day. Examples include the child/adolescent using the phone, watching TV, using the car, being able to go outside, and playing computerized games.

3. The parent(s) do not nag the child/adolescent or remind him/her of behavior expectations. Simply inform the child/adolescent that he/she has earned or lost a privilege when behavior expectations are either met or not met. One privilege is earned or lost for each behavior expectation met or not met.

4. Privileges are earned or lost for only one day, provided the child/adolescent fulfills the behavior expectation the following day. A day consists of the time between waking up and going to sleep.

Daily Behavior Contract: Example

Behavior expectations	Privileges earned sometime over the next day	Privileges lost for the next day
1. Be home at 7:30 P.M.	1. Stay up 15 minutes later usual	1. TV
2. Homework before 8:00 P.M.	2. 30 minutes extra phone time	2. Nintendo
3. Brush teeth	3. 30 minutes special time with parent	3. Outside privileges
4. Feed the dog	4. Favorite supper	4. Phone

Terms: For every expectation that is met, one privilege is earned over the next day.
            For every expectation that is not met, one privilege is lost for the next day.

Signatures: 1. _____

            2. _____

            3. _____

            4. _____

Daily Behavior Contract

Behavior expectations	Privileges earned sometime over the next day	Privileges lost for the next day
1.	1.	1.
2.	2.	2.
3.	3.	3.
4.	4.	4.

Terms: For every expectation that is met, one privilege is earned over the next day. For every expectation that is not met, one privilege is lost for the next day.

Signatures: 1. _____

2. _____

3. _____

4. _____

Guidelines for Monitoring Contract

1. Parent(s) and child/adolescent discuss and specify those specific problem behaviors that the parent(s) will be monitoring. Examples of the specific problem behaviors include behavior at school, whereabouts when outside the home, which friends the child/adolescent is with, what time the child/adolescent comes home at night, etc.

2. The parent(s) use whatever means is necessary to monitor the child's/adolescent's behavior. If a child/adolescent is restricted from a certain area (e.g., a park), the parent(s) should periodically check to see if he/she is there. The parent(s) may require a child/adolescent to call home every 2 hours to tell parent(s) his/her whereabouts. The parent(s) may need to call school every day to see if the child/adolescent is truant, etc.

3. The parent(s) and child/adolescent discuss and specify those specific privileges that will be lost if the parent(s) observe the child/adolescent engaging in any of the problem behaviors that are being monitored. The specific privileges lost should be of equivalent value to the problem behavior observed. For example, if a child/adolescent is caught with friends whom he/she is not supposed to be with, the privilege lost may be 3 days' worth of driving time. If the problem behavior infraction is of much greater magnitude, however, then the loss of privilege may be of a greater magnitude as well. For example, if a child/adolescent engages in vandalism, the child/adolescent may lose the privilege of going outside for 1 week and be required to reimburse someone for the destroyed property. The amount of time for each privilege lost should be specified on the contract.

4. The terms of the contract are on the basis specified by the parents and adolescents.

Monitoring Contract: Example

Problem behavior parent(s) will monitor

1. Do not go to Grandview Park.

2. Do not skip school.

3. Do not hang around with Tony.

4. Call home every 2 hours to tell mom where you are.

Privileges lost for specific amounts of time if problem behavior is observed

1. No telephone for 3 days.

2. Grounded to house for 3 days.

3. Grounded to house for 5 days.

4. No driving privileges for 3 days.

Terms: The parent(s) will monitor the child's/adolescent's behavior. Every time one of the problem behaviors is observed, a privilege will be lost for the specified time.

Signature: 1. _____

2. _____

3. _____

4. _____

Monitoring Contract

Problem behavior parent(s) will monitor

1.

2.

3.

4.

Privileges lost for specific amounts of time if problem behavior is observed

1.

2.

3.

4.

Terms: The parent(s) will monitor the child's/adolescent's behavior. Every time one
                  of the problem behaviors is observed, a privilege will be lost for the specified
                  time.

Signature: 1. _____

                  2. _____

                  3. _____

                  4. _____

Family Problem-Solving

1. Stop! What is the problem we are having?
    *   Try to avoid blaming individuals.
    *   Focus on how each family member is interacting and causing problems together.
    *   State specifically what the problem is so that everyone agrees.

2. What are some plans we can use?
    *   Think of as many alternative plans as possible.
    *   Don't evaluate or criticize any family members' ideas.

3. What is the best plan we could use?
    *   Think of what would happen if the family used each of the alternatives.
    *   Think about how each alternative would make each family member feel.
    *   Decide which alternative is most likely to succeed.
    *   Reach an agreement by most or all family members if possible.

4. Do the plan.
    *   Try the plan as best the family can.
    *   Don't criticize or say "I told you so," etc.

5. Did our plan work?
    *   Evaluate the plan.
    *   Determine if everyone is satisfied with the way the problem was solved.
    *   If the solution didn't work, repeat the entire family problem-solving process again.

Note: Try to stay focused on the here and now. Do not bring up old issues when trying to do family problem-solving.

Communication Skills

I. *Be brief*
  A.   Make statements very short, preferably ten words or less.

II. *Make "I" statements*
  A.   Stay away from "you" statements like "You should do. . . ."
  B.   Instead, say things like "I would like it if you. . . ."

III. *Be direct*
  A.   State exactly what you want or need from another person. Avoid being vague or confusing in stating what you want.
  B.   State specific behaviors you want someone else to do. For example, "I want you to be in at 10:30 and, if you will be late, you will have to call me."

IV. *Congruence*
  A.   Communicate the same message on verbal and nonverbal levels. For example, the statement "I love you" should be said in a calm, sensitive manner, and not by yelling and pounding one's fist on a table.

V. *Give feedback*
  A.   After someone has spoken to you, say it back to him/her. This will let the other person know that you understood him/her. This also gives the other person a chance to clarify anything you did not understand correctly.

VI. *Make impact statements*
  A.   Tell the other person what effect his/her behavior or statements have on you. For example, "When you do . . . , I feel. . . ."

VII. *Be an active listener*
  A.   When someone is speaking to you, let him/her know you are really listening. This can be done by maintaining good eye contact, nodding, leaning forward, and giving feedback.

Family Anger and Conflict Management

1. *Recognizing anger/conflict*—Each family member should learn to recognize when they or others are so angry that effective problem-solving and communication are impossible. Family members should be aware of destructive anger signals such as loud voices, facial expressions, body posture, destructive communication, and angry thoughts.

2. *Coping with anger/conflict*—The family should agree ahead of time that when they recognize destructive anger/conflict, they will take a previously agreed on break (e.g., separate for 10 minutes). Each family member will then try to cope with anger through relaxation, deep breathing, and coping self-statements ("I'm going to try to stay calm," "I'm going to try to think of constructive ways to get my point across to him," etc.).

3. *Constructive problem-solving and communication*—The family should reunite and try to resolve conflicts using family problem-solving and communication skills. Family members should try to be assertive, not aggressive, in getting their points across to others.

Plan Movie Script: Example

Title: Return of the monster brother

Star: _____Diane_____   Role: _____Diane_____

Co-stars:

1. _____Dan_____   Role: _____Monster brother_____
2. _____Shelly_____   Role: _____Mother_____
3. _____   Role: _____

No-plan script: I'm watching TV. My brother comes home from school and turns the TV to another channel. I get really mad and punch him. My mom comes in and yells at us.

Plan script: I'm watching TV. My brother comes home from school and turns the TV to another channel. I get really mad. I use a cool–down plan to calm down. Then I use a plan and decide to ask him to turn it back or I'll tell mom.

Plan Movie Script

Title: _____

Star: _____   Role: _____

Co-stars:

1. _____   Role: _____

2. _____   Role: _____

3. _____   Role: _____

No-plan script: _____

_____

_____

_____

_____

_____

Plan script: _____

_____

_____

_____

_____

_____

Guidelines for Collaborative Plans
(When Using Stop, Think, and Use a Plan Chart for Child)

1. When a problem emerges, the adult(s) suggest to the child that they use a collaborative plan together. The adult(s) and child should try to "discover" the five steps to solve a problem together. It may be necessary to remind the child that he/she can earn a reward for helping to figure out a collaborative plan. It is helpful to use the words "we," "us," and "our" frequently when using a collaborative plan. See the "Stop, Think, and Use a Plan Chart: Collaborative Plan Example" chart for examples. If a child is judged to be belligerent or resistant to using a collaborative plan, then the adult(s) would want to discontinue prompting the child and use some other means to solve the problem.

2. After the adult(s) and child have successfully used a collaborative plan, the adult(s) and child complete the "Stop, Think, and Use a Plan Chart." The adult(s) or child can write on the chart. The adult(s) and child together should state what the problem was and identify whose idea it was to use the plan. Then the adult(s) and child should together rate how well they used the plan on a scale of 1–4, on the bottom of the chart.

3. At the end of the week, the child should receive credit on the "Tally for Using Plans (Weekly or Daily)" chart for the collaborative plans just as he/she would for child plans.

Stop, Think, and Use a Plan Chart: Collaborative Plan Example

Name: _____

Date: _____

On this chart, write what the problem was and whose idea it was to use a plan. Than rate how well the plan was used.

	Fighting with a friend	Arguing about when to do dishes	Negotiating bed time
What was the problem			
Whose idea was it to use a plan?	Mom	Child	Dad
How well was the plan used? Rate it 1, 2, 3, or 4.	4	4	2

Rating scale:

1	2	3	4
Didn't use plan at all for problem	Tried a little, but didn't really work	Tried hard and used a plan, but for less than 1 minute	Tried really hard and used a plan for 1 minute or more

Note: School-relevant content problems could be focused on when school personnel are using collaborative plans with a child.

Suggestions for Classroom Teachers of ADHD Elementary School Students

Leslie Laub
Lauren Braswell

The following list is based on the current research literature and on the suggestions of 450 teachers who were asked to share suggestions about methods they had found most useful in working with Attention-Deficit Hyperactivity Disorder (ADHD)-type students.

Obviously, each suggestion would not be appropriate for use with every ADHD child. The decision to use a particular suggestion must be based on an understanding of that particular child's educational, behavioral, and emotional needs.

Physical Arrangement of Room

1. Use rows for seating arrangement. Avoid tables with groups of students, for this maximizes interpersonal distractions for the ADHD child.

- Where possible, it may be ideal to provide several tables for group projects *and* traditional rows for independent work.
- Some teachers report that arranging desks in a horseshoe shape promotes appropriate discussion while permitting independent work.

2. Whatever arrangement is selected, it is important for the teacher to be able to move about the entire room and have access to all students.

3. Have distractible students seated near the teacher (as close as possible without being punitive).

4. Locate the student's desk away from both the hallway and windows to minimize auditory and visual distractions.

5. Keep a portion of the room free of obvious visual or auditory distractors. For example, have one area of desks that doesn't have interesting objects hanging over it that invite the child to study them rather than his/her work.

6. Use desk dividers and/or study carrels. Be sure to introduce their use as a "privilege" or pair appropriate carrel usage with reinforcement, so these study aids are not perceived as punishment.

7. Seat appropriate peer models next to the ADHD child.

8. Stand near the student when giving directions or presenting the lesson. Use the student's worksheet as an example.

9. Provide comfortable lighting and room temperature.

10. Use individual headphones to play white noise or soft music to block out other auditory distractions. Be sure the music is not too "catchy" or interesting so that it becomes yet another distraction. Also, introduce headphones as a privilege or pair appropriate use with reinforcement.

11. Provide a quiet, carpeted space in the room as a special study section for independent reading, etc.

Lesson Presentation

1. Provide an outline, key concepts or vocabulary prior to lesson presentation.

2. Increase the pace of lesson presentation.

3. Include a variety of activities during each lesson.

4. Use a multisensory presentation but screen audio-visual aids to be sure that distractions are kept to a minimum. For example, be sure interesting pictures and/or sounds relate *directly* to the material to be learned and are not extraneous.

5. Make lessons brief or break longer presentations into discrete segments.

6. Actively involve the student during the lesson presentation.

   a. Have the ADHD student be the instructional aid who is to write key words or ideas on the board.

   b. Encourage the students to develop mental images of the concepts or information being presented. Ask them about their images to be sure they are visualizing the key material to be learned.

   c. Allow the students to make frequent responses throughout the lesson by using choral responding, frequently calling on many individuals, having the class respond with hand signals, etc.

   d. Employ role-playing activities to act out key concepts, historical events, social studies concerns, etc.

   e. Provide self-correcting materials.

   f. Use computer-assisted instruction.

   g. Use cooperative learning activities, particularly those that assign each child in a group a specific role or piece of information that must be shared with the group.

   h. Develop learning stations *and* clear signals and procedures for how students transition from one center to another.

    i. Use game-like activities, such as "dictionary scavenger hunts," to teach appropriate use of reference/resource materials.

    j. Interact frequently (verbally and physically) with the student.

7. Use the student's name in your lesson presentation.

8. Write personal notes to the student about key elements of the lesson.

9. Pair students to check work.

10. Provide peer tutoring to help students review concepts.

11. Let ADHD students share recently learned concepts with a struggling peer or youngerstudent.

12. When presenting a large volume of information on the chalkboard, use colored chalk to emphasize the key words or information.

Worksheets and Tests

1. Use large type.

2. Keep page format simple.

- Include no extraneous pictures or visual distractors that are unrelated to the problems to be solved.
- Provide only one or two activities per page.
- Have white space on each page.

3. Use dark black print. (Avoid handwritten worksheets or tests.)

4. Use buff-colored paper rather than white if the room's lighting creates a glare on white paper.

5. Write clear, simple directions.

6. Underline key direction words or vocabulary or have the students underline these words as you read the directions with them.

7. Draw borders around parts of the page you want to emphasize.

8. Divide the page into sections and use a system to cover sections not currently being used.

9. If possible, use different colors on worksheets or tests for emphasis, particularly on those involving rote, potentially boring work.

10. Have the students use colored pens or pencils.

11. Give frequent short quizzes and avoid long tests.

12. Provide practice tests.

13. Provide alternative environments with fewer distractions for test-taking.

14. Using a tape recorder, have the student record test answers and assignments or give the student oral examinations.

15. Shorten assignments. If the child can demonstrate adequate concept mastery in 10 or 20 questions/problems, don't require 30 or 40 problems.

16. If longer worksheets cannot be shortened, segment them by cutting them in half or folding them. Have the ADHD child complete one shortened segment first and return it to you and then give him/her the next segment.

Organization

1. Model an organized classroom and model the strategies you use to cope with disorganization.

2. Establish a daily classroom routine and schedule.

3. Show that you value organization by allowing 5 minutes each day for the children to organize their desks, folders, etc.

4. Reinforce organization by having a "desk fairy" that gives a daily award for the most organized row of desks.

5. Use individual assignment charts or stenography pads that can go home with the child and be signed daily by the parents if necessary.

6. Develop a clear system for keeping track of completed and uncompleted work such as having individual hanging files in which each child can place completed work and a special folder for uncompleted work.

7. Develop a color-coding method for your room in which each subject is associated with a certain color that is on that subject's textbook cover and on the folder or workbook for that subject. (This system has been used on a school-wide basis in some middle school settings in which children were struggling with locker organization.)

8. Develop a reward system for in-school work and homework completion.

- One example of a system that reinforces both work quantity and work quality involves translating points earned on such work into "dollars" to be used for a silent auction at the end of the grading period.
- For children needing more immediate reinforcement, each completed assignment could earn the child a "raffle ticket" with his/her name on it. Prizes (or special privileges) could be awarded on the basis of a random drawing held daily or weekly.

9. Write schedule and timelines on the board each day.

10. Provide due dates for assignments each day.

11. Divide longer assignments into sections and provide due dates or times for the completion of each section.

12. Use visual and/or auditory cues as signals prior to changing a task and to announce that the task will be ending.

13. Tape a checklist to the child's desk or put one in each subject folder/ notebook that outlines the steps in following directions or checking to be sure an assignment is complete.

14. Provide study guides or outlines of the content you want the child to

learn, or let the child build his/her own study guide with worksheets that have been positively corrected.

15. Be clear about when student movement is permitted and when it is discouraged, such as during independent work times.

Behavior

1. Keep classroom behavior rules simple and clear.
2. Have the class agree on what the rules should be.
3. Define and review classroom rules each day.
4. Implement a classroom behavior management system.
5. Actively reinforce desired classroom behaviors.

   - Use self-monitoring and self-reinforcement of on-task behavior during independent work time.
   - Use a kitchen timer to indicate periods of intense independent work and reinforce the class for appropriate behavior during this period. Start with brief intervals (5 to 10 minutes) and gradually increase the interval (to 20 to 30 minutes) as the class demonstrates success.

6. When necessary, develop contracts with an individual student and his/her parents to reinforce a few specific behaviors.

7. Set hourly, daily, weekly, or monthly goals depending on the reinforcement needs of the specific student. Provide frequent feedback on the student's progress toward these goals.

8. Provide a changing array of backup rewards or privileges so that students do not "burn out" on a particular system. Including an element of chance can also help keep students from becoming satiated with a particular reinforcement approach. For example, students can earn tickets for a daily or weekly raffle for the display of positive behavior. Children displaying higher rates of desirable behavior earn more chances but even the child earning just a few tickets has the opportunity to win the reward or privilege.

9. To improve out-of-the-classroom behavior, allow the class to earn a reward based on the compliments they receive on their behavior from other teachers, lunchroom staff, playground aides and principals.

10. Avoid giving the whole class negative consequences based on the ADHD child's behavior.

11. The ADHD child, as well as the whole class, can benefit from the implementation of a social skills curriculum for the entire class.

12. Modeling and requiring the children to use a systematic method of talking through classroom conflicts and problems can be particularly valuable for the ADHD child. To implement this, teachers are referred to the literature on cognitive–behavioral approaches to developing the child's self-talk and problem-solving.

13. Praise specific behaviors. Avoid general, global praise statements. For example, say "I like how you wrote down all your assignments correctly," rather than "Good boy!"

14. Use visual and auditory cues as behavioral reminders. These elements can easily be combined with classroom reinforcement systems. For example, have two large jars at the front of the room, with one filled with marbles or some other object. When class is behaving appropriately, move some marbles from one jar to the other and let the students know that when the empty jar is filled they can earn a reward (such as 10 minutes free time). If the class is starting to behave inappropriately, move some marbles back into the original jar.

15. Frequently move about the room so that you can maximize your degree of proximity control.

16. When appropriate, give students choices about several different activities they could choose to work on at that time.

17. With students who can be quite volatile and may initially refuse negative consequences (such as refusing to go to time-out), set a kitchen timer for a brief period (1 to 2 minutes) after the refusal has occurred. Explain that the child can use the 2 minutes to decide if he/she will go to time-out on his/her own or if a more serious consequence must be imposed. Several experienced teachers insist that this method has successfully reduced the extent to which they have had to physically enforce certain negative consequences with students and seems to deescalate the situation. They emphasize that it is important not to continue to give the misbehaving child attention during the decision interval but rather to continue with class to the extent possible.

References

Abel, E. L. (1981). Behavioral teratology of alcohol. *Psychological Bulletin, 90,* 564–581.

Abel, E. L. (1984). Prenatal effects of alcohol. *Drug and Alcohol Dependence, 14,* 1–10.

Abikoff, H. (1985). Efficacy of cognitive training interventions in hyperactive children: A critical review. *Clinical Psychology Review, 5,* 479–512.

Abikoff, H. (1987). An evaluation of cognitive behavior therapy for hyperactive children. In B. B. Lahey & A. E. Kazdin (Eds.), *Advances in clinical child psychology* (Vol. 10, pp. 171–216). New York: Plenum.

Abikoff, H., Ganeles, D., Reiter, G., Blum, C., Foley, C., & Klein, R. G. (1988). Cognitive training in academically deficient ADDH boys receiving stimulant medication. *Journal of Abnormal Child Psychology, 16,* 411–432.

Abikoff, H., & Gittelman, R. (1985a). Classroom observation code: A modification of the Stony Brook code. *Psychopharmacology Bulletin, 21,* 901–909.

Abikoff, H., & Gittelman, R. (1985b). Hyperactive children treated with stimulants: Is cognitive training a useful adjunct? *Archives of General Psychiatry, 42,* 953–961.

Abikoff, H., Gittelman, R., & Klein, D. F. (1980). Classroom observation code for hyperactive children: A replication of validity. *Journal of Consulting and Clinical Psychology, 48,* 555–565.

Abikoff, H., Gittelman-Klein, R., & Klein, D. F. (1977). Validation of a classroom observation code for hyperactive children. *Journal of Consulting and Clinical Psychology, 45,* 772–783.

Achenbach, T. M. (1978). The Child Behavior Profile: I. Boys aged 6–11. *Journal of Consulting and Clinical Psychology, 46,* 478–488.

Achenbach, T. M. (1987). How is a parent rating scale used in the diagnosis of attention deficit disorder? In J. Loney (Ed.), *The young hyperactive child* (pp. 19–31). Birmingham, NY: Haworth.

Achenbach, T. M., & Edelbrock, C. S. (1979). The Child Behavior Profile: II. Boys aged 12–16 and girls aged 6–11 and 12–16. *Journal of Consulting and Clinical Psychology, 47,* 223–233.

Achenbach, T. M., & Edelbrock, C.S. (1983). *Manual for the Child Behavior Checklist and Revised Child Behavior Profile.* Burlington, VT: T. M. Achenbach.

Ackerman, P. T., Anhalt, J. M., Dykman, R. A, & Holcomb, P. J. (1986). Effortful processing in children with reading and/or attention disorders. *Brain and Cognition, 5,* 22–40.

Ackerman, P. T., Anhalt, J. M., Holcomb, P. J., & Dykman, R. (1986). Presumably innate and acquired processes in children with attention and/or reading disorders. *Journal of Child Psychology and Psychiatry, 27,* 513–529.

Ackerman, P. T., Dykman, R. A., & Oglesby, D. M. (1983). Sex and group differences in reading and attention disordered children with and without hyperkinesis. *Journal of Learning Disabilities, 16,* 407–415.

Akiskal, H. D., Down, J., Jordan, P., Watson, S., Daugherty, D., & Pruitt, D. B. (1985). Affective disorders in referred children and younger siblings of manic–depressives. *Archives of General Psychiatry, 42,* 996–1003.

Alberts-Corusch, J., Firestone, P., & Goodman, J. T. (1986). Attention and impulsivity characteristics of the biological and adoptive parents of hyperactive and normal control children. *American Journal of Orthopsychiatry, 56,* 413–423.

Alexander, J. F., Barton, C., Schiavo, R. S., & Parsons, B. V. (1976). Systems–behavioral intervention with families of delinquents: Therapist characteristics, family behavior and outcome. *Journal of Consulting and Clinical Psychology, 44,* 656–664.

Alexander, J. F., & Parsons, B. (1973). Short-term behavioral intervention with delinquent families: Impact on family process and recidivism. *Journal of Abnormal Psychology, 81,* 219–225.

Alexander, J. F., & Parsons, B. (1982). *Functional family therapy.* Monterey, CA: Brooks/Cole.

Alexander, J. F., Waldron, H. B., Barton, C., & Mas, C. H. (1989). The minimizing of blaming attributions and behaviors in delinquent families. *Journal of Consulting and Clinical Psychology, 57,* 19–24.

Aman, M. G. (1980). Psychotropic drugs and learning problems: A selective review. *Journal of Learning Disabilities, 13,* 87–97.

Aman, M. G., & Werry, J. S. (1982). Methylphenidate and diazepam in severe reading retardation. *Journal of the American Academy of Child and Adolescent Psychiatry, 21,* 31–37.

American Psychiatric Association. (1968). *Diagnostic and statistical manual of mental disorders* (2nd ed.). Washington, DC: Author.

American Psychiatric Association. (1980). *Diagnostic and statistical manual of mental disorders* (3rd ed.). Washington, DC: Author.

American Psychiatric Association. (1987). *Diagnostic and statistical manual of mental disorders* (3rd ed., rev.). Washington, DC: Author.

Anastopoulos, A. D., & Barkley, R. A. (1988). Biological factors in attention deficit-hyperactivity disorder. *Behavior Therapist, 11,* 47–53.

Asarnow, J. R., & Callan, J. W. (1985). Boys with peer adjustment problems: Social cognitive processes. *Journal of Consulting and Clinical Psychology, 53,* 80–87.

Atkeson, B. M., & Forehand, R. (1981). Conduct disorders. In E. J. Mash & L. G. Terdal (Eds.), *Behavioral assessment of childhood disorders* (pp. 185–219). New York: Guilford.

Atkins, M. S., Pelham, W. E., & Licht, M. H. (1989). The differential validity of teacher ratings of inattention/overactivity and aggression. *Journal of Abnormal Child Psychology, 4,* 423–435.

August, G. J. (1987). Production deficiencies in free recall: A comparison of hyperactive, learning-disabled and normal children. *Journal of Abnormal Child Psychology, 15,* 429–440.

August, G. J. (1990). Functional neuropsychological assessment in child psychiatry. In B. D. Garfinkel, G. C. Carlson, & E. B. Weller (Eds.), *Psychiatric disorders in children and adolescents* (pp. 469–485). Philadelphia: W. B. Saunders.

August, G. J., Anderson, D., & Bloomquist, M. L. (in press). Competence enhancement training for children: An integrated child, parent and school approach. In S. Christenson & J. C. Conoley (Eds.), *Home–school collaboration: Building a fundamental educational resource.* Colesville, MD: National Association of School Psychologists.

August, G. J., & Garfinkel, B. D. (1989). Behavioral and cognitive subtypes of ADHD. *Journal of the American Academy of Child and Adolescent Psychiatry, 28,* 739–748.

August, G. J., & Stewart, M. A. (1983). Familial subtypes of childhood hyperactivity. *Journal of Nervous and Mental Disease, 171,* 362–368.

Ault, R. L., Mitchell, C., & Hartmann, D. P. (1976). Some methodological problems in reflection–impulsivity research. *Child Development, 47,* 227–231.

Baker, L., & Cantwell, D. P. (1982). Psychiatric disorder in children with different types of communication disorders. *Journal of Communication Disorders, 15,* 113–126.

Baloh, R., Sturm, R., Green, B., & Gleser, G. (1975). Neurophysiological effects of chronic asymptomatic increased lead absorption. *Archives of Neurology, 132,* 326–330.

Barabas, G. (1988). Tourette's syndrome: An overview. *Pediatric Annals, 17,* 391–393.

Barkley, R. A. (1977). A review of stimulant drug research with hyperactive children. *Journal of Child Psychology and Psychiatry, 18,* 137–165.

Barkley, R. A. (1981). *Hyperactive children: A handbook for diagnosis and treatment.* New York: Guilford.

Barkley, R. A. (1982). Guidelines for defining hyperactivity in children: Attention deficit disorder with hyperactivity. In B. B. Lahey & A. E. Kazdin (Eds.), *Advances in clinical child psychology* (Vol. 5; pp. 137–180). New York: Plenum.

Barkley, R. A. (1985). The social interactions of hyperactive children: Developmental changes, drug effects and situational variation. In R. McMahon & R. Peters (Eds.), *Childhood disorders: Behavioral developmental approaches* (pp. 218–243). New York: Brunner/Mazel.

Barkley, R. A. (1987). *Defiant children: A clinician's manual for parent training.* New York: Guilford.

Barkley, R. A. (1988a). Attention deficit disorder with hyperactivity. In E. J. Mash & L. G. Terdal (Eds.), *Behavioral assessment of childhood disorders* (2nd ed., pp. 69–104). New York: Guilford.

Barkley, R. A. (1988b). The effects of methylphenidate on the interactions of preschool ADHD children with their mothers. *Journal of the American Academy of Child and Adolescent Psychiatry, 27,* 336–341.

Barkley, R. A. (1989). Attention deficit–hyperactivity disorder. In E. J. Mash & R. A. Barkley (Eds.), *Treatment of childhood disorders* (pp. 39–72). New York: Guilford.

Barkley, R. A., Copeland, A. P., & Sivage, C. (1980). A self-control classroom for hyperactive children. *Journal of Autism and Developmental Disorders, 10,* 75–89.

Barkley, R. A., Costello, A., & Spitzer, R. (1989). *The development of the DSM-III-R criteria for the disruptive behavior disorders.* Unpublished manuscript, University of Massachusetts Medical Center, Worcester.

Barkley, R. A., & Cunningham, C. E. (1978). Do stimulant drugs improve the academic performance of hyperkinetic children? *Clinical Pediatrics, 17,* 85–92.

Barkley, R. A., & Cunningham, C. E. (1980). The parent-child interactions of hyperactive children and their modification by stimulant drugs. In R. Knights & D. Bakker (Eds.), *Treatment of hyperactive and learning disordered children* (pp. 219–236). Baltimore: University Park.

Barkley, R. A., Fischer, M., Newby, R. F., & Breen, M. J. (1988). Development of a multimethod clinical protocol for assessing stimulant drug response in children with attention deficit disorder. *Journal of Clinical Child Psychology, 17,* 14–24.

Barkley, R. A., Karlsson, J., & Pollard, S. (1985). Effects of age on mother–child interactions of hyperactive children. *Journal of Abnormal Child Psychology, 13,* 631–638.

Barkley, R. A., Karlsson, J., Pollard, S., & Murphy, J. U. (1985). Developmental changes in the mother–child interactions of hyperactive boys: Effects of two dose levels of Ritalin. *Journal of Child Psychology and Psychiatry, 26,* 705–715.

Barton, C., & Alexander, J. F. (1981). Functional family therapy. In A. S. Gurman & D. P. Kniskern (Eds.), *Handbook of family therapy* (pp. 403–443). New York: Brunner/Mazel.

Barton, C., Alexander, J. F., Waldron, H., Turner, C. W., & Warburton, J. (1985). Generalizing treatment effects of functional family therapy: Three replications. *American Journal of Family Therapy, 13,* 16–26.

Bauer, W., & Twentyman, C. T. (1985). Abusing, neglectful and comparison mothers' reactions to child-related and non-child-related stressors. *Journal of Consulting and Clinical Psychology, 53,* 335–343.

Bayles, F., & McCartney, S. (1988, April 4). Scientology group wages war against Ritalin "baby druggers." *Los Angeles Herald Examiner.*

Beck, A. T. (1976). *Cognitive therapy and the emotional disorders.* New York: International Universities.

Beck, A. T., Rush, A. J., Shaw, B. F., & Emery, G. (1979). *Cognitive therapy of depression.* New York: Guilford.

Becker-Mattes, A., Mattes, J. A., Abikoff, H., & Brandt, L. (1985). State-dependent learning in hyperactive children receiving methylphenidate. *American Journal of Psychiatry, 142,* 455–459.

Befera, M. S., & Barkley, R. A. (1985). Hyperactive and normal girls and boys: Mother–child interaction, parent psychiatric status and child psychopathology. *Journal of Child Psychology and Psychiatry, 26,* 439–452.

Berry, C. A., Shaywitz, S. E., & Shaywitz, B. A. (1985). Girls with attention deficit disorder: A silent minority? A report on behavioral and cognitive characteristics. *Pediatrics, 76,* 801–809.

Biederman, J., Baldessarini, R. J., Wright, V., Knee, D., & Harmatz, J. S. (1989). A double-blind placebo controlled study of desipramine in the treatment of ADD: I. Efficacy. *Journal of the American Academy of Child and Adolescent Psychiatry, 28,* 777–784.

Biederman, J., Gastfriend, D. R., Jellinek, M. S., & Goldblatt, A. (1985). Cardiovascular effects of desipramine in children and adolescents with attention deficit disorder. *Journal of Pediatrics, 65,* 1017–1020.

Biederman, J., Munir, K., & Knee, D. (1987). Conduct and oppositional defiant disorder in clinically referred children with attention deficit disorder: A controlled family study. *Journal of the American Academy of Child and Adolescent Psychiatry, 26,* 724–732.

Biederman, J., Munir, K., Knee, D., Armentano, M., Autor, S., Waternaux, C., & Tsuang, M. (1987). High rate of affective disorders in probands with attention deficit disorders and in their relatives: A controlled family study. *American Journal of Psychiatry, 144,* 330–333.

Bierman, K. L. (1983). Cognitive development and clinical interviews with children. In B. B. Lahey & A. E. Kazdin (Eds.), *Advances in clinical child psychology* (Vol. 6, pp. 217–250). New York: Plenum.

Bierman, K. L., & Furman, W. F. (1984). The effects of social skills training and peer involvement on the social adjustment of preadolescents. *Child Development, 55,* 151–162.

Bierman, K. L., Miller, C. L., & Stabb, S. D. (1987). Improving the social behavior and peer acceptance of rejected boys: Effects of social skills training with instructions and prohibitions. *Journal of Consulting and Clinical Psychology, 55,* 194–200.

Birmaher, B., Greenhill, L. L., Cooper, T. B., Fried, J., & Maminski, B. (1989). Sustained release methylphenidate: Pharmacokinetic studies in ADDH males. *Journal of the American Academy of Child and Adolescent Psychiatry, 28,* 768–772.

Block, G. H. (1977). Hyperactivity: A cultural perspective. *Journal of Learning Disabilities, 110,* 236–240.

Block, J., Block, J., & Harrington, D. (1974). Some misgivings about the Matching Familiar Figures test as a measure of reflection–impulsivity. *Developmental Psychology, 10,* 611–632.

Bloom, A. S., Russell, L. J., Weisskopf, B., & Blackerby, J. L. (1988). Methylphenidate-induced delusional disorder in a child with attention deficit disorder with hyperactivity. *Journal of the American Academy of Child and Adolescent Psychiatry, 27,* 88–89.

Bloomquist, M. L., August, G. J., & Garfinkel, B. D. (1991). *Cognitive–behavioral therapy for children with attention deficits and hyperactivity: Effects of parent involvement and methylphenidate.* Manuscript submitted for publication.

Bloomquist, M. L., August, G. J., & Ostrander, R. (in press). Effects of a school-based cognitive–behavioral intervention for ADHD children. *Journal of Abnormal Child Psychology*.

Bloomquist, M. L., & Braswell, L. (1989). *Multicomponent cognitive–behavioral intervention for attention-deficit hyperactivity disordered children*. Unpublished treatment manual, University of Minnesota, Minneapolis.

Borcherding, B., Thompson, K., Kruesi, M., Bartko, J., Rapoport, J., & Weingartner, H. (1988). Automatic and effortful processing in attention deficit/hyperactivity disorder. *Journal of Abnormal Child Psychology, 16*, 333–345.

Boudreault, M., Thivierge, J., Côté, R., Boutin, P., Julien, Y., & Bergeron, S. (1988). Cognitive development and reading achievement in pervasive-ADD, situational-ADD and control children. *Journal of Child Psychology and Psychiatry, 29*, 611–619.

Bowdan, N. D. (1977). Hyperactivity or affective illness? *American Journal of Psychiatry, 134*, 329.

Braswell, L. (1984). *Cognitive–behavioral therapy with an inner city sample of non-self-controlled children*. Unpublished doctoral dissertation, University of Minnesota, Minneapolis.

Braswell, L. (1988). *Classroom-based cognitive–behavioral intervention program targeting academic and social behavior*. Unpublished manuscript, North Memorial Medical Center, Minneapolis.

Braswell, L., & August, G. (1989). *Feasibility and outcome for a classroom-based cognitive–behavioral intervention program addressing academic and behavioral deficits in school-aged children*. Unpublished manuscript, University of Minnesota, Minneapolis.

Braswell, L., Bloomquist, M. L., & Pedersen, S. (1991). *An educator's guide to understanding and helping children with ADHD*. Minneapolis: Department of Professional Development and Conference Services.

Braswell, L., & Kendall, P. C. (1988). Cognitive behavioral methods with children. In K. S. Dobson (Ed.), *Handbook of cognitive–behavioral therapies* (pp. 167–213). New York: Guilford.

Braswell, L., Kendall, P. C., Braith, J., Carey, M., & Vye, C. (1985). "Involvement" in cognitive–behavioral therapy with children: Process and its relationship to outcome. *Cognitive Therapy and Research, 9*, 611–630.

Braswell, L., Koehler, C., & Kendall, P. C. (1985). Attributions and outcomes in child psychotherapy. *Journal of Social and Clinical Psychology, 3*, 458–465.

Braud, L. W. (1978). The effects of frontal EMG biofeedback and progressive relaxation upon hyperactivity and its behavioral concomitants. *Biofeedback and Self-Regulation, 3*, 69–89.

Breen, M. J. (1989). Cognitive and behavioral differences in ADHD boys and girls. *Journal of Child Psychology and Psychiatry, 30*, 711–716.

Breen, M. J., & Barkley, R. A. (1988). Child psychopathology and parenting stress in girls and boys having attention deficit disorder with hyperactivity. *Journal of Pediatric Psychology, 13*, 265–280.

Brody, G., & Forehand, R. (1986). Maternal perceptions of child maladjustment as a function of the combined influence of child behavior and maternal depression. *Journal of Consulting and Clinical Psychology, 54*, 237–240.

Brown, R. T., Borden, K. A., Wynne, M. E., Schleser, R., & Clingerman, S. R. (1986). Methylphenidate and cognitive therapy with ADD children: A methodological reconsideration. *Journal of Abnormal Child Psychology, 14,* 481–497.

Brown, R. T., Wynne, M. E., & Medenis, R. (1985). Methylphenidate and cognitive therapy: A comparison of treatment approaches with hyperactive boys. *Journal of Abnormal Child Psychology, 13,* 69–87.

Bugental, D. B., Collins, S., Collins, L., & Chaney, L. K. (1978). Attributional and behavioral changes following two behavioral management interventions with hyperactive boys: A follow-up study. *Child Development, 49,* 247–250.

Bugental, D. B., Whalen, C. B., & Henker, B. (1977). Causal attributions of hyperactive children and motivational assumptions of two behavior-change approaches: Evidence for an interactionist position. *Child Development, 48,* 847–884.

Cairns, E., & Cammock, T. (1978). Development of a more reliable version of the Matching Familiar Figures test. *Developmental Psychology, 5,* 555–560.

Cairns, E., & Cammock, T. (1984). The development of reflection–impulsivity: Further data. *Personality and Individual Differences, 5,* 113–115.

Campis, L. K., Lyman, R. D., & Prentice-Dunn S. (1986). The parent locus of control scale: Development and validation. *Journal of Clinical Child Psychology, 15,* 260–267.

Cantwell, D. P. (1975). Psychiatric illness in the families of hyperactive children. *Archives of General Psychiatry, 27,* 414–417.

Cantwell, D. P. (1980). A clinician's guide to the use of stimulant medication for psychiatric disorders of children. *Journal of Developmental and Behavior Pediatrics, 1,* 133–140.

Cantwell, D. P. (1985). Hyperactive children grown up: What have we learned about what happened to them? *Archives of General Psychiatry, 42,* 1026–1028.

Cantwell, D. P. (1987, June). *The clinical description of AD-HD individuals.* Workshop presented at the Conference on Attention-Deficit Hyperactivity Disorders in Children and Adolescents: Assessment and Intervention Techniques, Minneapolis, MN.

Cantwell, D. P., & Baker, L. (1988). Issues in the classification of child and adolescent psychopathology. *Journal of the American Academy of Child and Adolescent Psychiatry, 27,* 521–533.

Cantwell, D. P., & Carlson, G. (1978). Stimulants. In J. Werry (Ed.), *Pediatric psychopharmacology* (pp. 171–207). New York: Brunner/Mazel.

Cantwell, D. P., & Satterfield, J. H. (1978). The prevalence of academic underachievement in hyperactive children. *Journal of Pediatric Psychology, 3,* 168–171.

Carlson, C. L. (1986). Attention deficit disorder without hyperactivity: A review of preliminary experimental evidence. In B. B. Lahey & A. E. Kazdin (Eds.), *Advances in clinical child psychology* (Vol. 9, pp. 153–175). New York: Plenum.

Carlson, C. L., Lahey, B. B., Frame, C. L., Walker, J., & Hynd, G. W. (1987). Sociometric status of clinic-referred children with attention deficit disorders with and without hyperactivity. *Journal of Abnormal Child Psychology, 15,* 537–547.

Castenada, A., McCandless, B., & Palermo, D. (1956). The children's form of the Manifest Anxiety Scale. *Child Development, 27,* 317–326.

Chandler, M. J. (1973). Egocentrism and antisocial behavior: The assessment and training of social perspective-taking skills. *Developmental Psychology, 9,* 326–332.

Chandler, M. J., Greenspan, S., & Barenboim, C. (1974). Assessment and training of role-taking and referential communication skills in institutionalized emotionally disturbed children. *Developmental Psychology, 10,* 546–553.

Chase, S. N., & Clement, P. W. (1985). Effects of self-reinforcement and stimulants on academic performance in children with attention deficit disorder. *Journal of Clinical Child Psychology, 14,* 323–333.

Chess, S., & Thomas, A. (1984). *Origins and evolution of behavior disorders from infancy to early adult life.* New York: Brunner/Mazel.

Citizens' Commission on Human Rights. (1987a). *CCHR information letter #1: How psychiatry is making drug addicts out of America's school children.* Los Angeles: Author.

Citizen's Commission on Human Rights. (1987b). *CCHR information letter #2: Ritalin: A warning for parents.* Los Angeles: Author.

Cohen, H., & Minde, K. (1983). The hyperactive syndrome in kindergarten children: Comparison of children with pervasive and situational symptoms. *Journal of Child Psychology and Psychiatry, 24,* 443–455.

Cohen, R., & Schleser, R. (1984). Cognitive development and clinical interventions. In A. W. Meyers & W. E. Craighead (Eds.), *Cognitive behavior therapy with children* (pp. 45–68). New York: Plenum.

Coll, P. G., & Bland, R. (1979). Manic–depressive illness in adolescence and childhood. *Canadian Journal of Psychiatry, 24,* 255–263.

Comings, D. E., & Comings, B. G. (1984). Tourette's syndrome and attention deficit disorder with hyperactivity: Are they genetically related? *Journal of the American Academy of Child Psychiatry, 23,* 138–146.

Conners, C. K. (1969). A teacher rating scale for use in drug studies with children. *American Journal of Psychiatry, 126,* 152–156.

Conners, C. K. (1970). Symptom patterns in hyperkinetic, neurotic and normal children. *Child Development, 40,* 667–682.

Conners, C. K. (1973). Rating scales for use in drug studies with children: Pharmacotherapy of children. *Psychopharmacology Bulletin, 9,* 24–84.

Conners, C. K. (1980). *Food additives and hyperactive children.* New York: Plenum.

Conners, C. K. (1985). The computerized continuous performance test. *Psychopharmacology Bulletin, 21,* 891–892.

Conners, C. K. (1987). How is a teacher rating scale used in the diagnosis of attention deficit disorder? In J. Loney (Ed.), *The young hyperactive child* (pp. 33–51). Birmingham, NY: Haworth.

Conners, C. K., & Barkley, R. A. (1985). Rating scales and checklists for child psychopharmacology. *Psychopharmacology Bulletin, 21,* 809–851.

Conrad, M., & Hammen, C. (1989). Role of maternal depression in perceptions of child maladjustment. *Journal of Consulting and Clinical Psychology, 57,* 663–667.

Coons, H. W., Klorman, R., & Borgstedt, A. D. (1987). Effects of methylphenidate on adolescents with a childhood history of attention deficit disorder: II. Information processing. *Journal of the American Academy of Child and Adolescent Psychiatry, 26,* 368–374.

Copeland, A. P. (1979). Types of private speech produced by hyperactive and nonhyperactive boys. *Journal of Abnormal Child Psychology, 7,* 169–177.

Costello, A. J., Edelbrock, C., Kalas, R., Dulcan, M. K., & Klaric, S. H. (1984). *Development and testing of the NIMH Diagnostic Interview Schedule for Children (DISC) in a clinic population: Final report.* Rockville, MD: Center for Epidemiological Studies, NIMH.

Craighead, W. E., Meyers, A. W., & Wilcoxon-Craighead, L. (1985). A conceptual model for cognitive–behavioral therapy with children. *Journal of Abnormal Child Psychology, 13,* 331–342.

Cunningham, C. E., & Barkley, R. A. (1979). The interactions of hyperactive and normal children with their mothers during free play and structural task. *Child Development, 50,* 217–224.

David, O. J., Clark, J., & Voeller, K. (1972). Lead and hyperactivity. *Lancet, 2,* 900–903.

de Haas, P. A., & Young, R. D. (1984). Attention styles of hyperactive and normal girls. *Journal of Abnormal Psychology, 12,* 531–546.

Denckla, M. D., Bemporad, J. R., & MacKay, M. C. (1976). Tics following methylphenidate administration: A report of 20 cases. *Journal of the American Medical Association, 235,* 1349–1351.

Denson, R., Nanson, J. L., & McWatters, M. A. (1975). Hyperkinesis and maternal smoking. *Canadian Psychiatric Association Journal, 20,* 183–187.

Di Giuseppe, R. (1988). A cognitive behavioral approach to the treatment of conduct disorder children and adolescents. In N. Epstein, S. Schlesinger, & W. Dryden (Eds.), *Cognitive–behavioral therapy with families* (pp. 183–214). New York: Brunner/Mazel.

Dix, T. H., & Grusec, J. E. (1985). Parent attribution processes in the socialization of children. In I. Sigel (Ed.), *Parental belief systems: The psychological consequences for children.* Hillsdale, NJ: Erlbaum.

Dodge, K. A. (1986). A social information processing model of social competence in children. In M. Perlmetter (Ed.), *Cognitive perspective on children's social and behavioral development* (pp. 77–125). Hillsdale, NJ: Erlbaum.

Dodge, K. A., & Frame, C. L. (1982). Social cognitive biases and deficits in aggressive boys. *Child Development, 53,* 620–635.

Dodge, K. A., Murphy, R. R., & Buchsbaum, K. C. (1984). The assessment of intention-cue detection skills in children: Implications for developmental psychology. *Child Development, 55,* 163–173.

Dodge, K. A., & Newman, J. P. (1981). Biased decision-making processes in aggressive boys. *Journal of Abnormal Psychology, 90,* 375–379.

Donnelly, M., Zametkin, A. J., Rapport, J., Ismond, D. R., Weingartner, H., Lane, E., Oliver, J., Linnoila, M., & Potter, W. Z. (1986). Treatment of childhood hyperactivity with desipramine. *Clinical Pharmacological Therapy, 39,* 72–81.

Douglas, V. I. (1983). Attentional and cognitive problems. In M. Rutter (Ed.), *Developmental neuropsychiatry* (pp. 280–328). New York: Guilford.

Douglas, V. I. (1984). The psychological processes implicated in ADD. In L. M. Bloomingdale (Ed.), *Attention deficit disorder: Diagnostic, cognitive and therapeutic understanding* (pp. 147–162). New York: Spectrum.

Douglas, V. I., Barr, R. G., Amin, K., O'Neill, M. E., & Britton, B. G. (1988). Dosage effects and individual responsivity to methylphenidate in attention deficit disorder. *Journal of Child Psychology and Psychiatry, 29,* 453–475.

Douglas, V. I., Barr, R. G., O'Neill, M. E., & Britton, B. G. (1986). Short-term effects of methylphenidate on the cognitive, learning and academic performance of children with attention deficit disorder in the laboratory and the classroom. *Journal of Child Psychology and Psychiatry, 29,* 191–211.

Douglas, V. I., Parry, P., Marton, P., & Garson, C. (1976). Assessment of a cognitive training program for hyperactive children. *Journal of Abnormal Child Psychology, 4,* 389–410.

Douglas, V. I., & Peters, K. G. (1979). Toward a clearer definition of the attentional deficit in hyperactive children. In G. A. Hale & M. Lewis (Eds.), *Attention and the development of cognitive skills* (pp. 173–247). New York: Plenum.

Dubey, D. R., O'Leary, S. G., & Kaufman, K. F. (1983). Training parents of hyperactive children in child management: A comparative outcome study. *Journal of Abnormal Child Psychology, 11,* 229–246.

Dunn, H. G., McBurnery, A. K., Ingram, S., & Hunter, C. M. (1977). Maternal cigarette smoking during pregnancy and the child's subsequent development: II. Neurological and intellectual maturation to the age of 6½ years. *Canadian Journal of Public Health, 68,* 43.

Dupont, H., Gardner, O., & Brody, D. (1974). *Toward affective development.* Circle Pines, MN: American Guidance Service.

Dush, D. M., Hirt, M. L., & Schroeder, H. E. (1989). Self-statement modification in the treatment of child behavior disorders: A meta-analysis. *Psychological Bulletin, 106,* 97–106.

Dvoredsky, A. E., & Stewart, M. A. (1981). Hyperactivity followed by manic depressive disorder: Two case reports. *Journal of Clinical Psychiatry, 42,* 212–215.

Dykman, R. A., Ackerman, P. T., & McCray, D. S. (1980). Effects of methylphenidate on selective and sustained attention in hyperactive, reading-disabled and presumable attention-disordered boys. *Journal of Nervous and Mental Disease, 168,* 745–752.

D'Zurilla, T. J., & Goldfried, M. R. (1971). Problem-solving and behavior modification. *Journal of Abnormal Psychology, 78,* 197–226.

Edelbrock, C., & Achenback, T. M. (1984). The teacher version of the child behavior profile: I. Boys aged 6–11. *Journal of Consulting and Clinical Psychology, 52,* 207–217.

Edelbrock, C., Costello, A., & Kessler, M. D. (1984). Empirical corroboration of attention deficit disorder. *Journal of the American Academy of Child Psychiatry, 23,* 285–290.

Egeland, B., & Weinberg, R. A. (1976). The Matching Familiar Figures test: A look at its psychometric credibility. *Child Development, 47,* 483–491.

Epstein, N. E., Schlesinger, S. E., & Dryden, W. (1988). Concepts and methods of cognitive–behavior family treatment. In N. Epstein, S. Schlesinger, & W. Dryden (Eds.), *Cognitive–behavioral therapy with families* (pp. 5–48). New York: Brunner/Mazel.

Erenberg, G., Cruse, R. P., & Rothner, A. D. (1987). The natural history of Tourette's syndrome: A follow-up study. *Annals of Neurology, 22,* 383–385.

Eyberg, S. M., & Johnson, S. M. (1974). Multiple assessment of behavior modification with families: Effects of contingency contracting and order of treated problem. *Journal of Consulting and Clinical Psychology, 42,* 594–606.

Feindler, E. L., & Ecton, R. B. (1986). *Adolescent anger control: Cognitive-behavioral techniques.* New York: Pergamon.

Feindler, E. L., Ecton, R. B., Kingsley, D., & Dubey, D. R. (1986). Group anger-control training for institutionalized psychiatric male adolescents. *Behavior Therapy, 17,* 109–123.

Feindler, E. L., Marriott, S. A., & Iwata, M. (1984). Group anger control training for junior high school delinquents. *Cognitive Therapy and Research, 8,* 299–311.

Feingold, B. F. (1975). *Why your child is hyperactive.* New York: Random House.

Felton, D., Kia, H. F., Swanson, K., & Bloomquist, M. (1987, November). *Effects of a comprehensive school-based cognitive–behavioral intervention for non-self-controlled children.* Paper presented at the annual meeting of the Association for Advancement of Behavior Therapy, New York.

Felton, R. H., Wood, F. B., Brown, I. S., Campbell, S. K., & Harter, M. R. (1987). Separate verbal memory and naming deficits in attention deficit disorder and reading disability. *Brain and Language, 31,* 171–184.

Ferguson, H. B. (1986, November). Overview of biological research. In R. Milich (chair), *Biological Perspectives on Attention Deficit Disorder.* Symposium conducted at the Annual Meeting of the Association for Advancement of Behavior Therapy, Chicago.

Fiese, B. H., & Sameroff, A. J. (1989). Family context in pediatric psychology: A transactional perspective. *Journal of Pediatric Psychology, 14,* 293–314.

Firestone, P., Crowe, D., Goodman, J. T., & McGrath, P. (1986). Vicissitudes of follow-up studies: Differential effects of parent training and stimulant medication with hyperactives. *American Journal of Orthopsychiatry, 56,* 184–194.

Fish, M. C. (1988). Relaxation training for childhood disorders. In C. E. Schaeffer (Ed.), *Innovative interventions in child and adolescent therapy.* New York: Wiley.

Folks, D. G. (1983). Monoamine oxidase inhibitors: Reappraisal of dietary considerations. *Journal of Clinical Psychopharmacology, 3,* 249–252.

Forehand, R., Lautenschlager, G. J., Faust, J., & Graziano, W. G. (1986). Parent perceptions and parent–child interactions in clinic-referral children: A preliminary investigation of the effects of maternal depressive moods. *Behaviour Research and Therapy, 24,* 73–75.

Forehand, R. L., & McMahon, R. J. (1981). *Helping the noncompliant child: A clinician's guide to parent training.* New York: Guilford.

Foster, S. L., & Robin, A. L. (1989). Parent–adolescent conflict. In E. J. Mash & R. A. Barkley (Eds.), *Treatment of childhood disorders* (pp. 493–528). New York: Guilford.

Fras, I., & Karlavage, J. (1977). The use of methylphenidate and imipramine in Gilles de la Tourette's disease in children. *American Journal of Psychiatry, 134,* 195–197.

Gadow, K. D. (1985). Relative efficacy of pharmacological, behavioral and combination treatments for enhancing academic performance. *Clinical Psychology Review, 5,* 513–533.

Gadow, K. D., & Swanson, H. L. (1985). Assessing drug effects on academic performance. *Psychopharmacology Bulletin, 21,* 877–886.

Gan, J., & Cantwell, D. P. (1982). Dosage effects of methylphenidate on paired associate learning: Positive/negative placebo responders. *Journal of the American Academy of Child Psychiatry, 21,* 237–242.

Gard, G. C., & Berry, K. K. (1986). Oppositional children: Training tyrants. *Journal of Clinical Child Psychology, 15,* 148–158.

Garfinkel, B. D. (1987, June). *Treatment strategies for AD-HD.* Workshop presented at the Conference on Attention Deficit-Hyperactivity Disorders in Children and Adolescents: Assessment and Intervention Techniques, Minneapolis, MN.

Garfinkel, B. D., Wender, P. H., Sloman, L., & O'Neill, I. (1983). Tricyclic antidepressant and methylphenidate treatment of attention deficit disorder in children. *Journal of the American Academy of Child Psychiatry, 22,* 343–348.

Gastfriend, D. R., Biederman, J., & Jellinek, M. S. (1984). Desipramine in the treatment of adolescents with attention deficit disorder. *American Journal of Psychiatry, 141,* 906–908.

Gittelman, R., & Eskenazi, B. (1983). Lead and hyperactivity revisited: An investigation of nondisadvantaged children. *Archives of General Psychiatry, 40,* 827–833.

Gittelman, R., & Koplewicz, H. S. (1966). Pharmacotherapy of childhood anxiety disorders. In R. Gittelman (Ed.), *Anxiety disorders of childhood* (pp. 188–203). New York: Guilford.

Gittelman-Klein, R., & Feingold, I. (1983). Children with reading disorders: II. Effects of methylphenidate in combination with reading remediation. *Journal of Child Psychology and Psychiatry, 24,* 193–212.

Gittelman-Klein, R., Landa, B., Mattes, J. A., & Klein, D. (1988). Methylphenidate and growth in hyperactive children. *Archives of General Psychiatry, 45,* 1127–1130.

Gittelman-Klein, R., & Mannuzza, S. (1988). Hyperactive boys almost grown up. III. Methylphenidate effects on ultimate height. *Archives of General Psychiatry, 45,* 1131–1134.

Glow, R. A., Glow, P. H., & Rump, E. E. (1982). The stability of child behavior disorders: A one year test–retest study of Adelaide versions of the Conners Teacher and Parent Rating Scales. *Journal of Abnormal Child Psychology, 10,* 33–60.

Golden, G. S. (1974). Gilles de la Tourette's syndrome following methylphenidate administration. *Developmental Medicine and Child Neurology, 16,* 76–78.

Golden, G. S. (1986). Tourette syndrome: Recent advances. *Pediatric Neurology, 2,* 189–192.

Golden, G. S. (1988). The relationship between stimulant medication and tics. *Pediatric Annals, 17,* 405–408.

Goodman, R., & Stevenson, J. (1989a). A twin study of hyperactivity—I. An examination of hyperactivity scores and categories derived from Rutter,

Teacher and Parent Questionnaires. *Journal of Child Psychology and Psychiatry, 130,* 671–689.

Goodman, R., & Stevenson, J. (1989b). A twin study of hyperactivity—II. The etiological role of genes, family relations and perinatal adversity. *Journal of Abnormal Child Psychology, 30,* 691–709.

Gordon, D. A., & Arbuthnot, J. (1987). Individual, group and family interventions. In H. C. Quay (Ed.), *Handbook of juvenile delinquency* (pp. 290–324). New York: Wiley.

Gordon, M. (1979). The assessment of impulsivity and mediating behaviors in hyperactive and nonhyperactive boys. *Journal of Abnormal Child Psychology, 7,* 317–326.

Gordon, M. (1983). *The Gordon Diagnostic System.* Boulder, CO: Clinical Diagnostic Systems.

Goyette, C. H., Conners, C. K., & Ulrich, R. F. (1978). Normative data on revised Conners Parent Teacher Rating Scales. *Journal of Abnormal Child Psychology, 6,* 221–236.

Grenell, M. M., Glass, C. R., & Katz, K. S. (1987). Hyperactive children and peer interaction: Knowledge and performance of social skills. *Journal of Abnormal Child Psychology, 15,* 1–13.

Griest, D. L., Forehand, R., Wells, K. C., & McMahon, R. J. (1980). An examination of differences between nonclinic and behavior problems clinic-referred children and their mothers. *Journal of Abnormal Psychology, 89,* 497–500.

Gurucharri, C., Phelps, E., & Selman, R. (1984). Development of interpersonal understanding: A longitudinal and comparative study of normal and disturbed youths. *Journal of Consulting and Clinical Psychology, 52,* 26–36.

Halperin, J. M., Wolf, L. E., Pascualvaca, D. M., Newcorn, J. H., Healey, J. M., O'Brien, J. D., Morganstein, A., & Young, G. (1988). Differential assessment of attention and impulsivity in children. *Journal of the American Academy of Child and Adolescent Psychiatry, 27,* 326–329.

Hammill, D. D. (1985). *Detroit Tests of Learning Aptitude.* Austin, TX: Pro-Ed.

Harris, K. (1986). Self-monitoring of attentional behavior versus self-monitoring of productivity: Effects on on-task behavior and academic response rate among learning disabled children. *Journal of Applied Behavior Analysis, 19,* 417–423.

Harter, S. (1985). *The Self-Perception Profile for Children: Revision of the Perceived Competence Scale for Children (Manual).* Denver, CO: University of Denver.

Hartsough, C. S., & Lambert, N. M. (1982). Some environmental and familial correlates and antecedents of hyperactivity. *American Journal of Orthopsychiatry, 52,* 272–287.

Hartsough, C. S., & Lambert, N. M. (1984). Contribution of predispositional factors to the diagnosis of hyperactivity. *American Journal of Orthopsychiatry, 54,* 97–109.

Hartsough, C. S., & Lambert, N. M. (1985). Medical factors in hyperactive and normal children: Prenatal, developmental and health history findings. *American Journal of Orthopsychiatry, 55,* 190–201.

Hathaway, S. R., & McKinley, J. C. (1951). *Minnesota Multiphasic Personality Inventory: Manual.* Minneapolis: University of Minnesota Press.

Heffron, W. A., Martin, C. A., & Welsh, R. J. (1984). Attention deficit disorder in three pairs of monozygotic twins: A case report. *Journal of the American Academy of Child Psychiatry, 23,* 299–301.

Henggeler, S. W. (1982). The family–ecological systems theory. In S. W. Henggeler (Ed.), *Delinquency and adolescent psychopathology: A family–ecological system approach* (pp. 1–10). Littleton, MA: PSG.

Henker, B., & Whalen, C. K. (1989). Hyperactivity and attention deficits. *American Psychologist, 44,* 216–223.

Herjanic, B., & Reich, W. (1982). Development of a structural psychiatric interview for children: Agreement between child and parent on individual symptoms. *Journal of Abnormal Child Psychology, 10,* 307–324.

Hinshaw, S. P. (1987). On the distinction between attentional deficits/hyperactivity and conduct problems/aggression in child psychopathology. *Psychological Bulletin, 101,* 443–463.

Hinshaw, S. P., Buhrmester, P., & Heller, T. (1989). Anger control in response to verbal provocations: Effects of stimulant medication for boys with ADHD. *Journal of Abnormal Child Psychology, 17,* 393–407.

Hinshaw, S. P., & Erhardt, D. (1990). Behavioral treatment of attention deficit–hyperactivity disorder. In V. B. Van Hasselt & M. Hersen (Eds.), *Handbook of behavior therapy and pharmacotherapy for children: An integrative approach.* New York: Plenum.

Hinshaw, S. P., & Erhardt, D. (1991). Attention-deficit hyperactivity disorder. In P. C. Kendall (Ed.), *Child and adolescent therapy: Cognitive–behavioral procedures* (pp. 98–128). New York: Guilford.

Hinshaw, S. P., Henker, B., & Whalen, C. K. (1984a). Cognitive–behavioral and pharmacologic interventions for hyperactive boys: Comparative and combined effects. *Journal of Consulting and Clinical Psychology, 52,* 739–749.

Hinshaw, S. P., Henker, B., & Whalen, C. K. (1984b). Self-control in hyperactive boys in anger-inducing situations: Effects of cognitive–behavioral training and of methylphenidate. *Journal of Abnormal Child Psychology, 12,* 55–77.

Hinshaw, S. P., Henker, B., Whalen, C. K., Erhardt, D., & Dunnington, R. E. (1989). Aggressive, prosocial and nonsocial behavior in hyperactive boys: Dose effects of methylphenidate in naturalistic settings. *Journal of Consulting and Clinical Psychology, 57,* 636–643.

Hoberman, A., & Peterson, C. (1990). Multidimensional psychotherapy for children and adolescents. In B. D. Garfinkel, G. C. Carlson, & E. B. Weller (Eds.), *Psychiatric disorders in children and adolescents* (pp. 503–536). Philadelphia: W. B. Saunders.

Homatidis, S., & Konstantareas, M. M. (1981). Assessment of hyperactivity: Isolating measures of high discriminant validity. *Journal of Consulting and Clinical Psychology, 49,* 533–541.

Horn, W. F., Ialongo, N., Popovich, S., & Peradotto, D. (1987). Behavioral parent training and cognitive–behavioral self-control therapy with ADDH children: Comparative and combined effects. *Journal of Clinical Child Psychology, 15,* 57–68.

Horn, W. F., Wagner, A. E., & Ialongo, N. (1989). Sex differences in school-aged children with pervasive attention-deficit hyperactivity disorder. *Journal of Abnormal Child Psychology, 17,* 109–125.

Hudson, W. W. (1982). *The clinical measurement package: A field manual.* Chicago: Dorsey.

Hughes, H. M., & Haynes, S. H. (1978). Structured laboratory observation in the behavioral assessment of parent–child interactions: A methodological critique. *Behavior Therapy, 9,* 428–447.

Hughes, J. N., & Hall, R. J. (Eds.). (1989). *Cognitive–behavioral psychology in the schools: A comprehensive handbook.* New York: Guilford.

Humphrey, L. L. (1982). Children's and teachers' perspectives on children's self-control: The development of two rating scales. *Journal of Consulting and Clinical Psychology, 50,* 624–633.

Iversen, S. D. (1977). Behavior after neostriatal lesions in animals. In I. Divac & R. G. E. Oberg (Eds.), *The neostriatus* (pp. 195–210). Elmsford, NY: Pergamon.

Iwata, B. A., & Bailey, J. S. (1974). Reward versus cost token system: An analysis of the effects on students and teacher. *Journal of Applied Behavior Analysis, 7,* 567–576.

Jacob, R. G., O'Leary, K. D., & Rosenblad, C. (1978). Formal and informal classroom settings: Effects on hyperactivity. *Journal of Abnormal Child Psychology, 6,* 47–59.

Jacobvitz, D., & Sroufe, L. A. (1987). The early caregiver–child relationship and attention deficit disorder with hyperactivity in kindergarten: A prospective study. *Child Development, 58,* 1488–1495.

Jacobvitz, D., Sroufe, L. A., Stewart, M., & Leffert, N. (1990). Treatment of attentional and hyperactivity problems in children with sympathomimetic drugs: A comprehensive review. *Journal of the American Academy of Child and Adolescent Psychiatry, 29,* 677–688.

Jensen, J. B., Burke, N., & Garfinkel, B. D. (1988). Depression and symptoms of attentional deficit disorder with hyperactivity. *Journal of the American Academy of Child and Adolescent Psychiatry, 27,* 742–747.

Johnston, C. J., & Pelham, W. E. (1986). Teacher ratings predict peer ratings of aggression at 3 year follow-up in boys with attention deficit disorder with hyperactivity. *Journal of Consulting and Clinical Psychology, 54,* 571–572.

Johnston, C., Pelham, W., Hoza, J., & Sturges, J. (1988). Psychostimulant rebound in attention deficit disordered boys. *Journal of the American Academy of Child and Adolescent Psychiatry, 27,* 806–810.

Kagan, J. (1966). Reflection–impulsivity: The generality and dynamics of conceptual tempo. *Journal of Abnormal Psychology, 71,* 17–24.

Kagan, J., Rosman, B. L., Day, D., Albert, J., & Phillips, W. (1964). Information processing in the child: Significance of analytic and reflective attitudes. *Psychological Monographs, 78*(1, Whole No. 578).

Kaplan, B. J., McNicol, J., Conte, R. A., & Moghadam, H. K. (1989). Dietary replacement in preschool-aged hyperactive boys. *Pediatrics, 83,* 7–17.

Karoly, P. (1981). Self-management problems in children. In E. J. Mash & L. G. Terdal (Eds.), *Behavioral assessment of childhood disorders* (pp. 79–126). New York: Guilford.

Kashani, J., Chapel, J. L., Ellis, J., & Shekim, W. D. (1979). Hyperactive girls. *Journal of Operational Psychiatry, 10,* 145–148.

Kaufman, A. S., & Kaufman, N. L. (1983). *Kaufman Assessment Battery for Children: Administration and scoring manual.* Circle Pines, MN: American Guidance Service.

Kazdin, A. E., Bass, D., Siegel, T., & Thomas, C., (1989). Cognitive–behavioral therapy of children referred for antisocial behavior. *Journal of Consulting and Clinical Psychology, 57,* 522–535.

Kazdin, A. E., Esveldt-Dawson, K., French, N. H., & Unis, A. S. (1987a). Effects of parent management training and problem-solving skills training combined in the treatment of antisocial child behavior. *Journal of the American Academy of Child and Adolescent Psychiatry, 26,* 416–424.

Kazdin, A. E., Esveldt-Dawson, K., French, N. H., & Unis, A. S. (1987b). Problem-solving skills training and relationship therapy in the treatment of antisocial child behavior. *Journal of Consulting and Clinical Psychology, 55,* 76–85.

Kelley, M. L. (1990). *School–home notes: Promoting children's classroom success.* New York: Guilford.

Kendall, P. C. (1985). Toward a cognitive–behavioral model of child psychopathology and a critique of related interventions. *Journal of Abnormal Child Psychology, 13,* 357–372.

Kendall, P. C. (1989). The generalization and maintenance of behavior change: Comments, considerations and the "no-cure" criticism. *Behavior Therapy, 20,* 357–364.

Kendall, P. C., & Braswell, L. (1982a). Cognitive–behavioral assessment: Model, measures and madness. In J. N. Butcher & C. D. Spielberger (Eds.), *Advances in personality assessment* (Vol. 1, pp. 35–82). Hillside, NJ: Erlbaum.

Kendall, P. C., & Braswell, L. (1982b). Cognitive–behavioral self-control therapy for children: A components analysis. *Journal of Consulting and Clinical Psychology, 50,* 672–689.

Kendall, P. C., & Braswell, L. (1985). *Cognitive–behavioral therapy for impulsive children.* New York: Guilford.

Kendall, P. C., Cantwell, D. P., & Kazdin, A. E. (1989). Depression in children and adolescents: Assessment issues and recommendations. *Cognitive Therapy and Research, 13,* 109–130.

Kendall, P. C., Chawski, T. E., Friedman, M., Kim, R., Kortlander, E., Sessa, F. M., & Siqueland, L. (1991). Treating anxiety disorders in children and adolescents. In P. C. Kendall (Ed.), *Child and adolescent therapy: Cognitive–behavioral procedures* (pp. 131–164). New York: Guilford.

Kendall, P. C., & Siqueland, L. (1989). Child and adolescent therapy. In A. M. Nezu & C. M. Nezu (Eds.), *Clinical decision-making in behavior therapy: A problem-solving perspective* (pp. 321–336). Champaign, IL: Research.

Kendall, P. C., & Wilcox, L. E. (1979). Self-control in children: Development of a rating scale. *Journal of Consulting and Clinical Psychology, 47,* 1020–1029.

Kendall, P. C., & Wilcox, L. E. (1980). A cognitive–behavioral treatment for impulsivity: Concrete versus conceptual training in non-self-controlled children. *Journal of Consulting and Clinical Psychology, 48,* 80–91.

Kendall, P. C., & Zupan, B. A. (1981). Individual versus group application of cognitive behavioral strategies for developing self-control in children. *Behavior Therapy, 12,* 344–359.

Kidd, K. K., Prusoff, B. A., & Cohen, D. J. (1980). Familial pattern of Gilles de la Tourette syndrome. *Archives of General Psychiatry, 37,* 1336–1339.

King, C., & Young, R. D. (1982). Attentional deficits with and without hyperactivity: Teacher and peer perceptions. *Journal of Abnormal Child Psychology, 10,* 483–495.

Kinsbourne, M. (1977). The mechanism of hyperactivity. In M. Blaw, I. Rapin, & M. Kinsbourne (Eds.), *Topics in child neurology* (pp. 289–306). New York: Spectrum.

Kinsbourne, M. (1984). Beyond attention deficit: Search for the disorder in ADD. In L. M. Bloomingdale (Ed.), *Attention deficit disorder: Diagnostic, cognitive and therapeutic understanding* (pp. 133–145). New York: Spectrum.

Kirby, E. A., & Grimley, L. K. (1986). *Understanding and treating attention deficit disorder.* New York: Pergamon.

Klee, S. H., & Garfinkel, B. D. (1983). The computerized continuous performance task: A new measure of inattention. *Journal of Abnormal Child Psychology, 11,* 487–496.

Klein, D. F., Gittelman, R., Quitkin, F., & Rifkin, A. (1980). *Diagnosis and drug treatment of psychiatric disorders: Adults and children* (2nd ed.). Baltimore: Williams & Wilkins.

Klein, N. C., Alexander, J. F., & Parsons, B. V. (1977). Impact of family systems intervention on recidivism and sibling delinquency: A model of primary prevention and program evaluation. *Journal of Consulting and Clinical Psychology, 45,* 469–474.

Klein, W. L. (1963). *An investigation of the spontaneous speech of children during problem-solving.* Unpublished doctoral dissertation, University of Rochester, Rochester, NY.

Klorman, R., Brumaghim, J. T., Salzman, L. F., Strauss, J., Borgstedt, A. D., McBude, M. C., & Loeb, S. (1988). Effects of methylphenidate on attention deficit hyperactivity disorder with and without aggressive/noncompliant features. *Journal of Abnormal Psychology, 97,* 413–422.

Klorman, R., Coons, H. W., & Borgstedt, A. D. (1987). Effects of methylphenidate on adolescents with a childhood history of attention deficit disorders: I. Clinical findings. *Journal of the American Academy of Child and Adolescent Psychiatry, 26,* 363–367.

Kovacs, M. (1982). *The Children's Depression Inventory: A self-rated depression scale for school-aged youngsters.* Unpublished manuscript. University of Pittsburgh School of Medicine, Pittsburgh, PA.

Kruger, S. D. (1984). *The nosology of Tourette syndrome.* Unpublished doctoral dissertation, Yale University School of Medicine, New Haven, CT.

Krupski, A. (1986). Attention problems in youngsters with learning handicaps. In J. K. Torgesen & B. Y. L. Wong (Eds.), *Psychological and educational perspectives on learning disabilities* (pp. 161–192). New York: Academic.

Kuperman, A. (1988, November). *Understanding attention deficit disorder.* Workshop presented for the St. Cloud Public Schools, St. Cloud, MN.

Kupietz, S. S., Winsberg, B. G., Richardson, E., Maitinsky, S., & Mendell, N. (1988). Effects of methylphenidate dosage in hyperactive reading-disabled children: I. Behavior and cognitive performance effects. *Journal of the American Academy of Child and Adolescent Psychiatry, 27,* 70–77.

Lahey, B. B., Pelham, W. E., Schaughency, E. A., Atkins, M. S., Murphy, H. A., Hynd, G., Russo, M., Hartdagen, S., & Lorys-Vernon, A. (1988). Dimensions and types of attention deficit disorder. *Journal of the American Academy of Child and Adolescent Psychiatry, 27,* 330–335.

Lahey, B. B., Piacentini, J. C., McBurnett, K., Stone, P., Hartdagen, S., & Hynd, G. (1988). Psychopathology in the parents of children with conduct disorder and hyperactivity. *Journal of the American Academy of Child and Adolescent Psychiatry, 27,* 163–170.

Lahey, B. B., Schaughency, E. A., Hynd, G. W., Carlson, C. L., & Nieves, N. (1987). Attention deficit disorder with and without hyperactivity: Comparison of behavioral characteristics of clinic-referred children. *Journal of the American Academy of Child and Adolescent Psychiatry, 26,* 718–723.

Lahey, B. B., Stempniak, M., Robinson, E. J., & Tyroler, M. J. (1978). Hyperactivity and learning disabilities as independent dimensions of child behavior problems. *Journal of Abnormal Psychology, 87,* 333–340.

Lambert, N. M. (1988). Adolescent outcomes for hyperactive children: Perspectives on general and specific patterns of childhood risk for adolescent educational, social and mental health problems. *American Psychologist, 43,* 786–799.

Lambert, N. M., & Hartsough, C. S. (1984). Contribution of predispositional factors to the diagnosis of hyperactivity. *American Journal of Orthopsychiatry, 54,* 97–109.

Lambert, N. M., Hartsough, C. S., Sassone, D., & Sandoval, J. (1987). Persistence of hyperactivity symptoms from childhood to adolescence and associated outcomes. *American Journal of Orthopsychiatry, 57,* 22–32.

Lambert, N. M., & Sandoval, J. (1980). The prevalence of learning disabilities in a sample of children considered hyperactive. *Journal of Abnormal Child Psychology, 8,* 33–50.

Lambert, N. M., Sandoval, J., & Sassone, D. (1978). Prevalence of hyperactivity in elementary school children as a function of social system definers. *American Journal of Orthopsychiatry, 48,* 446–463.

Lefkowitz, M. M., & Burton, H. (1978). Childhood depression: A critique of the concept. *Psychological Bulletin, 85,* 716–726.

Levine, M. D. (1987). Attention deficits: The diverse effects of weak control systems in childhood. *Pediatric Annals, 16,* 117–130.

Linn, R. T., & Hodge, G. K. (1982). Locus of control in childhood hyperactivity. *Journal of Consulting and Clinical Psychology, 50,* 592–593.

Lochman, J. E. (1987). Self and peer perceptions and attributional biases of aggressive and nonaggressive boys in dyadic interactions. *Journal of Consulting and Clinical Psychology, 55,* 404–410.

Lochman, J. E., Burch, P. R., Curry, J. F., & Lampron, L.B. (1984). Treatment and generalization effects of cognitive–behavioral and goal-setting interventions with aggressive boys. *Journal of Consulting and Clinical Psychology, 52,* 915–916.

Lochman, J. E., & Curry, J. F. (1986). Effects of social problem-solving training and self-instruction training with aggressive boys. *Journal of Clinical Child Psychology, 15,* 159–164.

Lochman, J. E., & Lampron, L. B. (1986). Situational social problem-solving skills and self-esteem of aggressive and nonaggressive boys. *Journal of Abnormal Child Psychology, 14*, 605–617.

Lochman, J. E., Lampron, L. B., Gemmer, T. C., & Harris, S. R. (1987). Anger coping intervention with aggressive children: A guide to implementation in school settings. In P. A. Keller & S. R. Hyman (Eds.), *Innovations in clinical practice: A source book* (Vol. 6, pp. 339–356). Sarasota, FL: Professional Resource Exchange.

Lochman, J. E., Nelson, W. M. III, & Sims, J. P. (1981). A cognitive behavioral program for use with aggressive children. *Journal of Clinical Child Psychology, 10*, 146–148.

Locke, H. J., & Thomas, M. M. (1980). *The Locke Marital Adjustment Test: Its validity, reliability, weighting procedure and modification.* Unpublished manuscript, University of Southern California, Los Angeles.

Loeber, R. (1982). The stability of antisocial and delinquent behavior: A review. *Child Development, 53*, 1431–1446.

Loney, J., Langhorne, J. E., & Paternite, C. E. (1978). An empirical basis for subgrouping the hyperkinetic/minimal brain dysfunction syndrome. *Journal of Abnormal Psychology, 87*, 431–441.

Loney, J., & Milich, R. (1982). Hyperactivity, inattention and aggression in clinical practice. In M. Wolraich & D. K. Routh (Eds.), *Advances in behavioral pediatrics* (Vol. 2, pp. 113–145). Greenwich, CT: JAI.

Lopez, R. E. (1965). Hyperactivity in twins. *Canadian Psychiatry Association Journal, 10*, 421.

Lou, H. C., Henriksen, L., & Bruhn, P. (1984). Focal cerebral hyperfusion and/or attentional deficit disorder. *Archives of Neurology, 41*, 825–829.

Lou, H. C., Henriksen, L., Bruhn, P., Borner, H., & Nielsen, J. B. (1989). Striatal dysfunction in attentional deficit and hyperkinetic disorder. *Archives of Neurology, 46*, 48–52.

Love, A. J., & Thompson, M. G. G. (1988). Language disorders and attention deficit disorders in young children referred for psychiatric services: Analysis of prevalence and a conceptual synthesis. *American Journal of Orthopsychiatry, 58*, 52–64.

Lowe, T. L., Cohen, D. J., Detlor, J., Krimenitzer, M. W., & Shaywitz, B. A. (1982). Stimulant medications precipitate Tourette's syndrome. *Journal of the American Medical Association, 247*, 1729–1731.

Luria, A. R. (1961). *The role of speech in the regulation of normal and abnormal behavior.* New York: Liveright.

Luria, A. R. (1973). The frontal lobes and the regulation of behavior. In K. H. Pribram & A. R. Luria (Eds.), *Psychophysiology of the frontal lobes* (pp. 3–26). Orlando, FL: Academic.

Mahoney, M. J., & Nezworski, M. T. (1985). Cognitive–behavioral approaches to children's problems. *Journal of Abnormal Child Psychology, 13*, 467–476.

Malmquist, C. P. (1975). Depression in childhood. In F. Flach & S. Diaghi (Eds.), *The nature and treatment of depression* (pp. 73–98). New York: Wiley.

Mannuzza, S., Klein, R. G., Konig, P. H., & Giampino, T. L. (1989). Hyperactive boys almost grown up—IV. Criminality and its relationship to psychiatric status. *Archives of General Psychiatry, 46*, 1073–1079.

Markwardt, F. C. (1989). *Peabody Individual Achievement Test—Revised*. Circle Pines, MN: American Guidance Service.

Marshall, P. (1989). Attention deficit disorder and allergy: A neurochemical model of the relation between the illnesses. *Psychological Bulletin, 106*, 434–446.

Mash, E. J., Terdal, L., & Anderson, K. (1973). The response-class matrix: A procedure for recording parent–child interactions. *Journal of Consulting and Clinical Psychology, 40*, 163–164.

Masten, A. S., & Braswell, L. (in press). Developmental psychopathology: An integrative framework for understanding behavior problems in children and adolescents. In P. R. Martin (Ed.), *Handbook of behavior therapy and psychological science: An integrative approach*. New York: Pergamon.

Mattes, J. A., & Gittelman, R. (1981). Effects of artificial food colorings in children with hyperactive symptoms. *Archives of General Psychiatry, 38*, 714–718.

Matthews, W. (1988). Attention deficits and learning disabilities in children with Tourette's syndrome. *Pediatric Annals, 17*, 410–416.

McClure, F. D., & Gordon, M. (1984). Performance of disturbed hyperactive and nonhyperactive children on an objective measure of hyperactivity. *Journal of Abnormal Child Psychology, 12*, 561–571.

McGee, R., & Share, D. L. (1988). Attention-deficit hyperactivity disorder and academic failure: Which comes first and what should be treated? *Journal of the American Academy of Child and Adolescent Psychiatry, 27*, 318–325.

McGee, R., Williams, S., Moffitt, T., & Anderson, J. (1989). A comparison of 13-year-old boys with attention deficit and/or reading disorder on neuropsychological measures. *Journal of Abnormal Child Psychology, 17*, 37–53.

McGee, R., Williams, S., & Silva, P. A. (1987). A comparison of girls and boys with teacher-identified problems of attention. *Journal of the American Academy of Child and Adolescent Psychiatry, 26*, 711–717.

McMahon, R. J. (1980). Genetic etiology in the hyperactive child syndrome: A critical review. *American Journal of Orthopsychiatry, 50*, 145–150.

McMahon, R. J., & Forehand, R. (1988). Conduct disorders. In E. J. Mash & L. G. Terdal (Eds.), *Behavioral assessment of childhood disorders* (2nd ed., pp. 105–153). New York: Guilford.

McMahon, R. J., & Wells, K. C. (1989). Conduct disorders. In E. J. Mash & R. A. Barkley (Eds.), *Treatment of childhood disorders* (pp. 73–132). New York: Guilford.

McMichael, A. J., & Baghurst, P. A. (1988). Port Pirie cohort study: Environmental exposure to lead and children's abilities at the age of four years. *New England Journal of Medicine, 319*, 468–475.

Meichenbaum, D. H., & Goodman, J. (1971). Training impulsive children to talk to themselves: A means of developing self-control. *Journal of Abnormal Psychology, 77*, 115–126.

Mendelson, W., Johnson, N., & Stewart, M. (1971). Hyperactive children as teenagers: A follow-up study. *Journal of Nervous and Mental Disease, 153*, 273–279.

Meyers, A. W., Cohen, R., & Schleser, R. (1989). A cognitive–behavioral approach to education: Adopting a broad-based perspective. In J. N.

Hughes & R. J. Hall (Eds.), *Cognitive–behavioral psychology in the schools: A comprehensive handbook* (pp. 62–84). New York: Guilford.

Meyers, A. W., & Craighead, W. E. (Eds.) (1984). *Cognitive behavior therapy with children.* New York: Plenum.

Middlebrook, J. L., & Forehand, R. (1985). Maternal perceptions of deviance in child behavior as a function of stress and clinic versus nonclinic status of the child: An analogue study. *Behavior Therapy, 16,* 494–502.

Milich, R., & Dodge, K. A. (1984). Social information processing in child psychiatric populations. *Journal of Abnormal Child Psychology, 12,* 471–490.

Milich, R., Loney, J., & Landau, S. (1982). The independent dimensions of hyperactivity and aggression: A validation with playroom observation data. *Journal of Abnormal Psychology, 91,* 183–198.

Milich, R., Roberts, M. A., Loney, J., & Caputo, J. (1980). Differentiative practice effects and statistical regression on the Conners Hyperkinesis Index. *Journal of Abnormal Child Psychology, 8,* 549–552.

Minde, K., Lewin, D., Weiss, G., Lavigueur, M., Douglas, V., & Sykes, E. (1971). The hyperactive child in elementary school: A five-year controlled follow-up. *Exceptional Child, 38,* 215–221.

Moos, R. H., & Moos, B. (1981). *Revised Family Environment Scale.* Palo Alto, CA: Consulting Psychologists.

Morris, S. B., Alexander, J. F., & Waldron, H. (1988). Functional family therapy. In I. R. H. Falloon (Ed.), *Handbook of behavioral family therapy* (pp. 107–127). New York: Guilford.

Morrison, J. A. (1980). Adult psychiatric disorders in parents of hyperactive children. *American Journal of Psychiatry, 137,* 825–827.

Morrison, J. A., & Stewart, M. A. (1973). The psychiatric status of the legal families of adopted hyperactive children. *Archives of General Psychiatry, 23,* 888–891.

Morton, T. L., Twentyman, C. T., & Azar, S. T. (1988). Cognitive–behavioral assessment and treatment of child abuse. In N. Epstein, S. Schlesinger, & W. Dryden (Eds.), *Cognitive–behavioral therapy with families* (pp. 87–117). New York: Brunner/Mazel.

Mouton, P. Y., & Tuma, J. M. (1988). Stress, locus of control and role satisfaction in clinic and control mothers. *Journal of Clinical Child Psychology, 17,* 217–224.

Munir, K., Biederman, J., & Knee, D. (1987). Psychiatric comorbidity in patients with attention deficit disorder: A controlled study. *Journal of the American Academy of Child and Adolescent Psychiatry, 26,* 844–848.

Naeye, R. L., & Peters, E. C. (1984). Mental development of children whose mothers smoked during pregnancy. *Obstetrics and Gynecology, 64,* 601.

Nasby, W., Hayden, B., & DePaulo, B. M. (1980). Attributional bias among aggressive boys to interpret unambiguous social stimuli as displays of hostility. *Journal of Abnormal Psychology, 89,* 459–548.

Newcorn, J. H., Halperin, J. M., Healey, J. M., O'Brien, J. D., Pascualvaca, D. M., Wolf, L. E., Morganstein, A., Sharma, V., & Young, J. G. (1989). Are ADDH and ADHD the same or different? *Journal of the American Academy of Child and Adolescent Psychiatry, 285,* 743–748.

Nichols, P. L., & Chen, T. C. (1981). *Minimal brain dysfunction: A prospective study.* Hillsdale, NJ: Erlbaum.

Nieburg, P., Marks, J. S., McLaren, N. M., & Remington, P. L. (1985). The fetal tobacco syndrome. *Journal of the American Medical Association, 253,* 2998–2999.

Nieman, G. W., & Delong, R. (1987). Use of the Personality Inventory for Children as an aid in differentiating children with mania from children with attention deficit disorder with hyperactivity. *Journal of the American Academy of Child and Adolescent Psychiatry, 27,* 381–388.

Nomellini, S., & Katz, R. C. (1983). Effects of anger control training on abusive parents. *Cognitive Therapy and Research, 7,* 57–68.

Novaco, R. (1978). Anger and coping with stress: Cognitive–behavioral interventions. In J. Foreyt & D. Rathjen (Eds.), *Cognitive–behavior therapy: Research and application* (pp. 135–173). New York: Plenum.

Nowicki, S. Jr., & Strickland, B. R. (1973). A locus of control scale for children. *Journal of Consulting and Clinical Psychology, 40,* 148–154.

O'Brien, M. A., & Obrzut, J. E. (1986). Attention deficit disorder with hyperactivity: A review and implications for the classroom. *Journal of Special Edcuation, 20,* 281–297.

Parker, J. G., & Asher, S. R. (1987). Peer relations and later personal adjustment: Are low-accepted children at risk? *Psychological Bulletin, 102,* 357–389.

Pastor, D. (1987, April). Response to questioning. In S. Beaver (Chair), *Answering Parental Questions.* Symposium conducted at the meeting of the Minnesota Association for Children with Learning Disabilities, Minneapolis.

Paternite, C. E., Loney, J., & Langhorne, J. E. (1976). Relationship between symptomatology and SES-related factors in hyperkinetic/MBD boys. *American Journal of Orthopsychiatry, 46,* 291–301.

Patterson, G. R. (1972). The aggressive child: Victim and architect of a coercive system. In E. J. Mash, L. A. Hamerlynck, & L. C. Handy (Eds.), *Behavior modification and families* (pp. 267–316). New York: Brunner/Mazel.

Patterson, G. R. (1982). *Coercive family process.* Eugene, OR: Castalia.

Patterson, G. R., & Bank, L. (1989). Some amplifying mechanisms for pathologic processes in families. In M. Gunnar & E. Thelen (Eds.), *Minnesota symposium on child psychology: Systems and development* (pp. 167–209). Hillsdale, NJ: Erlbaum.

Patterson, G. R., Ray, R. S., Shaw, D. A., & Cobb, J. A. (1969). *Manual for coding of family interactions* (rev. ed.). New York: Microfiche Publications.

Patterson, G. R., Reid, J. B., Jones, R. R., & Conger, R. E. (1975). *A social learning approach to family intervention: Families with aggressive children* (Vol. 1). Eugene, OR: Castalia.

Patterson, G. R., & Stouthamer-Loeber, M. (1984). The correlation of family management practices and delinquency. *Child Development, 55,* 1299–1307.

Pauls, D. L., Hurst, C. R., Kruger, S. D., Leckman, J. F., Kidd, K. K., & Cohen, D. J. (1986). Gilles de la Tourette's syndrome and attention deficit disorder with hyperactivity: Evidence against a genetic relationship. *Archives of General Psychiatry, 43,* 1177–1179.

Pelham, W. E., Atkins, M. S., Murphy, H. A., & White, K. S. (1981, November). *Operationalization and validation of attention deficit disorders.* Paper presented at the Annual Meeting of the Association for Advancement of Behavior Therapy, Toronto, Ontario, Canada.

Pelham, W. E., & Bender, M. E. (1982). Peer relationships in hyperactive children: Description and treatment. In K. Gadow & I. Bialer (Eds.), *Advances in learning and behavioral disabilities* (Vol. 1, pp. 365–436). Greenwich, CT: JAI.

Pelham, W. E., Bender, M. E., Caddell, J., Booth, S., & Moorer, S. (1985). Methylphenidate and children with attention deficit disorder: Dose effects on classroom academic and social behavior. *Archives of General Psychiatry, 42,* 948–952.

Pelham, W. E., & Milich, R. (1984). Peer relations in children with hyperactivity/attention deficit disorder. *Journal of Learning Disabilities, 17,* 560–567.

Pelham, W. E., Milich, R., Murphy, D. A., & Murphy, H. A. (1989). Normative data on the Iowa Conners Teacher Rating Scale. *Journal of Clinical Child Psychology, 18,* 259–292.

Pelham, W. E., & Murphy, H. A. (1986). Attention deficit and conduct disorders. In M. Hersen (Ed.), *Pharmacological and behavioral treatments: An integrative approach* (pp. 108–148). New York: Wiley.

Pelham, W. E., Schnedler, R. W., Bologna, N. C., & Contreras, J. A. (1980). Behavioral and stimulant treatment of hyperactive children: A therapy study with methylphenidate probes in a within-subject design. *Journal of Applied Behavior Analysis, 13,* 221–236.

Pelham, W. E., Walker, J. L., Sturges, J., & Hoza, J. (1989). Comparative effects of methylphenidate on ADD girls and ADD boys. *Journal of the American Academy of Child and Adolescent Psychiatry, 28,* 773–776.

Piers, E. V., & Harris, D. B. (1969). *The Piers–Harris Self-Concept Scale.* Nashville: Counselor Recordings and Tests.

Pisterman, S., McGrath, P., Firestone, P., Goodman, J. T., Webster, I., & Mallory, R. (1989). Outcome of parent-mediated treatment of preschoolers with attention deficit disorder with hyperactivity. *Journal of Consulting and Clinical Psychology, 57,* 628–635.

Pliska, S. R. (1987). Tricyclic antidepressants in the treatment of children with attention deficit disorder. *Journal of the American Academy of Child and Adolescent Psychiatry, 26,* 127–132.

Porrino, L. J., Rapoport, J. L., Behar, D., Ismond, D. R., & Bunney, W. E. (1983). A naturalistic assessment of the motor activity of hyperactive boys. II. Stimulant drug effects. *Archives of General Psychiatry, 40,* 688–693.

Porter, B., & O'Leary, K. D. (1980). Mental discord and childhood behavior problems. *Journal of Abnormal Child Psychology, 4,* 287–295.

Poznanski, E. O., Cook, S. C., & Carroll, B. J. (1979). A depression rating scale for children. *Pediatrics, 64,* 442–450.

Prendergast, M., Taylor, E., Rapoport, J., Bartko, J., Donnelly, M., Zametkin, A., Ahearn, M. B., Dunn, G., & Wieselberg, H. M. (1988). The diagnosis of childhood hyperactivity: A U.S.–U.K. cross-national study of DSM-III and ICD-9. *Journal of Child Psychology and Psychiatry, 29,* 289–300.

Price, R. A., Leckman, J. F., Pauls, D. L., Cohen, D. J., & Kidd, K. K. (1986). Gilles de la Tourette's syndrome: Tics and central nervous system stimulants in twins and nontwins. *Neurology, 36,* 232–237.

Prinz, R., Connor, P., & Wilson, C. (1981). Hyperactive and aggressive behaviors in childhood: Intertwined dimensions. *Journal of Abnormal Child Psychology, 9,* 191–202.

Prior, M., & Sanson, A. (1986). Attention deficit disorder with hyperactivity: A critique. *Journal of Child Psychology and Psychiatry, 27,* 307–319.

Prior, M., & Sanson, A. (1988). Attention deficit disorder with hyperactivity: A reply. *Journal of Child Psychology and Psychiatry, 29,* 223–225.

Puig-Antich, J., Ryan, N., & Rabinovich, H. (1985). Affective disorders in childhood and adolescence. In J. Weiner (Ed.), *Diagnosis and psychopharmacology of childhood and adolescent disorders* (pp. 151–177). New York: Wiley.

Quay, H. C. (1989). The behavioral reward and inhibition systems in childhood behavior disorder. In L. J. Bloomingdale (Ed.), *Attention deficit disorders* (Vol. 3, pp. 186–223). New York: Pergamon.

Ramsey, E., & Walker, H.M. (1988). Family management correlates of antisocial behavior among middle school boys. *Behavioral Disorders, 13,* 187–201.

Ramsey, E., Walker, H. M., Shinn, M., O'Neill, R. E., & Stieber, S. (1989). Parent management practices and school adjustment. *School Psychology Review, 18,* 513–525.

Rapoport, J. L., Buchsbaum, M., Zahn, T. P., Weingartner, H., Ludlow, C., & Mikkelsen, E. (1978). Dextroamphetamines: Cognitive and behavioral effects in normal prepubertal boys. *Science, 199,* 560–562.

Rapoport, J. L., Donnelly, M., Zametkin, A., & Carrougher, J. (1986). "Situational hyperactivity" in a U.S. clinical setting. *Journal of Child Psychology and Psychiatry, 27,* 639–646.

Rapport, M. D. (1987). Attention deficit disorder with hyperactivity. In M. Hersen & V. B. Van Hasselt (Eds.), *Behavior therapy with children and adolescents: A clinical approach* (pp. 325–361). New York: Wiley.

Rapport, M. D., Jones, J. T., DuPaul, G. J., Kelly, K. L., Gardner, M. J., Tucker, S. B., & Shea, M. S. (1987). Attention deficit disorder and methylphenidate: Group and single-subject analyses of dose effects on attention in clinic and classroom settings. *Journal of Clinical Child Psychology, 16,* 329–338.

Rapport, M. D., Murphy, A., & Bailey, J. S. (1980). The effects of a response–cost treatment tactic on hyperactive children. *Journal of School Psychology, 18,* 98–111.

Rapport, M. D., Murphy, A., & Bailey, J. S. (1982). Ritalin versus response cost in the control of hyperactive children. *Journal of Applied Behavior Analysis, 15,* 205–216.

Rapport, M. D., Quinn, S. O., DuPaul, G. J., Quinn, E. P., & Kelly, K. L. (1989). Attention deficit disorder with hyperactivity and methylphenidate: The effects of dose and mastery level of children's learning preference. *Journal of Abnormal Child Psychology, 17,* 669–689.

Rapport, M. D., Stoner, G., DuPaul, G. J., Birmingham, B. K., & Tucker, S. (1985). Methylphenidate in hyperactive children: Differential effects of dose on academic, learning and social behavior. *Journal of Abnormal Child Psychology, 13,* 227–244.

Rapport, M. D., Stoner, G., DuPaul, G. J., Kelly, K. L., Tucker, S. B., & Schoeler, T. (1988). Attention deficit disorder and methylphenidate: A multilevel analysis of dose–response effects on children's impulsivity across settings. *Journal of the American Academy of Child and Adolescent Psychiatry, 27,* 60–69.

Reeves, J. C., Werry, J. S., Elkind, G. S., & Zametkin, A. (1987). Attention deficit, conduct, oppositional and anxiety disorders in children. II. Clinical characteristics. *Journal of the American Academy of Child and Adolescent Psychiatry, 26,* 144–155.

Reynolds, C. R., & Richmond, B. O. (1985). *Revised Children's Manifest Anxiety Scale Manual.* Los Angeles: Western Psychological Services.

Reynolds, W. M., & Stark, K. D. (1986). Self-control in children: A multimethod examination of treatment outcome measures. *Journal of Abnormal Child Psychology, 14,* 13–23.

Richard, B. A., & Dodge, K. A. (1982). Social maladjustment and problem-solving in school-aged children. *Journal of Consulting and Clinical Psychology, 50,* 226–233.

Richardson, E., Kupietz, S. S., Winsberg, B. G., Maitinsky, S., & Mendell, N. (1988). Effects of methylphenidate dosage in hyperactive reading-disabled children: II. Reaching achievement. *Journal of the American Academy of Child and Adolescent Psychiatry, 27,* 78–87.

Riddle, M. A., Hardin, M. T., Cho, S. C., Woolston, J. L., & Leckman, J. (1988). Desipramine treatment of boys with attention-deficit hyperactivity disorder and tics: Preliminary clinical experience. *Journal of the American Academy of Child and Adolescent Psychiatry, 27,* 811–814.

Roberts, M. A. (1990). A behavioral observation method for differentiating hyperactive and aggressive boys. *Journal of Abnormal Child Psychology, 2,* 131–142.

Roberts, M. A., Milich, R., & Loney, J. (1985). *Structured Observations of Academic and Play Setting (SOAPS): Manual.* (Available from Mary Ann Roberts, PhD, Psychology, Hospital School, University of Iowa, Iowa City, IA 52242.)

Roberts, M. A., Milich, R., Loney, J., & Caputo, J. (1981). A multitrait–multimethod analysis of variance of teachers' ratings of aggression, hyperactivity and inattention. *Journal of Abnormal Child Psychology, 9,* 371–380.

Roberts, M. A., Ray, R. S., & Roberts, R. J. (1984). A playroom observational procedure for assessing hyperactive boys. *Journal of Pediatric Psychology, 9,* 177–191.

Robin, A. L. (1981). A controlled evaluation of problem-solving communication training with parent–adolescent conflict. *Behavior Therapy, 12,* 593–609.

Robin, A. L., Fischel, J. E., & Brown, K. E. (1984). The measurement of self-control in children: Validation of the Self-Control Rating Scale. *Journal of Pediatric Psychology, 9,* 165–175.

Robin, A. L., & Foster, S. L. (1989). *Negotiating parent–adolescent conflict: A behavioral–family systems approach.* New York: Guilford.

Robin, A. L., Kent, R., O'Leary, K. D., Foster, S., & Prinz, R. (1977). An approach to teaching parents and adolescents problem-solving communica- skills: A preliminary report. *Behavior Therapy, 8,* 639–643.

. N. (1966). *Deviant children grown up.* Baltimore: Williams & Williamm, M., & Baker, E. (1984). Self-control behavior in hyperactive ~ vperactive children. *Journal of Abnormal Child Psychology, 12,* 303–

Ross, D. M., & Ross, S. A. (1982). *Hyperactivity: Theory, research and action* (2nd ed.). New York: Wiley.

Rosvold, H. E., Mirsky, A. F., Sarason, I., Bransome, E. D., & Beck, L. H. (1956). A continuous performance test of brain damage. *Journal of Consulting Psychology, 20*, 343–352.

Rotter, J. B. (1966). Generalized expectancies for internal vs. external control of reinforcement. *Psychological Monographs: General and Applied, 80* (Whole No. 609).

Rutter, M. (1977). Brain damage syndromes in childhood: Concepts and findings. *Journal of Child Psychology and Psychiatry, 139*, 21–33.

Rutter, M.L. (1983a). Behavioral studies: Questions and findings on the concept of distinctive syndrome. In M. Rutter (Ed.), *Developmental neuropsychiatry* (pp. 259–279). New York: Guilford.

Rutter, M.L. (1983b). Low level lead exposure: Causes, effects and implications. In M. Rutter & R. R. Janes (Eds.), *Lead versus health: Sources and effects of low level lead exposure* (pp. 333–370). New York: Wiley.

Rutter, M., Chadwick, O., & Shaffer, R. (1983). Hyperactivity and minimal brain dysfunction: Epidemiological perspectives on questions of cause and classification. In R. A. Tarter (Ed.), *The child at psychiatric risk* (P. 80–107). New York: Oxford University Press.

Ryan, E. B., Week, K. A., & Short, E. J. (1986). Cognitive–behavior modification: Promoting active, self-regulatory learning styles. In J. K. Torgesen & B. Y. L. Wong (Eds.), *Psychological and educational perspectives on learning disabilities* (pp. 367–397). New York: Academic.

Ryan, N. D., Puig-Antich, J., Rabinovich, H., Fried, J., Ambrosini, P., Meyer, V., Torres, D., Dachille, S., & Mazzie, D. (1988). MAOIs in adolescent major depression unresponsive to tricyclic antidepressants. *Journal of the American Academy of Child and Adolescent Psychiatry, 27*, 755–758.

Safer, D. J. (1973). A familial factor in minimal brain dysfunction. *Behavior Genetics, 3*, 175–186.

Safer, D. J., & Allen, R. P. (1975). Side effects from long-term use of stimulants in children. *International Journal of Mental Health, 4*, 105–118.

Safer, D. J., & Allen, R. P. (1976). *Hyperactive children: Diagnosis and management.* Baltimore: University Park.

Safer, D. P., Allen, R. P., & Barr, E. (1972). Depression of growth in hyperactive children on stimulant drugs. *New England Journal of Medicine, 287*, 217–220.

Safer, D. P., Allen, R. P., & Barr, E. (1975). Growth rebound after termination of stimulant drugs. *Pediatrics, 86*, 113–116.

Sameroff, A. J. (1987). Transactional risk factors and prevention. In J. A. Steinberg & M. M. Silverstein (Eds.), *Preventing mental disorders: A research perspective* (pp. 74–89). Rockville, MD: U.S. Department of Health and Human Services.

Sandberg, S. T., Rutter, M. L., & Taylor, E. (1978). Hyperkinetic disorder in psychiatric clinic attenders. *Developmental Medicine and Child Neurology, 20*, 278–299.

ndoval, J., Lambert, N., & Sassone, D. (1980). The identification and labeling of hyperactivity in children: An interactive model. In C. K. Whalen & B.

Henker (Eds.), *Hyperactive children: The social ecology of identification and treatment* (pp. 145–172). New York: Academic.

Sarason, I. G., & Sarason, B. R. (1981). Teaching cognitive and social skills to high school students. *Journal of Consulting and Clinical Psychology, 49,* 908–918.

Satterfield, J. H., Cantwell, D. P., & Satterfield, B. T. (1979). Multimodality treatment: A 1-year follow-up of 84 hyperactive boys. *Archives of General Psychiatry, 36,* 965–974.

Satterfield, J. H., Satterfield, B. T., & Schell, A. M. (1987). Therapeutic interventions to prevent delinquency in hyperactive boys. *Journal of the American Academy of Child and Adolescent Psychiatry, 26,* 56–64.

Schachar, R., Rutter, M., & Smith, A. (1981). Situationally and pervasively hyperactive children. *Journal of Child Psychology and Psychiatry, 22,* 375–392.

Schachar, R., Sandberg, S., & Rutter, M. (1986). Agreement between teachers' ratings and observations of hyperactivity inattentiveness and defiance. *Journal of Abnormal Child Psychology, 14,* 331–345.

Schachar, R., Taylor, E., Wieselberg, M., Thorley, G., & Rutter, M. (1987). Changes in family function and relationships in children who respond to methylphenidate. *Journal of the American Academy of Child and Adolescent Psychiatry, 26,* 728–732.

Schachar, R., & Wachsmuth, R. (1990). Hyperactivity and parental psychopathology. *Journal of Child Psychology and Psychiatry, 31,* 381–392.

Schleifer, M., Weiss, G., Cohen, N., Elman, M., Cvejic, H., & Kruger, E. (1975). Hyperactivity in preschoolers and the effect of methylphenidate. *American Journal of Orthopsychiatry, 45,* 38–50.

Schleser, R., Meyers, A. W., & Cohen, R. (1981). Generalization of self-instruction: Effects of general versus specific content, active rehearsal and cognitive level. *Child Development, 52,* 335–340.

Schleser, R., Meyers, A. W., Cohen, R., & Thackwray, D. (1983). Self-instruction interventions with non-self-controlled children: Effects of discovery versus faded rehearsal. *Journal of Consulting and Clinical Psychology, 51,* 954–955.

Seidel, W. T., & Joschko, M. (1990). Evidence of difficulties in sustained attention in children with ADDH. *Journal of Abnormal Child Psychology, 18,* 217–229.

Shapiro, A. K., & Shapiro, E. (1981). Do stimulants provide, cause or exacerbate tics and Tourette's syndrome? *Comprehensive Psychiatry, 22,* 265–273.

Shapiro, E., & Shapiro, A. K. (1989). Gilles de la Tourette's syndrome and tic disorders. *Harvard Medical School Mental Health Letter, 5,* 4–6.

Shaffer, D., Campbell, M., Cantwell, D., Bradley, S., Carlson, G., Cohen, D., Denckla, M., Frances, A., Garfinkel, B., Klein, R., Pincus, H., Spitzer, R., Volkmar, F., & Widiger, T. (1989). Brief communication: Child and adolescent psychiatric disorders in DSM-IV: Issues facing the child psychiatry work group. *Journal of the American Academy of Child and Adolescent Psychiatry, 28,* 830–835.

Shaywitz, B. A., Shaywitz, S. E., Byrne, T., Cohen, D. J., & Rothman, S. (1983). Attention deficit disorder: Quantitative analysis of CT. *Neurology, 33,* 1500–1503.

Shure, M. B., & Spivack, G. (1972). Means–end thinking, adjustment and social class among elementary school-age children. *Journal of Consulting and Clinical Psychology, 38,* 348–353.

Shure, M. B., & Spivack, G. (1978). *Problem-solving techniques in child rearing.* San Francisco: Jossey-Bass.

Smith, L. (1976). *Your child's behavior chemistry.* New York: Random House.

Sobol, M. P., Ashbourne, D. R., Earn, B. M., & Cunningham, C. E. (1989). Parents' attributions for achieving compliance from attention-deficit disordered children. *Journal of Abnormal Child Psychology, 17,* 359–369.

Spivack, G., Platt, J. J., & Shure, M. B. (1976). *The problem-solving approach to adjustment.* San Francisco: Jossey-Bass.

Spivack, G., & Shure, M. B. (1974). *Social adjustment of young children: A cognitive approach to solving real-life problems.* San Francisco: Jossey-Bass.

Sprague, R. L., & Sleator, E. K. (1977). Methylphenidate in hyperkinetic children: Differences in dose effects on learning and social behavior. *Science, 198,* 11274–11276.

Stark, K. D., Reynolds, W. M. & Kaslow, N. (1987). A comparison of the relative efficacy of self-control therapy and a behavioral problem-solving therapy for depression in children. *Journal of Abnormal Child Psychology, 15,* 91–113.

Stark, K. D., Rouse, L. W., & Livingston, R. (1991). Treatment of depression during childhood and adolescence: Cognitive–behavioral procedures for the individual and family. In P. C. Kendall (Ed.), *Child and adolescent therapy: Cognitive–behavioral procedures* (pp. 165–206). New York: Guilford.

Steinhausen, H. C., Göbel, D., & Nestler, V. (1984). Psychopathology in the offspring of alcoholic parents. *Journal of the American Academy of Child Psychiatry, 23,* 465–471.

Steinhausen, H. C., Nestler, V., & Huth, H. (1982). Psychopathology and mental functions in the offspring of alcoholic and epileptic mothers. *Journal of the American Academy of Child Psychiatry, 21,* 268–273.

Steinhausen, H. C., Nestler, V., & Spohr, H. L. (1982). Development and psychopathology of children with the fetal alcohol syndrome. *Journal of Developmental and Behavioral Pediatrics, 3,* 49–54.

Steinhausen, H. C., & Spohr, H. L. (1986). Fetal alcohol syndrome. In B. B. Lahey & A. E. Kazdin (Eds.), *Advances in clinical child psychology* (Vol. 9, pp. 217–243). New York: Plenum.

Stewart, M. S. (1980). Genetic, perinatal and constitutional factors in minimal brain dysfunctions. In H. Rie & E. Rie (Eds.), *Handbook of minimal brain dysfunctions: A critical review* (pp. 186–223). New York: Wiley.

Stewart, M. S., Pitts, F. N., Craig, A. G., & Dieruf, W. (1966). The hyperactive child syndrome. *American Journal of Orthopsychiatry, 36,* 861–867.

Still, G. F. (1902). The Coulstonian lectures on some abnormal physical conditions in children. *Lancet, 1,* 1008–1012, 1077–1082, 1163–1168.

Strecker, E. A., & Ebaugh, F. G. (1924). Neuropsychiatric sequelae of cerebral trauma in children. *Archives of Neurology and Psychiatry, 12,* 443–453.

Streissguth, A. P., Barr, H. M., & Martin, D. C. (1983). Maternal alcohol use and neonatal habituation assessed with the Brazelton Scale. *Child Development, 54,* 1109–1118.

Streissguth, A. P., Martin, D. C., Barr, H. M., McGregor-Sandman, B., Kirchner, G. L., & Darby, B. L. (1984). Intrauterine alcohol and nicotine exposure:

Attention and reaction time in 4-year-old children. *Developmental Psychology, 20,* 533–541.

Streissguth, A. P., Martin, D. C., Martin, J. C., & Barr, H. M. (1981). Seattle longitudinal prospective study on alcohol and pregnancy. *Neurobehavioral Toxicology and Teratology, 3,* 223–233.

Sullivan, M. A., & O'Leary, S. G. (1990). Maintenance following reward and cast token programs. *Behavior Therapy, 21,* 139–149.

Sverd, J., Curley, A. D., Jandorf, L., & Volkersz, L. (1988). Behavior disorder and attention deficits in boys with Tourette's syndrome. *Journal of the American Academy of Child and Adolescent Psychiatry, 27,* 413–417.

Swanson, J. M. (1985). Measures of cognitive functioning appropriate for use in pediatric psychopharmacological research studies. *Psychopharmacology Bulletin, 21,* 887–890.

Swanson, J. M., Kinsbourne, M., Roberts, W., & Zucker, K. (1978). Time-response analysis of the effect of stimulant medication on the learning ability of children referred for hyperactivity. *Pediatrics, 61,* 21–24.

Swanson, J. M., Sandman, C. A., Deutsch, C., & Baren, M. (1983). Methylphenidate hydrochloride given with or before breakfast. I. Behavioral, cognitive and electrophysiological effects. *Pediatrics, 72,* 49–55.

Tannock, R., Schachar, R. J., Carr, R. P., Chajazyk, D., & Logan, G.D. (1989). Effects of methylphenidate on inhibitory control in hyperactive children. *Journal of Abnormal Child Psychology, 17,* 473–491.

Tant, J. L., & Douglas, V. I. (1982). Problem-solving in hyperactive, normal and reading-disabled boys. *Journal of Abnormal Child Psychology, 10,* 285–306.

Taylor, E. (1986). Childhood hyperactivity. *British Journal of Psychiatry, 149,* 562–573.

Taylor, E. (1988). Attention deficit and conduct disorder syndromes. In M. Rutter, A. H. Tuma, & I. S. Lann (Eds.), *Assessment and diagnosis of child psychopathology* (pp. 377–407). New York: Guilford.

Taylor, E., & Sandberg, S. (1984). Hyperactive behavior in English schoolchildren: A questionnaire survey. *Journal of Abnormal Child Psychology, 12,* 143–156.

Taylor, J. F. (1980). *The hyperactive child and the family.* New York: Random House.

Thackwray, D., Meyers, A., Schleser, R., & Cohen, R. (1985). Achieving generalization with general versus specific self-instructions: Effects on academically deficient children. *Cognitive Therapy and Research, 9,* 297–308.

Thomas, A., Chess, S., & Birch, H. G. (1968). *Temperament and behavior disorders in children.* New York: New York University Press.

Thorley, G. (1984). Review of follow-up and follow-back studies of childhood hyperactivity. *Psychological Bulletin, 96,* 116–132.

Thorndike, R. L., Hagen, E. P., & Sattler, J. M. (1986). *Stanford–Binet Intelligence Scale* (4th ed.). Chicago: Riverside.

Trites, R. L., Dugas, F., Lynch, G., & Ferguson, B. (1979). Incidence of hyperactivity. *Journal of Pediatric Psychology, 4,* 179–188.

Trommer, B. L., Hoeppner, J. B., Lorber, R., & Armstrong, K. (1988a). The go–no-go paradigm in attention deficit disorder. *Annals of Neurology, 24,* 610–614.

Trommer, B. L., Hoeppner, J. B., Lorber, R., & Armstrong, K. (1988b). Pitfalls in the use of a continuous performance test as a diagnostic tool in attention deficit disorder. *Developmental and Behavioral Pediatrics, 9,* 339–345.

Twardosz, S. R., & Nordquist, V. M. (1987). Parent training. In M. Hersen & V. B. Van Hasselt (Eds.), *Behavior therapy with children and adolescents: A clinical approach* (pp. 75–105). New York: Wiley.

Ullmann, R. K., Sleator, E. K., & Sprague, R. L. (1984). A new rating scale for diagnosis and monitoring of ADD children. *Psychopharmacology Bulletin, 20,* 160–164.

Ullmann, R. K., Sleator, E. K., & Sprague, R. L. (1985). A change of mind: The Conners Abbreviated Rating Scales reconsidered. *Journal of Abnormal Child Psychology, 13,* 553–565.

Urbain, E. S., & Savage, P. (1989). Interpersonal cognitive problem-solving training with children in the schools. In J. N. Hughes & R. J. Hall (Eds.), *Cognitive–behavioral psychology in the schools: A comprehensive handbook* (pp. 466–497). New York: Guilford.

Varley, C. K. (1983). Effects of methylphenidate in adolescents with attention deficit disorder. *Journal of the American Academy of Child and Adolescent Psychiatry, 22,* 351–354.

Varni, J. W., & Henker, B. (1979). A self-regulation approach to the treatment of three hyperactive boys. *Child Behavior Therapy, 1,* 171–192.

Vincent Roehling, P., & Robin, A. L. (1986). Development and validation of the Family Beliefs Inventory: A measure of unrealistic beliefs among parents and adolescents. *Journal of Consulting and Clinical Psychology, 54,* 693–697.

Vygotsky, L. S. (1962). *Thought and language.* New York: Wiley.

Wahler, R. B., & Afton, A. D. (1980). Attentional processes in insular and non-insular mothers: Some differences in their summary reports about child problem behaviors. *Child Behavior Therapy, 2,* 25–41.

Wahler, R. G., & Dumas, J. E. (1989). Attentional problems in dysfunctional mother–child interactions: An interbehavioral model. *Psychological Bulletin, 105,* 116–130.

Walker, H. M. (1970). *The Walker Problem Behavior Identification Checklist.* Los Angeles: Psychological Services.

Wallander, J. L., & Hubert, N. C. (1985). Long-term prognosis for children with attention deficit disorder with hyperactivity (ADD-H). In B. B. Lahey & A. E. Kazdin (Eds.), *Advances in clinical child psychology* (Vol. 8, pp. 113–147). New York: Plenum.

Wechsler, D. (1974). *Wechsler Intelligence Scale for Children—Revised Manual.* New York: Psychological Corporation.

Weinberg, W. A., & Brumback, R. P. (1976). Mania in childhood. *American Journal of the Disturbed Child, 130,* 380–385.

Weiss, G. (1975). A natural history of hyperactivity in childhood and treatment with stimulant medication at different ages: A summary of research findings. *International Journal of Mental Health, 4,* 213–226.

Weiss, G., & Hechtman, L. T. (1986). *Hyperactive children grown up: Empirical findings and theoretical considerations.* New York: Guilford.

Weiss, G., Minde, K., Werry, J. S., Douglas, V., & Nemeth, E. (1971). Studies on the hyperactive child. VII. Five-year follow-up. *Archives of General Psychiatry, 24,* 409–414.

Wender, P. H. (1987). *The hyperactive child, adolescent and adult: ADD through the lifespan.* New York: Oxford University Press.

Wender, P. H., Reimherr, F. W., & Wood, D. R. (1981). Attention deficit disorder (minimal brain dysfunction) in adults. *Archives of General Psychiatry, 38,* 449–456.

Werner, P. H., & Smith, R. S. (1977). *Kauai's children come of age.* Honolulu: University of Hawaii Press.

Werry, J. S. (1968). Developmental hyperactivity. *Pediatric Clinics of North America, 19,* 9–16.

Werry, J. S. (1976). Food additives and hyperactivity. *Medical Journal of Australia, 2,* 281–282.

Werry, J. S. (1988). Drugs, learning and cognitive function in children—An update. *Journal of Child Psychology and Psychiatry, 29,* 129–141.

Werry, J. S., & Wollersheim, J. P. (1989). Behavior therapy with children and adolescents: A 20-year overview. *Journal of the American Academy of Child and Adolescent Psychiatry, 28,* 1–18.

Whalen, C. K., & Henker, B. (1987). Cognitive behavior therapy for hyperactive children: What do we know? In J. Loney (Ed.), *The young hyperactive child* (pp. 123–141). Birmingham, NY: Haworth.

Whalen, C. K., Henker, B., Buhrmaster, D., Hinshaw, S. P., Huber, A., & Laski, K. (1989). Does stimulant medication improve the peer status of hyperactive children? *Journal of Consulting and Clinical Psychology, 87,* 545–549.

Whalen, C. K., Henker, B., & Dotemoto, S. (1981). Teacher response to the methylphenidate (Ritalin) versus placebo status of hyperactive boys in the classroom. *Child Development, 52,* 1005–1014.

Whalen, C. K., Henker, B., & Granger, D. A. (1989). Ratings of medication effects in hyperactive children: Viable or vulnerable? *Behavioral Assessment, 11,* 179–199.

Whalen, C. K., Henker, B., & Hinshaw, S. P. (1985). Cognitive–behavioral therapies for hyperactive children: Promises, problems and prospects. *Journal of Abnormal Child Psychology, 13,* 391–410.

Whalen, C. K., Henker, B., Swanson, J. M., Granger, D., Kliewer, W., & Spenser, J. (1987). Natural social behaviors in hyperactive children: Dose effects of methylphenidate. *Journal of Consulting and Clinical Psychology, 55,* 187–193.

Whisman, M. A. (1990). The efficacy of booster maintenance sessions in behavior therapy: Review and methodological critique. *Clinical Psychology Review, 10,* 155–170.

Wilcox, A. J. (1983). Intrauterine growth retardation: Beyond birth weight criterion. *Early Human Development, 8,* 189–193.

Willis, T. J., & Lovaas, I. (1977). A behavioral approach to treating hyperactive children: The parents' role. In J. B. Millichap (Ed.), *Learning disabilities and related disorders* (pp. 119–140). Chicago: Year Book Medical.

Wirt, R. D., Lachar, D., Klinedinst, J. K., & Seat, P. D. (1981). *Multidimensional description of child personality: A manual for the Personality Inventory for Children.* Los Angeles: Western Psychological Services.

Wong, B. Y. L. (1985). Issues in cognitive–behavioral interventions in academic areas. *Journal of Abnormal Child Psychology, 13,* 425–442.

Woodcock, R. W., & Johnson, M. B. (1977). *Psychoeducational battery.* New York: Teaching Resources.

World Health Organization. (1978). *Glossary of mental disorders and guide to their classification: For use in conjunction with the International Classification of Diseases* (9th rev.). Geneva: Author.

Yarrow, L. (1960). Interviewing children. In P. Mussen (Ed.), *Handbook of research methods in child development* (pp. 561–602). New York: Wiley.

Zametkin, A. J., Nordahl, T. E., Gross, M., King, A. C., Semple, W. E., Rumsey, J., Hamburger, S., & Cohen, R. (1990). Cerebral glucose metabolism in adults with hyperactivity of childhood onset. *New England Journal of Medicine, 323,* 1361–1366.

Zametkin, A. J., & Rapoport, J. L. (1986). The pathophysiology of attention deficit disorder with hyperactivity: A review. In B. B. Lahey & A. E. Kazdin (Eds.), *Advances in clinical child psychology, 9,* 177–216. New York: Plenum.

Zametkin, A. J., Rapoport, J. L., Murphy, D. L., Linnoila, M., & Ismond, D. (1985). Treatment of hyperactive children with monoamine oxidase inhibitors: I. Clinical efficacy. *Archives of General Psychiatry, 42,* 962–969.

Zametkin, A. J., Rapoport, J. L., Murphy, D. L., Linnoila, M., Karoum, F., Potter, W. Z., & Ismond, D. (1985). Treatment of hyperactive children with monoamine oxidase inhibitors: II. Plasma and urinary monoamine findings after treatment. *Archives of General Psychiatry, 42,* 969–973.

Zentall, S.S. (1985). Stimulus control factors in search performance of hyperactive children. *Journal of Learning Disabilities, 18,* 480–485.

Zentall, S.S. (1986). Effects of color stimulation on performance and activity of hyperactive and nonhyperactive children. *Journal of Educational Psychology, 78,* 159–165.

Zentall, S. S. (1989). Self-control training with hyperactive and impulsive children. In J. N. Hughes & R. J. Hall (Eds.), *Cognitive–behavioral psychology in the schools: A comprehensive handbook* (pp. 305–346). New York: Guilford.

Zentall, S. S., & Meyer, M. J. (1987). Self-regulation of stimulation for ADDH children during reading and vigilance task performance. *Journal of Abnormal Child Psychology, 15,* 519–536.

Zentall, S. S., & Shaw, J. H. (1980). Effects of classroom noise on performance and activity of second-grade hyperactive and control children. *Journal of Educational Psychology, 72,* 830–840.

Ziegler, R., & Holden, L. (1988). Family therapy for learning disabled and attention-deficit disordered children. *American Journal of Orthopsychiatry, 58,* 196–210.

Index